Angels In The Dust A Novel Of The First Crusade

ANGELS IN THE DUST

ANGELS
IN THE DUST

A NOVEL
OF THE FIRST CRUSADE

BY ZOFIA KOSSAK

AUTHOR OF
BLESSED ARE THE MEEK

Roy Publishers, New York

1947

Contents

BOOK I

BOOK II

CONTENTS

BOOK III

BOOK IV

◇◇◇

BOOK ONE

1.

The Good Knights of Silesia

ONCE AGAIN THE LAST OF THE RIDERS TURNED TOWARD THE MONASTERY. "God be with you!" he called.

The Prior, who was still standing at the gate, shouted back, "God speed to you!" but added under his breath: "And, pray, good Lord, lead them astray! Leave not our wrong unavenged!"

Sandals clattered behind him. Without turning his head, the Prior listened to the doleful report of the cellarist: "All our bread is gone . . . and three sheep . . . six score eggs . . . all the bacon . . . a pig, a head of fine cheese, a bag of groats . . ."

"Rascals! Robbers!" the Prior groaned wrathfully.

"A barrel of mead, two vats of beer, ten measures of oats, half a stack of hay . . ." the cellarist continued in a low monotone.

"Why did you give so much?" grumbled his superior.

"We tried to hold back, Reverend Father. Aah, we tried. But it was no use; their men were famished and their mounts starved."

"Aye," the Prior admitted. "Their lordships fell to as though they would never get their fill. St. Lambert, our good patron! Why, we could have lived four weeks on what they swallowed in one day."

"Five or six weeks, more likely," the cellarist said bitterly, thrusting his emaciated hands into the loose sleeves of his dark-gray frock.

"Did the villains betray whence they came?" the Prior asked confidentially.

The steward glanced at him, the corners of his mouth turned down in a sly smile. "So, Father! you haven't heard the news?"

"News?" said the Prior. "I asked the lords, but they only scowled and went on eating. Wouldn't say a word . . . Bad-tempered brutes!"

"Just the same in the kitchen. You would have thought they'd lost their tongues. But I took one of their lads into the cellar and gave him a drop or two and—"

"What did he tell you?" The Prior frowned impatiently.

"They came all the way from Krushvitsa, riding like all the devils, without a halt the whole way. Seems there was a battle . . . a mighty fierce battle . . ."

"At Krushvitsa? St. Lambert! Have the Pomeranians reached Krushvitsa?"

"Pomeranians, ho! They fought the Prince!"

"The Prince?"

"Aye, our own Prince, Ladislas! The lords brought Zbignev from Saxony and would have put him on the throne, but Shechec's men routed them."

"God have mercy on us! Another rebellion! Will there never be peace again! This is dreadful news, my brother! But," the Prior hesitated, "are you sure the man was not lying?"

"Why should he lie? He spoke the simple truth. Fools can't lie."

The Prior stared dully at the ground. Then, overcome by the sudden realization, he shouted: "We took the rebels in! We gave them food!

"Indeed, if we had known sooner—"

"We should have refused to let them in, to open the gates! Babylonians! Foul Ahabs! They would not have devoured our poor sustenance. Nay! And to boot, we shall hear from the Prince. O, we shall hear from the Prince," he said ominously, shaking his head from side to side.

"And the Abbot, as luck would have it, still away . . ." the cellarist said reflectively, stealing an amused glance at the Prior. "Aye, we are in for it this time! We are really in for it—"

The Prior began quickly pacing the narrow courtyard, seething with anger, chafing the more for want of someone on whom to vent his spleen; for who could be blamed for the misfortune? Surely no one at the monastery, save, perhaps, St. Lambert, who had failed to warn his faithful servants in good time! When a strong band of the foremost

Silesian lords had ridden up to the gates and demanded that they be opened, a band headed by Ostoy, who only the year before had been appointed by the Prince guardian and defender of the monastery, how could the Prior have refused to let them in and to give them food and fodder? Why, they would have torn the place to pieces, had he not done as he was bidden. O, how he reviled them! O, the curse of God! O— In impotent rage he shook his fist at the forest into which the last of the cavalcade had just disappeared.

"May the earth swallow you, accursed tribe!" he shouted. "May you never find your way home!"

Meanwhile, those whom he cursed rode single-file along a narrow forest trail toward Silesia, their home. Smashing through the underbrush, climbing hillocks scented with thyme, golden with orpine, they plunged again into ferns that reached to the horses' ears, splashed across shallow, spreading forest pools overgrown with trees and bushes, and startled grunting herds of boars, and single-bearded bull aurochs grazing in the glades. They spurred their mounts mercilessly on; for deep in their hearts they felt that only on their own soil would they recover the sound judgment that would tell them what to do now, after their defeat.

Now no one spoke. Loquacity never becomes a warrior, and, indeed, what were they to talk about? Were they to fret because Zbig[n]ev, for whom they had fought, whom they had tried to restore to his rights and make heir to the crown, had abandoned them at the crucial moment and surrendered to his father, drawing half his partisans after him? It was their own fault! They should have foreseen that that callow youth, now presumptuous, now humble, lending ear to everyone, would behave just as he had done.

But the defeat at Krushvitsa was not the only reason for those jaws being clamped in stubborn silence, nor for all their headlong flight. The whole knighthood was prey to an inner strife, to a restlessness produced by a sense of degradation and frustration that gnawed at their hearts, for they had all too freshly in mind those recent days of royal might when Poland, although it had been a Christian country for a mere hundred years, stood among the foremost powers of the world, when it was the key to European politics, an invaluable ally that both the Pope and the Emperor strove to win to his cause.

These were the days when the Holy Father sent envoy after envoy to the court of Boleslas, calling him in his missives "beloved son" and "Excellency," an honor theretofore reserved for the Emperor and the Basileus, since the French king was addressed merely as "His Eminence" and the King of England only as "His Magnificence." Between the two of them, Pope Gregory and Boleslas cornered Henry IV like a wild boar in a thicket, and on the very day when, defeated, he stood barefoot and freezing in the snow at the gates of Canossa, fifteen Polish, Saxon, Hungarian, and Italian bishops in the cathedral of Gniezno crowned Boleslas king. Then Polish princesses sat on the thrones of distant Norway and Denmark, and when Ladislas, the royal prince of Hungary, was brought to Cracow Castle, retinues of Polish knights escorted him to the steps of the throne. Aye, those were the days . . . In far-away, unknown England, bards sang of the valor of the Polish knights who dwelled in the deep black forests on the banks of the Vistula. While as for the Russian princes, rulers of boundless domains, the Polish king pushed them to and fro as he pleased, returning from each of his eastern expeditions loaded with priceless treasures and booty. In addition to riches, the knights who accompanied the King brought back a sense of inner growth, of exultation at the discovery that the world beyond their own forests and clearings was so vast, so infinitely varied. It challenged them, it awakened a craving to know, to encompass, to possess it all, and back in their manors and castles they were unable to think of anything but the wonders that might be theirs. They mused over that variegated, many-hued life; they turned it over in their minds, chewed it over like a cud, till it swelled into a yearning for yet another royal summons.

And now, after only a few years, the dreams had vanished. And whose fault? . . . Their evil fate's, no doubt, but also their own. They never spoke of it, but deep in his heart each felt a gnawing responsibility for the evil that had befallen. How could they have allowed their King to be banished from Cracow? Why had they not followed him to Hungary? Had they been but more vigilant, murderers sent by Ladislas would not have caught Boleslas while he was hunting alone! And, afterwards, they had even failed to guard the royal orphan.

And it was they, they alone, who were to blame . . .

The three Strzygonia brothers rode at the tail of the cavalcade, where the way was broken wide across the brush and hazels, pounded smooth and soft by the horses' hoofs, so that all three could ride abreast. The brothers, though they used the same war-cry and branded the same device, three horseshoes pierced by an arrow, upon the backs of their slaves and the flanks of their horses and cattle, and though they cut the same mark on the border trees of their domains, were not in the least alike. Now as they rode between the dense walls of the forest, pressed so close that their knees, hands, and shoulders touched, their minds were far apart.

The eldest, a man with hair already hoary, a huge head and powerful shoulders, was named Vitoslav—a name handed down to the first born in each generation. It would not be seemly, however, to have such a venerable name bandied about in trivial, daily use lest, God forbid, its power be drained and its splendor dulled. Hence the man who in war and council and upon important family occasions bore the name of Vitoslav, in everyday life was simply addressed as "Glovach," or Headman.

Although cheerful by nature, Glovach's disposition had been of late beclouded by care: his wife, though a robust woman of good family, bore him only daughters—six already. Not knowing how to break the evil spell, he offered gifts to the gods of old and made vows to the new One —all to no avail. Indeed, there were some who tried to comfort him by saying that should a seventh girl be born, she would, no doubt, grow to be a seeress able to tell the future and to see other things concealed from mortal eyes. Such an oracle, they said, might be of great profit to the clan. But Glovach only shook his huge, grizzled head at such talk. "I shall sow my seed till I get me a son," he repeated doggedly.

Zbylut, who came next in age, and rode now by Glovach's side, was still unmarried, though black bristles had long ago overgrown his chin and cheeks. He had fierce black eyes glowing in deep sockets under heavy brows. His red lips curled in a contemptuous sneer, particularly whenever he happened to catch sight of the youngest of the three brothers, Imbram; for there was no love or understanding lost between these two—the ill-tempered, hot-headed Zbylut, and the gentle, soft, and yielding Imbram. It was said that when Imbram—or Imko, as he was generally called—was a tiny baby, a fairy had tried to bewitch him. Though she was driven away in time, it seemed that her touch or perhaps even her gaze had been enough to befuddle the lad's mind with strange fancies, for to this day he was inordinately fond of songs and story-telling. He was also deeply in love with his wife, whom he had married but a year before, and at this very moment his anxiety on her account, for she was about to be confined, drove him on far more than the fear of pursuit.

Unable to restrain his impatience, he rode out a few steps ahead of his brothers to catch up with his kinsman and friend, Zavora.

Now there were two Zavoras. The elder was nicknamed "Momot," the "Mumbler," because he stammered, and while stumbling and mumbling, he twisted his head in a ludicrous fashion; yet the words he uttered with such difficulty were weighty and full of sense, and he was held in great respect. The younger Zavora was tall and thin with a small, round head, and a wide, always laughing mouth and beardless chin, set upon a very long neck with a protruding Adam's apple. His foolish appearance had earned him the derisive nickname of "Yashek," a mocking reference to one of the ancient pagan gods, powerful once, but now despised. It was with him that Imbram had sworn eternal friendship on the last Friendship Sunday.

"Home is no more than three leagues away," Imbram said in a low voice to Yashek. "I am tempted to push ahead and see how it is with my Ofka."

"Why not?" said Yashek.

Imbram cast a significant glance at his brothers. "They will rail."

"Let them rail. They will not eat you up, will they?"

"True," Imko admitted. Pleased to have found a supporter, he turned to Glovach and shouted, "Goodbye! I'm riding on ahead."

Glovach waved his hand desperately. "Don't you dare, changeling! Want to bring misfortune upon the house?"

But Imbram neither heard his voice nor saw his gesture. Pressing spurs into his horse's flanks, he had already left the trail and turned into the forest, to cut past the long line of riders.

"A grown man, and hare-brained as a wench," Glovach muttered irritably. He cast an apprehensive glance at the treetops, as if he expected to discover there the malevolent forces that, aroused by this unseemly haste of Imbram's, might follow him to the manor. "He is forever making trouble," he said angrily to his brother. Zbylut did not answer.

2.

The Son

THE BABY WAS CRYING. ITS LOUD WAILS ROSE FROM THE WICKER BASKET, suspended from the rafters on four bast ropes, in which it lay. The shutters were tightly closed, the room was murky and stiflingly hot, and although it was broad daylight outside, a burning wax taper stood in the corner. Flies buzzed monotonously in the shaft of sunlight that seeped through a crack in the shutters.

Ofka, Imbram's wife, leaned out of bed, and tenderly drew the crib to her side. The baby's tiny puckered face was turning blue from screaming; cautiously the mother took up the small, stiff doll wrapped in multicolored swaddling bands, its arms tightly bound to its body, and with nimble, swift motions unwrapped it. No wonder her darling was crying! The piece of iron, a broken horseshoe, that had been wrapped in the swaddling clothes as an indispensable protection against evil spells, had slid under the tiny back, against the skin. "O, the poor darling!" she said to him. And to think that Bogucha, her sister-in-law, had told her again and again that the swaddling must on no account be removed from sunrise to sunset!

Ofka moved over to the edge of the bed and laid the child comfortably upon a pillow stuffed with hay. The tiny arms and legs, at last free of bonds, waved happily, and Ofka lost herself in contemplation of tiny pink fingers, of fingernails no bigger than millet seeds. Could it be, she marveled, that some day they would become the gnarled claws of a mighty knight? She was so engrossed in her thoughts that she did not notice the creaking of the door when Bogucha entered the chamber. The nine days' period of confinement had not yet elapsed, and only three chosen women were allowed to see the mother and the baby. Separating Ofka and the crib from the rest of the room was a broad sheet, and before she was aware of her sister-in-law's presence, the sheet was brusquely

lifted and, "Mercy!" hissed the newcomer. "Are you out of your mind?
How many times have I told you not to anger the evil powers?"

"O, Bogucha! The knife is here, and the taper, and the herbs . . . !"

"Wrap that child up! Hurry! Hurry!"

Big and strong, dressed in a bright woolen skirt that spread wide over
her hips, Bogucha stood guard over the bed while Ofka reluctantly began to swaddle the baby. The pink knees, still bent as they were in the
womb, refused to unfold, the arms would much rather hold the tiny
fists close to the face. Stubbornly, with unwavering eyes, Bogucha looked
at her nephew and at his tiny male organ, like a quivering worm . . .
the magic charm that made a child welcome in the family and his
mother honored and revered by all. Would she, Bogucha, ever live to see
a son of her own? Oh! Fate . . .

"It is a sorry sight the way you go about it," she said scornfully, and,
pushing Ofka's fumbling hands aside she proceeded to swaddle the baby
herself. With sure, practiced fingers she quickly overcame the infant's
resistance and quickly had him bundled tightly, horseshoe and all. As
he burst into a fresh fit of screaming, Ofka gave him her breast. Then
Bogucha bustled out, soon to return, dragging the butter churn from
the adjoining room. She seated herself before the sheet partition, as if
to prevent any new foolishness on Ofka's part. "The knife will protect
you in some ways, but not altogether," she said, only now replying to
Ofka's earlier protests. "By tomorrow the evil time will be over. Can't
you keep still till then?"

"Is the christening set for tomorrow?" Ofka asked, alarmed.

"Aye. The Abbot said he would wait no longer."

"And Imko? Will he baptize him without Imko?"

"Imko need not be present at the christening, only at the churching.
And what are you afraid of? That he will disown him, afterwards?"

There was a touch of bitterness in Bogucha's voice, but Ofka only
burst into laughter. "Disown him? Nay, my little lamb! Your father
will acknowledge you, never fear! He will lift you up high, high up,
to the very beams, then he will lower you to the threshold, and again
raise you so you may grow as tall, as tall . . ."

Bogucha pursed her lips. "Go on. Talk. Talk. Provoke the evil
powers."

Ofka sighed and was silent. Bogucha continued to pound steadily with
the beater, but when the butter refused to form, she rose, squared her

shoulders and indignantly flipped her apron several times to drive away the sprite who, no doubt, must have been sitting on the beater and interfering with the churning. Then, calm once more, she sat down, carefully arranged the folds of her voluminous skirt, and resumed her work, while Ofka reverently followed each motion. Bogucha filled her with a mixture of admiration and awe; she marveled at her self-possession and her ability to cope with all the hidden forces that ruled the lives of men. And there was so much to know! Even such household furnishings as the kneading trough and the pail, though outwardly seeming common enough, were actually endowed with a profound meaning closely related to the most intimate bodily matters and had to be treated with respect, even though the Abbot grew angry. With what dignity and skill Bogucha moved among these everyday yet sacred objects, conjuring up any household sprite she chose.

It was fate's cruel jest that this wise and stately matron should have been denied what so easily, almost casually, was granted to her young sister-in-law: a son and heir. Who more deserved to be the mother of the robust little lad who was now falling asleep at the maternal breast: the wise Bogucha or the flighty Ofka, as immature as Imko, always ready to burst into tears or laughter, now frightened by a trifle, now, with complete unconcern, provoking the mighty, dark powers that were so jealous of every human happiness and joy?

The child was asleep, the butter made. Bogucha took up the churn and departed. Left alone, Ofka lay on her back, her head propped up on the hay-stuffed pillows, gazing idly at the ceiling, darkened with age, and thinking that as soon as Imbram returned she would be able to leave this stifling room, and go out into the open, into the sun, into the sweet-smelling wind. There would be no more need to shut the windows tight, to stuff the chimney, to beware of the moon, and forever burn the taper. No more gloomy evenings, lugubrious as a wake, when the flame flickered, moths flew in circles and dropped to the floor with singed wings, shadows lurked on the walls, and something knocked and creaked in the rafters, while the wife of old Pobieda, the steward, snored in the corner. No longer would she be cut off from the world or have to submit to the restrictions that bound a woman in the last month of pregnancy. She was not allowed then to attend to household duties; she could not prepare meals; she must not sit on the threshold or fetch water, not even carry in her apron apples, pears, or eggs. But she had to conceal a heavy piece of iron in her bosom under the shift and never part with a knife that had been twice blessed at Easter. But now this was all behind her, for it concerned only first childbirths.

She stretched with pleasure and folded her arms behind her head. How blithesome and yet how almost incredible it seemed, that from now on she would no longer be a bride-wife, a stranger at the family hearth who had no right to speak to anyone unless spoken to. Now, as the mother of the first-born of the new generation, she would hold the foremost place in the household. Aye, she would take precedence over the wise and stern Bogucha. She laughed aloud at the very thought. How pleased Imko was going to be. O! if only he would return soon, that beloved, sweet husband of hers, her master and best friend. How she wished that she knew some way to call him from afar, to conjure him to make haste and come to her side.

She stretched her arms as though in invocation, and suddenly recalled that last winter a monk who wandered from monastery to monastery and who spent two weeks at the manor waiting for a cold spell to subside had taught her an incantation which, he said, never failed. Painstakingly she began to go over it word by word in her mind, for no incantation worked unless it was accurately repeated. At last she sat up in bed, cocking her ears for the sound of approaching steps (God help her if Bogucha ever found out!), and in a voice muffled with emotion began to recite:

> "Morning lights, sisters o' mine,
> Mount a piebald horse,
> Bring the one for whom I pine,
> Bring him to these doors.
> Whatever he may do
> Wherever he may be.
> Morning lights, sisters o' mine,
> Bring him back to me!
> One . . . two . . . three . . . Now!"

She listened. There was no sound. Only birds chirped outside, and from the hall where Glovach's daughters were playing came the twitter of childish voices. Undaunted she repeated her incantation, but still nothing of the sound she awaited. She began for the third time, saying each word very slowly, carefully, and with such confidence that she was not in the least surprised when, just as she reached the end, horse's hoofs clattered in front of the house and the watchdogs burst into joyous yelping. She could hear the patter of scurrying feet and Bogucha's voice calling:

"Welcome! Welcome home! And where is my man tarrying?"

Ofka fell back on the pillows weak with joy. So he had come! He was here! The charm had worked!

A strong hand yanked at the door so that it nearly fell off its creaking hinges, and Imko burst into the chamber. But Bogucha was close at his heels. She seized his shoulder, wheeled him about, and now stood facing him, stern and menacing, like the very incarnation of Law.

"You are not to see her until after the christening and the churching," she declared, still gasping for breath after having run to overtake him.

"Oh! Come . . . Just a glimpse. If you would only draw that sheet aside just a little . . ."

"Are you out of your senses? Want to bring on misfortune?"

"Nah! Right away misfortune?" Imko muttered, peevishly. He was deeply chagrined at the prospect of not seeing Ofka, yet he realized that these were matters not to be trifled with.

Bogucha shrugged contemptuously.

"You two are fine parents for a child!" she mocked, wagging her head. "As though you'd never heard what happened to the Rogalas! And for the same reason, too! The father saw the mother, and before they knew it, the boy's back grew all crooked so that they had to cast him out into the weeds."

"Rogala said he was born that way."

"He was not. The crone who tended Rogala's wife told me so herself. The lad was as straight as this one here, when she took him out."

"Ha! If so . . . Have it your way. Isn't Ofka even allowed to talk?"

"Talk? Yes, she may talk."

"Ofka, why don't you say something? I am here."

Indeed, Ofka knew that her beloved was there, but overcome with joy, she could not utter a sound. She heard his voice, she could even smell the mixture of his sweat, of the horse, of leather, and of forest.

"You are here," she repeated at last, in a voice so small that he was barely able to hear her.

He was alarmed. "What is wrong, Ofka? What is the matter?"

"Nothing . . . I just feel faint."

"Faint? Why? Are you sick?"

"No . . . Because I am so happy!"

"Oh! My very own!"

Bogucha spat violently. First under her feet, then over her right shoulder, then over her left. Didn't they know how dangerous it was to admit aloud that one was happy?

Imbram, attempting to pacify her, put an arm about her broad shoulders.

"Show me at least the little one so I may acknowledge him?"

"Will you not wait for the others?"

"The christening can wait. But acknowledge him I will, at once."

"As you please."

She disappeared behind the partition to fetch the child. Ofka caught her hands.

"Little sister, my lovely, my sweet!" she implored. "Have mercy! Leave but the tiniest opening, so I too can see. Please, just a tiny one, no bigger than the tip of my finger."

After brief deliberation, Bogucha gave in. Be it so, Ofka may see Imko as long as he does not see her. In the seam of the curtain she ripped a tiny aperture, to which Ofka put her eye. She could see now. She saw Bogucha place the baby, still asleep on the table, and unswaddle it solemnly under its father's eyes so he might see for himself that it was, indeed, a son that his wife had borne him. Aye, a fine boy! Red as a beet and no bigger than your fist, but straight legs, those broad shoulders.

The baby did not cry. Glad to be rid of the swaddling cloth, so full that his little belly swelled under the linen strip that bound it, he turned towards the light eyes as blue and turbid as those of a puppy. With those eyes he still saw fairies and brownies, trolls and nymphs, all that is hidden from the eyes of men. Not till tomorrow, when the Abbot poured water over his head, would that world of the unknown vanish, and a new world, the world of his father, open before his eyes.

Cautiously, Imbram picked up his son in his big, warrior's hands. Bogucha, full of solicitude, instructed him how to support the head with his fingers so that it would not tilt backwards. Thus. See? And the father lifted up the babe as once his own father had lifted him, so high that the light down that covered the little head touched the carved beam at the spot where the family crest, three horseshoes pierced by an arrow, was cut in the timber. Three times he lifted him thus, so that the spirits of the departed forefathers who dwell in the beam might know that this babe was his, Imbram Strzygonia's, true son and heir.

Now, twice again he bent to the ground and touched the frail body to the doorsill, that sacred threshold, the abode of home sprites and the spirits of stillborn babes. Here, likewise, dwelled the souls of children cast out into the woods who though their heads had been wrapped in a shroud, had found their way home after death. All of them must be propitiated by a low bow, so that they might be friendly to the new member of the family whose little feet would soon begin to toddle and step over the sill, who later, in years to come, would ring silver spurs against it. Might they serve him faithfully, and prevent ill luck from entering the house! And in return, the father, bowing three times, pledged his son to guard and respect all home spirits and powers.

And while thus, without a word, he raised the babe, now lowered him to the sill, the two women—Ofka hidden behind the curtain, and Bogucha standing with arms hanging limply beside her body—watched him in breathless suspense. Neither was able to utter a sound, Ofka for joy, Bogucha for grief, for never, so far, had Glovach lifted any of her children. And whom was he to lift up, indeed? A girl? A tear trickled down her strong, stern face. She wiped it quickly away and took the now screaming child from Imko's hands. Let Ofka quiet her son.

"I will not let you stay here a minute longer," she told Imko in a voice that had once more regained its composure. "You two fools are not to be trusted. Come along."

"I'm coming," Imko said meekly. "Only—you, Ofka, tell me that you are glad."

"I am glad. Ever so glad . . ."

"There you go again!" Bogucha muttered irritably, and pushed her brother-in-law out the door.

"Go and take a look at the Byzantine mare's colt. It's mighty handsome, too," she called after him by way of consolation.

3.

The Christening

THE KNIGHT, NOVINA, SURNAMED "THE BABBLER" BECAUSE OF HIS LO-
quacity, flung a handsome belt studded with gold plates onto the
pile of presents. His brother—Novina the Oak—a misericorde upon a
golden chain. The three Osventas added a silver goblet, a broadsword,
and a breadth of brocade. The Ogonziks brought a handsome colt, raising a stir of admiration by the magnificence of the gift.

Following the nobles came the plain men at arms and they, too, deposited their offerings on the sheet spread at Imbram's and Ofka's feet.
Unable to afford costly objects bought from foreign merchants or won
in distant expeditions, the men at arms threw on pelts, horseshoes,
battle-axes, and bows laboriously bent and seasoned until they were
stronger than steel. Others brought bowstrings, or arrows, or quivers
made of beech bark or beautifully wrought in leather.

Two sheets were spread side by side. First the gift-bearers would stop
before one, saying: "To Vitoslav, Imbram's son, here is for luck, for
fortune, for a long life!" and on that they would throw anything: a
broken twig, a few pine cones, a blind kitten, or a warped tin cup. Moving over to the second sheet they would say: "Here I cast what is un-
profitable, unworthy, useless. Take it who will," and they deposited
their real gifts. This was done in order not to arouse the envy of the
evil powers by the sight of offerings too magnificent.

Hardly visible behind the pile of gifts sat Imbram and Ofka, side
by side. On her head Ofka wore a thin kerchief white as snow; she
was dressed in a tight-fitting bright blue gown finished with a fringe,
which, like the kerchief, had come long ago from Kiev and was the
product of Greek workmanship. The baby, tightly swaddled to a carved
beechwood board and covered with a rich gold brocade coverlet, lay in
her lap.

Imbram kept his hands motionless in his lap; his hair, smoothed and plastered down with lard, shone in the sun. Ofka darted sidelong glances at him and tried to assume the same detached expression that his face bore, but in vain. Joy, rapture, curiosity, and childish pride flitted across her small face, still pale, as fast as clouds flit over a spring sky. Her breasts, swollen with milk, were painfully heavy and pressed against the tight blue bodice of her gown as though they would burst its seams, and this only served to increase the sensation she felt of not being able to contain herself within her old form, of growing, expanding beyond her own self. Once more she glanced at Imbram, but he did not move or change his expression; only a slight flicker of his eyelids told her that he had seen her glance and that he shared her joy.

The men at arms had passed. Now came the free settlers, not attached to the land but tilling the lord's fields with their own farm gear. Behind them, and far more numerous, came the peasants, the serfs. Hastily they threw their humble gifts on the sheet, and while they mumbled the formula of offering they greedily sniffed the smell of roasting meat which the breeze wafted in from the yard. Stacks of bread and casks of beer stood nearby. Eyeing them, the serfs, for the first time in their lives perhaps, felt a soothing sense of good will toward their masters, and even of gratitude toward that little creature, thanks to whom they would be able to eat and drink their fill for the next three days. But even this gleeful prospect was tinged with regret at the thought that the human belly could only hold so much and no more. Try as he might, a body could never wolf down all the victuals prepared for the occasion. And so, scratching their heads, they moved on toward the boards and their load of good cheer.

Last in the procession of gift-bearers came the masters of hounds, the beavermen, the beekeepers, and the fishermen. These were no common laborers. Each was a master in the craft he had inherited from his father and wise in the lore of nature. They carried pitchers of honey and mead, rounds of wax, beaver skins, and dried and smoked fish.

Before the last gift had been dropped, the clatter of hooves rang out in the yard. A belated guest? No, it was Zbylut, whom Glovach had sent on to Breslau to represent the family at the council held by Paladin Magnus. He was evidently the bearer of some portentous tidings, for he was gasping for air and his road-weary mount looked no better than a jade. Hastily dismounting, he threw the reins to a servant and advanced on foot toward the festive throng.

At once Glovach broke away to meet his brother alone, out of the others' hearing. As he walked toward Zbylut he was aware of a strange feeling of reluctance: the sight of his brother had brought back painful memories and sore misgivings that he had tried to put out of mind for the past two days. On his return home he had forbidden the servants to mention the defeat at Krushvitsa; even Bogucha must not know of the threat that hung over the household. It would be fatal, indeed, if such misgivings were to mar moments that were to influence the whole life of the newborn babe, and though Glovach might grieve at heart that this long-desired son and heir should have been bestowed upon his younger brother and not upon himself, nevertheless he was too generous a man not to do justice to the new family seedling.

Ofka, too, watched Zbylut as he approached, but with altogether different feelings. To her, his arrival meant the last drop in her already overflowing cup of happiness, the final touch to her triumph. Now, at last even that sullen, contemptuous, scoffing brother-in-law of hers would see her in all her glory, as the beautifully adorned, resplendent, revered mother of little Vitoslav. O, let him stare! Let him marvel!

Since her marriage, Zbylut had treated her with silent indifference, even scorn. And she often wondered why; for in the old days when she was still a maiden running about with long-flowing hair, she had sometimes felt that he liked her better than any other girl. Once, in fact, during the frolics on Midsummer Night, he had even caught her hands and, without a word, had dragged her into the woods. His eyes glowed like a werewolf's. She had been dreadfully frightened, and she broke loose and fled.

Now, blushing with pleasure, she gave him a haughty stare. He answered her challenge with a twisted smile that was half pity, half malice. He knew what the news he brought would mean to her. Ofka dropped her eyes and unconsciously grasped Imbram's hand and Zbylut cast his brother a venomous glance.

"If you hold life dear," he said in a low voice, "dismiss these people and come with me to the hall. We are gathering for a council."

"I will follow you anon," Imbram replied serenely, and did not stir from his seat.

He waited until the last offering was laid down, and only then rose and bade the gift-bearers partake of the banquet and be of good cheer. Servants were already collecting the presents and rounding up the live-stock brought by the guests, while Pobieda, the steward, eagerly collected the more valuable objects to carry them to the upper chamber of the manor. Ofka clung to Imko's breast; her earlier joy and self-assurance had vanished as though swept away by a gust of cold wind.

"I am afraid, Imko," she whispered, "I am horribly afraid."

"Of what, my pretty? There is nothing to fear. Look at that baby, he has gone to sleep. See how soundly he sleeps? Better take him home."

"Will you come soon?" she insisted, still reluctant to leave.

"I will, dearest, very soon."

But he did not come soon, and well into the night she awaited him, pacing the chamber in her long linen shift. To and fro she walked, now stopping by the window to watch the moon struggle with the clouds, now by the bed to peer at the child sound asleep in his wicker basket. Desperately she strained her ears for the murmur of the distant voices that were sometimes wafted from the hall, but silence fell again and she heard nothing but the creaking of the house. At last she heard footfalls approaching. Imko was coming. But even as she listened to his heavy, slow steps she was filled with forebodings and stood motionless with dread.

He stood looking at her for a moment, then stepped forward and took her hands. "Listen," he began.

And carefully choosing his words so that she might understand, he told her of the help they had given to the accursed fool Zbignev, of the defeat at Krushvitsa, and of the news just brought by Zbylut. Disastrous news it was, indeed. Shechec had connived with the Czechs and was approaching Silesia from every side, swearing upon his broadsword that he would not rest till he had slain every one of Zbignev's partisans and thrown their kin into his dungeon. He had already besieged the Ostoy, killed the elder, and, far worse, had captured the younger, and sold him into slavery. When they heard this—Imbram told Ofka—they all sprang to their feet shouting that it could not be true, but Zbylut pounded his breast with his fists, roaring that true it was! In the face of such infamy even the Bilinas and the Avdanyets, who had had a feud for two generations, swore to forego their enmity and join hands against the common foe. For the present, it was decided, they must seek refuge in Hungary, and there gather strength and await their chance.

"For if we remain here, Shechec will pick us out, one by one, like eggs from a nest," Paladin Magnus had said.

Here Imbram broke off, for he was loath to add to Ofka's grief; and so he did not tell her that, according to Zbylut, the Paladin had gone on to say that anyone who would rather not flee could make his peace with the Prince. Since Zbignev had been the first to leave and so had betrayed them, no dishonor would hold to this; and Ladislas was not bloodthirsty; he would willingly forgive. "Mayhap I shall do so myself," the Paladin had said, "for, as the saying goes, 'What you cannot climb over—crawl under,' and perhaps luck will turn, and I shall yet lock Shechec in my dungeon before he locks me in his." So, the knights could take their choice: either to flee to Hungary or make peace with the Prince. There was no third way. Such had been the decision of the council at Breslau.

With his arm around Ofka, Imbram remembered bitterly how, on hearing of the decision, he had wanted to rise and tell the others he was for making peace with the Prince; he remembered how Zbylut looked at him, leering, and said: "Hearken to Imbram. He is doubtless ready to humble himself and lick Ladislas' boots, so he can stay with his wife and child." Furiously angry, though that was just what he had been thinking, he rose to his feet and swore upon his knightly honor that, since he was the youngest, he would do whatever the elder brothers decided was best.

And they had decided to go.

Very likely Glovach would have remained had it not been for Zbylut taunting and goading and shaming them all till they forgot what they wanted to do. They were going to Hungary and Imko no longer had any choice in the matter.

"I could weep for sorrow," he confessed sadly. "Not such a mighty journey, but who can tell when we shall return? By Christmas," he hesitated, "perhaps not until next spring!"

Ofka lay in his arms, overcome by the suddenness of the blow, stricken dumb by despair.

Alarmed by her silence, Imko pressed her more closely to him and strained to see what her face would tell, but the dark was too thick, the clouds had hidden the moon. He felt a surge of infinite tenderness toward her, and he felt wretchedly sad, both for himself and for her. Lightly he stroked her face with his fingers, like a blind man trying to memorize a beloved form. She surrendered passively to his caresses, limp with grief. "Hush! Hush!" he whispered, though she had said nothing. In the timber of the walls something creaked. Throughout all the sleeping house rose strange whispers, knocks, rustles . . . Someone was stealing along the walls. Who had entered the house? "Hush! Hush!" he whispered again.

4.

Fare Thee Well!

R UBBING HIS BALD PATE AND RUNNING HIS FINGERS THROUGH HIS WREATH of hair, Abbot Guido meditated upon the plans of the Silesian knights. It would certainly be best if they made peace with their Prince; as long, however, as those mule-headed warriors would not hear of that —why! let them go, rather than begin a civil war here! No matter what uncertainty of outcome there might be for the knights, a war could have but one result for the common folk: destruction, hunger, and suffering. So . . . let them go! by all means let them go. God bless the wise man who had conceived that plan. Only . . . Hungary was too near, almost next door, a two weeks' journey, and nothing could keep such voluntary exiles there for long. Fretting over the fate of their domains, easily reached by rumors, they would be back in no time. Ah, no, he thought, they must go somewhere far away, so that they would not be able to return for at least a year.

So, when the knights who had gathered in the hall of the Strzygonia manor turned to him for advice, he began to urge them not to sit idly in Buda, but instead to undertake a pilgrimage to the tomb of St. Gilles in Provence. Such a pilgrimage expiated all sins—aye, it could even lift the ban of excommunication; such a pilgrimage was a deed worthy of a knight, combining as it were, the salvation of one's soul with an opportunity to see the world.

The Abbot, who had come from Provence many years before, spoke with great eloquence, but they were not convinced. Someone mumbled that it was no use—none of them knew the way to those distant lands; they would soon get lost.

The Abbot shrugged his shoulders. "Lose your way?" he exclaimed. "Nonsense! Anyone can show you the way. It is as simple as the royal highway to Cracow. Across Hungary, Croatia, Istria, to Venice—from

there to Provence, only a step! Do you think that none from Poland
has made the journey before you? Scores," he said loudly, "scores of
others have made that holy pilgrimage. In the olden days, when Rome
was under the German hand, the bishops from Poland went to Provence
to be consecrated. And even lately—you have heard, of course—Ladislas
sent envoys to St. Gilles to ask for a son by his new Czech wife, Judith?
And what happened? They went and in less than nine months they
were back. For no sooner was the service performed, no sooner had they
presented the Prince's offerings—a child's figure wrought in gold, ca-
lixes, surplices, and a mantle—than the monks came to them and said:
'You may go home. The Princess has conceived.' And so it was. Just
before winter sawing, Boleslas was born. Now the lad is already big
enough to mount a horse, and the envoys are still telling the wonders of
their journey! Thus, too, shall you come back, covered with glory, full of
wondrous tales. And victorious, too, if you obtain Shechec's death. St.
Gilles never refuses a pilgrim's plea; and surely, it will be easier for him
to destroy a warrior than to raise a babe in the womb of a barren woman
who has a slothful husband to boot. If he has done one, he will do the
other."

The knights listened in rapt attention to these supremely sound considerations. Nevertheless, they were unable to make up their minds.
Provence was too far. From Hungary they could always keep an eye
on Shechec, and be back quickly to thwart any new foul deed.

"That's just the trouble," the Abbot told himself; "'quickly,' indeed,"
and promptly began to assure them that none would dare to touch the
property of pilgrims, for the Church punished such a crime by excommunication, and St. Gilles by a mortal paralysis of all the limbs, as many
had learned to their sorrow. Ladislas and Shechec, in particular, could
ill afford to harm them, for they needed the benediction of the Holy
See and its gift of powerful relics for the new cathedral.

Still unconvinced, they voiced another objection—their fear of the
witch of longing who in far foreign lands was known to devour a man's
heart. There was no remedy, they had heard, for the dreadful illness
the witch induced. The shadow of the victim left his body and returned
home, and everyone knew what a man was worth when deprived of
his shadow. —Soon enough, he would turn into a shadow himself.

Aye, that was a dreadful affliction—the Abbot knew it well, better
than any of them. He still remembered the years when he had wandered

about like just such a shadow, unable to sleep, to eat, to pray. All that had passed now, but he remembered.

Nevertheless, he warmly denied the very existence of the witch. The sense of strangeness, the longing for one's land, he declared, were peculiar only to war prisoners and men of base extraction; a knight need not fear them—all the world stood open to him. Wherever he went, he would find a country and a family that were his by right, for the Christian knightly order united all nations, and it was in this, precisely, that lay its greatness and its glory. And he began to tell them of the magnificent reception that awaited them in Provence and of the unheard-of wonders they would see there.

But the good knights still seemed unable to make up their minds. They were loath to venture alone into such distant parts. It would be the first time they had set out in a small group, with no king to lead them, no strong forces of which they would be part, and they would wander about like exiles, uncertain of return. And disheartened, perhaps for the first time in their lives, at a loss what to decide, they tugged at their long, drooping moustaches and exchanged uneasy glances.

At last Glovach rose to his feet. "Either way we must journey through Hungary. You said so yourself, my Lord. Once in Hungary, we will decide whether we should make the pilgrimage or not."

"No doubt, no doubt," the Abbot agreed absently, rubbing his eyes which were dazed by the vision of his native land. He had been so completely lost in remembering it, that he had almost forgotten what he had been attempting. And what did it matter anyway? . . . Ah! *Belle Provence* . . .

The other knights sighed with relief. True, once in Hungary, they would decide one way or another. It was clever of Glovach to have thought of that.

They left the hall in a body: three Strzygonias, two Zavoras, two Novinas, three Osventas, and one Nagodzits—eleven in all.

Outside, on the turf of the front yard, sat waiting about thirty men at arms and servants who would accompany them, silent, neither conversing nor deliberating, for they had nothing to do with the choice of a destination and felt nothing but gloom to be leaving.

Pobieda, the steward, walked among the sturdy, solid-wheeled well-greased carts and sighed. He felt the leather pouches that held the money needed for such a long expedition, to see if they had been properly tied. Alas! Once upon a time, knights used to bring money home, now they were carrying it away. What was the world coming to?

Next to the money, and packed in similar cowhide pouches to protect them against rain and humidity, lay marten pelts, bolts of fine linen, and salt, all of them to be used as gifts or in barter, for there were many localities where folk did not know the use of coins and would accept none, though they gladly traded food and fodder for such precious goods as these.

Other carts, carefully covered with hides, were loaded with dry barley cakes, smoked meat, small barrels of lard which would serve both in cooking and to plaster down unruly hair, wolfskins and bearskins for use as bedding, spare thongs, quivers, bows, bundles of arrows. On top, easily accessible, lay the big lances and oblong shields.

The lances were spiked with iron on both ends so that a mounted knight could drive the reverse into the ground by his charger's side while he rested. The shields were worn suspended from the neck on a wide strap, while inside a loop was securely fastened, through which the left arm was thrust during combat.

These heavy weapons were to be carried on carts. It would have been easier to make the same disposition of helmets and suits of armor, cumbersome as they were on a long journey undertaken in the midst of summer heat. But this the travelers might not do, for how then were strangers to know that they were belted knights? And at any rate their armor was light, no longer the full plate-armor their forefathers used to use. Instead of breastplates, they wore knee-length hauberks of mail, with sleeves that reached to their finger tips and fastened at the waist by a knightly girdle of silver or gold. Helmets were round, with labra and a mail hood for the back of the head and neck. An unsheathed broadsword hung at each belt; the misericorde dangled from the neck. A leather jerkin worn under the hauberk, and a mail hose of lighter iron mesh than the hauberk completed their accoutrement.

The gold of their belts and chains flashed in the sun, as they stood, ready to depart. The wise Momot stuttered that it was time to be off; they would gain nothing by tarrying. And he was right. If leave they must, the sooner the better. The bay oxen already stood by the carts, the caparisoned chargers snorted impatiently. Men at arms were shouldering bows and quivers and adjusting their swords. Servants picked up the axes and flint-set staves that served them for weapons.

The time had come, indeed! Their hearts were immeasurably heavy. When would they see again their own Silesian forests, when step once more across the sacred thresholds of their homes? Perhaps their bones would whiten in some faraway land while the spirit alone returned. Who could tell?

"Oh, that I were dead!" lamented Ofka in the keening voice of a mourner, as she clutched at Imbram's arms. "Could I be turned into a hawk and fly after you . . . Could I be turned into a blade of grass and wilt by the roadside until you came past . . . Imko, Imko, I summoned you to my bedside and you came . . . O, you came, Imko . . . But how will you ever hear my call so far in Hungary, so far away, Imko? How can I summon you?" She choked in her sobs as he caressed her head helplessly.

In a calm voice Glovach was giving last-minute orders and instructions to Bogucha and Pobieda: what crops were to be sown, and where, out of which bin they were to take the seed for winter sowing; the white mare was to be bred to the chestnut stallion, and the red heifer to the white-faced bull. And mind they did not let the place run to seed.

"Have no fear, I know, I know," Bogucha said, and Glovach nodded.

Now all was ready. The Abbot lifted up his crooked staff to give the departing knights a solemn blessing. Ofka wept softly, pressing her face to Imbram's breast, her fair hair catching in the iron mesh of his hauberk. With his mailed hand he tried clumsily to draw up the white kerchief that had slipped back from her hair. Zbylut watched them with his usual sardonic expression. Yashek Zavora smiled his usual vague but friendly smile and his elder brother, Momot, kept quiet, also as usual. The Babbler was silent for once and, like the others, he kept his eyes fixed on the forest, pretending not to notice Imbram's unseemly weakness. Now Ludobir Osventa began to grow impatient: "Let's be off! Let's be off!" The steward came running, carrying a jug of mead. Glovach's daughters had already brought crocks that were to be used as stirrup cups.

The knights first poured off a few drops for the *lares,* then drained their cups, flung them to the ground, and stamped on the shards. Bowing low from the waist, they took leave of the doorstep, the walls, the thatched roof, then they sprang into their saddles.

Yokes creaked, cartwheels, though well greased, began to squeak balefully.

"Weep not, Ofka! We shall soon return," Imbram called from the gate.

"Don't turn around," Glovach growled. He was furious with his brother. No knight was he! That witch's changeling! That lout! But Imbram paid no heed. "Weep not! It won't be long!" he shouted once more.

Alas! Pomian, the mischievous spirit, had caught the unguarded words. From the black wall of the forest they drifted back now, mocking: ". . . long . . . long," as the first of the knights disappeared among the trees.

All this took place on the sixth day of July, in the year 1095 Anno Domini, on the day which in the Catholic calendar is devoted to the memory of Saint Pulcheria, virgin and martyr.

5.

The Truce of God

THE SUMMER SUN WARMED THE SADNESS OF THE EXILED KNIGHTS; THEY rode to the great Hungarian city of Buda, on the Danube River. There they joined the court of King Ladislaus, and made a friend in the knight, Moymir Stiborovits, a countryman who had fled into exile years before with the late Polish king, Boleslas. There also they saw knights preparing for a journey to Clermont, in faraway France. Pope Urban II had sent messengers to Ladislas, announcing a council at Clermont. Restless, unhappy, full of energy that should have been poured into their fields and crops at home, the Polish knights decided to join the envoys. Moymir Stiborovits told them it was a journey just long enough to use up the time they must remain away from Poland and so, with the royal ensign to lead them, they set out in the month of August. Imbram, regretful that he had not the courage to turn homeward and make a separate peace, rode with his brothers and thought of Ofka.

In September they crossed the Alps to Italy. Snow struck them among the mountains; blizzard gales tried to force them from the narrow trail into abysses. Their guide, riding a mule, led them slowly to the pass of Mount Jervis where they stayed at a monastery which one day was to house a young man fleeing from his own wedding, a young man named Bernard, who would become a saint and give his name to the pass.

At the monastery they met other travelers, two Provençal knights named Roger de Foix and Gaston d'Armillac, who were returning to their liege lord, Count Raymond St. Gilles of Toulouse, having carried the dowry for Raymond's daughter Giselle to the German margrave she was to wed.

When the storm passed they rode together into Italy, into a land so warm and ancient that the Polish knights wondered how history could

26

be so aged and climate so pleasant. But there was famine in the valleys and quiet on the ruined Roman roads.

The royal arms, raised high on its staff, glittered in the warm sun over the heads of the Hungarian emissaries. Upon white limestone rocks lizards basked in the sunshine. Everywhere one looked, the whiteness of the rock broke through the red soil, red soil upon white rock, like dried blood smeared upon a bleached skull. Cicadas buzzed their endless tune, on and on from dawn to dusk, until one could almost believe it was the old, rich Mediterranean soil itself that was singing.

Oak forests grew everywhere in this fertile land, but the trees themselves were unlike the ones the good Silesian knights had been used to at home, much lower and with leaves more sharply cut and tough as leather; and besides the oaks, the countryside was covered with fig and olive groves. As the cavalcade passed by, deep purple fruits swollen with sweetness would fall from the trees and burst at the horses' feet.

Where no olive or fig tree grew, where no oak spread its mighty roots, the soil was at once invaded by the maqui, a wild tangle of vegetation, a maze of perfumed evergreens with small narrow leaves and inch-long thorns, which neither man nor beast could penetrate.

Each year, with the first breath of spring, the maqui burst forth into bloom like a cloister courtyard, shimmered with the pale pink of rockroses, sparkled with the golden cascades of laburnum, and upon every patch free of the brush spread a carpet of wild tulips, hyacinths, and saffron. Fair as a dream was the land of Provence at such times; and the ancient Mediterranean world seemed as new as though it had just left its Creator's hands.

But when the torrid, relentless summer had turned the rustling grass to ashes, when the maqui had shed its bloom and revealed its hidden thorns, when the brilliant green of the leaves had vanished under a coat of dust, when olive trees had turned gray and in the whole landscape no color remained but the red of the soil and no sound but the endless fiddling of the cicadas, then, indeed, this world seemed old and weary of the burden of so many ages, peoples, and religions.

As the good Polish, Hungarian, and Provençal knights proceeded now along the wide tracks with which the Roman Empire had crisscrossed the land, they encountered at every turn shattered remains of overturned statuary, old relics of dead faiths, lying mutilated in the tangle of the maqui or in the shade of oak groves, the light gold of their marble, so different from the deathly white of limestone, shining in the dusk.

Here and there, upon weedless hillocks overgrown with thyme, rose the ruins of some ancient structure, graceful pillars supporting richly carved crossbeams, all wrought in that same golden marble.

"These are pagan Roman temples and idols," Roger de Foix informed his new friends, and spat in disgust.

The Silesian knights stared curiously at the strange Roman deities, so unlike the wooden blocks and shapeless figures clumsily hewn in stone that once were worshipped in their old homes.

There must have been a great many of these Roman temples and idols that were so strange to the Polish visitors, since almost every wayside chapel (and these, too, were innumerable) was built of their remains. From under the thick layers of plaster which covered these primitive structures there everywhere peered rich capitals with beautifully carved profiles, masks, and acanthus leaves. Among them, under the heavy, clumsily vaulted arch of the Romanesque portal, the holy guardian of the nearby bridge or hamlet kept watch. There he stood, stiff, austere, awesomely different from the laughing faces that surrounded him on every side, staring straight ahead in stern meditation. He was called the good Bishop Martin, Guy, Lambert, Gilles, or Mamert and was piously honored by all men, even though the same who knelt at his feet would afterwards steal into the woods to worship the ancient idols that now lay broken on the ground.

The broad, diagonally grooved slabs of the Roman road no longer lay flat on the ground. Dislodged by the roots of trees that grew on either side, lifted by the swelling of the ground, they presented an uneven surface that was becoming increasingly unsafe for travel, particularly at night. How could it be otherwise? For centuries now no one had tended the Imperial highways—no one, that is, save that single guardian: a stone saint in an arched wayside chapel.

None of the chapels was more carefully adorned than those that kept watch over the bridges thrown in bold Roman arches over rivers and streams. Though from a distance these bridges looked as stout as ever, in reality they were unfit to cross. The stone surface had worn off, leaving gaping holes that could readily swallow both horse and rider. In vain did the Church promise the redemption of sins to anyone who would undertake to repair them; the people preferred to find fords or to build ferries.

At every ford sat a toll collector, exacting his dues. There were many of them, far too many. Every baron, bishop, or abbot through whose domains the highway ran levied a toll, fixing the amount arbitrarily. In return, they presumably took it upon themselves to patrol the highway and protect travelers from robbers, but this they seldom did. For though his Lordship never failed to collect his due, the safety of wayfarers was the least of his concern.

According to the prevailing custom, knights and the clergy paid no tolls; servants and bondsmen on foot were charged half the normal rate, horsemen and carts the full amount; merchants paid double, and Jews four times over. The toll was seldom taken in coin; the collectors preferred to take it out in goods. If the cart happened to be loaded with wine the collector was entitled to open every cask, sample the contents, and only after due consideration and often long deliberations with his cronies, make up his mind which one he was going to keep. The same held true of other goods: honey, fish, leather, and bolts of woolen cloth or silk, from which a malicious collector could order a length cut out of the very middle.

Since neither the stone saints nor flesh-and-blood toll collectors provided much safety along the roads and since the impassable cover of the maqui swarmed with outlaws lying in wait for merchants' caravans, the number of men bold enough to travel with goods grew smaller every year. A trade route once crowded with traffic became deserted, and townships famous in Roman days for their wealth and civilization turned into mean and squalid little boroughs.

"It's less than a month since a fellow merchant of mine, a good Christian he was, mind you, was slain by bandits on the road to Toulouse while carrying Eastern spices," a merchant from Paris, whom the knights met on the road, said bitterly. "It befell near the castle, so we went to the Lord to complain that under his very nose, the robbers had acted so boldly. 'And when did it happen?' asked his Lordship. 'Even as the church bells were ringing for Angelus,' said we. 'The Angelus?' said his Lordship. 'Then what are you pestering me about? Since the mishap befell after sundown, it is none of my business. I guard the road in the daytime, not at night.' And he sent us away empty-handed and would not even return the toll he had taken."

This melancholy tale was told not to the knights, who would have no intercourse with merchants, but to the squire, Saint-Pierre de Luz, who passed it on. This Saint-Pierre was an interesting and not unusual unfortunate of the times. Though squire to Sir Roger de Foix, he was no mere stripling, as most squires were, but a mature man with grizzled temples. He came of noble blood, and the fact that despite his great valor and his friendship with Sir Roger he had not yet won his silver spurs and that he continued to hold a post intermediate between that of servant and companion was a sore spot with him, which he tried to conceal by jesting and making sport of himself.

"My Lord, you see, is the liegeman of the Count of St. Gilles," he told the Strzygonia brothers. "But that is no dishonor, since the Count himself is of royal blood. But look at me . . . I am the liegeman of my lord though his birth is inferior to mine . . . Hah! So be it. My belly has grown hollow with hankering after a knight's girdle. It's not meant for me. I daresay I shall knock about as a poor squire as long as I live."

"Can it be that you have had no opportunity yet to show your valor?" Zbylut inquired in a tone of incredulity.

"Opportunity! Opportunity I had in plenty. More, in fact, than I can boast hairs on my head. Ask Sir Robert! But it's not that. Noble birth and valor are not enough to make one a knight. No, a man needs substance; wealth alone lends splendor to lineage. In Toulouse, you will see scores of elderly men, like myself, who will never reach out for the silver spurs. They cannot afford the price."

He broke off, and seeing that the Silesian knights had not understood, he grew annoyed.

"Listen," he resumed. "What is a knight to live on? His family estates have shrunk, wasted away, till they bring next to nothing. War, likewise, is becoming less and less profitable. You were surprised to hear that a knight will plunder in league with outlaws, but, pray, what else is he to do? It's not proper to work . . . What else remains? Hunting or war. Once a man wins his spurs, he must either stay buried in his manor, eating barley cakes and game, and unseasoned game at that, or if possible he will by some means get hold of enough money to set out with a retinue and join some baronial court where there are tourneys and hunts, rings and love courts—where there is life! I have been told, indeed, that some scribe has deduced and described at length the twelve delectations or pleasurable pursuits which a lord of the manor may enjoy. These, as I recall, are: hunting, fencing, chess, good cheer, guzzling, lying with his wife's wenches, listening to minstrels, bear baiting, sitting by the fireside, holding court over his vassals, blood-letting in the spring, and watching it snow in wintertime. But all this, my good friends, is little, very little, indeed. . . . Not enough to keep a man at home. The wide world calls, but how is one to set forth without gold?"

The Silesians, however, were more puzzled than ever. They could not grasp his meaning and blamed it on their inadequate knowledge of the language. Why, they wondered, should anyone bother to enumerate, let alone describe, such simple, obvious things as hunting or sitting by the fireside? And why, on the other hand, had the real, the greatest pleasures of manorial life, such as sawing, harvest, and haying, not been mentioned at all?

"In our land the lord of the manor will have nothing to do with chores which by right belong to the peasants," Saint-Pierre de Luz informed them with an air or superiority when he discovered what was on their minds. "He leaves it to the tenant farmers. They, in return, pay him a fee or rent—and a high one, at that."

"Why, then, did you say there was a dearth of denarii in the manor?"

"Because the lord of the manor usually collects his fee ten years in advance, and the denarii vanish in no time."

Thus they conversed, as in company they proceeded toward Clermont, where Pope Urban was to hold council a month later. On their road they halted at wayside inns where young wine foamed in tall crockery pitchers. But beer and mead there was none, and their absence annoyed the Polish knights. Reluctantly and with distaste they tried now to grow accustomed to wine, of which there was an unheard-of profusion. The reddish soil spread upon white rock must have been ideal for vine growing, for wherever the eye turned, vineyards dotted the landscape. Grape gathering was long since over, and only here and there, upon less sunny slopes, the fruit hung in heavy, scented clusters, while in the village the ripe, mellow grapes, heaped in huge vats, were being trodden by bare feet. The white thighs of girls flashed from the brownish, bubble-covered liquid. They stood in twos, facing each other, their arms entwined, drunk with the vapors of the musk that spurted from under their feet. As the cavalcade appeared on the road the villagers would promptly vanish around the corners of the houses (for who can tell what fancy may enter a lord's mind?), and only the treaders remained in the square, bare to loins, seemingly absorbed in their work, yet stealing sidelong glances at the passing men at arms. The Provençals laughed and beckoned to them but the Poles and Hungarians turned their eyes away, scandalized. A naked wench was good enough in bed or in the bath-house, but here, by the road-side . . . Faugh!

Sometimes in the small towns they happened upon festivals celebrated in honor of the ancient god of wine, Bacchus. A naked old man bedecked with vine-leaves was driven around in a wagon to which young lads dressed in goatskins were hitched. A host of girls completely naked but adorned with garlands surrounded the procession. They ran dancing, shouting, slapping their thighs, while shepherds who accompanied them blew bark trumpets and drew from their flutes weird tunes, the meaning and purpose of which had long since been forgotten. This ancient custom survived, though no one knew any more whence it came nor whom the naked old man in the wagen might represent. Nor did anyone know why priests and monks grew so angry over the custom and threatened those who took part in it with doom and eternal fire, and at the sound of approaching hoof beats the revelers hastened to disband, running like stalked deer, to hide in the bushes.

The bells of a nearby monastery were just ringing for evensong when the cavalcade halted for the night before a wayside inn. Two days before, at Avignon, they had crossed a large river called the Rhone, and were now proceeding upstream along the valley in the direction of Saint-Etienne.

The inn, like most of the buildings in this land, was constructed from the ruins of a pagan temple, or perhaps of a Roman palace. An exquisite capital protruded from its crooked wall just above the ground; a bearded giant with stooped shoulders supported the eaves of its flat and flimsy roof. The door was open, and a gaunt, flat-chested monk on the threshold watched with obvious approval the innkeeper, who had just brought out a pail filled with raw meat and was flinging its contents with unwonted vigor into a small brook that flowed past the inn.

"What is wrong with that meat?" asked Saint-Pierre de Luz, approaching. "Gone bad?"

"God forbid, Your Honor. In my inn, the Lord be praised, there is no fear of that. But as the fast day is close at hand, it is befitting not to keep flesh in a Christian house. Let the fishes eat it!"

"Aye, aye," the monk nodded with quick approval. "Better not to keep it, lest one be led into temptation. Like those vagrants last week: they stole a steer on Friday and devoured it at once, mindless of the fast day. Thy could not even wait until Sunday!"

He sighed over this depravity, bowed to the newcomers and departed, his sandals clattering on the stones. The knights dismounted and took their seats on wooden benches, crowding around a table that had been set under the trees.

"Here you're throwing meat to the fishes, and we starving to death!" Sir Roger observed sourly.

The innkeeper cast a prudent glance around.

"Not so, my Lord, I'll pull it out directly. I have a little cave there under that stone, a cool spot where the meat keeps better than indoors."

"Ah, ha, you deceitful knave," the knight said with a laugh.

"It's always best to keep on good terms with the abbey, my Lord. As for the meat, I shall fetch it quickly."

"Wait! First bring us wine. And see that it is good."

The innkeeper vanished inside and presently reappeared with wine and clay mugs. As he was placing them on the table, the door opened again from within and a tall, graying knight, evidently attracted by the noise of the conversation outside, appeared on the threshold. His gaunt frame was enclosed in well-worn mail adorned only by a rich girdle. He bowed to the company assembled under the trees, holding up, as he did so, both palms towards them to show that he held no weapon and planned no treachery. The others rose to their feet, and likewise showed their palms in a forthright, knightly salute.

"My name is Gouffier de la Tour," the tall knight introduced himself. "Are you, noble lords, on your way to Clermont?"

"We are," Roger de Foix told him. "We are all going to Clermont. Even these noble knights here who come from a land so distant that Saxony seems close in comparison."

Gouffier de la Tour nodded in approval. "Yes. All the world is coming to Clermont. I too am bound there, though not from so far. And where, tell me, did you hear him?"

"Hear whom?" they asked, surprised.

"Why, him who has called us all to Clermont."

"Pope Urban, you mean? Is he already here?"

"No, it's not Pope Urban I have in mind, but Brother Peter, the one who discoursed last Sunday at Avignon."

"We never heard of him."

"Never heard of him?" repeated Sir Gouffier, incredulously, scanning their faces with eyes as blue as cornflowers. "You have not heard him and yet you are going to Clermont?"

"These noble lords are on a mission to the Holy Father, who will be there. And we are hastening to rejoin Count Raymond of Toulouse, whose vassals we are."

"Oh? Then surely you must have wondered why everyone else is likewise hastening to Clermont?"

"Hardly. Why should we, since the Council has been called?"

Sir Gouffier shrugged impatiently.

"The Council, forsooth! There has been many a council and men have never flocked as they flock now. They go because *he* summons them to Clermont."

"He? You mean that monk?"

"Yes, Peter. No one knows whence he came. Some say from Amiens, not that it matters. A puny little man, mere skin and bones, who wears a bedraggled cloak with a cowl that hangs to his heels. But when he begins to speak, men's hearts stand still. And mine, too, stood still. . . ."

His listeners were convinced that Sir Gouffier was drunk, yet none showed the slightest sign of harboring such a thought.

"And of what, tell us, did he speak?" Sir Roger inquired politely.

"Of Jerusalem, of course. What else? Of Jerusalem and the cruel plight of our Lord. It's enough to make one's heart weep bloody tears to hear—and yet here we sit and drink, as though . . ."

"Oh!" interrupted Sir Roger, disappointed. "He is not the first to have told of Jerusalem."

"Quite so, good sirs. Many have told of it before. Yet, since the Saracens overran the Holy Land, he is the first to have come back alive."

"You say he was there?"

"That he was. . . . With his own eyes he saw the degradation, the infamy to which Our Lord has been subjected . . . Now he commands all good Christians to gather at Clermont. We shall learn why in good time . . ."

He lowered his head and remained absorbed in thought. Through the open door came the clatter of vessels and the odor of scorching olive oil. Suddenly . . . "Hi! Hi! The Normans are coming!" the innkeeper screamed shrilly behind their backs.

"Where? Where?"

"Down that hill! Look at the emblems! Normans!" and he vanished as though the ground had swallowed him.

Two black-eyed girls ran out of the kitchen and hurriedly gathered the cups and bowls in their aprons. The knights quickly buckled their girdles and drew their broadswords; their eyes never left the approaching cavalcade, already descending the hill. A pennant bearing the emblems of the Vikings floated over the riders' heads. Aye, these were Normans—there could be no doubt of it. Their faces were harsh and bold, their eyes blue, their hair red. They stared straight ahead with the arrogance of men who had vanquished the world. Had they not but lately conquered Sicily and England? And not so long ago they had devastated Gaul, Burgundy, and Provence itself. The memory of those days still rankled. Ah! the wanton destroyers of churches, the foul persecutors of holy relics! Was there anyone in these parts who did not recall with horror how blessed bones and ashes had been carried from monastery to monastery, from church to church, in a mad flight from the pursuing invaders who cared nothing for their sanctity and coveted only the gold and gems of the reliquaries? No, these were not things easily to be forgotten; and though the Normans were now allies, and presumably good neighbors, De Foix, De La Tour, and D'Armillac watched the approaching group with a hatred that seemed quite incomprehensible to the Polish knights, who saw nothing unusual in the newcomers. In fact, they were amazed to observe that the emblem displayed on the Norman pennant was the same as that used in their own country by those good knights, the Yashcholts, whose forefathers, it was said, had long ago come in dragon ships from far across the sea. What they felt about the Normans, however, was not of the slightest consequence; it would never do to decline an armed encounter, and so, like the rest, they stood ready.

The Normans halted. There were not many of them—five knights and about twenty servants, some mounted, some on foot. Now the eldest of the knights called out in a ringing voice: "Ho, there! Make room in the inn for the true vassals of the good knight and noble prince, Robert Curthose, Lord of Normandy!"

"The inn is already occupied by rightful emissaries of the King of Hungary and good knights of Poland and Provence."

"If so, it must be vacated."

"By Christ's Passion—it shall not!"

At once the Normans turned and withdrew some twenty paces to make room for the charge, while their opponents hastily mounted their horses, which the servants, seeing how matters stood, had already brought around. On both sides squires, clutching battle-axes and shields, ranged themselves behind the horses; they could hardly wait for the moment when their masters would close in and it would be their turn to lash out with their broad, double-edged axes against the shields of the opposing squires. Meanwhile, behind them, the shutters of the inn flew shut with a bang. The two maid servants who but a moment before had collected the crockery jumped out through the kitchen window and raced for the brook. They waded across, squealing with fright, and hid in the woods beyond. The innkeeper, sweating and terrified, thrust his round head through the venthole to watch. The visors of helmets snapped shut. The Normans, their lances held ready on a level with their horses' ears, waited, as custom demanded, for their opponents to make ready. The latter had already deployed themselves in a single file, a thin formation called "the hedge." Only the Hungarians, with the Zupan Geza, Sukki de Szuka at their head, though likewise mounted and ready, kept to one side; for as long as their mission was not completed they had no leave to take part in any encounter.

"By God, are ye ready?"

"By God, we are!"

Pressing the flanks of their mounts with their thighs so that the beasts groaned, they flung themselves powerfully against each other, but before they had time to close in and lash out with their lances a tremendous thunder of hoofs broke upon them from the side. Mounted upon a magnificent bay stallion, Albert, Bishop of Nîmes, brandishing his crozier, rushed between them. He was followed by a host of armed men, mounted and on foot—the holy militia of peace. They wedged themselves between the combatants, unmindful of the fact that they might be trampled and speared from both sides.

"Hold! *Treuga Dei!* The Truce of God!" roared the bishop. "In the name of Our Lord Jesus Christ and His vicar on earth, Urban the Second, I enjoin you: Cease!"

"Begone, Bishop!" the Normans growled. "And make haste, lest we run our spears through you." They had reined in their chargers so abruptly that bloody froth dripped from their mouths, but they still held their lances ready.

"We need no defenders," fumed the Provençal knights. "We can take care of ourselves."

"The Truce of God!" the bishop repeated vehemently, and being a man of great physical strength, he began to knock up their lances with his bare fist.

"Since when is God's Truce in force on Thursdays?"

"Friday is come already. The Angelus has long since rung. Raise your lances, I say. For shame! Are you Christians or heathens? Instead of making for Clermont in a body as you should, here you fall upon each other."

"To Clermont!" repeated De La Tour and was the first to raise his lance.

"We too are bound to Clermont," the Normans admitted sullenly.

"Why then must you pick quarrels on the highway?"

"They would not make room for us at the inn."

"If such be the case, pray accept the hospitality of my own house. I shall welcome you with all my heart."

Slowly, with obvious reluctance, the knights signified that they would not engage in combat, not for the present, at least. The squires morosely stuck their axes into their belts and threw their shields over their shoulders. As the two parties were about to set off in peace, the bishop blessed them, and pointing to the North, called once more:

"To Clermont!"

A gold and crimson twilight richly stained the gray olive groves of Provence. The two knightly bands had already vanished in the distance, and the bishop, satisfied, had also ridden away. Only the holy militia of peace still lingered by the inn. Well pleased with themselves for having so stoutly defended the Church's peace, they haughtily summoned the host to stand them wine. Seeing that they were numerous and had no thought of paying, he demurred, whereupon they broke down the door and looted the cellar. Then, in high spirits, they first smashed mugs on each other's heads, and next proceeded to demolish the tables and benches. The host, following the example of the maid servants, waded across the brook and hid in the brush. There, tearing his hair in anguish, he cursed them one and all—knights, bishop, and holy militia.

6.

Clermont

GOUFFIER DE LA TOUR SOON BECAME THE CONSTANT COMPANION OF THE three youngest Silesians: Imbram, the Momot, and Yashek. There was a strange affinity between the gaunt, blue-eyed giant and these "changelings," as their elders called them. Perhaps he, too, had been once almost bewitched by a fairy, for, despite all his tremendous strength, he was incredibly gentle and fond of animals and children. In fact, he swore by the sacred seamless robe of Argenteuil that God, too, must love babes and beasts best, since of all His creatures they were the most innocent. Aside from that, he was a man of great learning, knew more than many an abbot, and gladly told his new companions of the history of the lands through which they were traveling. Thus the Polish knights, whose grandfathers still remembered the days of omnipotent pagan priests, were surprised to learn that the lands of the Mediterranean coast had been Christian for over eight hundred years. But what astounded them even more, was to hear of the terrible persecutions that had taken place here in Roman days, how virgins had been torn by wild beasts, how dung was thrown at Christians, and how they were forbidden entrance to public buildings and baths. It sounded utterly fantastic to the Silesians, who had known Christianity only as a ruling faith imposed from above and stoutly guarded by mighty kings and bishops. How could Christ, they wondered, permit such outrages to be visited upon His own? It must be that He had been still young and weak in those days, and it was not until later that He had grown so strong and powerful that He could overthrow creeds and smash the idols, which here in Auvergne were strewn along the roads and on top of mounds as plentifully as they had been in Provence.

For they were in Auvergne now, and the soil all around was no longer red, nor were the rocks white, but both were black, grayish black. On the horizon rose strangely shaped hills with abrupt slopes and flat brows, looking as though their summits had been sliced off. That these were dead volcanos, that once upon a time a live and terrible fire had spilled from those levelled crowns into the valley below and later turned into a black and fertile soil, none of the riders ever suspected.

Though it was late autumn, the weather was dry and the highway, along which so many men, horses, and carts had passed in the last few weeks, was covered with a thick layer of dust looking like ashes and leaving an ashy taste in one's mouth.

The nearer they drew to Clermont, the larger grew the number of travelers hastening in the same direction. Peter the Hermit, whose name was on everyone's lips, preceded them by a day. At every halt they were told that he had just ridden off on his mule, and the local people never tired of describing to the new arrivals his paltry, sickly figure in the tattered cloak and overlong cowl for which children called him "Peter Cuculla," "Peter-with-the-Cloak." He had tramped it, it was said, all over France, Normandy, Brittany, and Picardy, up and down, north, south, east, and west, and everywhere, it was said men spoke of him as they seldom do of mortals; they brought him gifts of cloth, gems, and choice morsels of food, which he, however, immediately distributed among the poor. He reconciled broken marriages and bade masters be gentle with their servants. But chiefly he spoke of Jerusalem and of the dreadful plight of the Holy Sepulcher and told his listeners to set out at once for Clermont, where the Holy Father would devise some way to erase the frightful indignity. It was said that his throat was so inflamed from this constant haranguing that he spoke in a hoarse, barely audible whisper. But let him only stand in the market place, and the spirit of the Lord would descend upon him, and his voice would ring out so you could hear it all over the square. After he had spoken, some charitable woman would give him warm water with olive oil or a drink of goat's milk, for he often clutched his breast in pain. Sometimes he drank it, sometimes he would not even see what was handed to him. There was but one thing that enraged him. That was having people pluck the hair of his mule and hide it in their bosoms as a holy relic. Then he would thunder and shout in wrath. Otherwise he was as gentle as a lamb and only bade everyone set forth at once for Clermont, where great things would come to pass. .

What these things might be, none knew; but they all tied their bundles, ready to start on their way.

Some who knew Peter's own folk or came from his parts recounted how in the past he used to be like any other man, with a wife and three children. Yet even in those days he would run away from his family and dwell all by himself in some miserable hut of branches he would build in the woods. This love of solitude had won him the nickname of "The Hermit." His wife used to track him down, and when she had discovered his hiding place, she would drag him home, to the delight of the entire village. But at last his wife died, his children grew up and went their own ways, and the Hermit, too, vanished from the neighborhood, leaving behind all his possessions—which consisted of a wretched hut, a goat, and a mangy cat.

No one knew whether he had hidden in the woods or had wandered away somewhere beyond the confines of the Vermandois country. But, as it turned out, he had wandered much farther than his countrymen could ever have imagined, all the way to the Holy Land, and whether somewhere on his way he had taken monastic vows, no one knew.

These tales of Peter's countrymen met with little favor among his ardent followers. Shaken to the marrow by the Hermit's oratory, they did not like to hear of his humble past. For them he had begun to exist the moment he set foot in Jerusalem, and only then.

Yet some of his hearers felt strangely baffled, even as the Silesian knights had felt baffled when listening to Sir Gouffier's tales. Hitherto they had never given Jerusalem a thought; it was Rome that they looked upon as the most sacred spot, the very center of Christianity and of its mighty power. Now, they were told that holy places more important, more sacred than Rome itself had fallen prey to the heathen, that God had been defeated and had surrendered His Own Sepulcher to His foe. The realization of such an outrage filled them with horror and shame and, at the same time, the Saracens, those who had defeated God himself, rose in their eyes to the stature of evil giants, with whom it would be both awesome and glorious to strive.

Whatever their feelings, they all hurried to Clermont, pushing hand-carts laden with their children and their goods, and driving before them their goats, which there was no one left at home to tend. Forced to make way for lordly retinues, they abandoned the highroad and spread over the fields in search of short-cuts and ungathered turnips. A cold, sweeping wind from the north urged them on. And along the highway rode endless cavalcades of knights who, as they passed each other, raised open palms, exchanged family calls, the names of their liege lords and countries, and even snatches of conversation.

Two German knights, named Gottschalk and von Emich, hearing that the Silesians understood their language, begged leave to travel with them, for, knowing no Latin, they felt completely lost. Glovach and Moymir consented, though reluctantly, for the appearance of the two German knights was strangely unprepossessing.

Another time, Bishop Lambert of Arras, who was related to Sir Roger de Foix, catching sight of his kinsman, called to him to ask whether he knew why such throngs were bound for Clermont? What was going to happen to them? And who was that monk, Peter? Was he preaching at the Pope's bidding or at his own? It all seemed strange indeed, since none of the matters to come before the council called for such an unusual assemblage.

"I wonder," the bishop ran on, glad to have found a listener. "As far as I know we were to consider first whether or not to double the anathema laid upon the Emperor Henry and King Philip. I trust we shall. These godless rebels must be curbed. Next, we were to settle the dispute as to whether St. Dennis, the good bishop and patron of Paris, was one and the same with St. Dionysius the Areopagite whom St. Paul converted in Athens. A monk from the south, no doubt moved by envy, insists that if he was, he must have lived three hundred years. And why not, I ask you? Why should a great saint not live three hundred years? What is there to marvel at? Nevertheless, the good inhabitants of Paris are justly vexed at such doubts, so the Council has promised to settle the matter once and for all . . . And last of all, we were to promulgate the Peace of God in triple form, namely: *Pax Dei*, that shall at all times and in all places protect monks and nuns, the clergy, widows, orphans, minors, and old people; *Asilium Dei*, that will shield anyone who seeks refuge in a church or any other consecrated place; and *Treuga Dei*, forbidding all strife in Lent, Advent, on Holy Days and Holy Day Eves, and every week from Thursday night until Monday morning . . ."

"Marry!" Sir Roger interrupted with a chuckle. "What will there be left for us then?"

"Nothing!" shouted the bishop. "Nothing, but to fight the enemies of the Church. For once we shall put an end to your eternal quarrels!"

He would have gone on, but at that moment their attention was drawn by the appearance of a strange figure who came striding down the middle of the road. He was a man of gigantic stature, dressed in a worn leather jerkin, horseless and spurless. Instead of a dagger, a huge broadsword dangled from his neck.

"Indeed, there will be no one missing in Clermont if even he is coming," the Bishop observed.

The giant, whose fame had spread far and wide, called himself "Walter the Penniless," and was the bastard offspring of high, some even said of royal, lineage. Years ago he had been unjustly refused the silver spurs and, infuriated at the slight, had sworn he would do without them forever. Wearing his sword belt round his neck, he began to associate with the rabble or else wandered alone, poor, hungry, and independent. His reckless bravery soon brought him fame, and King Philip of France offered him the spurs he had once coveted. But he declined the honor, and continued to roam the world, his broadsword dangling from his neck, solitary and knowing no master but himself.

The walls of Clermont were surrounded by a crowd so dense that it was difficult to push one's way into the town. The suburbs, the market places, and even a marshy lowland that stretched off to the west, were covered with swarming encampments, dotted with the white pavilions of the high nobility, barons, and dukes. In the most convenient site, near the gate of St. Honoré, the camp of the delegation sent by the Basileus Alexius, surnamed "*Isapostolos*" or "The Equal of Apostles," glittered and dazzled the eye, and overhead shone the Imperial labarum with its two-headed eagle. The pavilions, all the equipment, and even the carts surpassed in wealth and beauty anything that had ever been seen before, and the camp of the Greek envoys was constantly surrounded by a throng of curious onlookers. Close by, the court of Swennon, the royal prince of Denmark, had pitched their leather tents, and though the tents themselves were few and modest enough, the huge scarlet standard cut in four by a white cross was famous the world over and attracted general attention. Among the throngs which overflowed the valley there were visitors from every land: knights and commons, monks and wandering jugglers, tramps and fugitive slaves who hid their brands under rags and were only too glad to disappear in a multitude among which they could not easily be found. There were servants and clerics, students forever on the watch for a chance to play a prank or create a disturbance, trollops, mountebanks, and Jews in peaked caps and with the compulsory yellow patch sewn upon their left sleeves.

Calling to each other in every Gallic dialect, hawkers sold fish and smoked meat, cheese, olive oil and wine, goats and cattle, herbs, cakes, medicines, spices, salt, hemp, flax, Picardy wool, Flemish linen, Spanish and Genovese leather, pelts, and even gems. Money changers stood gravely by their scales. In a corner there was even a booth where were to be found encaustic, gilt, paints, and parchment, both new sheets and old ones from which the Roman texts had been erased. The stocks of parchment being limited, the sheets could not be sold to anyone (in the unlikely event that an eager purchaser happened along) until the Archbishop himself had descended in state from his castle to buy the annual supply for the entire diocese. This moment was anxiously awaited in many a monastery by copyists and illuminators, who were painstakingly adorning the final sheets of the former year's supply and dreaded to interrupt a task which was not only life's passion but also constituted the surest passport to salvation, since for every letter traced in a holy book the Church redeemed one venial sin, and for every elaborate initial fifteen.

As was their habit, the most powerful of the barons were the last to arrive, reaching Clermont only a week ahead of the Holy Father himself. Each brought along a multitude of servants, vassals, squires, falconers, scribes, lutanists, and singers. Once in town they stopped wherever they pleased, while their servants, armed with cudgels, drove away the common rabble, and cleared space for the pavilions of their masters. And as the place was already overcrowded and ejected unfortunates had nowhere to go, there would on every such occasion arise a terrific din of wails and protests, which at once proclaimed to the good town of Clermont that some new important personage had arrived within its precincts.

None of these late arrivals could vie in the magnificence of their retinues with Raymond St. Gilles, hereditary lord of Toulouse. His men and horses alike sparkled with gold, shimmered with brilliant colors. One would have thought that the resplendent train was on its way to some courtly tournament, and not about to spend several autumnal weeks in a suburban encampment. Raymond himself, now nearing middle age, was a handsome man, chivalrous and open-hearted, generous to a fault but brooking no opposition. He was accompanied by his young wife, Elvira, the daughter of the king of Castille and reputed to be the most beautiful and the proudest lady in the land. Haughtily she gazed from under long, dark lashes upon the world, and knight or servant were one to her. Why, indeed, should she make any distinctions between these who in her eyes were nothing and deserved no more attention than a speck of dust or a wisp of straw? Her stepdaughter, Giselle, who had been married to a German margrave, often told how her stepmother even kept her husband waiting at their chamber door and forced him to follow the prescribed etiquette. Six pages accompanied the beautiful lady wherever she went, two holding up the gold-embroidered train of her robe; the others following with her perfume, handkerchief, and mirror, or, at night, carrying torches. All were sumptuously and fancifully dressed in the colors of the kingdom of Castille, wearing striped tights and split sleeves that were so long that they reached the ground. The fairest maidens were chosen to be Elvira's ladies-in-waiting and followed their mistress in pairs, their eyes piously cast down.

Far more modest than Raymond's was the retinue brought by the two young dukes of Lorraine: Godfrey of Bouillon and Baldwin of Lorraine. The elder of the two dukes, Godfrey, of whom it was said that he had never known a woman and led the life of a monk, was a quiet, gentle man, grave of mien and steadfast of purpose. The long, fair beard that he wore only served to accentuate the austerity of his face. The gay, high-spirited Baldwin, with his swarthy complexion and aquiline nose, seemed at least ten years his junior, though in truth the two brothers were only a few years apart. Baldwin's youthful appearance contrasted even more vividly with that of his wife, Gontrane, who was gaunt, vindictive, and bitter, a veritable virago.

On the heels of the two dukes of Lorraine arrived Hugh of Vermandois, the brother of the king of France, an indolent, frivolous youth. For all his giddiness, however, the young prince lacked neither generosity nor courage when occasion demanded. With him came Stephen, Count of Blois, famed for his wealth and learning, a nobleman who had actually mastered the difficult art of writing and could compose stanzas no worse than those of any troubadour. Though known for his wisdom and fairness, Stephen found little favor in the eyes of his peers, who saw something not quite virile in his learned accomplishments.

It was true, of course, that the scholarly count could hardly compare with that paragon of all manly virtues, Robert, Duke of Flanders, surnamed, "the Lance and Sword of Knighthood." Robert, whose small but carefully picked train was composed of the finest soldiers, set up his camp a good distance from the town, in order not to expose his brave Frisians and Flemings to the provocations of southerners.

Last to arrive were the Norman dukes. They came in force, leading hosts of magnificently armed, well-disciplined, and seasoned troops. There were three of them: Robert Curthose, the Conqueror's first-born; William, called the Red; and the youngest, Henry. They were neither handsome of face nor pleasant of manner, since each in one way or another took after their grandfather, Robert the Devil, and their grandmother, a crafty peasant girl from Falaise; short-legged they were, with big heads and a tendency to obesity inherited from their father. Yet, since they represented a power which none could contest, they were surrounded with respect and honor.

No sooner had the Normans set up camp than the Holy Father, Pope Urban II, arrived in the town. And it seemed as though the council were about to begin, when an unfortunate mishap caused its opening to be postponed:

The men of Hugh, the French King's brother, fell to quarreling with some burghers who allegedly refused to sell them certain merchandise. They thrashed them soundly, and when the fleeing burghers took refuge in the cathedral, the vindictive bravos would not leave them even there, but dragged them out into the square and cut them to ribbons, thus committing a flagrant breach of *Asilium Dei*. The aged Archbishop of Clermont, Durand, took the incident so much to heart that on that very night he died. He was an old, old man, to be sure, more than fourscore, some said, and overworked with preparing for the council, so perhaps it was not unnatural that this last straw should have proved too much for him. In any case, it was now out of the question to open the council. First, the deceased prince of the Church must be buried in state, a vicar must be elected in his place, and the cathedral, polluted by crime, must be purified while Hugh's men, barefoot and in sackcloth, made public penance in the square. So the opening of the council was postponed for a fortnight and everyone was left to his own devices to fill the days as best he could.

Luckily for the Silesian knights, the camp of Raymond St. Gilles happened to be only a short distance from the spot where the Hungarian mission had set up its pavilions, so that the friendly relations which had developed during the journey between the three young Poles and De Foix, De La Tour, and D'Armillac need not be interrupted. The Provençal knights visited them almost daily and took Imbram, Yashek, the Babbler, and sometimes even the others, to their own camp, which at any time of the day or night rang with music and song. Because of the mourning for the archbishop, Count Raymond, who had a passion for music and play, was unable to indulge in the sumptuous banquets, the tournaments, and dances for which his court was famous. Still, the ban did not apply to a favorite court game called "The Besieging of the Fortress of Love," and in this the gay Provençals engaged almost daily.

The game called for a strange structure, somewhat like a tower but more like a large barrel with openings cut all around it. This was set in the middle of the courtyard, and Lady Elvira's comely maidens were locked inside it, their rosy, laughing faces peering through the openings. It was upon these fair prizes that Raymond's brave knights flung themselves with tremendous zest. The maidens defended themselves as best they could, throwing missiles that in the summertime consisted of flowers, and now were of oak leaves and skeins of tangled, multicolored silk. According to the rules of the game a knight who had been hit by a missile, be it ever so lightly, must stand aside and recite something artful and amorous, preferably of his own composition, although in case inspiration should fail him he was allowed to quote someone else's song or stanza. Only after thus having paid his forfeit could he re-enter the fray. A knight who succeeded in catching the hand of a maiden before she hit him would pull her out through the opening and carry her away. She was his captive. The companion of the fair prize defended her obstinately, holding fast to her legs and squealing with glee. Raymond St. Gilles roared with laughter till tears came to his eyes, and urged his knights on to even more fervent attacks. The beautiful Elvira, her head adorned with a coif two feet high, her robe glittering with gems like a reliquary, and an ermine-lined mantle, which, being a royal princess, she was entitled to wear, wrapped around her shoulders, smiled in her own impersonal and haughty way. When all the maidens but one had been dragged out of the tower, the last to remain was presented with a crown of virtue. If the truth be told, however, none of the gay young maidens craved the honor; each would rather feel hard, knightly arms about her.

The Silesians watched the game curiously but from a distance, feeling not in the least inclined to join in the sport. Such frolicking, they thought, was good enough for youngsters on a Midsummer Night, but why should grown knights indulge in it? Besides, the game was pointless; the captor did not lie with his captive. So what was the use?

Even stranger and more senseless they found those recitations of songs and stanzas in which the Provençals took such pleasure. Although by now they had acquired a fair command of Romance, the Poles understood none of that elaborate poetry, and, besides, they deemed the very idea of composing verses improper. Truly, they too knew many a song, betrothal songs and wedding chants, bridal songs and dirges, but these had come down the ages, handed on from one generation to the next, unaltered, formal, fixed like a sacred rite. It would never have occurred to anyone to change even the most insignificant word.

Among the brilliant, gaily attired ladies of Elvira's court, there were two who attracted attention because of the strange contrast they made with the rest. The black coif of the elder forever veiled her face. And while the younger, who never left her companion's side, was comely enough, her face was sullen and her dark eyes brooding. Sir Gouffier de la Tour told his friends that the elder was Madame Salviac de Viel, and the younger her daughter Blanche. Blanche, it seemed, had been given in marriage several years before to Sir Hugh de Montbeliard, a knight famed for his wanton cruelty. He tortured her so that at last her mother, gentle and pious widow though she was, could no longer endure to watch the torment of her only child, and poisoned her son-in-law. So Montbeliard died, to the intense relief of everyone, including his own kin. This general rejoicing was, in fact, so sincere that although everybody knew how his death had been brought about, no one came forth with an outright accusation. And as, according to law, no trial could be held without a formal accusation, both mother and daughter had so far escaped judgment and the punishment, which, in the case of husband-slaying, consisted of cutting off the guilty wife's limbs and burying the rest of her body alive. The case against them, however, could be opened at any time, should an accuser appear. And so Blanche and her mother lived in constant terror lest they should incur someone's ill-will or anger, and wished for nothing except to be forgotten. In addition to that, the mother, a gentle and pious creature, was sorely tormented, not by remorse, but by the lack of it. In vain did her confessor urge her to repent her evil deed. She could not. Every time she recalled the pale, wicked eyes of her son-in-law and his wily, cold-blooded cruelty, she felt with a sinking sense of despair that she would not hesitate to poison him a second, a third, and yes, if need be, a tenth time, that again she would go in the dead of the night to pick the henbane blossom and catch the asp among the rocks. And though, as well she knew, God must condemn her for such feelings, she was unable to admit that she had done wrong.

Amidst the general gaiety of Raymond's court the two unfortunate ladies, wrapped up in their bitter sorrow, seemed strangely out of place. They were kept at court out of pure pity, since the powerful baron's protection constituted the best safeguard against any attempt on the part of human malice to bring the two unfortunates to their doom. No one, however, sought out their company, or tried to draw them into the general life of the court. And so they wandered about the magnificent camp like two souls in pain.

The only man who understood them and was glad to be with them was a knight of Picardy by the name of Raoul de Beaugency, who wandered aimlessly among the various encampments. Concerning him too, strange stories were whispered about. It was said that to avenge himself on an ignoble old miser who was his uncle and guardian, the young knight had sold his soul to the Devil. And so he had. He had gone at midnight to the Devil's crossroads, where witches offer the Evil One scrambled eggs so that he may give them power over the hens of their neighbors, and there had summoned the Prince of Darkness by a magic incantation. True, the Evil One did not appear. But a week had not passed before Raoul's miserly uncle had suddenly died, so it was plain that Satan, though invisible, had been present at the crossroads and had accepted the bargain. By the terms of the bargain Raoul had forfeited his soul to the power of hell in return for the privilege of forever watching the torments inflicted upon his uncle's sinful soul.

But as time went on and the memory of his hated kinsman began to fade, the prospect of such sweet revenge no longer held any of its anticipated delight, and only horror remained. What would Raoul not give to erase that moment when he had stood at the crossroads asking for the Evil One's help! But no power can obliterate a moment that has gone by.

Mournful and embittered, Raoul de Beaugency sought company, in the vain hope that by another's side he might forget his plight. But people avoided him. Satan, watchful guardian that he was, was certain to be hovering around a man who by right belonged to him and he might easily pounce upon anyone who came near. It was safer, much safer, to keep away from hell's prey.

Only the tragic Blanche, obsessed every night by a horrible dream in which the executioner heaped earth upon her young and quivering body, and her old mother, the unrepenting murderess, did not shrink from the hapless knight. For, though they had not deliberately sold themselves to the Devil, they too were irrevocably doomed and nothing they might do could make their lot any the worse.

7.

The Envoy from the East

STRATEGOS ARGYROS, THE GREEK ENVOY, HIDING A YAWN WITH THE PALM of his hand, went on speaking without betraying the boredom he felt.

With a careless gesture of hand to shoulder he kept readjusting the round gold clasp that fastened his outer garment, cut like a cloak from cloth of gold of Bagdad and woven with a pattern of peacocks and griffons. Against the golden background, the griffons spat fire from ruby jaws, while the tails of the peacocks glittered with the blue-green light that was reflected from their countless eyes. Here indeed was a ravishing garment, and at the sight of it even the proud Elvira, daughter of the King of Castille, might well have lost her usual cold indifference. For of such stuff was it made that no woman of the West had ever seen its like. Under his peacock cloak the Greek dignitary wore a white tunic, sheer as gossamer, and, under that, a still finer, whiter shift, stitched at the neck and wrists with golden thread.

The inside of his pavilion matched the richness and elegance of his attire. Low gilded stools; rugs of a silken sheen, strewn with innumerable cushions filled with down and covered, in royal purple, with silk and gold-tooled leather. Against the walls, pitchers of wrought silver for wine and olive oil and rose-water, each pitcher protected by a case of painted leather. A carved chest displayed the quite comprehensive reference library that accompanied the Strategos on all his journeys. Here were geographic descriptions of the several lands of Europe, translated from the Arabic; volumes containing countless prayers and exorcisms for every occasion; scientific treatises; descriptions of the weather and the change of the seasons in many lands; and above all, two most highly prized and essential works: *Ceremonials at the Court of the Basileus*, set down a century earlier by order of the Emperor Constantine VII

50

Porphyrogenitus for the use of his son, Romanus, together with a volume entitled *"Oneirokritika,"* compiled by the great Artemideros, which provided an interpretation of every dream, even the most uncommon.

Behind the shot silk curtain of changing hue which divided the interior of the tent and which had been drawn aside to provide a passage, shone silver and copper vessels for foot-baths and the complicated equipment required for the indispensable Armenian steam bath, including a portable folding stove for heating water. At the entrance of the pavilion a half-naked servant boy, as beautiful as a heathen idol, was sprinkling the glowing coals of a tripod with beads of resin, to fill the air within with the tangy breath of a pine forest. Deep in the interior, against the main wall, and gleaming with all the splendor of gold, enamel, and precious stones, stood a small altar in two sections. In the upper shone an ikon representing the Most Blessed Virgin Mary, the miraculous *Panago, Theotokos, Blacherniotissa,* the Patroness of Byzantium; in the lower, a similar ikon, only smaller, depicting the Most Enlightened, Most Pious, Equal-to-the-Apostles Basileus, Autocrator, Alexius Commenus, Porphyrogenitus. On the altar, between the two ikons, rested a tiny reliquary containing the Most Holy, Most Distinguished, Most Venerable Splinter of the Cross.

Not only the members of his retinue but even the Strategos himself took particular pains to bow low when passing before this tiny shrine, in simultaneous tribute to the Holiness of God and that of their great Autocrator.

At the present moment, however, the Strategos, stifling a yawn and toying with his clasp, was unburdening himself to a group of men sunk in a sea of cushions before him. The group consisted of Imbram, Zbylut, Yashek Zavora, the two Novinas, a Hungarian named Bakocz, and the Provençal knights, De La Tour and D'Armillac.

These gentlemen were not following his words attentively; instead, they kept exchanging among themselves glances of uneasiness and embarrassment. Never before had they sat upon anything so soft, and the very lack of a firm support for their posteriors filled them with apprehension. Even at the court of Count Raymond of Toulouse, famed for its luxurious appointments, there was no covering on the hard, unplaned benches except a single thickness of stiff gold brocade. And if in certain castles feather pillows were actually to be found, the feathers in them were invariably so tightly packed that the pillows hardly differed at all from the usual ones, which were stuffed with hay. Beds, as they knew them, even royal beds, were nothing but ordinary straw laid on boards, over which was spread a more or less costly coverlet. Startled by the unexpected comfort which now assailed them, the knights, with their rough hands, suspiciously fingered the smooth, glossy surface of the cushions, and dared not move for fear of sinking still deeper into that sea of down. With brooding eyes they followed the hands, which, with evident pleasure, the Strategos used to emphasize certain words, or more elaborate periods, of his speech. White, beringed, and pampered hands they were—hands soft and smooth to the touch, and graced with long, polished nails.

And the knights, whose own fists and uplifted forearms resembled knotty, mace-like clubs, and whose fingernails, as hard as hoofs, were bitten off short (they swallowed the fragments in order to prevent their possible use in witchcraft), regarded the hands of the Greek patrician with profound distaste, as one might look upon an unfamiliar reptile or monster. These cushions, these hands, the very voice of the Greek—how was it, they wondered, that such a stout man with such strong features and such bushy eyebrows should at the same time possess so thin and womanish a voice? In that shrill and high-pitched voice of his, the Strategos was indulging in one of his stock harangues, couched in studied Latin, developing each sentence with artful deliberation.

"Thus it is, O bravest of the brave," he was saying, "thus it is, noble knights, O pride of the Latin world . . . ! With humble admiration and inexpressible longing, from the welter of dark oppression that encompasses us, we come to you to implore the aid of your valiant arms. You and you alone, O Christian knights, whose fame reaches to the very stars, are called by the Creator to preserve the fruits of His handiwork. In the name of Christ the Most High, we pray you, consecrate yourselves to this holy task without delay! Tarry not a single day. No words, howsoever eloquent, can depict the dire plight of Christians now threatened by the Agars. In truth, with more safety should they seek repose in the embrace of a lion than within the bounds of the Holy Empire. Far more hope of life was Daniel's in the den of wild beasts than is ours at this moment. The Agars surround us. Already they have torn from our grasp such lands as Cappadocia, Phrygia, Bitynia, the Troad, Pontus, Lybia, Pamphilia, Isauria, Lisos, the islands of Chios, Mytilene, Lesbos. . . . Not long shall it be before 'the city guarded by God' will be left to stand

alone. Within this very year the accursed monsters have treacherously
snatched from us the Propontis and the Euxine . . . Today they stand
at our very gates! And worse still . . . For now they have discovered
the secret of the liquid fire which alone has thus far held them off. That
holy weapon, which for a thousand years and more has protected the
walls of Byzantium, has now been turned against us. In the face of that
frightful danger, our doom is sealed, unless the West come to our rescue.
The way whereby those sons of Satan have learned the secret of liquid
fire is unknown . . . On no occasion were the artisans who prepared
the thunder-breeding liquid ever permitted to leave the scene of their
labors. True, when they were too old and decrepit to continue their toil,
they were sent away, but not before their eyes and their tongues were
torn out to prevent them from betraying the secret or showing anyone
the way to the workshop. Yet, despite all our precautions, the Agars have
acquired the formula . . . Doubtless by means of witchcraft . . . Alas
for our people!"

"This that you tell of the Agar is new to us," Sir Gouffier de la Tour
remarked. "We have heard only of Saracens."

"They are one! 'Agar' is our name for all infidels—as sons of the sinful
goddess Agar . . . What does the name matter? Saracen, Arab, Turk—
all assail our Holy Faith. Tears forbid me to tell of the countless daily
torments inflicted upon Christ our Lord, personified by His faithful.
Driven by blasphemous hatred, the Agars are determined to possess all
the priceless relics that remain in our care, in order that they may defile
them. It is for those holy relics' sake that we implore your aid. It is they
which are the source of our constant anxiety. Our thoughts are not for
our miserable lives, which each of us stands ready to sacrifice in the
unequal fight—it is the sacred treasures entrusted to us by our Creator
which cause our chief concern. Should Byzantium fall, the holy faith
will perish! And with her the priceless treasure of our temples! The
column to which Christ our Lord was bound . . . the lashes which
scourged His flesh . . . Yea, the lashes on which His Precious Blood
remains to this day; miraculously fresh, uncongealed . . . The scarlet
robe which the soldiers put on Him in mockery . . . The crown of
thorns, the scepter of reed . . . More than half of the Most Holy Cross
. . . The very nails used in the Crucifixion . . . The shroud He cast off
in the Sepulcher . . . Twelve baskets in which lay the loaves He so
miraculously multiplied . . . The head of St. John the Baptist, un-

scathed by time . . . The bodies of countless holy martyrs, youths and virgins alike.

"Whose soul would not shudder at the thought of permitting such holy fountains of Divine Grace to fall into the hands of Satan? O valiant knights, let not this come to pass, we beseech you! Rise like St. George who vanquished the dragon! Let not the greedy hands of the accursed infidels fall upon our Christian treasure! I pray you believe me, the riches of Solomon were as nothing compared with those which God has entrusted to our care. And they will be yours. With joy shall we deliver them up, begrudging you no one of them, caring but for the preservation of Christianity and content in the knowledge that the memorials left to us by God are safe. The riches won by your deeds will descend with your line for years to come . . . Pray, feast your eyes upon the contents of this coffer . . ."

He motioned to the servant boy at the tripod to raise the lid of a heavy oaken chest bound with silver trimmings. Instantly the eyes of the assembled knights were blinded by a blaze of gold and precious stones, by a superb display of belts, and clasps, and necklaces, and rings.

"And now, good knights, it is yours to choose from these at will. Some trifling keepsake, a small token of the wealth awaiting the final victor. Take them, noble knights. And if you care not for gold, let me tell you in your ear that these jewels are but toys compared with the fairness of our women. Greek women are known the world over for their charm and their artful love-making; and in God's name, I assert that their fame is well deserved. With no other women may a knight find as great pleasure as with them . . . And being, as they are, true Christians to the last, and holding as they do the Holy Faith dearer than life, I leave it to you to imagine how tenderly they will greet and reward their noble defenders! To refuse you will never lie in their hearts . . ."

The Strategos smiled, slyly narrowing his eyes, then stifled another yawn. Oh! how it bored him day after day to repeat the same speech to successive groups of simpletons, with masterly skill to appeal to the faith and the greed of these barbarians who stank of sweat and leather, to rouse them to the point where they would finally act. Few men could perform the task as well as he. And Strategos Argyros swelled with admiration for his own willingness to serve his native land, no matter at what sacrifice. In appointing him envoy, the noble Pantaleonos, Superior

of the Logothesios by the will of the Basileus, together with the Great
Protosebastos of the Court, could never have hit upon a happier choice,
and Strategos Argyros was fully confident that those mighty dignitaries
would never permit his efforts to fail of appreciation or due reward.

The barbarians, however, heard him through without comment. With
childish admiration they gazed at the jewels held out to them, but when
these were laid in their hands, they merely nodded their heads with
majestic indifference. They had become aware, at this point, of a growing sense of distaste and distrust, without quite comprehending its
source. So elegant, so learned was the envoy's discourse—what bishop
could have uttered finer words!—and yet the unmistakable instinct of
simple primitive folk warned them away.

At last they departed, solemnly escorted by enormous, fully armed
protospatarii. It was with a sense of relief that they handed over the
envoy's gifts to their own squires, who awaited them outside the pavilion. At the edge of the Greek camp they encountered a group of
knights wearing leather breastplates, silver helmets, swords, and double-
edged battle-axes slung from their belts. The sound of their animated
conversation brought the Polish knights to a sudden halt and left them
rooted to the spot with astonishment.

Kinsmen . . . Russians!

They stood there, overjoyed, yet uncertain, not knowing whether to
greet the strangers. Were these men knights or mercenaries, or possibly
only prisoners?

The situation was soon saved for them, however, when the group,
having likewise recognized them as friends and neighbors, advanced
with welcome glowing in their faces.

"We are free knights, serving the Basileus by our own will," they said
in greeting.

No longer afraid, and delighted at meeting men of their own blood,
the Polish knights extended their hands with upturned palms, and once
again they seemed to see the golden gates of Kiev, marking an age of
wars and glorious exploits. Taking leave of the Provençal knights, they
went with their kinsmen to their tents.

Russians! How did they come come here?

The Greek wine, so heavy and sweet, which the Strategos had given
them, reminded them of the mead they had known—O! how long ago

—at home. Its first effect had been to create nostalgia; it now served to loosen their bound tongues.

"We are here in strength," their hosts explained, "and we come from all the corners of the earth. The standards we serve under are Greek, it is true, but the only Greeks you will find among us are there by chance. But there are Bulgarians, Danes, Hungarians, Swedes, Avars, Pieczengs, Huns . . . Even Saracens and Turks!"

"Heathens?"

"Aye, heathens! Most of us are true Christians, of course, but we have no lack of heathens, Waregs in particular. The Greeks have a way of saying that it is God who guards their city; aye, but when it comes to raising an army, they question no man's faith, caring only for his strength as a warrior. They shrug at the matter of religion. The Devil himself could find his way into their ranks."

All crossed themselves and, in haste, spat thrice.

"Why don't they do their own fighting?"

"Ho! They were never born to fight! Such drones as they are! Life, not war, lies closest to their hearts. Not one will risk his head."

"Then what do they do with themselves?" the guests asked in astonishment, for to them fighting was the very essence and beauty of knightly existence.

"What indeed? They toss balls to each other. They are ravished by racing—horse races, chariot races. They bathe, they read like monks, write, sing, feast, gabble! What a way to live! But they seem to thrive on it."

"Never!"

"Seems incredible, doesn't it? Why if it weren't for outlanders like ourselves, the Saracens would have eaten them up years ago. And now the Greek is back again, whining at our doors for help. We've heard that the Strategos has given the Basileus his solemn oath that he will not return without further aid from us. He has probably been trying to persuade you, too?"

"Of course. With gracious gifts for us all."

"Ha, gifts he makes in plenty, but they are only lures to catch fish with! And he can afford to be lavish, for the riches that lie behind him are such as have no like. His land is a land of gold—gold roofs, gold ceilings, gold floors. Gold garnered from every quarter of the world lies piled in Greece. And it is all that gold that has made the Greek the simpering fop that he is! Well, we shall see what success will reward his pains. He is a shrewd devil, even though an ox."

"An ox? He seems no dullard!"

"It is not his head I had in mind, but that which makes an ox an ox." The others failed to understand.

A single word, accompanied by an appropriately brutal gesture, at once made the meaning clear, and when they recoiled in horror and disgust, their hosts broke into peals of ribald laughter.

"Ho, it is not uncommon practice amongst the Greeks, my friends!" the speaker went on to explain. "Consider all the Emperor's bastards, who must be prevented from claiming the throne! And the slaves who are kept to watch over the wives of the nobility!"

"Come now, you are making sport of us!"

"No, indeed, I speak the truth, so help me God! My comrades here will bear me out. Men thus deprived of manhood—eunuchs, we call them—stand watch over the womenfolk. But it is a poor watch they keep, for the little beauties slip out in spite of them. At dusk our legion's quarters swarm with ladies of high station . . . You can well imagine the rest!"

"And their husbands . . ."

"Feign ignorance. After all, what does it matter to them? For themselves, they prefer young boys."

"Boys?"

"Of course! They take a foul pleasure with lads of tender years. Why do you gape so? If the Strategos has his way with you, you shall see for yourselves!"

After thus delivering himself, Oleg, son of Oleg, scion of an ancient line of Russian princes whose grandfather had taken part in Sviatopelk's memorable expedition against Byzantium, angrily threw his goblet to the ground and crushed it under his feet.

"Dirty scoundrels! That's what they are," he shouted. "If I were not held to my pledge, I would take my men and return home this very day. But a knight's word must be kept, and I must stick it out, honestly, to the bitter end. O, yes, gold you may find in plenty in their service, I grant you, but glory there is none. And what is gold worth without glory? Once, it seems, they had Kings with fighting blood in their

veins: the Bulgar-slayer, Nicephorus, Phocas, Cimisces . . . But no
more. All they want is peace. Scheming—that's what they are good at:
they wag their tongues, they wag their heads, they hold councils, they
write parchments, they fling gold around—anything to avoid fighting
and to find someone to protect them. The bastards!"

Their heads swimming with the strong Greek wine and with too
many impressions which they could neither comprehend nor assimilate,
the Silesians returned to their own camp. Here they were met by an
unusual commotion. The whole place buzzed with irate voices. Momot,
stammering more than ever in his excitement, told them what had
happened.

The two German knights, Gottschalk and Von Emich, whom Glovach
had quite unnecessarily admitted to their company, had proved to be
shameless liars, unworthy of the silver spurs. They had, it seemed, tried
to negotiate a loan from a Jew of the place, named David Kalonymos.
The prudent Jew, naturally enough, wanted security, for though in case
of default a debtor became the slave of his creditor, no one would dare
to lay hands on a knight. A knight pledged his servants in his place and
how many he pledged depended on the amount of his debt. Gottschalk
and Von Emich had assured the Jew that the entire Polish camp belonged to them; they pretended to be rich men when they owned nothing but what they wore on their backs, two old nags, and a bleary-eyed,
game-legged servant. The wary Jew, before he delivered over the money,
had sent an agent to the camp to check on the truth of their statements.
The agent was promptly thrown out and threatened with a flogging—
for how dare a Jew set foot in a knightly encampment? But the news
of the intended deceit soon spread from the servants to their masters,
causing an outburst of righteous indignation. For the world of those days,
though it had countless faults and failings, though it was harsh, ruthless,
cruel, and greedy, yet faithfully kept its own supreme commandment:
it was trustworthy. A knight did not lie. No surname was held in
greater esteem than that of *"preux," "probus."* No shame greater than
that of a man whose words were false to his thoughts or whose deeds
were false to his words. Save in the one case excepted by the chivalrous
Latins, that in which the honor of a lady was involved, a knight caught
in a lie forfeited both honor and spurs.

And so the indignant Silesians and Hungarians swore to chastise the unworthy Germans. The latter, however, must have caught wind of what lay in store for them, for they did not set foot in the camp again. Probably their bleary-eyed servant had warned them. Indeed, in the company of other squires he cursed them roundly. Still . . . they were horses of the same color . . .

8.

Old Friends

A COLD, NORTHERLY WIND SWEPT OVER THE CASTLE OF THE LATE ARCH-bishop Durand, whistling round the window openings. But in the tower where they were talking neither Pope Urban nor the companion of his monastic years, Adhemar de Monteuil, Bishop of Puy, felt the cold. Taking advantage of the last free moments at their disposal before the Council opened on the morrow, they were enjoying each other's company, after long years of separation.

The Pope, slender and stooped, briskly paced the floor of the small chamber. Now and again he stopped at the high, narrow window, and thrusting his head through the opening, exposed his hollow, rugged cheeks to the icy blasts. Standing thus, he could see, down below in the translucent darkness of the night, the town and the great multitude of people which surrounded it on every side. Thousands of fires, lighted as a protection against the cold of the night, glittered toward him, as if in expectation. In the sky, though night had long since fallen, there still lingered, as though forgotten, streaks of red, and he pointed out the belated light to his friend:

"Look, Brother, did you ever see such a glow at this hour? It is said that before Caesar died the sun set in a red halo, and that the halo remained in the sky long after sundown, even as today, when the Western world is about to break from its roots and fall upon the East."

"Do you indeed believe that it will?"

Shaking his head in doubt, Adhemar de Monteuil moved closer to the window. He was just a head taller than his friend, and because he had been a knight before he ever became a monk and a bishop, each of his movements still showed martial strength and determination.

Now, standing side by side, they both watched that sea of flickering light as though they were peering into the abyss of the human soul.

"For what reason did you bring all these conflicting elements together here?" Adhemar asked. "No good will come of it. What bond can there be between Robert Curthose, the grandson of the Devil, and that mad Raymond of Toulouse? Instead of going forth together as you wish them to, they will be at each other's throats whenever they get a chance. They will destroy each other and each other's men before they reach the frontier."

"They are destroying each other as it is, though perhaps more slowly. But you are mistaken, Adhemar; they will go. They may kick and rear against the bit, but go they will. And they will get there. They must go! Only hear what Alexius' envoy is saying. The fall of the Byzantine Empire is not a matter of years, but months. And when the Empire falls, who will check Mohammed's triumphant progress? Feeble Russia? Bulgaria, Hungary, or kingless Poland? The day Byzantium falls, the Saracens will throw all their power against the Slavs, against Italy and the Pyrenees. They will overrun France, occupy Rome! They boast already that Turkish horses will soon graze on the deserted grave of the Apostle. And so they shall, you will see, if we do not move against them while there is yet time!"

"It may be so. But, supposing that the knights will go, of what use is the rabble? Why did you summon them all here? Are they also to go?"

"You have said it—they shall go."

"Have you lost your mind, Odo? What do you expect an unruly mob to accomplish?"

"No, I have not lost my mind, Brother. Be patient, and let me explain. Do you think that the Saracens are the only threat to Christendom? Do you believe there is nothing worse than they? Look around you! Do you not see that the world is dying? Decaying and dying? Look, look at the universal poverty, dirt, laziness, violence, persecution, indifference to spiritual things. Each year they grow worse and worse; each year it becomes harder to live. All this will tumble about our heads some day, if we do not bring it a new life. The whole rotten structure must be shaken, moved, stirred to its very foundations; a fresh wind must blow in. That's why I have summoned them here. I wish to lead them somewhere—away from themselves! Do you understand?"

"Do I understand? Do I see that the world is rotting? Odo! I only think—it is not worth saving."

"And Christianity?" the Pontiff cried out with alarm.

For a moment they were silent.

"Do you remember," Adhemar resumed in a low, passionate voice, "how five hundred years ago people believed that the Roman Empire and Christianity were one and the same? If the Emperor fell—Christ would fall. Bishops excommunicated those who surrendered their towns to the barbarians. Yet Caesar fell—and Christ remained. Will it not be the same today?"

The Pope made a gesture of violent protest.

"No, no! You cannot compare these things. If today's society, today's world, were to fall—it would be the end of the Church."

Adhemar smiled bitterly.

"The Church . . ." he repeated. "I recall a number of our bishops, of our abbots . . ."

"Stop! I know what you have in mind. But despite all, they are the Church, and the Church and Christ are one."

"Are you so sure of that?"

The Pontiff wheeled to face his friend. His cheeks were as white as his kerchief.

"Listen," he whispered. "Listen. Even on a night like this, when we are alone and no one can hear us but these four walls and God above, you cannot admit such thoughts. I will not have it! I forbid it! Beware! It is as your superior that I command you! You are in error, in grave error. You have acquired too much knowledge, you have been reading too many Roman and Greek philosophers."

"There can never be enough knowledge."

"You are wrong, Brother, there can be. Too much knowledge fills a man with over-confidence. He wants to comprehend what is beyond comprehension, and he goes astray . . . Like those absurd people, the Gnostics, with their cult of Eons, and their faith in their own ability to become invisible. That is what too much learning leads to."

"I shall never agree with that. And you yourself held other thoughts in the past days. Rome has changed you. Let us drop the subject . . . So you would become another Moses? You would drag those ignorant, quarrelsome, hungry wretches across the desert, even as he dragged Israel? Forget not, however, that Moses had help from the Lord."

"And why should not the Lord likewise help me? In His eyes the present and the past are one."

"You have kept your faith in miracles, Odo."

"Why, Brother—have you lost yours?"

"I do not know. I still believe in God's eternal mercy. I believe as deeply and as firmly as I did in those days when you and I meditated together. I believe in the meaning and purpose of creation, even though it is so distressingly concealed from our eyes. I could not live without that faith . . . Nor could I live in this dour, wicked world, were I not certain that close beside a merciful, not a stern or rancorous God, there reigns an incarnate deified Motherhood, to whom one can run for safety, even as a child runs to his mother's side. I believe that these ever watchful Holy Powers do not despise even the most miserable human dust. Only with such a conviction can one live in this world without going mad. I believe too in miracles, although I doubt if they are as numerous as people say. But, for all that, Brother, I do not believe in your foolhardy plan. And why? Because it often seems to me that Christianity has fallen upon human nature even as an angelic flower might fall upon hard rock. It has not taken root, because it cannot take root. Anyone with common sense, of course, even a heathen, will agree that Christianity is the only remedy for the world's evils: To love instead of to hate . . . To create, instead of to destroy. Christianity, why, it means to care for women and children, for the old and the feeble. It means that the strong and mighty should submit, of their own free will, to the bonds of their conscience. Would not the world then become that promised Kingdom of Heaven? But human nature has not accepted Christianity, and it will not accept it. As for your plan, do you know what would be needed to carry it out? That at least half of these people should feel themselves Christians at heart. Do you understand what that means?"

"We must trust that they will . . ."

"God grant it! And who is going to lead them? This monk, Peter?"

"No, indeed! Peter, bless his soul, is but God's flint that strikes the holy spark. The leader ought to be a king, so that our barons will accept his command. I have in mind Ladislaus of Hungary, a just ruler and a true knight. As long ago as last summer I sent a secret mission to sound him out. He agrees, he is ready to go. His envoys have just arrived, bringing a group of Polish knights . . ."

The wind had grown increasingly cold and the two friends retired from the window.

"So Ladislaus of Hungary is to be the leader . . . It is fortunate that there is still one king not under an anathema. Otherwise, you would be in a quandary," Adhemar observed, bitingly.

"Who is to blame?" the Pope irritably retorted.

"Nevertheless, our bishops abuse their power of excommunication, and often needlessly."

"What can they do? What other measure do you propose, to hold men in check?"

"Rather tell me, Odo, was Martin, the good Bishop of Tours, at whose voice heathen idols fell, truly a saint or not?"

"Why! He was one of the greatest!"

"And did not Martin say: 'Even thou, wretched Satan, wouldst thou but cease to destroy souls, couldst obtain Christ's mercy'?"

"Yes," Urban agreed, rubbing his cheek thoughtfully. "He did. And it is said that Satan then wept for the first time since his fall, and fled . . ."

"You see! That means contrition is enough, and punishment unnecessary. Why do we threaten with damnation and refuse absolution for trifling offenses?"

"I do not thus!"

"That I know. But the others? Is not theirs the same teaching as Martin's?"

"Yes. The same. But you see, Brother, sometimes it is easier to shame the Devil than to shame man . . ."

"Wrath will not better anyone."

"How can I better them, then?"

"You cannot, Odo. Get it out of your head that this world can be changed. It cannot. Your plan is sheer madness, and I wish to have nothing to do with it."

"What else but this madness remains to save us from destruction?"

"It will not save us . . . Ah, Brother! When shall we rest at last? If only we might go away, somewhere in the mountains, or to some desert shore and dream that the world is happy and sinless, as it was on the day of creation, and know nothing of anyone and anything, save God."

9.

The Crusade Is Born

THE WIND THAT BLEW FROM THE BLACK, SCORCHED HILLS WAS STILL BIT-
terly cold, but the people, standing shoulder to shoulder in a vast
throng, did not notice it. What kept them warm was not only one
another's proximity but also an inner glow of impatient curiosity. The
strain of so many weeks of expectation had made every thought as taut
as the string of a bow, and that sense of strained expectancy was further
increased by monks and other papal emissaries who circulated among
the crowd telling of strange and awesome signs, of which both the sky
and the earth had lately been full . . . The Bosphorus had frozen over
. . . the Nile last winter was covered with floating ice. People who had
never heard of the Bosphorus or the Nile crossed themselves fearfully
at the sound of the foreign names. With no less trepidation they listened
to the news that in Burgundy a hail of stones had fallen from the skies,
each marked with the sign of the cross . . . Flaming stars were raining
upon the earth. A comet, an ominous portent, hung every night over
Byzantium. A calf with two heads had been born in Paris. All these
were certain signs of divine wrath and presages of dreadful events soon
to come. Other speakers pointed out the hard lot of the yeomanry—
nothing but work and want—and promised an easier life full of God's
blessings.

The crowd lent eager ears to all such news, quite anxious to believe
in the coming of some great change in their existence. It did not seem
possible that, once the Council was over, a man should return home as
if nothing had happened and lead the same old life as before. They stood
on that wide windswept slope as if facing some great door into the
future, ready to accept whatever awaited them beyond—waiting only
for the word that would tell them what to do. They did not even realize
how definitely in the course of the last few weeks, in their unconscious

readiness to start on a tremendous journey into the unknown, they had broken away from their previous miserable existence. The vision of that tomorrow set their thoughts on fire, stirred their imaginations—the more so, since few had any reason to regret the past they were to leave behind.

They had been waiting since dawn. Some even had risen while it was still night, in order to secure the best posts in which they could see and hear everything that would happen, not on the ground, of course, where the nobles would be sure to dislodge them in no time, but in trees, on nearby roofs, and on top of the city walls,—humble vantage points that no noble would covet. The rest milled about in an endless throng. The solemn, long-awaited meeting was to be held near the gate of St. Horatius. At first it had been planned to hold it in the great market place. The Holy Father, however, did not deem it fit for the occasion, because of ruins of a pagan temple that still stood in its center. Heathen demons, who undoubtedly still clung to the old ruin, might easily exercise an evil influence upon the course of the debate.

Moreover, the gate of St. Horatius presented another advantage; just outside it there began a long, gentle slope toward the valley that stretched all the way to Montferrand. This slope made it possible even for those standing far away to see the figure of the Holy Father standing on a purple-covered wooden dais, with Peter the Hermit at his side. Aye, all would see them, but would they hear? No, it was impossible; no human voice was strong enough to carry across a wide pasture thronged with a hundred thousand people. Only those nearest the gate would hear. No matter—those who heard would repeat it to the others. Besides, it was really for the Holy Father to decide. Since he had summoned them here he would see to it that each knew what was expected of him.

Behind the raised dais glimmered the tents and the two-headed eagle of the Greek envoy. On the right flamed the red of the Danish standard cut in four by a great white cross. In front of the dais a large square space had been left empty, it was surrounded by notables on horseback or on raised seats. As the Holy Father did not arrive (he was still in the Cathedral lost in prayer) and the cold was growing bitter, people talked vigorously and moved about to keep warm.

From where they stood the Polish knights saw Swennon, the royal prince of Denmark, preceded by four knights, push his way through

the crowd towards them; evidently he was anxious to meet the knights
of the country from which his grandmother, Storrada, had come. He
stared at them with childish curiosity, asking questions in Latin and
blushing like a girl, while they looked at him with tenderness and envy.
The prince was so handsome, so young! Why could they not claim him
for their own? A sudden roar announced the arrival of the Holy Father;
Swennon turned quickly and walked away. The throng was straining
forward now, it pushed him and his knights from their course toward
a dais scarcely lower than the papal one and likewise upholstered in
crimson cloth, on which stood Philip, Duke of Burgundy, the mightiest
of all the French barons. At his side sat his daughter Florine, curious
and eager, leaning over the railing. Her long fair tresses, made still
longer and stiffer by intertwined ribbons of gold brocade, hung over the
heads of the crowd. Framed by these two ropes of hair shone a rosy,
childish face, with big blue eyes and tiny parted lips. The long tresses
lightly touched Swennon's head, and, startled, he looked up. His eyes
met hers and suddenly he stood still. The Duke of Burgundy stroked
his moustache, and, smiled; he was not displeased to see a king's son
stand as though bewitched before his little pet. And she unconsciously
twisted and untwisted the stiff braid of her hair as if trying, with that
symbol of virginity, to defend herself against her mounting confusion.
Now because Duke Philip was a man with a practical turn of mind,
he immediately began from that chance encounter of the two young
people to evolve a host of sound considerations. A royal prince—Denmark was far away to be sure, but then royal blood was royal blood
. . . And the court was reputedly rich. So why not? It would never do
for the Duke of Burgundy to give his daughter in marriage to anyone
but an emperor or king. Why not? If only one knew with whom that
Danish King was friends and with whom foes? Could such a son-in-law
be of any use against that detestable hobbledehoy, the King of Paris?
With his eyes still on Florine, the royal prince bowed courteously to her
parents, her mother a huge woman wearing a tall headdress that framed
her triple-chinned face, and departed. Following him with his eyes, the
Duke decided as soon as possible to see Arnuld, the sly chaplain of
Robert of Normandy, who knew all about those northern countries,
and to learn more from him about the Danish court.

A sudden mighty shout interrupted his train of thought. It rose above

the din of thousands of conversations, and boomed with strange so-
nority across the open space.

"Ye people! Ye Christian people!"

Whose voice was this? Surely not Peter the Hermit's, who stood on
the papal rostrum, a tiny, barely visible figure, grotesque in his big hood
and with his beetle-like movements? Yes, it was his voice, but repeated
by three hundred relays, strategically placed over the wide field. Standing on logs or overturned barrels, they had been trained to repeat every
word of the speaker without fault or change and as loud as they could.
They stood in ever-widening circles, so that the voice of the tiny man
in the long-hooded cloak seemed to ring out from everywhere at once,
as if falling from the sky.

"People who wait here!

". . . Christian people, do you know what those terrible signs in the
sky and on earth portend?

". . . The bones of the Great Pope rattle in his grave . . .

". . . In Asia Minor the earth has been trembling for two months
past, so that houses, trees, and rocks fall down. As the Pope's bones
tremble underground, so the earth quakes in fear and foreboding. Over
the Holy Land stands a star with a flaming tail, a certain omen of destruction. Whose destruction, I ask you, whose? What do these signs
mean?

"Christians! They mean God's wrath because of the terrible profana-
tion of holy places. Christ's Sepulcher is desecrated by heathen hands.
Hearken to the Archangel, the very same Archangel who will call you
on Judgment Day. 'Where are the Christians?' he shouted. 'Are there no
Christians left in the world?' Answer, Christians, and hearken. Aye,
hearken to me, for I speak at the Archangel's command. I shall tell you
what I saw with my own eyes, touched with my own hand, heard with
my own ears . . . I was in Jerusalem . . . I was there, I who stand
before you . . . With these feet I trod the Holy Land . . . With these
eyes I wept . . . These hands touched the rock of Golgotha torn asunder . . . And I saw! . . . I saw! . . . I saw! . . ."

His small voice struck weakly against the ears of the first circle of relay
men. Instantly they roared his words to the second circle of relays, who
shouted them to the third circle. Those at the edge of the field, glimpsing
Peter, heard his phrases as loudly as if they had been thundered by an
angel.

"I saw Christians whipped and beaten and denied entrance to the city where their Saviour died!

"I saw them kicked, flogged, starved, abused. . . .

"I saw the earth Christ trod rubbed into their faces. I saw iron crosses hung on their necks in mockery—crosses that bent them double as they walked. . . . They have forgotten how to smile or how to hope. . . .

"Yet not a month passes but the Patriarch finds on the altar of the Basilica a letter, written by the Archangel and signed by the Holy Virgin, or by the Saviour Himself, saying, 'Come and liberate the place where I died . . . I will not have it polluted by heathen . . .'"

The voices of the relay men rose, and the blood of the listeners quickened. Infidels! Heathen! Idolators!

"'If Christians will not come to liberate My home, I will no longer intercede for them in Heaven' . . . so say the letters . . ."

The crowd moaned. "Lord! Lord!"

"I bring you this message. . . . I who was there. . . . Go to Jerusalem and liberate the Sepulcher of Christ!"

"To Jerusalem!" shouted the relay men.

"To Jerusalem!" the crowd whispered to itself.

"I bring you this message from the Archangel himself," cried Peter. "Will you go?"

"Will you go?" roared the relay men.

"Yes!" shouted someone in the crowd. "We will go!"

Quickly the cry was taken up: "We will go! We will go! We will go!"

"Go to the Holy Land!" cried Peter. "Arise and march to the East. Have no fear—the time of great miracles is again at hand. The Star of Bethlehem will appear and lead you! The burning cloud will show you the way. Take your sword, your axe, your spear! Let us go East!"

"East!" roared the relay men.

"East!" rumbled the crowd. "East to Jerusalem . . . Christ has commanded it. . . ."

Peter, exhausted and reeling, stumbled from the rostrum. Instantly his place was taken by Urban. Dressed in a monk's white frock, with a triple crown of gold on his head and a golden cross in his hand, the slender Pope raised his arms and swung the cross, blessing the entire field. The gold glistened in the cold, sharp sunshine.

"Brothers in Christ!" he cried. "Brothers in Christ!

"Peter, who is God's servant, has spoken. I, who am Christ's Vicar on earth, tell you truly: This is the day which has long been a-coming, the day when all must go to the East!

"This is an hour that comes once in the time of man. You who are here at this moment are chosen for blessedness and battle.

"You Franks, Burgundians, Provençals, Germans, Hungarians, Poles —your swords were long ago marked for sacred tasks. Until this hour you have drawn them against each other, and the land has been unhappy and hungry because of it.

"Henceforth they shall be sheathed except in the cause of your new Commander, Who is Jesus Christ, the only Son of the Living God!"

The crowd drew in its breath at the impact of the words. Except for a personal visitation by Almighty God no greater wonder could have befallen them. Out of eternity and in a time of misery and famine the hand of Christ had touched them; they had been picked by the Holy Ghost. Next to those who walked with Jesus, they were the chosen of all humanity.

"Out of the East has come a pagan race," said Urban. "The ramparts of heaven are held by its legions from hell. . . ."

The crowd shuddered. In the cold sun the chemistry of its temper changed; it moved together in a thought; it put on the garment of a new desire. Its thinking could almost be heard: We are not lost; we are saved and anointed. We have something to do beyond fighting for food and waiting to die. We are known to God and *we shall see heaven!*

"You will go, you will go! I know that you will go!" cried Urban. "I brought you this summons for I knew that you would go! You will defend the Cross! You will liberate the tomb of Christ! You will win heaven from the armies of Lucifer! I know you will do it, for God wills it! *Dieu lo vult!* God wills it!"

"*Dieu lo vult!* God wills it!" shouted the relays.

"*Dieu lo vult!* God wills it!" rumbled the crowd. "God wills it. . . . God wills it. . . . *Dieu lo vult!* . . . God wills it. . . ."

Once more the Holy Father lifted his arm.

"Silence!" shouted the relay men.

"Beloved brothers, hearken to my words, the words of Christ's Vicar on earth: Whoever goes to defend the cross becomes a free man and none has any right over him. He shall be free, a soldier of Christ, a son of the Cross—a crusader! As Christ's Vicar on earth I cancel all bonds, obligations, and debts. I loose monastic vows. Whoever joins the standard of the Cross shall be free as a bird is free. He shall be absolved and pardoned. Repent and pray, and I will do more than that. I will lift the burdens from your consciences so that you shall set forth whiter than snow, pure as angels . . ."

"Repent and pray," cried the relays.

And like a field of wheat suddenly struck by a mighty gust of wind the multitude bent to the ground. Some fell to their knees, others threw themselves prostrate, sobbing, moaning, stricken with the awareness of their innumerable sins.

Cardinal Gregory Papereschi came forward and knelt down before Urban. He prayed aloud and in unison the multitude repeated after him:

"Confiteor Deo omnipotens . . ."

Those who stood farther away picked up the words of those in front, till there were no lips which did not profess with quivering exultation their faith in God's great mercy, their repentence for all sins committed in thought, word, or deed.

The tremendous wave of voices swelled at Urban's feet, and he, as if overwhelmed by its power, stretched his arms before him . . . "May God absolve them from whatever sins they have committed . . . May they become, as He has said, whiter than snow . . . In the name of the Father and of the Son and of the Holy Ghost . . ."

A sigh of deep blissful relief rose from the hillside. Raoul de Beaugency, who had sold his soul to the Devil and was now recovering it, burst into tears; Madame de Viel, who had poisoned her cruel son-in-law, pressed her brow to the ground in mute thanksgiving.

And the Pope continued. Slowly, word after word, so that the relay men would not miss a syllable:

"You shall all go. Free and equal. Would that I could go with you! Would that I might lead you, ye warriors of Christ. Alas, that joy is not for me. I may not leave Rome. Thence I shall follow you with my thoughts and prayers. Your spiritual leader will be Our Lord Jesus Christ Himself. He will direct your steps. He will lead you to your destiny. And as His representative I name Ladislaus, King of Hungary, a prince who is indeed the mirror of all knightly virtues . . . Under his command you shall go safely to the Holy Land, as God wills!"

"I take the cross! *Dio li volt!*" the hearty voice of Raymond, Lord of Toulouse, boomed out.

"I take the cross! *Dieu le veult!*" the two Lotharingian princes exclaimed simultaneously.

"*Dieu le veult!*" the Normans repeated in unison.

"God wills it! God wills it!"

Like a sea stirred to its very depths the whole field swayed and heaved. Knights and villeins alike surged toward the Holy Father, begging for a sign that would mark them as crusaders. Someone produced scissors, and the bishops who stood at the Holy Father's side began to tear off the crimson cloth that covered the dais. Out of that cloth they cut out crosses. Each man pinned a crimson cross to his right shoulder. Hundreds of hands stretched out for more. And another hundred, and a thousand, ten thousand . . .

Thus these knights took the vow to go to Jerusalem: De Foix, De La Tour, the latter weeping with exaltation, D'Armillac, De Beaugency, Hugh, the king's brother, and the scholarly Stephen, Robert Curthose and Robert of Flanders, Omer and Wilfred Guillebaut, the twin brothers Salviac de Viel Castel, and Count d'Haineault. Also the youthful knight Engelram, fair as a cherub, and his old guardian Anselm de Ribeaumont, Roger de Berneville, Fulgence de Guines, Swennon of Denmark, and Imbram Strzygonia.

The latter had stood for a time undecided, looking around with burning eyes. One thing he saw plainly: that all the evil, all the misery on earth were due to the hateful pagan forces which had overrun the world. It was they who had torn him from home and tossed him into this wide, strange world. It was they who had captured the Holy Sepulcher and threatened Christ Himself. Therefore, his duty was to help free the Sepulcher and drive out the enemies of God. Then there would be no more misery and separation in the world . . . No more of Ofka's tears, no more longing . . . Aye! He must go! And, unmindful for the first time in his life of what his elder brothers would say, he raised his hand to take the vow. Immediately Yashek Zavora followed suit. It was his wont to do whatever Imbram did. Next, the Babbler, and all around them arms were raised, as many uplifted arms as there were heads. A noise like thunder rolled and heaved over the field. The bishop's hands grew numb with fatigue. The crimson cloth was gone long since. The Holy Father stood on bare planks, while squires dragged fresh bolts from the town: first red, then—when no more red was to be found in the booths—other colors. Presently the people apportioned colors among themselves according to their speech: the French taking red, the Frisians and Flemings green, the English white, the Germans black, and all the others yellow. Soon not a scrap of cloth would be left in all the town. The colored shreds were pressed to reverent lips; trembling fingers pinned them to shoulders.

Before long all the nobility were wearing the sacred emblem. All, that is, except the Duke of Burgundy. He was still deliberating, tugging at his moustache.

He wished to go but he was loath by his departure to gladden the heart of that despised kinsman of his, the king of Paris. It was hard indeed to make up one's mind.

A sudden hush fell over the first rows, a silence of awed amazement. For out of the crowd stepped Elvira, the fairest, the proudest lady in France. Behind her, six pages elbowed their way through the crowd. Elvira stepped in front of the Holy Father and in a calm voice vowed to take the cross and with her husband to go to the Holy Land.

As though only awaiting that signal, other ladies followed. Lady Salviac de Viel with her daughter, Blanche. The pale, indifferent Willibald, wife of Omer de Guillebaut; the gaunt, vindictive Gontrane. And, before Philip of Burgundy had time to interfere, his only child, his beloved darling, Florine. With her restless fingers twisting her fair braids and her blue eyes fixed on the royal prince of Denmark, who at that very moment was pinning the cross to his shoulder, she vowed in a thin, childish voice, to go to the defense of the Holy Land. Bystanders smiled, the Duke of Burgundy gaped and knew not what to say, but his lady, the big woman with a triple chin, burst into loud wails.

10.

Who Shall Lead Them?

THE THIN TRIANGULAR FACE OF URBAN II GLOWED WITH THE WHITENESS of heated iron. He no longer knew whether his feet still touched wooden boards, or whether he was floating on air. With a motion of his hand he summoned the Greek envoy, who stood nearby. The Strategos, though still his usual elegant and courtly self, plainly did not share the general enthusiasm.

"My son," the Pope turned to him, and spoke in hurried, feverish tones, "hasten back to Byzantium and give Alexius the glad tidings. Tell him what you have seen: the whole Western world is on its way to defend the Cross."

The Strategos did not stir.

". . . Good tidings . . ." he drawled. "Your Holiness, we are terrified. We neither wished nor expected anything of this sort . . ."

The Pope recoiled.

"Do I hear rightly? Did you, or did you not, ask for help?"

"Help—yes. But surely not for an invasion of a motley crowd, incapable of anything except looting! I shall hasten back indeed, but only to warn my master. Who can hold these mobs in check? Woe, if they enter within the walls of the 'City protected by God.' Once the sight of its riches fires the greed of these wretches, what will happen then?"

The Pope drew his brows together in an angry frown.

"These throngs have no thought of looting. And, besides, with them there will be the well-disciplined men at arms of the barons."

"What barons?" exploded the envoy. "Have we not been told that Boemund of Tarentum is on his way! Boemund, son of that criminal, Guiscard, who threatened the Holy City? He among the defenders— he, whose very name is a supreme insult to the holy person of the Basileus!"

"That will do!" snapped the Pope. "Enough! You have been whining here, begging for help, pretending that you were Christians with nothing but the safety of the Cross at heart. Now we know what your faith is worth—*graeca fides,* as they call it all over the world. You have given yourself away. It is not the Cross you have at heart, but your gold. You have used Christ's name to foster your ends! But what is done is done. This mighty wave shall roll past your doorstep and as far as Jerusalem, whether you wish it or not! It will swell like a sea, and beware lest it sweep you away! In God's name, what is that . . . ?"

They both broke off and listened. A weird sound, the sound of trumpets approaching, pierced the tumult which surrounded the dais with a strident, heart-wringing wail. At once men who a moment before had been snatching crosses of cloth from each other's hands grew still, their eyes on a strange cavalcade.

About twenty riders were approaching. Their winded mounts were covered with caparisons of tow; the riders' armor was sheated in sackcloth. They rode with bare heads, their faces smeared with dust. Over them floated a pennant bearing the emblem of the white stag of the Arpads.

"By the wounds of Christ! What has happened?" the Zupan Sukki de Szuka cried, in horror.

The crowd drew back to let the riders pass. Without looking at anyone, as though blind to the world, they advanced slowly toward the Holy Father. Stopping in front of the bare dais, they raised their lances and shouting in unison: "Our King is dead! Our King is dead!" they flung their lances to the ground.

The crowd pressed closer. The Hungarians, shaking with fear, pushed their way through the throng.

"Dead? Our King dead? Ladislaus dead? Speak up, for God's sake!"

"Ladislaus is dead . . ."

"Where? When?"

"In Buda. Some six weeks ago . . ."

"O woe! O woe!"

With a terrific clatter the Hungarian knights threw their helmets to the ground. They tore their hair, and seizing fistfuls of dust from the ground rubbed it into their faces. In dead silence the crowd watched their despair.

The Greek envoy made a deep bow, and with a malicious smile disappeared unobserved.

Urban stood as if thunder-struck. At once voices began to rise from the crowd.

"Who will lead us now?"

"Who will command?"

"Who is to be the leader?"

Robert Curthose banged his lance on his shield to attract attention.

"Now that the king of Hungary is dead," he shouted, "who is to lead the holy expedition? Faith! If the noble knights so desire, I will!"

And he glared belligerently around, as if looking for anyone rash enough not to so desire. His partisans applauded. But not Raymond St. Gilles; he snatched his lance and shaking it called:

"No Frank shall win salvation under a Norman's command. I will lead!"

"Right! Never shall a Norman lord it over the Provençals!"

"Never!"

"Long live our leader Robert Curthose!"

"A pretty leader indeed! Grandson of the Devil, son of a bastard!"

"Step out, you barking dog!"

"Anyone will tell you the same!"

"Shame! Shame! Normans! Stand by!"

"Long live Raymond St. Gilles!"

"Neither Robert nor Raymond! Long live the Lord of Flanders, the spear and shield of knighthood!"

"Flanders! Flanders!"

And at once, all the lances were snatched up from the ground and began to quiver in feverish hands. Horses, feeling the pull of the reins, snorted. Reined back, they pushed into the crowd, which retreated in panic and pressed in every direction. Thus the knights made room for the approaching combat, while the rabble, safely perched on trees, shouted with delight.

Amid the general tumult Urban II alone sat silent. His face had turned as white as his robes. Was the whole stupendous venture about to collapse? O Death! What hast thou done? How hast thou dared run counter to the dispensation of Providence? Hast thou not heard: God wills it so?

The field was already seething with the tumult of battle. The Pope arose and raised the Cross. He motioned to the relay men. Let them out-shout the hubbub:

"Silence, Christians! Silence!"

"Lord Jesus Christ," prayed the Pope aloud, "Thou who art the Heavenly commander of this multitude. They have given themselves to Thee. Appoint Thy representative, direct who shall lead them—in Thy name."

A silence full of expectation fell over the field.

"Send him, O Lord, we wait."

Silence, while thousands upon thousands held their breath in suspense.

"Most merciful Lord Jesus Christ," and the voice of the Pope broke in a sob, "signify who shall lead this people."

"O Lord! Thou hearest. We wait!"

"No more waiting! Normans! Normans!"

"Stand by, Provence!"

"Stop!"

"I shall lead!"

Someone mounts the steps of the platform. Someone stands in front of Urban II. Adhemar de Monteuil, Bishop of Puy, his face strong and bright, his eyes deep and shining . . .

"Give me your blessing, Holy Father, I will lead the Crusade . . ."

"You, my friend. You?"

"What would you? Must all be undone?"

And the Pope, rising, put his arm around him, turned him to face the throng, marked him with the sign of the cross, and giving him his blessing, cried out that here was their commander and the representative of the Church, and whoever should not obey this leader would be as guilty as if he had not obeyed our Lord and Saviour Himself. Adhemar, Bishop of Puy, the leader of the Holy Crusade . . .

The knights, taken aback, were silent. What? A shaven cleric to lead them? Nothing of the sort had ever happened before. They made no objection, however, because each felt that, of the two, a bishop would be a lesser evil than another baron. Besides, they had no doubt that his would be a weak command, and that once out of the country they would have no trouble keeping him in his place.

And so, after a moment's hesitation, they drove their lances into the ground, and stretched out their unarmed palms, in sign of agreement.

11.

The Future Crusaders

MANNA WILL FALL FROM HEAVEN . . . THIS BLESSED PROMISE OF THE Hermit was already being fulfilled. It had become a fact, a reality. Clermont and its vicinity were suddenly overflowing with food within the reach of everyone. Prices, once exorbitant, now fell to levels so low that their like had not been seen or heard of in years. While a week before men had to pay thirteen denarii for one sheep, today for one denarius he could have thirteen. Everyone was selling out stocks of food and provisions in order to buy arms. The market place thronged with herds of cattle, driven from everywhere to be sold for anything they would fetch, and if no buyer appeared they were simply given away. Now that one and all were about to set forth on a long journey, who would bother about an old cow or goat? The same was true of grain. The price of bread had fallen to a small fraction of what it had been. Rumor had it that Wilbert, the miller, the richest man in the town, who had bought up all the grain from the surrounding countryside and filled his storehouses to the beams, counting on famine during the council, had hanged himself in despair.

For the first time the multitude, gorged with food, was in high spirits, and their camps buzzed merrily, like beehives.

The knights deliberated over their venture in one way, and the rabble in another. The nobles knew that they must take along their troops, servants, and horses, as well as their falconers and masters of hounds. They knew that they must provide themselves with money, food, and guides. They wondered where they might obtain interpreters. Not so the carefree rabble. They were ready to start at any time, tonight after supper if need be. No one planned to take anything with him, save perhaps his wife and his children. At present they were eating, making merry, and thanking the Lord for His bounty. This first of the

78

foretold miracles, the miracle of cheap food, was proof enough that others would follow in good time. What mattered most was that they were free! Since they had pinned the cross on their shoulders, they had become their own masters. No more toil, no more rising at daybreak to till the lord's fields. True, in the inns and around camp-fires, some already croaked that the barons were sorely angry with the Holy Father for freeing them from serfdom and were going to ask him to withdraw his promise. The abbots, too, were angry, for all the monks had taken the cross, and who would now remain in the monasteries?

"Aye, aye, soon they will surely begin to round up their own," said the timorous ones, glancing around. Alas! If only, besides receiving the Papal liberation, they could tear off that accursed brand, that loathsome mark on the shoulder which bore witness that they once belonged to this or that lord! Could they but cut it out, skin and all!

But others laughed at such fears. They were gorged with food, and therefore strong and confident. Just let the lords try to drive them back to toil! Let them try! Indeed, it would be easier to turn back a swollen river that has left its bed than to drive back into bondage men, conscious of their strength, who already looked upon themselves as free!

Peter Bartholomew of Marseilles, the jolly seminarian, drummed with his heels upon an empty keg on which he sat astride. He knew not himself whether he was glad to go. Would he find, wherever he went, wine, blessed wine, and maidens as comely and willing as here? He berated himself for these sinful thoughts and tried to turn his frivolous little soul to the Lord, to that oppressed Lord Jesus whose Sepulcher had been defiled. All in vain. His unruly thoughts continued to whirl and dance. Like his feet, the thoughts of Bartholomew, the seminarian, could never keep still. Already his speculations rushed forward: when would they start, what sights would they see first?

By his side two farmers, Macar and Jacob the Pimple-faced, discussed in low voices whether it would not be better to remain behind. In that throng even God could not have noticed their voices, so surely there would be no sin if they were to withdraw now. To stay might prove worthwhile, for men would be scarce here, and whatever is scarce becomes valuable.

With dancing steps, changed beyond recognition, Blanche de Montbeliard passed nearby. Joyfully she touched the cross pinned to her shoulder. Here was her shield, her protection. O! beloved Saviour!

To be free of the haunting executioner, she would in return gladly have walked to Jerusalem on her knees.

Walter the Penniless, the knight without belt or possessions, gathered around him bands of young and healthy men. Scornfully he drove away women, tonsured monks, and striplings. He would have none but the strong. "I shall turn you into troops that will put the Normans to shame," he promised. Serfs and servants willingly flocked around him, for they knew that he was poor and hated the rich as much as did they, and as for his strength and prowess—Good Lord! Just look at him!

The dishonest knights, Gottschalk and Von Emich, also talked a lot and summoned men to their side, all the while watching carefully lest in the throng they should encounter Hungarians or Poles, trying to persuade all who would listen that the sooner they started on their way the better. It was true, they said, that the Holy Father and the Bishop of Puy every day repeated through relay men that all should wait in peace until knightly retinues had gathered to lead the way, but would this waiting turn to the good of the common man? Everyone knew that the clergy always played the nobles' game, that they thought only of the rich, never of the poor. And did not the nobles wish to keep the fairest booty and fame for themselves?

"It irritates the noblemen that so many of you have taken the cross!" shouted Emich (in which he was not far from the truth). "Now they too must go, whether they like it or not . . . What would they do, if they were to stay? Till the land with their own hands? But pay them no heed."

"Neither them, nor you," voices rose from the crowd. "Who are you? A belted oppressor of poor folks, just like the others."

Huddled on a couch in the corner of her tent, Willibald, wife of Omer de Guillebaut, brooded over her vow. A sorrowful and unfortunate lady, Willibald was. Because Sir Omer, before he married her, had had another wife who gladly looked upon pages and the handsomer squires, he would no longer trust any woman. He was suspicious and cruelly jealous. It was in vain that Willibald never looked at anyone. She sat at banquets as if carved in wood, and never took part in dances or courtly games. All in vain . . . The more reserved and modest her deportment, the more suspicion of guile and betrayal it aroused in the gloomy Norman's heart. Neither Willibald's humility nor her sweetness could dispel his long-nourished bitterness against his former spouse and, whenever he left the castle, Omer would first with his own hands bind his poor lady with an iron-padlocked belt, called a *garde-vertu*. This was torture to a woman. The iron links bit into her hips, and her tender flesh, constantly chafed by rawhide, festered and stank. Despite all efforts, her walk revealed the humiliating truth. Because of this, whenever her husband was absent, Willibald never left her chamber. She was ashamed before people, ashamed to get out. She could not understand how other women could bear it, for she noticed that they did not seem to be much upset by the shameful device.

In fact, a friend, the chatelaine of Bois-Roche, once revealed to her that she possessed a second key to the padlock and simply took off the *garde-vertu* as soon as her husband was outside the gate.

"All you must remember," she informed her, "is to keep the belt and key always with you, in case your lord should unexpectedly return."

"But how is one to obtain a second key?" Willibald inquired.

"A locksmith made it for me, a youth. He took an imprint in wax and . . ." Noticing the astonished and horrified look on Willibald's face, she burst into laughter. "Faith! he did not do it for nothing. Well, if someone had found out, he would have been put on the rack. I rewarded him . . . What of it? All of us do likewise; you should try, too."

But Willibald would not even hear of it. She was at once too proud and too fearful. Besides, she had no desire to be untrue to her husband, she wished only to be left in peace. But at times there would mount within that gentle and naturally loving creature such hatred toward Sir Omer that it seemed to her the passion of it would tear her asunder. With set teeth she hated him till she longed to do murder. She would rue it, but she could not still her hatred. Would that cruel man never take pity on her? Did he not see her wounds whenever he took off the disgusting chains?

And that was why she took the cross. At the thought that he would go to the Holy Land for God knows how long and leave her behind, girdled in the *garde-vertu*, she was seized with such terror that, heedless of what she was doing, she had vowed to go with him.

Her husband did not take kindly to her decision. "Why did you do it?" he asked. "You are awkward, unused to travel. You will be nothing but an encumbrance to me."

"I want to serve God, and would rather not part with you, my lord."

The explanation did not satisfy him. He left the tent, suspiciously turning his head to right and left and considering which one among the knights of their acquaintance was responsible for his wife's rash step.

That young fop, always reeking with perfume, Alberon the archdeacon, was just passing by the tent and it occurred to Omer de Guillebaut that it might be he. As far as he knew, Willibald had not met Alberon, but how could one be sure whom a woman, that perverse and utterly false creature, had or had not met. In any case he was determined to keep an eye on them.

Nearby, in the magnificent quarters of the Duke of Burgundy, the beautiful Florine combed her golden hair, long, soft, and fair as silk; and fair too were her thoughts, fluttering ceaselessly around the figure of the foreign prince. He and she would ride away together on some distant expedition. Where? Florine hardly knew, but it did not matter. Father Placid, her confessor, would tell her. What mattered most at present (though her confessor need not know) was whether she would often see that handsome, that charming prince. O! how she wished that she knew what he was thinking of, what he was doing right now in that leather pavilion of his under the standard cut in four by the cross!

Indeed, the prince was thinking of her, and also of fame. Those two lovely themes wove themselves into a pattern like a troubadour song, into a glorious melodious call which filled him with delight and wonder.

Meanwhile, Philip, Duke of Burgundy, had at last made up his mind! He would remain. Philip of Paris, fool though he was, could not be taken too lightly. It was enough that Florine should have taken the cross. Surely no evil could befall that beloved child of his. With Raymond's Elvira and so many other noble ladies going, she would have proper company and care. Nor would she lack anything: he meant to send her off with a train that would befit the only child of the mightiest of French lords. Then, there was that royal prince of Denmark. The information supplied by the crafty Arnuld, chaplain to the Norman prince, had turned out to be favorable to Swennon, son of Olav.

Arnuld, who knew the intrigues of every European court, was at that moment closeted with Robert Curthose, in the latter's pavilion. Master and servant glared at each other furiously. In low voices, with their heavy-jowled faces almost touching, they exchanged bitter reproaches. And all because the rash Robert, finding himself short of money for the expedition, had on the spur of the moment pledged Normandy to his brother William. The Red had gladly assented, and within a week the money would be delivered. Arnuld was beside himself with indignation.

"O, it was easy to pawn, my Lord, but only try to get it back. Of what use was it to raise your sword against your late father, to spill so much blood, for a duchy that now, at a moment's notice, without consideration, without taking counsel, is to be given away? William will never return what he has taken."

Veins swelled in Robert's neck.

"He will not, say you? Sword in hand I shall tear it out of his throat, if need be."

"Back from one war, and embark upon another and a worse? Faith! my Lord! What do you keep me for? Have not my counsels always stood you in good stead? And you, my Lord, must decide a matter, such an all-important matter, in a flash of an eyelash without even asking my advice. Yet even a blind man would see that it would be safer to pawn with an enemy, a Jew, anyone, rather than your brother! A stranger, once paid, must take himself away. Not so one's own blood. Mark my word, my Lord, William will never let you sit again upon your ducal throne."

"Chaplain, you exceed the measure," Robert exclaimed angrily.

"Probably, probably, when I no longer know what I say for grief. Through your own remissness you have already forfeited the crown of England. And now your heritage! Such a duchy! Such a magnificent duchy!"

"Stop croaking. No one is taking it away yet."

"May I prove an untrue prophet! But I doubt if you will ever see it again. It would have been better if you had given it to your brother outright, in return for ready cash. Then at least it could be said of you that you are magnanimous and ready to make any sacrifices for the sake of the Holy Sepulcher. As it is, do you know, my Lord, what will be said?"

"That I am a blockhead—so? Let anyone dare!"

Arnuld did not answer, but his silence was eloquent enough. Robert leaped to his feet and began to pace in circles around the tent. He knew that his chaplain was right, for he had done a stupid thing, and through no fault of his own. The Red had hoodwinked him by sly talk, by tempting him with money. May his eyes rot out. May he perish before he takes the duchy over . . .

The learned Stephen, Count of Blois and Chartres, sat on a bench close by his wife Adele, an arm about her swelling waist.

"Pregnant women cannot join the expedition," he was saying, "and so you shall stay behind, my love. How I envy you! My only hope is that they will change their minds as quickly as they made them up, and perhaps we shall not start at all."

"Why did you offer to go, my Lord?"

"I had to," he sighed. "You know how it is. There would have been an outcry. They would say—and your brother Robert first of all—that I am a coward."

Imbram paced back and forth in front of the tent. He was not certain whether his brothers already knew that he had taken the vow. He must tell them. They would rage, no doubt, but ah! well, let them rage! They were no longer in Silesia, in the ancestral manor where the authority of the elder was sacred. Here, in this strange land, so far from home, customs were different. Glovach's scoldings or Zbylut's derision no longer mattered. He would tell them at once.

And while he deliberated with himself how best to break the news to his brothers, his heart once more flared up with rapture. Surely once Christ's Sepulcher was freed, He the Everlasting Kindness, the Eternal Goodness would rule over all the world. Gone would be ghosts, phantoms, and all dark powers, gone perpetual fear and anxieties. The endless traps of evil demons would no longer threaten the world. If only he, Imbram, should live to see that day! That wonderful day, when there would be nothing to fear, no need to part with those that one loved. He must help bring that about. He would help to free Christ's Sepulcher and restore Christ's rule to the world.

But even before he began to speak (for these were not easy things to put into words), Glovach forestalled him. Imko, it seemed, had taken the cross. That was good, very good, indeed. For once in his life he had acted wisely. In fact both Zbylut and he, Glovach, were likewise on their way to take the vow. So was Nagodits and the Novinas, so were the three Osventas.

Imbram was dumbfounded. The news was the last thing he had expected.

Glovach, however, went on explaining that with the Hungarian messengers of death there had arrived a Pole, the good knight Belina, bringing the latest news from Silesia. Ladislas, it seemed, had proclaimed that unless the knights who had fled the country returned before Christmas they would be sentenced to death and their domains confiscated and turned over to whomever the Prince might choose, which—no doubt—meant Shechec.

"But, mind you, Imko," Glovach continued, "we have in no wise fled the country. We have taken the cross, and that is an altogether different matter. No one dare harm us, and least of all Ladislas, who next spring intends to send envoys to Rome to fetch holy relics for the cathedral. I have already found a monk here who is to write that all of us are going, and the Holy Father, himself, will confirm it with his seal. Belina can take it to Lord Magnus. Then let Ladislas try to play us false. The bishop said that whoever wronged a crusader would be excommunicated. But take the vow we must. God knows when we shall return. Still, booty there ought to be aplenty, what with the Greeks or those other Saracens."

Thus Glovach. But Imbram hardly listened to him. He sat on the bench pulling his long, flaxen moustache that was lighter than his suntanned face. What was the matter with him, he wondered. He ought to be glad that instead of rebuke he had been given praise, and that they would still continue on their way in a body, as they had before. And yet he felt strangely bereft. In the face of Glovach's sober, common-sense arguments that earlier inner glow, the rapture he had experienced only a few minutes before, had gone out like the flame of a candle. It had seemed to him, fool that he was, that he was doing something great, so great, indeed, that it was beyond comprehension. He had thought that for the sake of the common good he was sacrificing Ofka, his love of her and his longing. And lo! as it turned out, he had taken the only sensible course. By acting as he had, he was merely safeguarding their common possessions. In a way it was all for the best and, surely, he ought to thank God. Yet, somehow, it seemed a pity . . .

In his tent Hugh de Vermandois lay upon a soft bed of bear skins. It was his habit whenever he was not on horseback to stretch out com-

fortably, for Hugh was lazy and as fond of comfort as a Greek, though
he had none of the Greek craftiness and greed. Indeed, it was common
knowledge that anyone could obtain from the lord of Vermandois anything that his heart desired. As a result, the good knight was always penniless and plagued with debts. He had already sold the better part of
his duchy and at the moment he was awaiting the return of messengers
he had despatched with a letter written by the learned Stephen to his
royal brother, Philip. By God, he said to himself, Philip ought to do his
share; since he was not going himself, he ought at least assist his brother
with his purse! Hugh was well aware that the royal purse was as empty
as his own princely one, but he reckoned that Philip, exultant as he
would be at the thought that all the rapacious wolves who surrounded
his tiny kingdom would be off wandering somewhere overseas, might
find some way to procure him the money.

So, with hands comfortably crossed under his head, he gazed at the
roof of the tent and waited.

"And how will the good Lord William de Melun manage to collect
a fighting force?" he asked suddenly. "For denarii are even scarcer in
his belt than they are in mine."

The knight, De Berneville, who was sitting with him, rose at the voice
of his prince.

"Lord William," he explained, "has gathered a good band of men and
ambushes merchants on the highway. And he says to his captives: 'I
am about to set out on a holy expedition and you are not. For the sake
of Jesus our Lord, share with me whatever you have.' "

"Ho, a capital thought!"

"Indeed, my Lord, it seems that he has collected a good deal already.
To be sure, some refused to give willingly, so he had them cut to
ribbons."

"They deserved it, too, the accursed enemies of the Holy Sepulcher!
Ha, if Philip sends nothing, perhaps we shall choose a bush opposite De
Melun."

"We had better not wait too long," remarked De Berneville. "Sooner
or later the merchants will grow wise and give up traveling."

Hugh yawned in reply.

The Count d'Haineault held his wife's hand in silence. The hearts of
both were almost breaking at the thought of parting so soon and they

looked at each other in mute adoration. They loved each other like Tristram and Isolde, with a bitter, conscious, consuming passion, for both had once known the poison of other, loveless bonds. Scarcely a year had passed since they were married. And now they must part. Ida, like Adele, the wife of the learned Stephen, was with child, and her time would come about Shrovetide. The son of the Count d'Haineault could not be born in a wayside inn; there was no choice: she must remain; he must go. One is not a knight for nothing. God and glory must take precedence over love . . .

Brother Hyacinthus, copyist and illuminator, writhed in an agony of indecision. What did the Lord wish him to do? How could he be sure? Which way lay the salvation of his soul? Should he continue to copy, remain in his beloved cell within the safe orbit of parchment, paint pots and brushes, or set out on this holy expedition, sally forth into a strange foreign world, which to his myopic eyes, to the mind of a recluse, appeared now like a terrifying whirlpool, now like an insoluble labyrinth? Enviously he watched a band of novices, cheerfully prattling about the journey. They, at least, had no misgivings. Pledged to monastic life since childhood, and some even before birth, they were leaving with joyous hearts a life that they had never desired.

Baldwin of Lorraine wondered how he could persuade the Pope to forbid women to take the cross, at least, not without their husbands' consent. What need was there for them to go? What need, say, for Gontrane? He had thought he would be rid of her for the time being, at least, but, no! she was coming. Damn the woman! She loathed him, held him in contempt, and on the slightest provocation covered him with abuse, and yet she would not let him alone. But he would have company: she was the same to everyone, vindictive, bitter, always irritable, a real shrew. Almost no one remembered that a few years before she had been a young, beautiful maid with gentle dark eyes.

There was but one man who could check Gontrane's outbursts of savage rage. That was her brother-in-law, Godfrey, whose exemplary, almost monastic life, calm and dignity, commanded everyone's respect. But unfortunately he seldom heeded Baldwin's pleas when the latter asked him to intervene in his domestic bickerings.

Leaning against a fence, Baldwin heaved a deep sigh. How beautiful would be the prospect of a journey into those unknown, far lands if only Gontrane would remain at home! Well, it could not be helped. Let that thorn come too, if it could not be otherwise.

He began to wonder how Godfrey would solve the problem of money. They had none, for Baldwin was altogether too fond of the tourney and the hunt, and Godfrey carried charity and generosity to a fault. They had been obliged to pawn table silver with the Jews of Metz, even to come here, and how many bags of good ducats would they not need now for such an expensive expedition? The Bishop of Verdun, it seemed, wanted to buy the Duchy of Lorraine. Baldwin had also heard that the people of the good town of Metz would be glad to buy their freedom and possess the town in their own name! Crafty burghers! Godfrey had always felt sorry for them and refused to molest them with taxes; and look how much gold they had amassed! It would be interesting to know how much they would offer. And what about the bishop? Probably Godfrey would not sell, merely pledge. But who could tell? Perhaps he would sell after all. Oh well . . . Let him do as he saw fit. Baldwin did not care. He had a sword and would carve out for himself in that distant world another, a better, dukedom. He smiled dreamily as he counted the spires of his dukedom to be.

Godfrey was not thinking of the price the Bishop of Verdun would offer him on the morrow for his heritage. He lay prostrate in prayer on the cathedral floor. Though the cold of the flagstones pierced his body, it failed to cool his burning head, and he was thanking God from the bottom of his soul for the great change He had wrought in his life, for this sacred summons, for this chance to tear himself away from loathsome worldly things. At last it would be granted him to forget all else and plunge into battle. "For Thy Sepulcher, O Christ . . . For Thee."

In this prayer he was not alone. Although the morning service was long since over, the Cathedral teemed with knightly figures. Raymond St. Gilles was there, and Robert of Flanders, De La Tour, Beaugency who no longer feared the devil, and De Luz (though he was not belted), the De Viel twins, Ribeaumont, the Counts de Grai and de Montaigue, Henry and Godfrey de Hache, Peter and Paul de Toul, and a host of others. All those, in fact, who had taken the vow for no other reason than their sincere love of Christ. They were all there praying, giving thanks, crying, and taking vows, each according to his lights. Thus one swore to abstain from wine, another not to touch a woman till he had returned from a liberated Jerusalem. And as they made those pledges aloud, others heard them and followed their example, taking the vow of chastity for the whole duration of the expedition. To this some added other privations: One would not have his hair cut until his head touched the stone of the Holy Sepulcher, another would not take off his clothes before he reached Jerusalem, yet another would not wash the dust of pilgrimage from his feet until he stood under the walls of the Holy City. With his sword clattering, Raymond St. Gilles rose from his knees. In a voice strong and resonant, though quivering with emotion, he vowed to Almighty God that in return for the supreme favor of seeing the Holy Sepulcher, he was ready never to set eyes again upon his native Toulouse . . . never to return to his own fair land! He renounced it willingly, so that he might gain in return the name of a defender of the Sepulcher, the greatest distinction any good knight could crave.

And as he stood there with his hands stretched out toward the altar as though upon his palms he was offering his very heart, sobs resounded throughout the church. Others rose, vowing likewise to renounce their homes. Let nothing hold them here, let nothing draw them back, neither their native soil, nor their paternal castles, nor their booty, nor their possessions. They would willingly strip themselves of everything, if only God would bestow upon them the only favor they craved, to free the Holy Sepulcher! To tread with their own feet upon the sacred soil, to see it freed from the infidel, to behold the sites where once Christ had lived and suffered, grant it, O Lord, to Thy good, Christian knights!

Heads that had never known tears were shaken with sobs; hands shook that had never once trembled before.

In the dark nave the flames of wax tapers flickered like so many glittering, golden bees. The misty breath of the praying knights rose in the air and spun rainbows over their heads. They knew that they were standing on the brink of a tremendous mystery; God had chosen them, elevated them, made them different from other men. Their breasts swelled with pride; exultation filmed their eyes, and it seemed to them that already they had passed the boundaries of mortality.

12.

First Throes

IT WAS A COLD AND BUSY WINTER. FROST WAS IN THE GROUND BEFORE Christmas, but the activity of summer filled the holidays and welcomed the year 1096. Adhemar was buying up food supplies and storing them in churches. Armorers were busy at their forges. Swordsmanship and archery were practiced, wills were executed, horses were trained, and in the great castles accounts were put in order, jewels were traded for gold, and chastity belts were fitted to flinching, frightened wives.

In Clermont the common people formed themselves into military companies and dreamed of the battles they would win. Adhemar tried to get knights to command them, but the belted gentlemen refused; they offered to belt any squire and to give him armor and a sword and girdle if he would lead the peasants. Many accepted the offer, and were dubbed on St. Paul the Hermit's Day by Adhemar himself.

All over the land tales of wonder were told. Stars fell from the sky and were turned into knights as they touched the ground. Lights like will-o'-the-wisps rose at night to guide crusaders on the road. A troubadour beset by wolves saw them lie down at his feet, yelping, because of the cross of his arm. Kings and saints rose from their sepulchers to set forth for Jerusalem; St. Martin walked in the square of Tours at dusk; St. Guy paced the walls of his abbey.

In the sky, clouds piled into ramparts and castles, with heavenly garrisons sent by the Lord. In Jerusalem a letter fell in the Basilica of the Holy Sepulcher; it was written by the Saviour Himself. A squire dreamed of his brother, long dead—the brother said he was taking the cross. Word swept over the countryside that graves were emptying to fill the ranks of God's army. Every stranger was anxiously examined to discover whether he were man alive or phantom quit of purgatory by dint of the general indulgence.

It was too much for the peasant soldiers. When spring came they wanted to be on their way. Jerusalem was over the hill and God had His arms outstretched. Why wait for the knights? Von Emich and Gottschalk urged them on. Wait for the knights, they said, and you will again be enslaved. The peasants asked Peter the Hermit to lead them. When he hesitated, Walter the Penniless and the German knights stepped forward with offers to take command. Peter, still frightened but now envious, capitulated. They would set forth immediately; he would walk at their head.

Adhemar tried to hold them; he begged that they consider the crops they would ruin by their early-season marching—there were a hundred thousand of them. They listened and did as they pleased. They broke into the churches, stole the carefully gathered food, and set off singing and shouting prayers; bawds, whores, cutpurses, ne'er-do-wells, minstrels, ribalds, beggars, cripples, blind men, peasants, housewives, children, and fresh young knights with new swords and great hopes. They drank wells dry, trampled fields, ruined vineyards, broke fences and wells, set fires, and scattered their food like manna. "Take it," they said to those they met. "When it is gone, God will give us more."

They moved in three groups, one under Peter, one under Walter the Penniless, and one under Von Emich and Gottschalk. When food gave out they stole, looted, and sacked. Thousands starved. The strong in Peter's band dispersed to raid and forage. Walter, a good soldier, kept military discipline and saved the core of his company. Von Emich, younger son of a German knight, a fugitive from Holy Orders, led his people against the nearest and most obvious target, the Jews.

In the town of Spira only the smoking ruins of the ghetto remained. They had left amidst the charred debris a score of Jews butchered like sheep on the steps of the Synagogue, and the naked body of a Jewish girl who had stabbed herself when they had tried to baptize her by force. The recollection of freshly shed blood made the men's nostrils quiver. Mounted on a beautiful stallion requisitioned without its owner's consent from a nearby castle, Von Emich stood on a hillock, stoutly addressing his men:

"God points to us the way we must follow. Hearken to me, brethren!

Hearken, you, Christian warriors! Is it not right that before we set
forth to free the Holy Sepulcher we should first punish the rascals who
have slain our Lord! We have set out against the Saracens, but who are
Saracens? Foul heathen they are, yet not as foul as the Jews! It was not
they who nailed Christ to the cross! It was not they who put Him to
death! And yet, mind you, while we, in bitter hardship and want tramp
across the world, ready to give our lives for Our Lord, these scoundrels,
these murderers of Our Sweet Saviour go about free and wax rich on
our heart's-blood. Is this fair? Should it be so? Down with the Jews! God
wills it so!"

"God wills it!" bellowed the mob.

"We march in sweat and toil, hungry, often forced to take the last
crumb from our fellow Christians while meantime the accursed Jews sit
upon bags of gold! Can this be God's will? Is it not our duty to take
these treasures from them to turn them into provender for our Holy
Campaign?"

"It is! Let's take it! God wills it!"

"You have seen with your own eyes that possessed wench who preferred to take her life rather than receive the blessing of Holy Baptism.
How are we to punish such accursed resistance? Only by death. It's
our duty to avenge this insult to Our Lord!"

"It is! So it is! Down with the Jews!"

Gottschalk nodded his big head in approval. He stared at the speaker
with open admiration. He was clever, Von Emich! Look how he could
talk. Gottschalk could not. The dull-witted, red-headed giant knew only
how to beat and plunder. He was incapable of cunning, not because he
despised ruse but because to save his life he could not invent a lie.

To Von Emich deceit presented no difficulty. By birth the younger
son of a knight, he had been destined to take orders, but still as a half-
grown lad he had fled the despised walls of the convent. To the warped
mentality of the unfrocked monk, he joined the bitter vindictiveness of
a weakling whose bodily growth had been stunted by monastical fasts
and privations. His mind was tortuous and dark, his heart filled with
hatred for everything that lived. The world had been cruel to him and
he hated the world.

It cost him nothing to pose in front of his followers as a true and
ardent Christian. With a great show of secrecy he let it be rumored
about that, still in Clermont, an angel had miraculously marked him

with a cross. It was common knowledge that on his shoulder, hidden under his clothes, he bore the sacred mark. Only he was not allowed to show it to anyone.

No one liked the Jews, no one would defend them. Those who needed them most were the loudest in their denunciations. Gruesome, blood-curdling stories were told of the dark multitudes shut in every city behind the gates of the ghetto. Stories of how, pagan-like, they worshipped the golden calf, even as their ancestors had done at the foot of Mount Sinai, of how every Saturday they drank Christian blood, of how they poisoned city wells with carcasses of dead dogs, and stole corpses from the church-yards to practice upon them abominable witchcraft, of how they kidnapped and murdered innocent Christian babes . . . such tales were Gospel truth to simple folk everywhere. No wonder lepers were more easily suffered than Jews.

Indeed, there was no one among the thousands that surrounded Von Emich and Gottschalk who would not welcome the summons:

"Beat the Jew! Avenge the death of Christ, Our Lord! God wills it!"

And while thus shouting they set off across the country, others promptly joined their ranks.

"To the Rhine! To the Rhine and its rich cities. Down with the Jews!"

Aye, Down with the Jews . . .

At Worms his men slew a thousand Jews. At Cologne everyone in the ghetto was killed. At Coblenz it became slaughter. At Neuse, Trevir, Wewelinghofen, Eller, Xantin, no Jews were left alive. At Mainz the archbishop took the fugitives into his castle; Von Emich's men surrounded it and formed to attack, faced only by the man of God.

A golden dalmatic sheathed the figure of the old archbishop. Gereon was old, very old indeed. The tangled locks of hair that framed his wrinkled face were white and the hand which held the shepherd's staff was shrivelled. But his eyes were keen and undaunted, as he stood there on a narrow log, alone, above the moat, before the castle.

"Hand over the Jews! God wills it!" men roared from every side; yet none made bold to step on the log.

"Hand over the Jews! How dare you protect the enemies of Christ! For shame!"

"Shame upon you, murderers! So long as I live, you shall not have these people. You have brought enough crimes upon yourselves as it is! Be gone! To church with you, and beg forgiveness!"

And with the golden crosier pointing directly at Gottschalk and Von Emich, he called so loud that an echo answered from the timbering below: "Woe to you, foul wretches, you who have turned God's children into the Devil's own! I curse you, evil-doers! I curse you whether sleeping or waking, whether alive or dying! I curse your souls! May you know no peace after death! May God in all His mercy forget you, then, amen!"

But at that moment, sweeping up from the outermost fringe of the mob, cries of anguish and fear grew and grew to drown whatever new curse the bishop might have called. For out of the dust had come another army, led by Godfrey of Bouillon and his brother Baldwin of Lorraine, on their way up the Rhine from Aix-la-Chapelle, the burial place of Charlemagne. They had gathered together the knights of Bouillon, Mons, Metz, Toul, and Verdun, and now, in savage anger, they smashed and scattered the peasant army, only at last to discover that Von Emich and Gottschalk had escaped.

In Hungary the crusaders under Peter and Walter found themselves escorted by soldiers who kept them from pillage and drove them to the Sava River, at the point opposite Belgrade. On the other side waited Greek mercenaries, sent to guide them to Constantinople. They were ferried across—all but the lepers, the beggars, and the cripples. These were kept until last, and forced to man the oars themselves.

This they did gladly, expecting no better treatment. But as they neared the opposite shore a strange thing happened. The centurion in charge of the Greek soldiers spoke to the honorable Tatikios, who had come as representative of the Basileus to meet the first crusaders and keep an eye on them. The Tatikios gave an order. The centurion spoke to Walter the Penniless, who nodded his head. Archers ranged themselves along the river and drew their bows. The centurion went to the water's edge and signalled the oncoming barges, waving them away from the shore. The wretches in the boats waved back, thinking they were being welcomed.

Then a two-wheeled cart was brought to the bank. It bore a serpentine pipe with a mouth formed like a calyx. Again the centurion waved and the wretches waved back. Suddenly there was an explosion, and from the calyx a dark mass burst. Instantly it began to glow. It fell on the water in flames, moving toward the barges. The water blazed.

It was Greek Fire, the military weapon which had made Byzantium impregnable for centuries, until the Saracens discovered it. A second missile landed closer to the barges. Now the wretches understood. They were not to be allowed to land. In panic they rowed toward the shore from which they had come. There the Hungarians raised their spears and shook them. They could not land. They were trapped in the swift current of the river. Suddenly they began to scream and weep.

Peter the Hermit, watching, was convulsed with agony. He pleaded with the centurion. He clawed at Walter the Penniless, tearing at the sword that hung around the knight's neck.

"The fault is yours!" he screamed. "You have killed them! You have condemned them to death! They are crusaders, Christ's soldiers! You have murdered them!"

Walter thrust Peter aside contemptuously. "The fault is not mine but yours, lout!" he grated. "Long enough has this vermin tortured our heels! Unless you now do as I say, you and your whole rabble will perish thus! We have stern business before us. The day of fools and beggars is done!" So saying, Walter strode off to greet the Tatikios, leaving Peter prostrate and moaning in the dust . . .

Thus the first wave of the Crusade swept over Europe and disappeared into the East.

13.

The West Has Broken Loose from Its Roots

FOUR TRAILS WERE TO LEAD THE NOBLE KNIGHTS TO THE HOLY LAND, AND this was right and wise, for the feeding of such large armies along a single way would have presented almost insuperable difficulties. Fortunately each group preferred to choose its own route. Godfrey of Bouillon proceeded from Cologne up the Rhine and on to the valley of the Danube, thus following the trail along which, only three months before, Peter's unruly bands had marched. Godfrey had finally sold his patrimony, the Duchy of Bouillon and of Lorraine, to the bishops of Liege and Verdun for 6,600 pounds of silver and five pounds of gold, and had allowed the townsfolk of Metz to buy their freedom for one thousand pounds of silver and a pound and a half of gold—a great fortune, indeed, and thanks to which his army presented a rich and imposing sight. Ten thousand mounted knights, fifty thousand bowmen, shieldmen, axemen, and attendants, all well fed, well armed, and well disciplined. They were taking few carts along to impede the march; instead they bought provisions on their way—bought, since Godfrey had a horror of violence and could not bear the tears and laments that followed looting. He himself set prices that his treasurer, however chagrined, was forced to pay.

In addition to his brother, Baldwin, and the acrimonious Gontrane, Godfrey was accompanied by his friends and faithful companions, Konon de Montaigue, Dudon de Contz, Wilfried d'Esch, Baldwin du Bourg, and the Count d'Haineault. Most of them were bringing their wives along; only the Count d'Haineault would have to wait till they reached Byzantium before he saw his beloved Ida again, for she had borne him a son that winter and had long ailed after the confinement. So, in order to spare her strength, it was decided to let her go by sea under the escort of a good company of knights. Costly as such a journey was, for the Genoese charged exhorbitant prices for the passage, it was shorter and less hard on a woman.

By sea, likewise, went Hugh de Vermandois, who, though a brave knight, was as lazy as a fat woman. His brother, King Philip, finding himself unable to supply him generously with money, had presented him instead with his own royal gilded galley. Besides his own retinue and squires, Hugh was taking along Sir Roger de Berneville and Sir William de Melun, nicknamed, "The Carpenter," because, whenever in the thick of the battle he began to hack with his mighty sword, heads and arms flew about like splinters under a carpenter's axe. The lord of Melun was famed not only for his strength but also because of his insatiable craving for food. It was a wonder how much Sir William would consume every day before he felt replete, but once he had his fill, he would whinny with joy like a horse and fling himself into battle, laughing at the death that circled around him.

Alongside the gilded galley of the royal brother sailed a mighty flotilla of sea brigands who had likewise taken the Cross. Their leader, Guynemere de Boulogne, surnamed, "The King of Pirates," was a cruel and brilliant rascal whose fierce rule extended over the entire French coast. He was sailing eighteen ships, each vessel carrying a crew that, under red or black kerchiefs tied around the head, showed fierce copper-colored faces of which the Devil himself might well have taken fright. White teeth glittered rapaciously at the sight of the gilded royal galley that sailed amidst their shabby, black-rigged crafts like a swan among a pack of hungry wolves, and, leaning over the railings, they stared incredulously at that beautiful, easy prize. It was hard to believe that they were to sail thus quietly by her side. Still Guynemere was their master and Guynemere had ordered them to respect the royal vessel; for the comfort-loving knight, stretched all day long upon a soft couch on the deck of the galley, was Guynemere's fellow crusader. Verily, all of them were likewise no longer pirates but crusaders. From now on they were to loot none but the Saracens.

In the French vineyards heavy, sweet clusters of grapes were already turning dark when Robert Curthose set out upon the Holy Expedition. In return for the pledge of Normandy he had received from his brother, William the Red, ten thousand pounds of silver and fifteen pounds of gold. For that money (even though his minions had in no time stolen nearly half of it) he had outfitted a magnificent army almost sixty thousand strong. As travelling companions he was taking along his inseparable chaplain and adviser, Arnuld de Rohes, the learned chronicler Foucher de Chartres, the two brothers Guillebaut, the royal prince of Denmark with fifteen hundred fair-headed, tight-lipped warriors, and Robert of Flanders and his heavy Frisians, whose valor and good sense had no peer the world over. They journeyed from Normandy to Rome so that they might spend the winter at the grave of St. Peter and at the break of spring, once more blessed by the Holy Father, start upon the last leg of their journey. This course was adopted at the advice of the crafty Arnuld de Rohes. "Let that credulous, straightforward Godfrey," he had said, "get to Byzantium first. Our trusted men will advise us how his relations with Alexius are shaping up; then we will know how it befits us to enter the Basileus' lands: as allies and friends or as conquerors."

It was the late summer when at last the band of Raymond St. Gilles, Count of Toulouse, made ready to leave their native land. There were almost a hundred thousand of them; all the knighthood of Provence, Languedoc, and Toulouse, in fact, and with them the Hungarian and Polish knights.

Meantime, a thousand knights of the highest rank and thirty thousand foot soldiers gathered in Italy at the summons of Boemund. A mighty lord was Boemund. His father, Robert Guiscard, had been the terror of the Greeks and Saracens alike and, but for his untimely death, might have ascended the Byzantian throne. The son was no less ambitious than the father. Handsome of features, tall of stature, he was reckless and cunning. Outwardly frank, impulsive and open-handed, he was in reality greedy, cool, and calculating. Each of his presumably spontaneous impulses or outbursts was the fruit of long and careful deliberation. That was why it was often said that the Devil himself had fled before Boemund lest he, too, fell prey to the wily prince. As he prepared now for the Holy Crusade, Boemund was assisted by his favorite nephew, Tancred.

Though Tancred bore a striking likeness to his uncle, it was in face and grace of figure only. By nature he was impulsive, noble, and completely guileless. Boemund looked upon him with a sense of his own superiority but not without love: deep at heart he felt a grudging admiration for the crystal-clear honesty of the youth. Tancred was the only man in the world whom Boemund trusted: he had never and he would never betray a trust.

The Norman-Italian armies of the two knights gathered in the sunny Benevento and Amalphi. In the first days of November they were to sail from three ports: Bari, Brindis, and Otranto to Durazzo and Valone. From there they would proceed by land following a trail close to that of Raymond St. Gilles, across the rocky Balkans and half-pagan Bulgaria.

One hundred thousand people had set forth with Peter the Hermit. Fifteen thousand with Gottschalk and Von Emich, ten thousand with Walter the Penniless. Sixty thousand with Godfrey de Bouillon. A hundred thousand with Raymond St. Gilles. Thirty thousand with Boemund and Tancred. Sixty thousand with Robert Curthose. These figures were set down and recorded by the chroniclers who took part in the expedition: Foucher de Chartres, Raymond d'Aguilers, and an anonymous knight of Boemund's retinue. Their statements were confirmed by the learned Anna Porphyrogenita who forty years later, described the reign of her father, Basileus Alexius, and by the wise Matthew of Edessa. They were also confirmed by the Arab historian Kemel-el-Din, Ib-al-Atyr, Abdul Mehacen, Ibn Giusi, and Abdul Feda. Incredible as it may seem, it must therefore be true—true that four hundred thousand men, a large portion of then sparsely populated Europe, had set forth in an outburst of faith, ambition, lust for power, and hope of a better fate, unparalleled in the history of mankind.

As Pope Urban II had said to Bishop Adhemar de Monteuil: The West had broken loose from its roots to fall upon the East.

◇◇

BOOK TWO

14.

The Werewolf

PAUSING EVERY NOW AND THEN TO MOISTEN HER FINGERS AND DRAW THE thread from the distaff, the Bulgarian woman chanted in a muffled monotone:

"Fifteen thousand of our band fell captive to the Caesar Basil.

"The eyes of the fifteen thousand were torn out at his word.

"Save for one eye spared to every hundredth man that he might lead ninety-nine of his comrades home.

"And so the sightless returned to Prince Samuel.

"Seeing his blind warriors, Prince Samuel tore his own eyes from his head and cast them into the Danube.

"Float on, O starry eyes, once falcon keen—float on to the Christian Emperor. I have no wish to gaze upon the world when its beauties are lost to my followers. And O, what now, my loyal band, now that we are blind? We shall sit about the fire and tell of our past glories. We shall keep the tale alive until our young have grown strong, and have forged strong axes, and have pointed many arrows. Until they take the field and avenge our loss."

The Silesian knights, seated about on benches, listened attentively but understood no portion of the Bulgarian woman's song. Only an occasional word borrowed from the Serbs struck their ears with a familiar sound. The air in the low hut was offensively close and smoke from the fire bit into their eyes. The figures of the spinners, of the hostess and her daughters, were barely visible, and the mournful tale concerning the cruel Emperor Basil, known here as the Bulgar-killer, seemed like an echo from another world.

The low door, wrought from a single slab of wood, gave a hideous squeak as it was jerked sharply open from without. Bending low, Imbram, De La Tour, and D'Armillac entered. They were breathless with excitement.

"What's happened?" the others asked, startled.

"We've seen a werewolf!"

"Holy Virgin! No!"

"We did! We saw him in the flesh! With our own eyes we saw him!"

"When? Where?"

"Only a moment ago. At the edge of the wood. Just behind the camp."

"God's mercy!"

"For a long time now the Canon d'Aguilers has been warning us to be on our guard, for the woods here are full of werewolves. He told us that even though these Bulgars are reputed to have been baptized, they are a loathsome pack of pagans devoted to witchcraft.

"And so we were coming along, talking about what he had said and a trifle uneasy because none of us had any relics. Then we talked a bit about the weather, saying it might be clearing, since the fog was beginning to settle, when we came upon Blanche de Montbeliard, strolling along. We wondered what she had done with her waiting women and said how unbecoming it was for such a high-born lady to be walking off by herself. Then all of a sudden in the underbrush by the road we heard a crash. 'De La Tour, hold your spear ready!' I said. 'Some kind of game is stirring. A wild boar, perhaps.' We all three made ready our spears, glad at the chance for a hunt—when straight from the thicket burst a werewolf!"

"What did he look like? For God's sake, tell us!"

"In the dusk he seemed as big as a cow. He reared on his hind legs, bared his teeth, and poured from his mouth both fire and stench. Then he flung himself on the lady."

"God's wounds! What did she do?"

"She stood stock still for fright. We too became weak with terror. But from somewhere De Beaugency suddenly appeared and flung his spear at the monster and caught him in the left arm."

"So!" Zbylut observed maliciously, "wherever Lady Blanche walks, Beaugency is sure to be found not far away!"

"And praise God this time that he was there," De La Tour remarked with a half smile.

"Well, the beast ran away squealing into the forest. And after that, we made the sign of the Cross upon the ground and ran straight here, we did!"

"We must keep our eyes open now," Glovach observed thoughtfully, "and see whether anyone around here suddenly starts nursing a wounded arm. If anyone does . . ."

"By the bones of St. Ives! You mean—?"

"Beyond all doubt. A very learned abbot named Guido once told me of a certain knight who was attacked by a werewolf. The knight struck off one of the creature's front paws. Shortly afterward his own uncle appeared at his castle with his left hand missing. 'I never expected,' the uncle remarked, 'to be wounded by the son of my own sister.' And his face wore such a queer look that the knight took fright. And, just as his uncle stood there, he walked out of the hall and away on a pilgrimage."

"God have mercy on us! I wish we were well out of this God-forsaken wilderness."

"Do you think, sir, that the land of the Saracen will be one whit better? There for a certainty the country bristles with evil spirits."

"But with Jerusalem near, the demons will have no power."

"Perhaps."

"Besides, according to Canon d'Aguilers, werewolves are worse than any demon and the country here is full of them. No sense delaying, we ought to start at once."

The knights glanced about them with unconcealed terror. They were strong, insolent men and brave, but confronted with witchcraft they became as timid as children. And here was a particularly horrid case. Familiar as the Polish knights were with a vast supernatural world of autumn witches, of ghosts and changelings, of nymphs and goddesses, of midnight phantoms and forest specters, they knew very little of werewolves—aware only, like the rest of Europe, that they were rare and extremely evil. Sitting there crossing themselves feverishly, the knights sighed for the hundredth time, longing for their journey's end. They had been on the way for almost seven months; it was October when they had set out, and now it was Eastertime. For seven long months they had been pushing their way through the wild mountains of Croatia, Serbia, and other Balkan lands, never knowing how far they would have still to go. All the way from Trieste they had skirted the sea, here and there coming upon old Roman ruins of cities and roads, finding within the beautifully arched walls of huge circuses, where once thousands of gaily dressed spectators had sat, squalid little settlements of mountaineers where skinny goats grazed in peace. Looking at these relics, the knights marveled at the greatness of the Roman Empire, which had reached even here. But even the still useful though ruined Roman road had ended when they entered the uninhabited Balkan mountains, so wild they were that it seemed as though no human foot had ever trodden them, so threatening that one might swear that only eagles could surmount them, and so grim that they might have been the very gates of hell.

Blizzards roared continually over the passes and gorges. Treacherous avalanches swept down the slopes, ready to bury them all in white graves; gales lashed their hands and faces; ice-covered ridges slipped under tired feet. What was worse—the mountains soon proved not to be as deserted as they had at first thought. They were inhabited by a tribe of wild, rapacious mountaineers of unknown language, who, lured by the helplessness and obvious wealth of the crusaders, laid ambushes along their trail and attacked them from the rear, spreading confusion and fear among the ranks. Seeing that his men were frightened and had begun to grumble, Raymond, Lord of Toulouse, took personal charge of the rearguard. In the company of D'Armillac, De Foix, De La Tour, and of the Polish knights, he strode on foot at the very tail while Bishop Adhemar led the van of the long, snakelike column. Closer to the van than to the center, liveried servants, swaying with weariness, carried upon numb shoulders the litters of ladies. In one such padded chair, Florine, the fair-headed daughter of the Duke of Burgundy, wept, shivered with fear, and hid her face in the bosom of her duenna. She had thought that she and the handsome Danish prince would ride off together, hand in hand, spur touching spur, across unknown and beautiful lands, and now the prince was not even in sight. He was with the Normans, she had been told, and they would not meet again till they reached Byzantium. And she was so lonely and cold, and so frightened! The grand adventure had become the sheerest woe.

The knights, however, who sat in the smoky hut upon piles of sheep-skin, had by now forgotten the werewolf and were discussing the further stages of their journey.

"Day before yesterday the Bishop said that the worst was over," Gouffier de la Tour informed his friends. "All we have to do now is cross the river Struma. That means we must again build barges, and no telling whether there will be any woods nearby. Still, once across the Struma, the road from the city of Seres to Byzantium is straight as a shot, according to the people who live about."

"Ah! The Bishop!" Glovach shrugged impatiently. "He's been saying that for the last four weeks. 'The worst is over,' he says, and yet we go on and on and the end of our troubles is not yet in sight."

"Never mind, we will get there. I wonder if the others have arrived by now?"

"No doubt the rabble who went with Peter must have perished on the way. That's what the Hungarians said. The dukes of Lorraine could already be in Byzantium, since they left before we did. And that fop who went by sea—what's his name?"

"Hugh, the king's brother."

"Aye, that's the one I mean. Well, if he did not drown, he will be the first to get there. The Normans and Boemund must be wintering in Italy. It will be a long time before we see them."

The low door squeaked again, and their Bulgar host, a gloomy, dark-eyed, bewhiskered man with a flat head, sharp-pointed ears, and a mis-shapen nose, slipped shyly and noiselessly inside. He leaned humbly against the wall and surreptitiously watched the knights.

"What a life! So many months and not a single battle! If the Bishop insists on waiting until the Normans come, we won't go into the field before summer."

"The Saracens will be dead and we gray-haired before we meet each other."

"O, that we should see that day!"

"Christmas! The werewolf!" Moymir Stiborovits suddenly screamed, leaping to his feet. The eyes of his companions followed his, and they grew numb with terror. The left hand of the man who stood so meekly by the wall was wrapped in a bloody rag.

"St. Gilles, our patron, protect us!"

"Do you see, good knights? I told you how he was!"

"Aye, and his left hand—it is bloody!" affirmed De La Tour, trembling from top to toe, as though he had caught a chill.

The glances they exchanged were desperate. Fear had overpowered them, fear which was turning to choking anger. Breathing heavily, they stared at the man, who stood motionless and dumb, as though he comprehended nothing. Across the room a spindle fell to the ground with a clatter. Their hands idle, the women peered uneasily through the haze of smoke.

"But perhaps he is not a werewolf after all," said the Babbler comfortingly. "Anyone might hurt his arm."

"But it's his left arm that is bloody!"

"Right arm, left arm—it could as well be either one. This fellow went to get wood; maybe a log fell on him."

"God grant you were right!"

"Mind you," Mamot sputtered, "the Canon says that the werewolf has certain marks on his body! A hollow under his arm pit! Hair on his belly!"

"Off with your clothes!" the knights shouted at the man.

He did not understand. They pantomimed their command. He did not move.

Sweating with fear, Moymir prodded him with the tip of his sword. With a scream of pain, the man threw off his sheepskin and his linen tunic and stood naked—his yellow, hairy body, with sunken and protruding ribs, exposed to sight.

The eight knights glared at the ugly, emaciated flesh as though they would pierce it with their gaze. But there was nothing—not one mark.

"Turn around!" they commanded, indicating with their arms what they would have him do.

But the man only braced his back more firmly against the wall. And now for the first time he opened his mouth to speak. He stammered something unintelligible, but turn around he would not.

Zbylut, his lips twitching with rage, responded by seizing a blazing log from the hearth and thrusting it between the wall and the nude figure of the man. Scorched, the Bulgar leaped away from the wall and, with an agonized yelp, fell face downward on the floor. And then it was they saw . . . Aye, with their own eyes, the eyes of good Christian knights, they saw . . . The man—he had—a tail!

At the end of his backbone, there projected a short finger-like stub, covered with long sparse hair.

A werewolf!

They stood motionless, petrified with fear. They did not dare to kill him with their swords lest the evil spell should slip along the blade and reach their hands. They were even afraid to move. Nor could they tear their eyes away from the clear sign of the terrible black magic. By the hearth the frightened women wept. The burning log thrown by Zbylut smoldered quietly against the wall.

Then Glovach saw a way to save them all. He seized the glowing log, whirled it over his head so that it would burst into flame, and threw it into the corner, where a pile of firewood lay. He snatched another brand from the hearth, threw it on the pallet, and leaped for the door.

The others understood and crowded after him. At last they were outside. They swung the door shut and propped their spears against it. Now it was barred, barred for good—forever. They crossed themselves and took a deep breath. From inside the hut came desperate screams.

"Even if they put the fire out, they will die all the same," Glovach said. "There is no other way out but the door."

"Well, they are not putting the fire out," Zbylut announced with satisfaction, as from the hut came the crackle of flames. The screams turned into inhuman howls. Smoke poured through the crevices of the walls.

"Everything is in order. W-we c-can leave n-now," the Mumbler said.

"Aye, we burned the fiend. But what about the women? How do we know they were guilty too?" De La Tour began to fret.

"Never mind the women. Since they lived with a werewolf, they must certainly have been witches."

"Thank God we escaped unharmed."

They strode off with light steps, glad that the muscles of their legs functioned as well as ever. They stretched their arms, squared their backs. No, they felt no ill effects. Behind them the fire shot out in a bright tongue of flame from the roof of the hut, brightening the evening dusk. Before the knights appeared their own long black shadows. They watched them with respect and sighed with relief. The shadow was an essential part of any human being. Thank God, that the werewolf had had no time to steal theirs.

The sound of running feet came to their ears. A group of knights and servants was hastening toward the blaze.

"Fire! Fire!" they shouted. "Come along, help put it out!"

"Leave it alone. Never mind it. It was we who burned a werewolf in that hut."

"How is that? A real werewolf?"

"Aye, a true wolf-man. We saw him ourselves."

"The very same one who molested Lady Blanche de Montbeliard this morning," Glovach added.

"What, our niece?" Paul and Stephen de Viel Castel exclaimed simultaneously. The two not only resembled each other, but always said the same thing at the same time.

"Our niece?" they repeated, and raised their eyebrows in surprise. "Why had we not heard before?"

Just then Blanche emerged from the dusk, walking with her usual quick step, with which the two waiting maids who accompanied her could barely keep pace. And now, much to everyone's surprise, Lady Blanche denied De La Tour's assertion.

"That was no werewolf. It was a dog," she said laughing. "A big dog that belonged to Lord Roger de Foix. Because of the mist, the Sire de Beaugency took it for a werewolf and he wounded it. Lord Roger is terribly angry about it."

"You are mistaken, my lady," De La Tour corrected her gently but firmly. "It was a werewolf. The good knight De Beaugency has saved you from a horrible fate. We recognized the werewolf later. He had a Devil's mark. A tail. We burned him in that hut that is blazing away now."

"Then it must have been another one."

"No, indeed—it was the very same one. His left arm was wounded by Raoul's spear."

"All I know is that the beast who jumped at me was a dog," Blanche insisted with a scornful shrug.

The argument was broken by the pealing of a distant bell. Ah! the blessed sound! All fell silent and listened with a deep sense of relief. It was thin and feeble like an infant's wail, yet how soothing, how safe. They suddenly recalled that it was Sunday; the Bishop was calling them to vespers.

"Because it is Sunday, the Lord helped us to overcome the fiend," Glovach said thoughtfully.

15.

Two Worlds Meet

THE SURMISES OF RAYMOND'S KNIGHTS PROVED CORRECT. GODFREY OF
Bouillon was the first to reach Byzantium. Unlike the hot-headed
Count of Toulouse, he had wisely selected the best land route in existence, the way which Syrian merchants were accustomed to use when
they proceeded westward to their trading posts in Kiev, Breslau, Or-
leans, and Lyons. This route, which did not deviate much from the one
chosen by Peter the Hermit, led them through Sofia, Philippopolis, and
Adrianople.

All through the long march Godfrey's troops kept perfect order. They
bought food on the way and paid its full value with their good coin of
Lorraine. This procedure, though just, was extremely costly and had
swallowed almost all of Godfrey's ready cash. The price he had received
for the duchies of Lorraine and Boulogne and for the city of Metz had
proved barely sufficient to get his army to Byzantium. In Godfrey's
coffer, which had once been so heavy that it took four horses to draw it,
the bottom was beginning to show. He had still enough to last them
another two weeks. And after that . . . what? With deep grief he
realized now that, exorbitant as the charges of the Genoese were, it
would have cost only half of what he had already spent, to transport
the troops by sea.

Along their way, talking with the local people, Godfrey and his men
gleaned more news about the throngs of Peter the Hermit, who had
passed that way the summer before. The news was vague, and often
contradictory. Nevertheless all reports agreed as to the dreadful conditions that had prevailed among the crusaders: nothing but hunger,
robbery, and bloody strifes.

"God has punished them for starting by themselves, without the

Bishop's permission," Godfrey said. "And yet, may God have mercy on them! No telling whether the same fate will not befall us in a few weeks when our money and our food gives out."

"It is your part to see that that does not happen," answered Baldwin with his usual unconcern.

"We are indeed in trouble," Godfrey complained. "How can we tell in what manner Alexius will receive us?"

Baldwin shrugged his shoulders, repeating that it was his brother's problem. Was not his brother the head of the expedition? Baldwin himself took nothing to heart; he was convinced that a true Knight had only to trust his sword to give him power in any strange land.

"What do you think, brother Godfrey? How far can it be from Byzantium to the infidels? Two days' journey? Three?"

"God grant it be near," Godfrey sighed.

A few days before Christmas, they halted, they had almost reached Byzantium. At that moment Raymond St. Gilles was still far away in Spalato, Robert of Normandy and Robert of Flanders were wintering in Rome; Tancred and Boemund had not yet left Amalfi. The hearts of the knights of Lorraine swelled with pride at the thought that they had arrived first. Exultantly they ascended a hill from the crest of which they hoped to see the city.

And indeed Byzantium lay in full view, almost at their feet. The knights gasped and stood motionless—transfixed with wonder. They had heard many a tale of the beauty and greatness of Byzantium, but none was prepared for what he saw now, though at that distance it was impossible to distinguish many details. All were struck at once by the height and length of the walls, by the enormous size of the city, larger than all the cities of France put together. The City Protected by God! Aye, indeed, and God likewise must have chosen its site! No capital in the world had a more commanding position. With the Sea of Marmora protecting it from one side, St. George's Arm from the other, the Golden Horn from the third, and the Black Sea behind, it had every reason to consider itself impregnable. The mighty western wall, which faced the crusaders, was double and covered at the top with copper plate. In the red rays of the setting sun the copper blazed like a streak of fire, like a magic band guarding the approach to the city. Behind the walls, buildings gleamed white, the gilded roofs of the countless temples and palaces

glittered and sparkled. The enormous cupola of the great church, Hagia
Sofia, blazed like another sun. The whole city seemed to bask in a
golden glow, which enveloped the entire peninsula between the two
dark arms of the sea.

Awed by the greatness of the sight, the knights descended in silence
from the hillock and proceeded on their way along a magnificently kept
highway, the like of which they had never before seen. All along this
thoroughfare, at regular intervals of about an hour's march, stood the
outposts of the Basileus' army. Each post consisted of clay living quarters
attached to a fairly high rectangular flat-roofed tower. These towers
were all alike, and the Latins had encountered them, standing thus at
regular intervals, ever since they had begun to descend from the mountain.

Every night at dusk the *warangs,* as the Basileus' troops were called,
climbed to the tops of these towers and lighted bonfires of hemlock and
dry branches. Then they covered the flame with screens of tin, some
plain, others with openings of various shapes and designs. Thus the man
on watch at the next tower would see the light appear in certain shapes
and at certain intervals. These shapes and intervals he immediately relayed to the next post.

As they proceeded along the highway, the knights had often watched
these strange proceedings, the meanings of which baffled them completely. They never suspected that, thanks to these light signals, the
Basileus had known for a long time of their coming and was even informed of their numbers.

It was also due to these signals that no sooner had Godfrey stopped to
pitch camp within a mile of the city, than Alexius sent his envoys to call
on him. They came in great pomp, sumptuously attired, escorted by a
large retinue and bearing gifts and greetings. They assured Duke Godfrey, in perfect Latin, that the Most High, Very Enlightened, and Perfectly Pious Basileus, Equal-to-the-Apostles, Autocrator, wished to welcome his new guest as soon as possible, and that the noble guest would
be received like a son.

With the Greek envoys came Hugh de Vermandois, the brother of the
French King Philip, who, having wisely chosen to travel by sea, had
arrived at Byzantium without any difficulty several months ahead of
them. The knights did not recognize him at first, for he was dressed in

the Greek fashion—in bright, sumptuous clothes, with gilded sandals on his feet, bracelets on his wrists, and rings loading his fingers.

"Look what Basileus Alexius gave me," he boasted, displaying the rich gems. "And I have many more in my quarters. Out here it seems you have only to praise a thing and it's given to you at once. And well they may! They have so much, that even if they gave half their treasures away they would still have more than all the rest of the world ever possessed. The Basileus once showed me his treasury. By St. Denis, it fairly turned my stomach to see so much wealth. I became nauseous just from looking at it. And not all the wealth is in his treasury. Every palace, every church here, holds more treasures than the whole of Paris.

"Well, you shall see for yourselves. But, pray, look at these things. They should give you some notion of what I mean."

The eyes of his listeners turned to where, in front of Godfrey, who was seated on a low camp stool, the Greek envoys were depositing their gifts. Here, indeed, was something to see. Carelessly tossed on the ground lay shimmering folds of golden brocade, beautiful and miraculously light gilded shields set with corals, swords, spears, artfully wrought breastplates, crystal goblets, ivory boxes filled with costly perfumes. At one side the servants had set tall amphoras of wine, and baskets filled with fruit cake and sweetmeats.

Godfrey thanked the envoys graciously while his eyes scanned the riches laid before him with complete indifference. The arms would be useful, he thought, and so would the wine and food, but what earthly good were this flimsy glassware or the fine clothes to a soldier? Such things were for fops like Hugh. Nevertheless, he thanked them courteously and promised to call on the Basileus on the morrow. Bowing low, the envoys prepared to leave.

Baldwin moved quickly to his brother's side. "What are you going to give them?" he inquired.

"I? I have nothing to give. Armor or sword I cannot give away."

"They will think that we are beggars."

"They may think whatever they please. Besides, what would you give? We have nothing worth offering."

"Well, Gontrane still has a pair of pearl earrings and a bracelet to match," Baldwin said with hesitation.

Godfrey scowled. "That would show our poverty even more plainly than if we sent no gift at all," he said. "What are our bracelets and earrings compared to these things here? Nothing at all. Besides," he added with a smile, "I doubt whether Gontrane would consent."

Baldwin unconsciously rubbed his neck with his palm, but he did not give in.

"If you asked her she would give them willingly enough," he insisted.

"But I shall not ask her, since I am against it myself."

"Baldwin is right," Hugh broke in; "you ought to send gifts. But Godfrey is right too; the earrings and bracelets will not do. They have such trinkets by the barrelful. They will throw them into their coffers without as much as a glance. I'll tell you what you can do: send them a few pretty wenches—that is what they like at the court of the Basileus. They have slaves from all over the world, but none from our land. They ought to be pleased."

"Sir, you must be out of your mind!" Godfrey hissed.

"I see that you brought quite a number, and some of them quite beautiful," Hugo continued unperturbed, pointing to Gontrane's maids-in-waiting, who from a distance were greedily eying the gifts brought by the Greeks. "Look at that black-eyed one, the one to the left. Not bad, not bad at all."

Baldwin blushed. "Gontrane will never part with that one," he replied quickly. "She is quite a favorite of hers."

"Then send the others."

But Godfrey angrily struck his knee with his open palm. "These maidens are daughters of freemen—not slaves," he shouted.

"Two of them are bondswomen," Baldwin retorted. "And of these one is very comely, and still a virgin, I am told."

"Enough! Bondswomen or not, I will not hand them over to Greek lust. I will hear no more of the matter."

There was so much sternness in Godfrey's usually gentle voice that both Baldwin and Hugh preferred to keep their peace. The envoys departed, escorted to the confines of the camp by four Latin knights. Hugh stayed behind.

"Now tell us," Godfrey turned to Hugh, "what manner of man is this Alexius? Will he help us or not?"

"Oh! he will give us anything we want!" Hugh assured him, swaying nonchalantly on the balls of his feet. "Why don't you, my Lord, order the goblets filled with the wine they brought? Very good wine it is. Yes, anything we wish. I got to know Alexius quite well. I can see right through him. Not a bad man at all—simple-minded, without an ounce of cunning. I can wrap him around my little finger. By and large, this famed Greek cunning . . . there is nothing to it. We are far keener than they are. That is why they listen with great respect to all that I or my knights have to say and never contradict anything. Not a bad people really, though dreadful milksops. You know, they have no tournaments here—don't even know what they are. Instead, they have a passion for racing. You know: either horse races or chariot races."

"Indeed," Godfrey interrupted impatiently. "But tell me, my lord, will the Basileus provide for our men?"

"I have already told you that he will give you whatever you may need or desire. Two weeks ago, as soon as the news of your coming arrived, Alexius said that he would give you supplies, take you across to Asia, and even send an army with you under Butumitos—this Butumitos is one of his captains. Meanwhile galleys with that accursed liquid fire of theirs will sail along the coast to give us support later on. Of course you have not heard, but they say here that the Holy Land is still a long way from Byzantium."

"But that's impossible!"

"I know, but they say that to come here from Italy or France is but a stroll compared to what still lies ahead of us."

"They speak so because they were never in France."

"Strategos Argyros was."

"And what about their troops? Any good?"

"Very good indeed. Beautifully dressed. Why, back home, dukes don't have such clothes. But they are good in battle too. Especially the regiments which they call *Athanatos,* or 'The Immortals.' Mercenaries, one and all. Every nation you can think of. Armenians, Arabs, Waregs, Russians, Scandinavians. The Greeks pay well. A brother of Boemund is Captain of the Imperial guard."

"Boemund's brother?"

"Well, his half-brother. Boemund was born of Alberta, and this one—Guy is his name—of Sykelgaita. A pleasant fellow. I am quite fond of him."

But Godfrey was struck by something else in what Hugh told him. "You said, my Lord, that Alexius knew two weeks ago that we were coming?"

"Aye, and he ordered his Chief Steward, the Parakimomenos, to tell me of it."

"But how did he know? I did not inform anyone."

"I have no idea how he knew," replied Hugh, with complete indifference. "But he knew. I was so glad of your coming that every day I asked the Parakimomenos how you were getting along. 'Yesterday they stopped in such-and-such a place,' he told me. 'Today they have covered almost six miles and halted at such-and-such a village.' And so it went every day."

"What could it be? Magic?"

"Magic, no doubt. They are a strange breed, but they certainly know how to live in comfort. What food! I've never tasted anything like it in my life. And would you believe, my Lords, that here everybody can read? Everybody, even women. They are forever reading and writing. It's a sort of madness with them. The other day Kuropastos asked me what I liked best to read. 'I like best to play with my sword,' I told him. 'Books are good for monks and scholars, not for knights. I can read as well as anyone else, and once I even spelled out the entire Psalter, but ever since I learned the Psalms by heart I have no need of reading. I never touch a book.' I told him that, and he said nothing. Probably he was ashamed of himself. They are a curious people. But they know how to live. You will see for yourself. Time never drags. It would not be a bad thing if we stayed here a couple of years."

"God forbid!" Godfrey protested with feeling. "Raymond St. Gilles and the Bishop will no doubt be here any day now, and so will the Normans. We must start as soon as they come. We did not come here just to look at Byzantium. We have lost more than a year already."

"You would not have lost so much if you had come by sea. I was here in September. Alexius welcomed me like a father, so I took the oath right away."

"What oath?" asked Godfrey, startled.

"The oath of allegiance to the Basileus. The same oath that you will take. So, as I was saying, I took it right away, and by October Guy and I were already hunting the deer. They have wonderful dogs here and . . ."

"Tell me what kind of oath it was," broke in Godfrey sternly.

"Just an oath of fealty and a vow that whatever we conquer shall be his. To go back to the dogs—once they catch the scent . . ."

"Pray, sir, forget the dogs. The other matter is more important. So Alexius demanded an oath of you?"

"Certainly he did. As soon as I arrived. Just as he will demand it of you tomorrow."

"I am not going to take it."

"Why not? You don't intend to betray him? You don't want to make war on him, do you?"

"No, I neither intend to betray him, nor have I any design upon his land. Yet I would rather die than take an oath."

"Why not?"

"Because I am a free soldier of Christ."

"The Basileus is not a pagan either. He is a Christian ruler, even though a schismatic."

"No matter what he is. I shall not take the oath. I did not renounce my patrimony in order to become anyone's vassal."

"Do as you please," Hugh shrugged, yawning. "Only in that case, better send someone to the palace at once and call off tomorrow's meeting. Otherwise they will be expecting you to take the oath."

"But the Greek envoys never mentioned a word of the matter to me."

"They did not mention it because, to tell the truth, I was supposed to tell you about it, only it completely slipped my mind."

"Good God! That anyone should forget such an important thing!" the exasperated Godfrey almost shouted.

But the handsome Hugh lost none of his usual nonchalance. "Send your men to the Basileus at once, or explain to him yourself," he said, pouting.

Godfrey leaped from his bench.

"Montaigue!" he called. "D'Esch! Du Bourg! Come here! Quick!"

The three knights thus summoned left the Greek arms, which they were inspecting at the farther end of the tent, and hastily approached.

"You will go to Byzantium at once," Godfrey told them. His usual calm had vanished, his eyes shone feverishly. "You will go as my envoys."

"I will go with you," Hugh offered. "Then you will be sure to be received at once."

"You go as my envoys," repeated Godfrey emphatically. "Tell the Basileus that I cannot take the oath and that I ask to be released from taking it. I mean no treason, nor do I covet anything that by right is his.

But, being a crusader, I have sworn allegiance to Christ and cannot now swear it to anyone else. God alone is my master. My ancestors have always been free and independent rulers. Nor was I ever any man's vassal. I am God's servant, not Caesar's. Nevertheless, he need not fear deceit from me. I am his friend, as true as sworn. Tell him that. Montaigue! I count on you; you will express it better than I do."

Konon de Montaigue, a tall man with a proud aquiline profile, nodded his head in understanding and approval.

"Leave at once," Godfrey insisted.

Hugh struck his forehead. "I have an idea. Why should you wait here and eat your heart out, fretting? Come with us to Byzantium. You can wait in the palace which has been assigned to me." (Hugh proudly stressed these words.) "In that way you will hear the answer sooner, and you and I can talk it over and decide what is to be done next."

"Thank you, I think I will," Godfrey replied after brief consideration. "Baldwin, you will remain in charge here, since I may not be back before tomorrow."

Baldwin made a wry face. He would rather have gone too. He was burning with curiosity to see the famous Byzantium, now so near at hand. To see with his own eyes the treasures of which Hugh had spoken, to talk with Boemund's brother, Guy. Because—who could tell? Perhaps . . . Baldwin had not forgotten his dream of an independent principality.

"How do you manage to provide for your men?" Hugh asked an hour later as he and Godfrey rode side by side toward the city gates. "It is wonderful what good order you keep in your camp."

"It will not last long if the Basileus refuses to provide us with food. I am down to my last thalers. A few more days, and the soldiers will begin to loot."

"He will give you food, never fear. And plenty of it. Even the good knight De Melun admits—and what an eater that man is!—that he has never eaten so much and so well in his life. Nor do they stint wine either. But, despite that, my soldiers are forever looting. Just for sport. I cannot stop them. They pay no heed to me."

Godfrey kept his peace, but Hugh, undaunted by his silence, prattled on: "What a country! One could learn many things from these Greeks. What palaces! What comforts! I never suspected such things could exist. And their women! If only we had such women back home! Comely, perfumed, and so skilled in love. They know artifices of which none of our women have ever heard. I can tell you, for instance . . ."

"I have vowed chastity," Godfrey interrupted him coldly.

"Egad! So you have, even like a monk. What a pity! Still, I trust that your brother at least will profit by my experience."

"My brother is married," retorted Godfrey, even more coldly.

"That's true. He has even brought his wife along. I mean no offense to your sister-in-law, but pray, my Lord, tell me what for? I left mine at home."

"Think you, my Lord, that distance dissolves vows?"

Oh! What a bore that paragon of virtue was! Hugh looked at him in disgust. A veritable monk! Why didn't the fellow shut himself up in a monastery? Baldwin fortunately was nothing like him.

The hoofs of their horses rang out under the great vaulted gate of the City Protected by God. *Warangs* standing guard recognized Hugh and lowered their halberds in salute.

16.

The City Protected by God

ONCE INSIDE THE CITY EVEN THE AUSTERE GODFREY FORGOT HIS TROUBLES, so absorbing were the sights that were unfolded before his eyes. Hugh, who by now was quite familiar with the city and who was delighted to act as guide and play host to his countryman, purposely led them by the most roundabout way, which practically circled the city. Before he plunged into the maze of streets, he pointed out in the distance, on the opposite shore of St. George's Arm, the city of Christopolis, and told them that there was their first sight of Asia. Hearing his words, the knights promptly crossed themselves; to them the word "Asia" was synonymous with "Holy Land."

Hugh smiled. "It's the same country as here. No difference at all. All the patricians have their summer homes there, since it's a little higher and therefore cooler than the city itself."

Then he turned and pointed in the opposite direction, toward the Golden Horn, and to the Genoese settlement of Galata, with its tall watch towers standing high on a hill.

"So there are Genoese here too?" Montaigue marveled.

"That plague? You'll find them everywhere. They have their own ships and warehouses here. It was because of them that my pirates—a dirty and evil-smelling lot but good fellows, all of them—could not remain in Byzantium. The Genoese hate them like poison and even though the Basileus gives them his protection, they would certainly have burned their ships. So the pirate's leader, Guynemere—he and I drank many a cup together—said: 'Good Christian that I am I shall not make trouble.' And he sailed away with his men along the Asiatic coast. He is awaiting us there. Look at that bridge! Did you ever see anything like it?"

But even more than by the great bridge that connected Byzantium with Galata, the knights were impressed by the enormous chain, famed the world over, which, in case of an enemy approach closed the entrance to the Golden Horn. At present no danger threatened, so the heavy chain, thick and slippery as a dragon, hung loose from iron pulleys that took fifty men to move, and dipped beneath the water. On the eternally calm waters of the canal, row upon row of the Basileus' galleys, the famed tridecked ships called *pyroforos,* or *igniferos,* because they threw the Greek Fire, stood at anchor, brilliantly painted and gilded, with tall prows carved in the likeness of eagles, dragons, angels, and griffins. From the midst of gilded and carved ornaments protruded funnels that seemed ready at any moment to spit an unquenchable jet of flame.

Of these vessels there were about three hundred. Around them swayed countless small pursuit galleys called *moneria,* with but one tier of oars. The rest of the surface of the water was covered with barges and small craft; light *monoxyles,* carved out of one tree trunk, Russo-Wareg *chaykas* supported by reed floats, and the heavy vessels of merchants who had come from every part of the known world: Asia, Greece, India, Bagdad, Cyprus, Rhodes, Egypt, Genoa, Kiev, and Novograd. The goods unloaded from these barges could be seen daily at the famous Byzantian market near the monastery of St. Mamasius, where, under the watchful eye of the tax collectors, they were sold. A colorful multilingual, noisy mob closely filled the square. The silken chlamyses of Greeks rubbed against the sheepskins of Finns, beautiful amphoras from Rhodes stood next to a pile of bearskins and wolfskins. In the middle of the square a scaffold was erected upon which the executioner burned out the eyes of those who were suspected of being dissatisfied with the blessed rule of the Most Enlightened, Most Pious, Equal-to-the-Apostles, Autocrator, the Basileus. In Byzantium, blinding was the favorite and most common form of punishment. A death sentence might endanger a man's soul, since he died in a state of sin, while blinding rendered him harmless, yet left him enough time to repent. Executions were carried out daily, as the *nyctoparkos,* or prefect of the city (literally "Night Guardian"), was never idle. His spies roamed everywhere, their ears pricked for the sound of a careless word, or even the shadow of a word. After all, the Nyctoparkos must prove that the mood of the city was still hostile to the reigning dynasty and that, save for his own vigilance, the Commenus might well lose the throne. So even now a group of men bound with ropes stood by the scaffold looking about for the last time in their lives. Never again would they see the light of day, the golden-hued city, the green waters of the sea, and the familiar motley crowds. One by one they were grabbed by the executioner's helpers and hoisted on to the scaffold. It took but a second. The executioner snatched a red hot brand from a pot of glowing coals. A piercing scream, a momentary struggle and already the victim was pushed off the platform and the next one took his place. The blinded man, still screaming, with two bloody wounds where his eyes had been, fell in a heap. He rose, tripped, tried to run and fell again. Watching his clumsy progress, men laughed and clapped their hands. As he frantically groped his way, they pushed unexpected obstacles in his path, until at last, evidently attracted by the noise, a monk emerged from the crowd, took the wretch by the hand and mercifully led him away.

"A cruel people," Godfrey said, averting his eyes in disgust.

"You are right," Hugh assented. "Back home we do not torture people in this way. Either they are flogged to death, or burned alive, or else off with their heads and that is the end of it."

"I wish it were so! Don't they bury them alive? Don't they dismember them?"

"But not for trifling offenses as they do here. Look over there, my Lord, see that church and castle, almost outside the walls? That's the Blakernos, the summer residence of the Basileus. It's in this church behind golden bars that they keep the miraculous image of the Most Holy Virgin, Panagia Blakernitissa, the most beloved patroness of the city."

They had left behind the noise of the market place and were now proceeding along evenly paved streets, swarming with traffic. Richly dressed patricians rode past, mounted upon Arabian horses, incredibly beautiful, though much smaller than the heavy chargers of the Latin knights. Here, powerfully built slaves, called *manglabitos,* ran with rhythmic steps, carrying the litter of some exquisite lady, perhaps the wife of a court dignitary. The chair, set with ivory and pearl, glistened like a gem. There, seated in a less ornate litter, a learned professor of the College of Philosophy or Geography was gliding by. Other ladies, no less fine than the first one, but evidently finding a litter too close for comfort, rode in silver-plated and enameled chariots, their faces veiled with thin gauze. Look out! A golden youth, outpacing everyone else, came darting by in a light two-wheeled chariot. He drove standing bolt upright. His cloak fluttered at the shoulders as the spirited horses rushed on, pulling at the golden reins. Then suddenly all street noises vanished, drowned by the rhythmic beat of marching feet. A detachment of soldiers was on the way to change guards around the Holy Palace. First came the *protospatarii* with spears and oblong shields that covered them from head to foot. Next, the *warangs* brandishing broadheaded halberds. Then the *Athanatos,* the "Immortals," whose gilded coats-of-mail shone and sparkled. They were chosen from among the most beautiful men, and, indeed, looked like Greek gods. Last came the *Archontopuls,* young boys destined to military service from childhood, and raised at the expense of the Basileus in the military school of Logothesion.

All around the troops, sedan chairs, and chariots surged a crowd of pedestrians similar to that of the market place, motley, multilingual, multicolored and sprinkled as with poppy seed by the black frocks of the orthodox monks.

Hugh was continually pointing out new sights. "Here is the Church of the Holy Apostles, where the Basileis are buried. Few of them die of old age or even in bed, but they all get a splendid burial. And this fair castle here is the Bukoleon, where the Basileus comes to live whenever he gets tired of the Holy Palace. Those mighty buildings over there are government offices. Nowhere in the world will you find as many magistrates as they have here. And, pray, tell me what for? They well might learn from us. The baronial court and a constable—what need is there for more? Here, everyone is forever running from magistrate to magistrate and scribbling on little cards. Would you believe that all the goods you saw in the market place are weighed and recorded? Aye, and the merchants must pay a stiff tax on every bolt or measure. Along the highways no one collects tolls. You can travel up and down the entire land and you won't meet a toll gate. But once they arrive here, the Basileus skins them properly. But watch now, my Lords, we are entering the Square of Augusteon, or the Agora, as they call it, which is supposed to be the fairest place in the world."

Indeed, nothing on earth could compare in splendor to the magnificent square framed on one side by the golden mosaics that covered the entrance to Hagia Sofia, on the other by the Senate, and on the third by the Holy Palace, which like the Hagia Sofia, had been built by Justinian. The fourth side was closed by a portico and columnade, each column supporting a gilded or silver figure—the statues of the Basileis and their wives. In the middle of the square rose the porphyry column of

Constantin the Great, bearing a golden cross and the inscription "Holy!
Holy! Holy!" It was on the wide steps of its pedestal that the Basileis
sat in their days of triumph, to watch the procession of throngs of
prisoners and hostages. It was here that the Autocrator without stirring
from his seat pressed his foot, shod in a golden sandal, upon the head
of the defeated chieftain who lay in dust at his feet, while horns blared
and the countless throngs that filled the square cheered and called:
"Long live the great Basileus, the most pious, unconquerable ruler. Long
live the Basileus, whom God has chosen and appointed. Long live the Basileus whom the Lord leads and always shall lead! Long live the Basileus
upon whose arm rests the fate of the world. Long live the Basileus who
humbles and destroys the enemies of the church and his own."

Godfrey listened to Hugh with growing weariness. His eyes were
fixed on the carved door of the great temple in which he longed to be,
alone with his thoughts.

"By all means, do," agreed the always amiable Hugh when he heard
this wish. "Go to the temple. By St. Denis, the place is worth seeing.
Meantime, I shall take the knights and turn them over to the *protop-
zoedzos,* and then I will return for you. From here we can go straight
to my palace."

Leaving his horse with his squire, Godfrey pushed the wicket cut in
the enormous golden door, crossed one vestibule full of beggars, then
another full of priests and monks, raised a heavy rustling curtain which
hid the interior, and stood still.

He found himself enveloped in a strange golden dusk into which
from somewhere, infinitely high above, seeped a pale blue light. The
temple was immense, vast enough to hold tens of thousands of people
and, thanks to the skillful planning of the walls, the depth and size of
vaults, and the harmony of its proportions, appeared a hundred-fold
more vast. The exquisitely high and lofty cupola which covered the
building seemed to embrace the whole world. The walls covered with
golden mosaics swarmed with saints and angels, and had the unearthly
beauty of something out of a dream that might vanish at the slightest
touch. On both sides of the nave stood columns brought from the temple
of Diana in Ephesus that had been burned down by Herostrates, and
from the mysterious, far-away Baalbek, of which none of the western
knights had heard. Six hundred golden candelabra hung on golden
chains from the high vault, and the silence and the sense of remoteness

from the world, was more profoundly moving than anything Godfrey had ever before experienced. This church, consecrated to the Divine Wisdom, seemed as perfect and as impossible to encompass as Wisdom itself.

Crushed by the awareness of his own smallness, he fell to his knees before one of the altars that shone and sparkled with precious stones, and tried to pray. He tried to call to mind the familiar faces of the Infant Jesus and the Mater Dolorosa, sweet, human, understanding faces, but no sooner were they called than they would vanish as if frightened by all this enormity and change once more into stiff, unfeeling figures that peered at him from the golden glory of the walls.

Steps, subdued and lost in the silence, sounded behind him. Not in the least awed by the surroundings, Hugh tapped him on the shoulder.

"They will be given an audience before nightfall," he announced. "That's a great favor, mind you. Oftentimes, even more distinguished envoys are made to wait several days. A beautiful church, eh? Even in Paris we have nothing like it. The Greeks look upon it as *asylum inviolatum*. Whoever hides in here is safe from pursuit: so that anyone with a guilty conscience hastens to it in the hope that he will not be molested. The Basileus observes this custom in minor cases, but not in major ones. I was told that when once a queen who had had her husband killed because he was old and she young hid here afterwards, the *parakimonenos* with his own hands tore her away from yonder column and dragged her out of doors. True, the man was a eunuch so her beauty could not move him to pity."

"Leave me here yet awhile, my Lord, I have not finished my prayers," Godfrey said softly.

In spite of what Baldwin had told Hugh, the black-eyed maiden who had attracted the latter's attention was not a favorite of her mistress. On the contrary, Gontrane considered her lazy and pert. But pretty she was, indeed, with her smooth, swarthy skin, black eyes, and black hair. Her name was Leone.

As she ran now toward the tent of her mistress, Baldwin, peevish and bored by the prolonged absence of Godfrey, stopped her, "The hem of my mantle is torn," he said. "Come over and sew it up."

Belying Gontrane's complaint that she was lazy, Leone darted like a deer to her tent to fetch thread and needle. Nor was there in her bearing, as she approached Baldwin, any trace of pertness, only willingness and devotion.

"Where is it torn?" she asked.

"Right here," said Baldwin throwing the skirts of his mantle wide open. When she drew nearer, he enveloped her with the folds and with both hands pressed her to himself.

"Let me go, my Lord," she whispered, not much frightened. "Lady Gontrane might see."

"No one will see. Lady Gontrane has retired to say her prayers."

"Old Helgund might see and report."

"That old hag? If she does I'll have her flogged to death."

Not releasing her from under his mantle, he dragged the half-frightened, half-coy girl in the direction of his pavilion.

"The brother of the French king wanted me to send you as a gift to the Greek emperor," he told her, patting her cheek.

"Mercy!" she stood still, this time genuinely frightened.

"Have no fear! I told him that Lady Gontrane would never part with you, that you were her favorite."

They both laughed.

"But what will happen now? Will you send somebody else?" she said anxiously.

"No, Duke Godfrey will not have it."

"He is a good master."

"Do you perhaps prefer him to me?" he teased, lifting the flaps of the tent. At once he stood still. Facing him, Gontrane, his lawful spouse, sat on a low stool.

Nimble as a weasel, Leone, moving backwards, slipped from under his mantle, threw her apron over her head and fled before Gontrane had time to recognize her.

Baldwin remained motionless, shamefaced and uncertain what next to do and say. Gontrane pursed her narrow lips, her eyes furious. "Will you kindly tell me, my Lord, with which of my wenches have I the honor of sharing my husband?" she drawled.

"You always think God knows what," Baldwin protested indignantly. "I called her to sew up my mantle. I've torn the fringe."

"Who was it?"

"None of your own damsels."

"I see, you called someone else's maid-in-waiting to sew up your mantle," she jeered.

"She happened by . . ."

Gontrane cast him a look full of contemptuous hatred.

"Will you answer me or not? Who was it?" she insisted in a tone of command. "Not by any chance Leone? I suspect it was she."

"I told you it was none of yours."

"You lie," she shouted. "Speak up. No strange wench ever comes here. I want to know. Which of my own maids lies in the Duke's bed in my place? Come, now. Say it!"

He was silent. At once her assumed calm vanished. She drew close to him with the stealthy steps of a wild beast and grabbed him by the shoulders. He could feel her tiny sharp nails digging into his flesh.

"What is it to you?" he muttered, giving up further attempts to defend himself.

"I will have her flogged to death," she hissed. "Right here, before your eyes! And if you refuse to tell, I'll have them all flogged, one after another! Accursed perjurer! You have a wife of noble blood, but must drag a wench to your tent! Know you no shame? I could spit in your face, you filthy beast! Speak up! Who was it?"

"I told you none of yours."

"You lie. A knight that lies! A fine knight indeed! It was Leone, I'm sure! Leone! I will have her flogged first. Helgund! Helgund!"

Helgund must have been eavesdropping for she appeared in the tent almost at once, small, skinny, with hands piously folded across her middle.

"Call a man with whips. A stout one. And have all the wenches come here at once," Gontrane ordered.

"You will call no man with whips!" Baldwin roared, enraged. "And get out of here, you old witch."

"Do as I tell you," Gontrane shouted. "Call a man this very instant."

"Get out of here, or else . . ." repeated Baldwin with such passion that the mistress of the robes thought better of it and quickly withdrew, throwing her mistress a doleful glance before she vanished from the tent.

"Why don't you kill me outright instead of bringing such disgrace upon me?" Gontrane continued to scream. "Here! take this knife! Stab

me! Stab, I tell you! Then you'll be free to lie with any trollop you
please!"

"Come to your senses, woman! Stop shouting," he pleaded. "Why
should the whole camp know what is going on between you and me?"

"Let them hear! Let the whole camp know how their Duke carries
on. Duke! Forsooth!"

"Be quiet, Gontrane. It's you who are the one to blame. No, don't
shout. It's you, I say, you alone. You have been driving me out of your
bed like a dog. It's more than a year since I slept with you. What am I to
do, woman? What can I do? I am not fit to live like a monk as Godfrey
does. You should have married him. You would have made a well-
matched couple, you two."

She staggered as though he had struck her. For a moment her face
froze, then once more she burst out shrilly: "So it's women you lust for
while going to the Holy War, you lecher! When every good crusader
has vowed chastity. . . . You goat! You dirty heathen!"

"Keep quiet, damn you," whispered Baldwin hoarsely, overcome with
rage. He felt an almost irresistible impulse to grab his wife by the throat
and wring her neck.

"Shut up, for Christ's sake or I won't answer for myself."

"I will not shut up. I will shout, I will scream until everyone hears
me!"

The clatter of horse hoofs rang out. Throwing the flaps of the tent
open with a quick motion Godfrey came in.

"A swineherd would be truer to his word," Gontrane was shouting at
the top of her voice. She did not even notice Godfrey's arrival. "The
word of Baldwin of Lorraine is nothing but filth! Worse than filth!
Ha! Ha! Ha!"

"That will do, Gontrane," Godfrey's voice was stern but calm. "We
have more important problems on our hands than to listen to your
unbecoming shouts. Pray, be quiet!"

He did not need to repeat it twice. At the sound of his voice Gontrane
fell silent at once. She let go of Baldwin's jerkin, grew suddenly meek
and tears appeared in her eyes. She withdrew quietly to the far end of
the tent and sat there, hunched on a rolled carpet while her eyes never
left Godfrey's face. Baldwin wiped the sweat from his forehead.

"Thanks," he said to his brother. "I thought I would kill her. If you
would only speak to her more often my life might be different."

Godfrey, however, paid no attention, as if he had not heard. Nervously tugging at his fair beard, he said, "Things look bad, Baldwin. We must talk them over at once and decide what is to be done. Come to my tent. No one will disturb us there."

And without a glance at the huddled figure in the far corner, he left the tent with Baldwin at his heels. As soon as they disappeared, Gontrane sprang up and ran to the entrance, parted the curtains and watched the retreating figures, standing there thus for a long, long time.

"What is wrong?" asked Baldwin when they were seated in Godfrey's pavilion with Montaigue, D'Esch and Du Bourg. "Is it about this oath?"

"Yes, about the oath," Godfrey nodded somberly. "I want you to hear what Montaigue has to tell."

"So you did see the Basileus?" Baldwin said with quick curiosity, turning toward the knight.

"Yes, my Lord, we saw him, and the wonders the French king's brother told us about still don't do him justice."

"You don't say! Were you admitted soon?"

"Quite soon. First we were made to wait in the blue and golden hall which they call . . . How do they call it, Du Bourg?"

"Never mind the details. You can tell them later," interrupted Godfrey impatiently. "Now let us hear only what is most important, what Alexius had to say."

"Well, we were told that we must prostrate ourselves before him even as a serf does before his master," began Montaigue slowly, carefully, so as not to omit anything. "But it did not look right to us so we told them that there is no such custom with us. So we only bowed and kissed his hand. Almighty Sovereign he looked. What grandeur! The throne—"

"You can tell us later about the throne, Montaigue," Godfrey reminded him. "Now tell us what you told the Basileus."

"So we did not prostrate ourselves. He scowled but not very hard. And soon he asked: 'When will the Duke of Lorraine come?' 'Great Emperor,' we told him, 'our lord and master, the good knight Godfrey, Duke of Lorraine and Bouillon, Lord of Metz, Toul, and Verdun, will come to pay you due respects, only, please, Your Majesty, to release him first from taking the oath which the Count de Vermandois spoke of, for it is not seemly for our Duke to take such a vow.'

"He grew angry, half-closed his eyes and said: 'How is this? Does your Duke mean to be my enemy?' 'No,' we answered. 'Nay, indeed.

Not an enemy, but a friend more true than one who might take the oath. But it is only that having once vowed to Christ, whom he is going to defend, he cannot vow to anyone else.'

"His face brightened at that. 'Is that the only objection? But verily Christ and I are one. The most beautiful title of a Basileus is that of Filochristos. Whatever Christ desires, I do too. Whatever He bids me to do, I accept in all humility. Indeed, a vow taken before me doubles the importance of a vow taken before our Savior.'

"Here he began to sigh deeply with his eyes on the picture of the Most Holy Madonna, and we said: 'Will your Eminence allow us to hear the words of this oath so that we may report them to our Duke?' Whereupon he beckoned to one of his courtiers who was attired all in gold, and the man read. These are the words of the oath:

" 'I call to witness, Our Savior, Pantocrator, Filantropos, Jesus Christ, the Most Holy Virgin, Panagia, Theotokos, Blakernitissa, the Holy Apostles, St. George, St. Theodore *megalomatyri*, and all the saints of the Lord, that I hereby vow true fealty to the Most High, the Most Pious, the God Chosen, Autocrator, Basileus Alexius. Spoils I shall win shall belong to him. Cities which shall surrender to me will be his. My vassals will be his subjects. I swear to honor and obey him even as my father and Lord and never to oppose his will. This I swear, and should I break this oath may God punish my soul with eternal damnation."

"An oath of subjection," sputtered Baldwin indignantly.

"So it is," Godfrey nodded. "Even worse than subjection—vassalage. And he wants me to take such oath? Never!"

"What happened next? What next?" Baldwin inquired impatiently.

"When he had done reading, we told him, 'We shall deliver faithfully these words to our Duke. He shall do as he sees fit, for whatever he does will be right and proper for a true knight.' We bowed then, ready to leave, but the Basileus spoke again: 'Go to your Duke and tell him that I shall expect him to abandon his unwise resistance and appear before me tomorrow for I love him like my son.' To which we replied, 'It is not for us to tell the Duke what he should or should not do, but this we know—he will not take that oath.' He winced at that and said: 'It will not be my fault if your Lord chooses to reject the fatherly hand extended to him. I was ready to show him all my kindness, even as I have done to the brother of the French king. You would have lacked nothing in that case. But if he chooses to be my foe, let him not expect anything from me, be it the smallest assistance. That is my last word.' Then we bowed and left."

"And what shall we do now?" Godfrey turned to his brother.

"This oath is impossible," replied Baldwin, scratching his head meditatively. "That much is certain."

"The very words would choke me! But what shall we do? In three days, four at the best, there won't be any money left."

"What of it?" Baldwin exclaimed defiantly. "There is plenty of gold around here. It will do the Basileus no harm if we skin him a bit."

"There will be no looting. I will not have it!"

"It would not be looting. You don't want us to starve to death!"

"No! No! Don't even mention looting to me! I could not bear such disgrace. I have another idea. I shall go to Galata to the Genoese. Perhaps as good Christians they will agree to take us across to Asia. We could pay them as soon as we win from the Saracens, and those are not far. We would start against them at once, without waiting for Raymond and the Normans."

The eyes of Baldwin and the good knights shone at the prospect. At last they would go into battle! They would be the first to engage the infidels! Would God that the Genoese agreed! Misers and skinflints though they were, perhaps they would take pity.

17.

The East Talks of the West

"HIS HIGHNESS, THE NOBLE SIMON DUKAS, SEBASTOCRATOR!" THE EUNUCH announced loudly from the doorway.

The master of the house, Pancrace Butumitos, captain of the empire's Eastern armies, rose swiftly to his feet to welcome the important guest, a member of the former ruling dynasty, who despite the change in government, had retained his old influence at court, thanks to his great administrative and political ability.

"What is the news?" asked Butumitos, in a confidential tone, after he had seated His Highness at the place of honor which befitted him. "Has anything happened?"

"Nothing so far. But the troops must be kept ready."

The noble Butumitos, captain of the Eastern armed forces; the noble Tatikios, captain of the Western armed forces; and the noble Euforbenos Kalatos, captain of the Southern armed forces looked up with interest.

"Why? Have the Latins made so bold as to attack?"

"They are becoming more and more restless. Today they even tried to charge the St. Roman Gate; Godfrey stopped them in time and he and his brother have quarreled over it. Tomorrow he may not be able to hold them back."

"All the trouble Strategos Argyros brought upon us!" Kalatos grumbled. "A pity he was ever sent to Gaul."

"Strategos Argyros is not to blame," said the master of the house. "His trip there had no influence whatever upon the subsequent actions of these madmen. He told me himself how terrified he was by what he saw there. It was all the Pope's doing, and the Pope sent them, no doubt, so that under the pretext of the defense of the Holy Sepulcher he might pull us from his rule.

"The Strategos went to Gaul," Butumitos went on to explain, "in order to recruit men for our legions. And the danger in which the city protected by God now lies he depicted with much eloquence so he might win over the mercenaries on cheaper terms. It was not his fault that all of Gaul, Italy, and the neighboring countries went mad and began this insane drift to the East; and that the help which they were to bring may now easily turn into a calamity. It is just to avoid such calamity that His Eminence, Our Lord and Master, the Basileus, may God grant him a long life, demanded an oath of the Duke of Lorraine."

"Is His Eminence not making a mistake?" asked Tatikios, prudently lowering his voice. "It seems to me it would be better to yield and give them provisions rather than to expose our suburbs and markets to the threat of such barbarians. Give them food, then let them stay or go away wherever the Parcae might lead them."

"What is the good of an oath anyway?"

The Sebastocrator looked at the three captains with the pity which the statesman feels for the soldier. "O! noble captains," he began sententiously. "Evidently you are not aware that all of Europe is up in arms and rolling upon us like a cloud of locusts. First to come were these noxious bands, well-known to the noble Tatikios here, who last summer polluted Byzantium. The ones led by that droll Kukupetros, the pseudo-saint, who in truth is just a fool and a dolt. We succeeded in pushing these bands across to Asia, where they are camped at Civitot. Now come the troops from Lorraine. But this is only the beginning. Hosts of Frankopulos are on their way here. Raymond St. Gilles is coming from the south, Flandrians and Normans from the north. Normans, mind you. How well we all remember them! Altogether they are more than three hundred thousand strong, I am told. What are we to do if instead of starting against the Saracens, they choose to take Byzantium? That is why His Eminence, the Basileus, may God grant him a long life, wants to bind each one separately with an oath before they all get here and become conscious of their might."

"What good will it do?" snorted Kalatos skeptically. "If the Frankopulos get into their heads to capture the city—the oath will not prevent them."

"That is where you are mistaken, my noble friend. Incredible as this may seem, these simpletons actually live up to their oaths."

"You don't say!"

"Aye! Except for Boemund, who has already acquired more artful notions as to how to rule a country, the other barons still keep their word. If they pledge themselves not to touch anything, you may be sure they won't. Which, of course, does not mean that there will be no cases of violence, thievery, and looting. After all, these men are savages who know no restraint, no discipline. Their leaders, however, will not turn against us, no matter what happens."

"How strange that their word should mean so much to them!"

"Well, it does. But for that very reason, it is essential at once to induce them, individually, to take the oath. According to the last pigeon post message, Raymond of Toulouse may be here in ten weeks, maybe a little earlier. Once he learns that the Duke of Lorraine took the oath, he won't be too reluctant to follow, the more so since Godfrey will urge him to do it. Otherwise they would incite each other to opposition, and meanwhile the Normans might come and—"

"No need to tell. We all know!"

"But what if Godfrey refuses?"

"By St. Theodora Stratilosa, how can I tell? I expect however that his own hungry men will force him to yield."

"Mighty dangerous to have hungry and well-armed men under your very walls," Butumitos observed, shaking his big round head.

"It's bad indeed."

All four fell silent, pondering upon these alien troops, these armed throngs that stood at the city's gates. It was not the first time that this had happened to Byzantium. Over three hundred years ago, in those terrible days when the Avars besieged the city, there had stood at its gates Slavs, Huns, Avars and Piechenegs, Bulgars and Waregs, Persians and Medes, and other tribes as well, whose very names had since vanished from memory. They had come as foes and stood there with terrible greed in their eyes as they gazed upon the City Protected by God.

Today another wave of peoples had arisen, and was sweeping upon them. True, they were coming as allies and protectors, but experience had taught the Byzantines caution. They knew all too well the irresistible temptation of gold, of which they had such profusion.

Skillful servants directed by the mere glance of the eunuch standing at the doorway, silently moved about carrying, on golden plates, tropical fruits, small bits of pastry savoring of honey and spices, sharp sheep cheeses, and in big gold and silver pitchers frozen wine, warm wine, and scented water and beer, which the Greeks had learned to use from their own Scandinavian, Russian, and Wareg mercenaries.

The adjoining room, as brilliantly lighted as the hall, belonged to the *gineceum,* the female part of the household. It was separated from the rest of the house by heavy silken curtains, by which stood two eunuchs dressed in white, swords in hands, and as stiff as statues. In the olden days it had been their duty to keep everyone away from the *gineceum.* Today they were only the evidence of the opulence of the household. The old custom was forgotten. How indeed could social and cultural life have existed without women? What charm could conversation hold if women took no part in it? Thus the higher the intellectual and artistic life of Byzantium became, the larger grew the influence and importance of women and the greater grew their independence. Nevertheless they preferred to retain this old form of separate quarters, since, though seemingly limiting their movements, it actually presented many advantages. According to the old customs and laws the *gineceum* constituted an independent, completely separate part of the household, inhabited by an unknown and varying number of women relatives, friends, itinerant nuns, servants, and slaves, a veritable state within the state, with an absolutely independent rule.

Noble ladies coming out of their quarters still covered their faces with gauze veils, light as a breeze, but these were the only sign of the old subjection. In reality women in Byzantium enjoyed greater freedom than anywhere else in the world, and they took advantage of it by playing an enthusiastic part in every phase of public life, politics in particular. Around the imperial throne, no matter who sat upon it, they were forever weaving intrigues, and many an event which was to resound later throughout the whole world could be traced to white and irresponsible feminine hands.

Because of these extensive activities, common domestic virtues were on the wane among the patrician women of Byzantium; only the old and the plain still practiced marital faithfulness. Yet, in some peculiar way they managed to reconcile this untrammeled mode of life with an extremely rigid and scrupulous form of piety. They never had more than one or two children and even that single child, as soon as it was born, was turned over to be nursed and brought up by a faithful slave.

Enamored of comfort, pleasure, and beauty as it was, the Byzantine society looked with smiling indulgence upon the charming little feminine sins. This tolerance, of course, was confined only to the members of the wealthy ruling class, for in regard to the plebs, laws were severe and strictly enforced. A woman of low birth was punished by death for breaking her marital vows, and even ladies of high birth were occasionally shrouded in a nun's veil and spirited away to a convent built on the gloomy rocky isle of Proti, the classic exile for beautiful sinners of high birth.

There thus was nothing surprising in the fact that in the palace of the noble Butumitos the curtains which divided the *gineceum* from the rest of the house were always parted and that the eunuchs on guard peered without misgivings upon the social gatherings which took place beyond.

There were seven women right now in the *gineceum* hall: the three daughters of Butumitos and four of their friends: Theodora, Zoë, Agatha, Praxeda, Irene, Eudoxia, and Anastasia; all of them young and endowed with the three principal virtues required of a Byzantium woman: beauty, elegance, and education. Their lithe bodies were beautifully cared for, their minds flexible and well-trained. They had studied many things and were able to converse freely upon such a variety of subjects as geography, history, mathematics, philosophy, theology, and poetry. No wonder, therefore, that not only fashionable youths, whose chief occupation in life was racing, but even the serious *logios,* or men of letters, were never bored in their company. The present gathering included two fashionable young men, Demetrius and Cleon, and three writers: John Italos, the learned scholar of Plato whose work he had recently transcribed to the great displeasure of the patriarch; the poet Prodomos, who was the idol of modern ladies though not the equal of the great and recently deceased Michael Psellos; and Basil Cheches, a well-known authority on Hesiod and Homer. And here too, as in the adjoining hall, the Latin army standing under the city walls furnished an inexhaustible topic of conversation.

"I would love to drive out and see them at close quarters only father won't let me," complained Zoë petulantly.

"There is nothing worth seeing about them," Italos assured her. "They are completely uncouth. Any slave here has more social polish. Withal, their conceit knows no bounds. Would you believe it, oh beautiful muses, that they look upon themselves as superior beings and consider us, aye! us! barbarians?"

The words were greeted with such an uncontrollable burst of laughter that in the adjoining room Butumitos scowled. He allowed his daughters to break the old customs but did not like it to be done in too glaring a way.

"So they consider us barbarians. How priceless! What a jest!"

"I see nothing droll about it," protested Cleon, the younger son of the *curopalat* of the Holy Palace. "They, themselves, are absolute brutes."

"I have heard the weirdest things about their customs," said Prodomos the poet, scanning rhythmically every word. "I have been told, for instance, that when a case is brought to trial among them, both parties a red-hot iron grab within their naked hands. And he who burns his hand is guilty; and that decides the case."

"But how is that possible? Don't they both burn?"

"Ah, then the both of them are punished. One because he did wrong and t'other—because he had no right to accuse him. And such a trial they call 'God's Judgment.' For they believe, you see, that God is always ready to solve their petty wrangles and that His Holy Justice could not allow an innocent to suffer. The same mentality as of our monks, only, dear friends, out there such tales find credence, even among the kingdom's foremost lords."

"How incredible."

"They are primitive and naive, no doubt," observed Cheches, who had hitherto remained silent. "Still there is a certain greatness about them. Or so it seems to me . . . Perhaps it's because I have had no personal contact with them so far. But from the stories I hear they remind me of the Homeric heroes, they have the same coarseness and courage, and same craving for independence, and, more than this, that strange urge to pursue in life certain high ideals, an urge which, alas, has died out completely among us, and which has caused them to abandon everything to come here to the rescue of the Holy Sepulcher."

"Nonsense," muttered Cleon. "They came here to loot and for no other reason. When you know them better, my Lord, you will soon see that they have nothing in common with the heroes of Homer. Dirty common thieves, greedy as ravens."

"Maybe so . . ."

"And the women? Tell us something about their women," exclaimed Agatha. "Have any of you seen them?"

"I have," boasted Demetrius. "I was twice in the Latin camp with our emissaries."

"Then tell us, quick! What sort of a camp was it? Did you see much splendor?"

"None at all. The place was wretchedly poor, pavilions small, cramped, unadorned. No comfort of any kind. They neither know nor crave it. And poorly dressed, too. You can hardly tell a knight from a squire, or a squire from a servant."

"But tell us about the women."

"They are even more uncouth than the men. They have no conversation. Indeed, I don't know what one could talk about with such ungainly creatures. I have seen the sister-in-law of Godfrey and she did wear a gown of heavy silk, but her hands were like a washwoman's, red, rough, chapped, untouchable. I am not certain whether she wore a shift under her outer garment or when she had bathed last. Probably not since she left home . . ."

"Don't be malicious, Demetrius."

"I am not being malicious. I purposely took a good look around the camp, but I did not see a single tub or bath, not even a wash pan. I was also told that feminine fashions change every hundred years or so, so that the granddaughters might wear out the dresses of their grandmothers. Such a thrifty people—how would you like that, my fair ladies?"

They giggled delightedly, for in Byzantium feminine fashions changed several times a year.

"It seems that they bear children constantly, like plebeian women. And they look upon sterility as a horrible disgrace. And besides this, they are virtuous."

"No wonder. Looking as they do, they cannot help it."

"They are virtuous," repeated Demetrius with great stress. "That's something we can envy the Latins."

He cast a meaning look at Praxeda to whom he was betrothed.

"Let us trade," she retorted archly. "Why don't you marry such an unbathed paragon of virtue, while I take one of the knights?"

"You would not like it, Praxeda."

"And why not, pray? They must have strong arms and loins."

He winced and grew red.

"I trust ours are no weaker. Besides I assure you, my dear, that you would not be able to bear even for an hour the company of such a hairy, evil-smelling lout. What do they know of the art and refinements of love? You might as well marry one of our mercenaries."

"Don't be wroth, Demetrius. I said it in jest, only to tease you."

"I should hope so," he exclaimed. "And their mental powers are likewise no better than a trooper's. They know nothing. The majority can't even read, and all they know is how to swill, gorge themselves, and fight."

"So that is the culture of the West. What then became of Rome?"

"Of Rome, you ask? Barbarians have annihilated it, even as their grandchildren would annihilate us now," Demetrius retorted bitterly and beckoned to a slave to refill his goblet.

18.

Basileus Isapostolos

GODFREY WAS STEEPED IN PRAYER. DURING THE LAST TWO WEEKS HIS FACE had grown dark and gaunt; he lived in a state of conflict and anxiety. The Genoese would not even hear of transporting his troops to Asia without immediate payment. They were merchants, nothing but merchants, they said, and none save business reasons could prevail with them. But the Duke of Lorraine had sold his patrimony and was in reality now but a penniless beggar. As for the booty which he hoped to win from the Saracens—such payment was doubtful enough. Who could tell whether it might not be easier for the Genoese to buy from the Saracens the booty which the latter might win from the crusaders?

So they refused. No use dreaming of help from these quarters. He had thought of building barges but all the woods in the immediate vicinity were the imperial property and strictly guarded. To obtain timber he would first have to engage in open battle, and thus break the last hope of coming to terms with the Basileus.

For over two weeks now Godfrey's men had lived on whatever they could obtain by begging or from the sale of their costlier possessions and better attire. Already once, Baldwin, heedless of Godfrey's wrath, had burned and looted the nearest suburb. It had taken Godfrey infinite pains to recall the men and lead them back to camp, for the knights were fuming with rage and openly demanded leave to go and fight for their food. In truth they were less concerned about their own hunger or that of their men than about their mounts, their most valuable possessions. The horses, gaunt and shaggy, turned their heads towards their masters and neighed anxiously, waiting to be fed, but there was no feed. So Godfrey prayed desperately, not knowing where to turn next.

Something stirred at the entrance. Reluctantly the knight turned his head, annoyed that his servant should disturb him again; then, with unconcealed surprise, he rose to his feet. It was not a servant, but his sister-in-law, Gontrane, who stood shyly at the entrance, nervously tugging at her long sleeves.

"Forgive me for coming, Godfrey," she said in a low voice. "But I thought it wise to ask you whether you know where Baldwin is right now?"

"I do not know," Godfrey retorted with unwonted harshness. He averted his gaze in order not to meet her eyes. "I do not know, and truly, Gontrane, I am surprised that foolish jealousy should have brought you here."

She lifted both arms in a gesture of protest. "Oh, but I do know where he is. This has nothing to do with me. I only wanted you to know."

"Well then, what is it? Speak up!"

Oh, if he only would look at her. But he did not. Never, within her memory, had he given her as much as a glance, and now he stared at the ground like a monk.

"Speak up!" he repeated impatiently.

"He went with Konon Montaigue, Wilfred d'Esch, and ten other armed men to steal the Miraculous Madonna from the Church of Blakernos."

"What did you say?" he cried horrified. "Say it again."

"He went to steal from the Church of Blakernos the Miraculous Image of the Madonna," she repeated slowly and distinctly. "He said that once it was in his hands he would have no trouble persuading the Basileus to release you from the oath and that it was not closely guarded."

"By the saint patrons of Lorraine! How long since they left?"

"Less than an hour."

"Perhaps I can still overtake them. Great God! My horse! My horse!"

He shivered with agitation and impatience, as he hurriedly buckled on his sword, and with fumbling fingers adjusted his helmet. At last the horse was brought, in the haste saddled not with the usual knight's high saddle but with a light one. Godfrey rushed out from the tent without armor, with his sword alone. Feverishly he grabbed the stirrup, and, not waiting for the servant to help him, leaped into the saddle, turned around, shouted, "God bless you, Gontrane," and galloped off at top speed.

He caught them soon; they were riding slowly in order not to draw attention. He passed them, turned, and halted.

"Turn back," he said. "I know everything. You cannot commit this sacrilege. It means eternal damnation."

"Let us be, Godfrey," Baldwin said. "The Basileus is letting us starve. When we have his relic for hostage, he will change his tactics."

"If you proceed," Godfrey said calmly, "I will run my sword through my heart."

"A good idea for a captain," Baldwin said. "What then will happen to your army? Would you have it stay here and starve or return home as best it can? My plan is better. Go home and pray while we attend to this business."

"I shall stab myself," Godfrey said.

Baldwin knew that he meant it.

"Then take your choice," he said angrily. "Give us food, allow us to execute this mission, or else I shall call out the troops and attack the city. We do not mean to starve for your stubbornness and the pleasure of the Basileus."

Godfrey saw his own determination reflected in the face of his brother.

"You shall eat, Baldwin," he said. "You shall eat no later than to-morrow. I will take the oath. It is a lesser evil than that which you propose to do."

"Suit yourself," Baldwin muttered. He turned and rode away with the three knights. "I think our way was better," he said to them.

"So do I," said Wilfred d'Esch. "It is a hard oath to take. I wonder who told Godfrey."

"If I knew, I would cut him in half," Baldwin said.

The enormous throne hall, called the *Christotriklinion*, was all aglow with a thousand candles gleaming in golden candlesticks. In their soft light, the walls, ceiling, and pillars shimmered with a rainbow of colors. Only gold, crystal, and precious stones had been used to adorn the hall: on the walls gold lay on top of gold, inlaid with gold, trimmed with gold, set with gold, carved with gold, woven with gold. The unparalleled artistry of craftsmanship vied with the richness of the material. Everything that the arts of Egypt, Babylon, Persia, and Greece, the youngest yet most perfect of them all, had produced and given to the world had been brought here and combined, merged, developed, to its logical conclusion to create this miracle of stately grandeur and mysterious harmony. Built by the master builders who had created Hagia Sofia, the Hall of *Christotriklinion* seemed to be a work of magic, as though left behind by some beings more perfect than the ordinary mortals.

At one-third of its length the hall was cut off by a golden tightly drawn curtain woven into great fantastic designs of beasts and griffons. The curtain flowed down from the ceiling in even folds, glistening like streams of water, and on both sides were great doors of ivory and gold, leading into suites of halls equally large, equally beautiful and rich. Against the background of golden mosaics loomed the figures of Basileis the victorious, Basileis the saintly, Basileis equal to the apostles, Basileis giving wise laws, Basileis fighting the enemies of the church, or overpowering raging lions. On the marble floor of one of the halls an enormous peacock fanned a tail sparkling with precious stones while in the four corners in richly decorated medallions, the masterful imperial eagles of Rome stretched their double necks, watching the East and West.

Beyond the peacock hall was the room of pearls, so called because of the multitude of pearls with which its walls were inlaid to give it a mysterious moonlight radiance. Beyond was the Basilissa's reception hall, the floor of which was described by chroniclers as a meadow strewn with flowers. Next came a hall with walls lined with green porphyry combined with white marble, conveying an impression of beauty so perfect that this room was called only "Harmony." Beyond that was the wedding hall with its great bed of solid gold, and the famed purple hall where the Basilissas lay in child bed. Children born here received the title, *Porphyrogeneti*, or born to the purple. But the truth was that it was not only on account of the costly purple of its walls that the hall deserved its name; blood had been often spilled here and the exquisitely beautiful halls of the Holy Palace held a host of bloody phantoms and many a blood-curdling memory. It was here in the Purple Hall that the eyes of the luckless emperor, Constantine VI, were gouged out at the order of and in the presence of his mother. It was here that five sisters of Emperor Roman knelt before their sister-in-law, the beautiful Teofano, vainly pleading that she would not condemn them in the bloom of their youth to life imprisonment in a convent dungeon. Indeed, few

Basileuses died of old age. Their demises were mostly sudden, the laby-rinths of halls in the Holy Palace providing good hiding places for con-spirators. And, anyhow, "purple makes a beautiful shroud," as the great Theodora, circus woman, street wench, and finally a famed Basilissa, once remarked.

In the great Hall of *Christotriklinion,* in spite of the throng of cour-tiers present, only the silk of the flowing state robes was to be heard. The court protocol, prescribing in minute detail the order of every possible event, reception, departure, arrival, gala, and celebration, was estab-lished for centuries and scrupulously observed. According to the proto-col, no one dared break the silence till the Basileus, still invisible behind the curtain, had first done so. Ranged in proper order they waited, the old Patriarch in a stiff golden dalmatic and surrounded by a host of deacons heading the principal dignitaries of the court.

Behind them stood a crowd of eunuchs in white robes and with golden bands on their heads. Among the latter were many imperial bastards who though born on the steps of the throne, were thus deprived of any hope of donning the purple. Though mutilated, they were not barred from holding high offices.

One side of the hall was reserved for the women, and here, in long even rows stood noblewomen—the *Zosta* or "dubbed ones"—who at any time of the day had access to the apartment of the Basilissa, all were wearing long court mantles of marvelous sheen and hue, and their hands and throats sparkled with gems. From their high, towerlike coifs, white transparent veils flowed over their backs. Behind them on a raised seat, resembling a throne, sat Maria Dalasenos, mother of the Basileus, an old woman of austere, almost stony mien. Since it was due to her indefatigable efforts, machinations, and intrigues that her son Alexius owed the throne, she considered herself entitled to voice her opinion in every affair of state, and her opinions were harsh indeed. At her side sat the oldest daughter of Alexius, Anna Porphyrogenita. Although only thirteen she was tall, with a well-rounded figure so that she gave the impression of a full-grown maiden. Two enormous black eyes glowed in her expressive, swarthy face and her swift, spirited motions were full of grace. Alexius adored her, he was proud of that brilliant firstborn of his, who at thirteen was studying rhetoric, philosophy, history, literature, geography, mythology, science, mathematics, geometry, music, and astronomy, who spoke Latin fluently and was familiar with all the ancient authors.

Beside Anna but on a slightly higher chair sat the heir apparent, her seven-year-old brother, John Porphyrogenitus, wrapped like a doll in the richest brocade, with an unhealthy yellowish skin, an abnormally broad skull, and the dull stare of a sickly child. Until his birth, Anna had been considered Alexius' successor, and the proud and ambitious girl could never forgive her brother for having been born.

An invisible orchestra composed exclusively of flutes began to play. All the court bowed almost to the ground and remained thus frozen, bent in two, while the gold and purple curtain parted slowly and the imperial couple, seated upon a high dais, appeared in the fullness of their glory. The Basileus, Alexius Commenus, wore a thick black beard which covered half his face; the gaze of his beautiful eyes, so like the eyes of his daughter, was very keen, hiding under an apparent benignity a great deal of shrewdness. By his side, upon a smaller throne, sat the Basilissa, Irene Dukas, daughter of the previous emperor. Though according to protocol, beauty was one of the essential attributes of Basilissa, Irene was not in the least beautiful. Marriage to her was of such political importance to Alexius, however, that he did not hesitate to overlook this detail; nor was it heeded by poets and flatterers who sang her praises, calling her the most beautiful rose of the world, the ornament of the throne, the pride of the purple cloth and the smile of the morning star. Actually Irene was small, skinny, gray, with an unpleasant and stubborn face. Unloved by her husband, tormented by her mother-in-law, she had become very pious and had surrounded herself with swarms of monks. Now she sat at Alexius' side, impersonal and aloof in her gorgeous, stately attire, so ill suited to her looks. Her hands, like her husband's, were folded in her lap; her eyes were vacant and lost in space. At the precise moment when the curtain parted, not a second sooner or later, from the opposite end of the hall, Duke Godfrey of Lorraine was ushered in. Two beardless eunuchs, looking like a pair of guardian angels in their white robes, led him carefully at each arm. Behind him marched Baldwin of Lorraine, Konon de Montaigue, Wilfred d'Esch, Paul du Bourg, and the Count d'Haineault, their swords clattering on the marble flags. In a proud gesture they had flung back their mantles over their shoulders to display the soldierly simplicity of their steel armor. The horrible conflict that had torn his soul in the last few days showed in Godfrey's gray and hollow-cheeked face and the deep shadows under the eyes. He walked because he was being led, his eyes fixed on the ground; he tried not to see anyone, to ignore the brilliant throng that stared at him so curiously. At last when he had reached the center of the hall, he was halted and the Patriarch moved forward with a cross. Godfrey heard the rustle of the stiff dalmatic, saw the enormous pearls sewed on the purple sandals, and laid his fingers on the cross, the infallible Friend who would never abandon him. In a slightly rasping voice he repeated the formula of the oath. Then the cross moved away from him and he arose, lifted to his feet by the two eunuchs. Now he was led on farther while his knights remained behind. He was to come close to the throne and kneel down again, but this time not before the cross. He must kneel before the Basileus, kiss his foot, knee, and hand, then kneel before the Basilissa, kiss her foot, knee, and hand. He—a free knight, independent of everyone—must humble himself as none of his kin had ever humbled himself before. A wave of terrible, wild hatred for the emperor swept over Godfrey and cold sweat broke out on his forehead. "For Thy sake, Christ! for Thee!" he repeated to himself, but the words refused to flow down from his lips to his heart, and had he not been led, he could not have walked a step farther.

He approached the throne, his face pale as death. And now he was only a step away. Two cushions marked the spots where he must kneel —and now the eunuchs had left him and he was alone before his ineffable humiliation. And suddenly there was an unexpected liquid rustle right behind the Duke's back and the golden curtain closed. He found himself in a small space filled with the smell of incense, alone with the two motionless figures.

Relieved in spite of himself to be free of the curious stare of hundreds of eyes, he looked up and to his amazement saw that the faces of Alexius and his wife had lost their impassivity, that they had become human and were smiling, Irene a bit sourly, perhaps, but Alexius with a wide friendly grin.

"We shall dispense with the genuflexion, my son," he said in Latin. "The oath is enough. Sit here by my side."

Blood rushed back into the Duke's heart, and he was filled with a sense of relief, exultation, and gratitude. He would have now gladly of his own accord kissed like a son the palm of this man who had freed him from torment. Still unable to speak he sat down on the low stool, and now the curtain parted again and once more the emperor and his wife froze into jewel-bedecked statues. Unconsciously following their example Godfrey looked with unblinking eyes at the hall, his gaze calm and serene. Gradually he was recovering his balance and his eyes swept over the court dignitaries, the eunuchs, deacons, Serbian and Bulgar princes, who stood at the back, until at last they rested on his own comrades. Then his face brightened in a smile and he thought how wonderful they looked standing there free and proud in their steel armors with their great swords pulling their belts on their hips, so different from the Greek courtiers, so familiar, his very own! With every muscle he felt that he belonged to them, his Latin brethren who, with him, had nothing in common with that alien Byzantine world.

19.

God or Satan?

PETER LAY SOBBING AT THE BISHOP'S FEET. HE CLUTCHED ADHEMAR'S ankles, kissed his sandals and, knocking his head on the ground, mumbled an incoherent stream of words.

The Bishop gazed at him with pity as he vainly urged him to compose himself and talk like a sensible being. At last he lifted the wretched little man and stood him on his feet.

"Sit down here," he pointed to a low box. "Sit down and tell me how are things with you? And take that cowl off your head. I can't hear what you are mumbling in there."

Hesitantly Peter pushed back the hood. His red eyes blinked like those of a bird unused to daylight. He looked punier and more wretched than ever, as he sat there, his eyes swollen, his face haggard and covered with unkempt tufts of hair, the expression of a frightened animal never leaving his face.

"Tell me all from the beginning," the Bishop commanded. "Well, was I right to forbid you to start without me?"

"Oh, you were right, Your Grace, how right, but it was not my fault. The people forced me to do it."

"Come, speak the truth! I remember you well. You were ready enough to lead them."

"It was my fault, yes," moaned Peter again, and dropped once more to his knees.

"Sit still and answer me. I've had enough of your lamentations. Now tell me the truth."

At last, with an obvious effort taking hold of himself, Peter the Hermit began to describe in detail what had happened to them on the terrible march through Hungary. He told of the drowning of three barge-loads of wretches in the Sava River. "A thousand men at least! A

146

thousand men at least!" he kept repeating, wringing his hands in despair. He told of the dour Walter the Penniless, before whom everyone trembled, and finally he told about their arrival in Byzantium.

"We set up camp right outside the city," he said. "There was plenty of food, thank God. The Basileus is generous that way, no denying it. But what of it? You cannot keep in hand people left idle. No sooner had they got their breath than they began to roam the suburbs and steal and pillage whatever they could lay their hands on. With so much gold everywhere, how could they resist the temptation, the more so since it all belonged to schismatics? At last they tore the lead roof from the imperial summer palace and sold it to the Genoese."

"The rascals! Shameful!" muttered the Bishop angrily.

"I am not to blame, Your Grace. No one will listen to me any more. They only jeer at me. And that Walter is nothing at heart but a bandit. He does not care with whom he fights as long as he fights and he bears the same malice toward everyone. He even says that he would rather fight the Greeks than the Saracens, since he would get more booty that way. It was not my fault."

"Go on. What next?"

"When the Greeks saw the palace without a roof, the Basileus' army surrounded our camp and ordered us aboard barges, and they had orders to kill whoever refused to go. But there were no more than half of the people in camp; the rest were roaming all over the place and we never saw them again, and we don't know what happened to them. Perhaps they are still hiding somewhere like criminals, perhaps they have been killed—no telling . . ."

"And you were taken across?"

"O yes, they took us across, and drove us with sticks like cattle to Civitot right by the Turkish border. A big camp they put us in, surrounded with a palisade, and it's there we've been living for almost half a year. Galleys bring us food every day. I came here on one of these galleys when I heard about your arrival, most blessed father."

"You suffer no hunger?"

"No, Your Grace, we don't. They bring us an abundance of everything."

"Then by and large you are not faring so badly?"

Peter covered his face with trembling palms.

"Oh! Your Grace! It could not be worse in hell," he cried. "There

would be nothing to complain of if people were different. No one goes
hungry. No one is driven to toil. Everyone is free. The river is close by,
they can bathe and wash their rags or catch fish; they can just sit and
bask in the sun all day. There are no wild beasts; the country is absolutely safe. It could be a wonderful life. But our people will not stay in
peace, not even for a day. They fight, they riot, they are forever at each
other's throats. Not one day goes by but several men are killed. And the
wantonness! Not one maiden still walks a virgin; they all have bastards.
And married women are no better; they live in open sin and make no
secret of it. Each comely one goes about followed by men like a bitch
by a pack of wolves. It's dreadful to tell what is going on. They have all
gone mad. The place is not a crusaders' camp but a filthy Devil's Sab-
bath."

"And what does Walter say to that? You told me the man had a
heavy hand."

"What does Walter care? He has his own twenty thousand men, well
armed and disciplined, whom he keeps in a separate camp. What are
we to him? Or vice? Or slaughter? Once long ago he might have had
some traces of a Christian conscience—but no more! He has picked for
his friend George Burel, a great rascal. And the man has completely
bewitched him. They drink together, they go out together on their
expeditions."

"Talk sense, man! What expeditions could they go on?"

"Across the Turkish border, Your Grace. Not a week goes by but
that they set out, sometimes to Nikomedia, betimes to Zerigordon.
Sometimes they even go all the way down to Nicaea."

"Then at least they are fighting the Saracens?" the Bishop remarked
with obvious relief.

"Would to God they did! But no, Your Grace. They leave the soldiers
alone; it's the simple folks they are after. The population there is Christian though for the last fifteen years it has been under the pagan's yoke.
The Saracens sit in their strongholds and never interfere. Why should
they not be glad that Christians, crusaders, about whom they have already heard, are murdering and destroying other Christians. Walter
never returns to camp without loot and prisoners. Everyone of these
prisoners carries a cross on his breast, and cries and invokes Christ's
help."

"And what does Walter do with them?"

"He sells them into slavery to the Greeks who bring our food on their galleys. For a cheap penny he sells brother Christians. What the Greeks do with them I do not know. It's rumored they resell them at a profit to the Saracens in Egypt."

"Oh God! Oh, God!" whispered Adhemar.

"Your lordship, father," Peter cried in despair, "it will be the same with you. Go back now while there is still time, before the Devil possesses you all. It's his doing, his, the sinful Archangel's! The whole crusade is nothing but the Fiend's temptation! It was not God who conceived it, but Satan!"

"Silence, Peter! Stop talking blasphemy!" Adhemar stamped angrily. "It is easy to blame Satan when oneself is at fault."

"You will see for yourself, Your Grace. You will see what will befall if you don't flee in time."

"You are mad, I tell you. Better go to church and pray."

"Long did I kneel and lay prostrate in churches! All in vain! He is after me because I saw through him and his infernal scheme. Because of him so many good Christians have perished and more perish every day. He is the father of the crusade."

"Go to church," repeated Adhemar. He lifted the weeping Peter to his feet, made the sign of the cross over him, gave him his ring to kiss and sent him away. Yet as he comforted the weeping Peter, his voice did not sound as firm and confident as usual. Was it, perhaps, because that very morning Sir Raoul de Beaugency had confided in him that he too was assailed by doubts as to whether the crusade was the work of God or the Devil.

Sir Raoul de Beaugency had once belonged to Satan, having of his own free will sold his soul for the price of avenging himself on his uncle. The taking of the cross had freed him from the devilish subjection. For more than a year afterwards he had felt free and blissfully happy. Yet now, since their arrival at Byzantium, he was torn by doubts whether he had really freed himself.

After taking the cross he had like many others vowed chastity. For a year this vow did not cause him much hardship, but recently strange things were happening to him. Every woman he saw filled him with desire, a desire stronger than he had ever felt before. At the very sight of the beautiful Greek harlots his knees trembled and he staggered like a drunkard. He tried to close his eyes and turn his head away, but in vain. The vision of their bodies was shameless, tempting, impossible to drive away.

It could not be anything else but a Devil's trick. Satan, disappointed because his prey had escaped him, was seeking to skewer it anew. Was he not the most shrewd of all creation? He, *Zabullus,* alias *Suggestor,* conveyor of bad counsel—he, the temptor, prince of falsehood, or simply the Evil One, *Malus,* the one who wanted evil, who consciously created evil—he was clutching Raoul again in his claws. "But how can he have access to me?" said the knight in despair. "Am I not a crusader? Should not Divine Grace guard and protect me?"

How could the Devil have access to a crusader? Here was a question which even the wise Bishop was not able to answer. Clearly, he should have had no access; but he had. Despite the hopes of Pope Urban, the taking of the cross had not changed human nature, and Divine Grace had been lost somewhere on their mighty journey.

The old doubts, the lack of faith in the success of the Holy Expedition, that he had discussed with Urban eighteen months ago in the lonely tower, were now returning more persistently and oppressively than ever. Torn by incertitude, Adhemar de Monteuil, Bishop of Puy, the leader of the holy crusade, could not bring himself to tell Peter or Raoul firmly that the Devil had nothing to do with the matter.

"God have mercy! What will happen if I, who am to lead them all, should begin to doubt?"

"You are already doubting," said a voice in his soul. Whose voice was it? Did it belong to the one whom Peter the Hermit considered the real leader and instigator of the crusade? "You already doubt, or rather, you never believed. You are too perspicacious not to know that what you are attempting is pure madness. Turn them back while there is still time."

"Turn back, Your Grace," the terrified Peter had implored.

"Turn back," whispered the counsellor in his soul.

To make matters worse, in the adjoining chamber Godfrey, Duke of Bouillon, who had just arrived to consult with Count Raymond of Toulouse was saying in a raised voice: "Believe me, my Lord, that harsh as the oath is, it's better to take it, so we might depart from here at once and flee as fast as we can from this luxury, this concupiscence—worse than pestilence itself. You have just arrived and may not realize what we who have been here for a long time know all too well. Believe me,

the Devil himself could have invented no better way to divert good
Christian soldiers from the path of honor than the hospitality of the
Greeks. I cannot recognize my own knights, for whom once I would
have gladly pledged my right hand, they have so changed. And, is it a
wonder? Let a man sleep in a soft bed of sinful down and he will never
like his hard knightly couch again. Let him get used to fancy dishes and
he will choke on camp rations. And how can a wife in a shift of un-
bleached linen remain dear to a man who has lain night after night
with shameless and perfumed whores? Some are already lost; nothing
will tear them away from here. They are doomed, gone completely
astray."

Hiding his face twisted by pain in his palms, Bishop Adhemar listened in horror. Satan. Satan again. Did not everyone say the same
thing? So the pious Godfrey, likewise suspected the presence of the
Evil Neighbor, the planter of the wicked tares . . .

"Even so I shall not take the oath," Raymond St. Gilles exclaimed
angrily.

"Believe me, taking it did not come easily to me either," Godfrey
assured him as though ashamed. "At first I said just what you say now,
but what else could I do? What other way out is there? We cannot get
across without the Basileus' assistance and yet we must flee from here,
at once, otherwise none of us shall ever behold the Holy Sepulcher."

"I will not take the oath," repeated Raymond shortly and passionately.

"Then what do you propose to do?"

"I don't know."

"Robert of Normandy, it seems, has already declared himself in favor
of taking the oath," a new conciliatory voice broke in. The Bishop
recognized the voice of Gouffier de la Tour.

"I know, I know," shouted Raymond. "And I also know that Boemund told the Basileus' envoys that he will take the oath gladly if they
give him in return the title of Protosebastos and a good annual pension.
Pugh! Let him! Provençals and Normans do not look the same way
upon honor."

"And how do we from Lorraine look upon ours, Count?" asked Godfrey in a strangled voice.

Now they will grab their swords, thought the Bishop. That's all that
we need at this moment!

But the peerless uprightness of Godfrey was known so well that Raymond St. Gilles took hold of himself and said almost gently: "Nothing can demean yours, my Lord, who are the paragon of knightly virtue."

"I am no paragon, indeed, but a sinner, desirous only to fulfill my vow as soon as possible."

"So am I. Nevertheless, I am not going to become anybody's vassal. Egad, I shall not!"

"But what other way is there?" asked Godfrey in an agonized voice.

"I ought to step in and settle the matter," thought the Bishop, "that's what I am here for." Yet he continued to sit with his face buried in his hands. He hardly knew what they should do. His own knightly blood seethed at the thought of pledging a vassal's allegiance to a schismatic emperor; nevertheless Godfrey was right. They had no choice. To strike in force against the Greek army and capture the fleet in order to cross to the Arm of St. George would mean open warfare now and the enemy at the rear in the future. It would deprive the expedition of guides, supplies, and the help of a fleet. No, they had no choice. They must either bow to the Basileus or turn back.

"The Duke of Normandy, the Duke of Tarentum, and the Count of Flanders are here," a servant said loudly, rushing in. The Bishop rose to his feet, his shoulders held high, his face composed, and went to preside at the council.

The council failed to reach a decision. Raymond and Tancred insisted that no power on earth could make them take the oath. They had set out to serve the Lord and deliver Jerusalem; they had no intention of becoming liegemen to a schismatic emperor along the way. He had asked for their help; now he barred their way to the Holy Sepulcher.

Adhemar tried to reason with them.

"Which do you consider more important," he asked, "your pride or the oath you took of your own free will at Clermont? If your pride is more important then there is nothing for you to do but return to your own lands. You need not consider it a disgrace so long as you believe it was Alexius who betrayed you."

Raymond was silent. He had sworn not to return to his home that the Holy Sepulcher might be freed. Adhemar went on, explaining why it was the better part of wisdom to take the oath and obtain help for the expedition, so that the ultimate goal might be reached. It was wrong, he said, to allow a great ideal to flounder in a sea of technical honor. Boemund smiled with pleasure. This was precisely the kind of reasoning he had always advocated. If you cannot climb over an obstacle, he theorized, crawl under it.

Noticing Boemund's smile, Adhemar paused in confusion. Only yesterday he had branded as a disgrace Boemund's readiness to take the oath in return for the title of Protosebastos. Was he not using part of the same cunning now?

In the silence Tancred stood up. Impatiently he stabbed a knife into the table.

"Let us decide something, for heaven's sake," he shouted. "Let us not sit here forever. Let us be off!"

"Yes, yes," said Godfrey. "Let us be off!"

"There is nothing to decide," Adhemar said to Tancred. "Only you and the Count of St. Gilles are holding us up. Take the oath and we shall be off to the Holy Land."

He looked at the stubborn pair hopefully then, as they remained silent, went on speaking.

"Consider this as a solution. From the moment we enter Asia I shall be your captain and supreme commander. The Holy Father decided this and you all agreed. Perhaps therefore the Basileus will consider it sufficient if I take the oath on behalf of all of you."

This suggestion suited no one.

"I am my own master and no one can take an oath for me," said Raymond.

"Nor for me," said Tancred.

"You are our true guardian but you have no power over us," said one of the others.

"I do not intend to interfere with you or your men," said Adhemar, "but a year and a half ago at Clermont you gave me your knightly pledge. Tell me, did not each of you lift his right palm in sign of consent?"

They were silent. They remembered.

"Sir," said Boemund, "I was not at Clermont."

The silence continued until it was ominous. Adhemar, unable to bear it, his conscience troubled by Boemund's taunting smile, adjourned the council until the next day.

20.

Boemund

IT OFTEN SEEMED TO THE SAD PALE-FACED WILLIBALD, WIFE OF OMER DE Guillebaut, that she would have done better to stay home and bear the indignity of the belt of chastity rather than venture on this expedition. The long trip on horseback had made her as sore and uncomfortable as the loathesome belt might have, and she had to suffer the continual presence and ill-will of her husband, the gloomy and suspicious Norman.

During the first part of the journey, her mount had gone lame and she had been forced to ride pillion upon her husband's charger. Such a mode of traveling, though customary in those days, was far from comfortable. The rump of the big stallion was broad, round, and slippery, the girth of Sir Omer too wide to put her arms about it. In order not to fall off she had to clutch at his tightly buckled leather belt which cut her fingers. At each turn Guillebaut poked her with his steel elbow-piece, and complained bitterly that she was nothing but a hindrance to him, yet when she begged him to let her ride behind a squire or another knight he only shrugged his shoulders and sneered. Nor would he allow her to walk though at the slow pace they were going she could have kept up with the riders. But, a noble lady could not amble on foot like a servant! So she arrived at Byzantium withered, embittered, forever inwardly cringing from the blows that life might still keep in store.

Once in camp, under the walls of Byzantium, she could rest at last and for days on end she did not leave her tent. Her own maids-in-waiting and her two friends, Guenon and Alberta, wives of Norman nobles, told her with rapture of the wealth and beauty of Greek life. She listened with bated breath, as one might listen to a fairy tale, not even dreaming to behold with her own eyes these wonders that lay so close to the camp. She well knew that Sir Omer would never permit it.

He himself rode every day to the city. For all his hatred and contempt for women, he craved their company. It did not take him long to discover the Byzantine districts where paid love was offered complacently to all comers. There he satisfied his gloomy lust, only to vent the contempt he felt for the Greek trollops upon the blameless Willibald. Time had not healed the wound inflicted by his first wife, the only being he ever loved and trusted, a beautiful woman who had betrayed him. On the contrary, as years passed, the sense of injury grew and rankled, adding gall to a naturally sullen disposition. This continual obsession with women, combined with the loathing of womankind had at last so warped Sir Omer's mind, that he began to ascribe all worldly evil to women and women alone. Lying in his tent, tormented by the recollection of the Greek wench he had possessed only a few hours before, he writhed with hatred for Willibald. She thought she could deceive him with her pretense of virtue, he said to himself, fiercely sneering in the dark—she thought she could outsmart him. Well, a Norman could be cheated only once, and with a threatening gesture, he shook his hand, in which he still felt the smooth roundness of the Greek woman's body, in the direction of the straw bed where his poor, tormented wife lay asleep.

Florine let her hands drop into the warm water. The boat glided swiftly, leaving behind a wake in the shape of a swallow's tail. It was one of the beautiful, narrow, light court boats, profusely gilded and carved, that the Basileus provided for the pleasure and comfort of his noble guests. The Danish royal prince Swennon sat by his betrothed's side so close that their shoulders touched. The moon, brighter than in France, stood high in the sky, filling with copper glow the furrow plowed by the boat, and all around lay the strange deep silence of a Byzantine spring night. The city walls which seemed to grow straight out of the sea glowed white in the moonlight and the dark waters were smooth and unruffled.

Florine's duenna, a stout woman of ripe years, dozed; the moon no longer affected her. Two pages crouching in the prow looked straight ahead at the distant city lights, so that the betrothed felt that they were quite alone in this night which had thrown about them a magic cloak of illusion, woven of moonlight, the pungent smell of herbs that grew on the shore, and the gentle splash of water. Every earthly thing had suddenly changed to beauty and, seen through this fairylike haze, the world was gloriously right and life an endless rapture.

In the steeples of monasteries, bells began to toll, calling the time of the first night watch and suddenly the two lovers were overcome with a craving for sacrifice; thankful for the bliss they had experienced, they wanted in turn to pay the highest price. In the fullness of their joy they felt the all-too-human urge to sacrifice their personal happiness for the sake of a great dream.

Moved by this quick, passionate hunger, Florine, the hot-headed Burgundian, who knew no restraint save that which was self-imposed, was the first one to draw away from her lover. "Do you not think, my Lord," she said quickly, "that we should vow not to touch each other until we enter Jerusalem?"

He glanced at her, full of admiration, but also of misgivings, and he was silent. He was afraid to take a vow so lightly and thoughtlessly, and then break it, in the way of this world.

"I do not know whether we will be able to keep it," he said hesitantly. "Better not vow at all than to break our oath afterwards."

"Oh! but we *will* keep it," she assured him with childish earnestness. "God will help us. Will you vow, my Lord?"

"Be it so!" he said slowly.

"Then let us take the vow together."

And heedless of the startled glances of the pages, they knelt in the boat and, taking each other by the hand, they said softly and solemnly:

"Jesus Christ, our Lord and Saviour, upon Thy Most Holy Wounds we vow not to embrace each other, not to kiss each other, and not to touch each other till we set Thy Holy Sepulcher free. So help us God. Amen."

They unclasped their hands and resumed their seats, but now their shoulders no longer touched. They were staring straight ahead at the water, at the golden trail of moonlight, filled with a sense of greatness, proud and yet a little frightened. And after a short while, they ordered the oarsmen to turn back.

The reception for the Latin barons was held in the Onyx Hall, a smaller, more intimate room than the great *Christotriklinion*. In the Onyx Hall guests were allowed to sit down. They had only to rise when answering questions put to them by the Basileus. They were allowed also to converse with members of the imperial family, provided, of course, that they were addressed by them first. An invitation to such an informal gathering was considered a great honor, and, as a rule, was reserved for visiting royalty.

All the barons but Tancred had taken the oath. Raymond St. Gilles had not altogether given in; for him the words of the oath had been changed to require only a promise that he would take no conquered lands for himself, and that he would not lift his sword against the Basileus. Alexius, a politician always willing to settle for the best he could get, had accepted the compromise. He wanted no further delay in getting rid of the crusaders, whose stay in Byzantium was costing him too dearly. But while the other barons and their knights were showered with costly gifts, Raymond and his men received nothing. Neither Raymond nor Tancred attended the reception.

The Basilissa Irene also was not present; she was exhausted due to overlong fasting. In her place at the side of Alexius sat his eldest daughter, Anna Porphyrogenita, once heiress to the throne. She regarded the Latins with scorn. Heedless of her father's angry glances she snickered as the harsh names were pronounced and smiled in amusement at Gontrane's dowdy dress, rough skin, and frost-bitten hands.

But as her eyes swept over the crowd she caught sight of Boemund. Here, she thought, is one who looks like a human being. She examined his handsome face, tall stature, wide shoulders, and slim hips. She noticed that he was more carefully dressed than the others, that his fingernails were clean and evenly trimmed.

Catching her glance, Boemund immediately went to her, bowed low, and broke ritual by addressing her first.

"You are wondering at these foreign knights, Madame? No doubt we seem terrible oafs."

She liked his voice; it was warm and melodious. Without thinking she said, "Oafs? Not you, certainly."

"We possess neither your treasures nor your wisdom," said Boemund. "But we possess youthful vigor and strength. To us will belong the world."

"The world belongs to us, the only rightful heirs to the mighty Roman Empire," Anna said.

"It is more apt to give itself to a bold conqueror than to the holder of a long extinct right," said Boemund.

He bent so close that she felt his breath. He whispered, "But you deserve to rule by the present right of your beauty."

He turned and lost himself in the crowd while she marvelled at his ability to strike the one vulnerable spot in her armor. She hated the brother who would precede her to the throne.

The Basileus charmed everyone. He beguiled Adhemar and Stephen with his learning, Godfrey with his piety, and the other barons with his knowledge of warcraft. He seemed affable, simple, and open-hearted. After a bit of hesitation he acceded to his own suggestion and took his guests to visit the secret treasure rooms of the palace.

They were hidden deep in the labyrinth of subterranean passages which lay under the great building. The slaves who had built them had not come out alive. Only the ruling emperor and a single guardian knew of their whereabouts.

The Western knights were lead through countless corridors, halls, and down dozens of passages and flights of stairs. Suddenly they found themselves standing beside a cistern so large that it seemed like an underground lake. Casually Alexius explained that the city had no water supply of its own. Aqueducts brought the supply from wells several miles away. In time of siege, the aqueducts could be broken. Therefore the city was honeycombed with cisterns for holding enough water to serve the populace for seven or eight years.

A barge carried them across the cistern, after which they went through more passages and down more steps until at last they reached the treasury. The guardian lit lamps suspended from the ceiling by golden chains. The walls were made of narrow bricks harder than granite, made from a secret formula. All over the floor lay strewn the most fantastic wealth possible to imagine, as if careless workmen had shovelled it up from a ditch.

Gold was stacked from the floor to the ceiling—in bars, in bricks, in ducats, in round discs that gleamed like yellow wax, and in piles like sand. Heaped up like grain were bushels of pearls, precious stones, and gems. Along the wall stood golden armor, golden statues, golden thrones, chains, and vestments. The visitors staggered and held their breath. Alexius walked about as if displaying pets in a barnyard.

"Please pick from here whatever strikes your fancy," he said. "I shall be glad to give it to you as a token of true friendship."

The knights pretended indifference and selected the smallest and least precious objects. But Alexius took more costly gems and put them in their hands. Boemund would take nothing.

"There is but one jewel I would accept," he said looking straight into the emperor's eyes. "It is the ring which Princess Anna wears on her finger."

Alexius flushed.

"You proceed swiftly, sir," he said. "Before yesterday you asked only for the title of Protosebastos. You should be aware that some goals are unobtainable."

"Not to one of my lineage," said Boemund.

Alexius turned away, angry at being reminded that Beomund's father, Guiscard, had almost captured Byzantium. Only a narrow military margin had prevented Boemund from sitting in Alexius' place. It was easy for Alexius to read his thoughts. He wanted to win the hand of Princess Anna, back her against her brothers, and get the throne for her, sharing it with her.

When the party again reached the Onyx Hall messengers were awaiting Alexius. Tancred, they said, had seized Genoese vessels, embarked his troops upon them, and sailed to the other shore. He had escaped to Asia without taking the oath. Alexius turned to Boemund.

"I am awaiting an explanation of your nephew's deed," he said. "You are responsible for him."

"My nephew is a dubbed knight and fully responsible for himself," said Boemund. "I knew nothing of his intentions."

Alexius smiled. "Not long ago in explaining Tancred's refusal to take the oath you described him to me as a callow youth completely dependent upon you. How easily you change your mind."

"Not as easily as you," said Boemund. "You would poison your own ally and a crusader to boot. Immediately upon my arrival you sent me a collation from your own board. Had not the Holy Virgin appeared to me and ordered me to fast that day, I would have eaten it. My dog did eat of it and died horribly of poison."

Alexius blushed. "Nonsense," he said.

Boemund smiled. "That is why Tancred escaped to Asia," he said. "He was afraid of your hospitality."

He strolled away and joined the other knights, who were talking of Tancred's feat. Alexius came and bade them all farewell. When they were gone he called his lieutenants.

"I thought we had decided not to poison Boemund," he said. "Who put it into his food?"

No one knew: an investigation was begun at once. When he was getting into bed the Basileus received a report. No poison had been put in Boemund's food. His men had eaten the collation sent to them with great relish and with no discomfort. Only Boemund himself had refrained. He had been afraid.

"Is that certain?" asked Alexius.

"Absolutely certain."

"Amazing," said Alexius. "The man is a true Ulysses . . . and to think that I believed him . . . perhaps his dreams are not so foolish after all."

21.

Satan Again . . .

AFTER MANY FRUITLESS ATTEMPTS, ADHEMAR DE MONTEUIL LOST HOPE OF
making the acquaintance of the Greek Patriarch Simeon. The old
dignitary of the Eastern Church felt a strong antipathy for the Latins.
Neither he nor his Acolytes would ever believe that if the Roman
Bishop wanted to meet them it was out of pure and friendly curiosity
and not with the hidden purpose of converting them back to Rome.
This fear was enhanced by an unconscious yet rankling sense of inferi-
ority with regard to the Mother Church which had remained independent of secular power and continued to defy it, while they, the eldest
among Christians, submitted slavishly to the will of the Basileus.

The aversion of the Greek high clergy was shared by monks, abbots,
and almost all lay dignitaries. Between the Latins and Greeks stood an
impassable wall of mutual prejudices which it would take long, long
years to overcome. Meanwhile, the best side of Byzantine life, its
science, learning, art, industry, commerce, and culture remained closed
to the crusaders. Only lust, tawdry love affairs, and luxury were open to
them, and they wallowed in them like flies in honey. Godfrey was not
the only one to complain bitterly that he no longer recognized his own
men. The tough warriors of the West disintegrated with surprising
rapidity in these new surroundings. Solemn vows were soon forgotten.
Many a knight who had vowed not to touch a woman before the Holy
Sepulcher was set free was seen time and again in the company of the
gay Greek women. They drank, they ate, they slept on such down as
they had never before known and, seeing that money made all these
comforts available, they began to value it as never before. Many thought
with grief of the moment when they would have to leave Byzantium
and wished they could stay here forever; they found endless excuses to

delay the moment of their departure for Asia, though actually no obstacles now stood in the crusaders' way.

At the head of these lovers of Greece and Greek women stood Hugh
de Vermandois and Robert of Normandy. And they could always
count on the debauched and crafty Arnuld de Rohes to suggest new
reasons for delay.

According to Arnuld, the crusaders ought to start at the same time as
the Basileus and not before. For the Basileus had promised solemnly to
follow them with his entire army led by Euforbenos Kalatos. The noble
Butumitos would start at the same time as the Latins; so would the fleet
which was to protect the shore.

"If we start first," Hugh and Robert told the council, "the rascal will
not move at all. He is only pulling wool over our eyes to get rid of us.
Once we go, he will never budge."

"If we wait till he gets ready, we shall waste months," the Bishop objected. "Guy, Boemund's brother, has told us how much time it takes."

And indeed, every trip the Basileus took required a remarkable
amount of time, preparation, and money. The rules and regulations per-
taining to such an expedition had been set down in detail in the Book of
Court Protocol compiled for Constantine VII, and not a particular
could be altered. According to this book the Most High Autocrator and
his field retinue required a thousand horses, a thousand mules, and two
thousand men. Several hundred officials as well as a few high field dignitaries such as the *Epict* equary, the *Drongario* guard, who received
personally from the Basileus the evening passwords, *idicos,* and the
oiciacos, or supervisors of the imperial kitchen—led this army, not less
important than the real one.

Horses and mules, caparisoned with purple and branded with imperial
insignia, carried huge loads of clothing, bedding, costly kitchen vessels,
tableware, and provisions. In addition to wine, olives, almonds, white
flour, cheese, fats, dried fruit, perfumes, oils, and rare delicacies carried
on horse or mule-back, herds of sheep and cattle followed the cortege,
along with wagons loaded with crates of chickens, hens, and geese. A
special team of fishermen with nets was entrusted with the daily task of
supplying fresh fish. On other carts came candelabra, lamps, candles,
books, clocks, rolls of parchment, medicines, salves, and balms. One of
the golden tents could be set up as a portable chapel complete with costly
vestments, chalices, statues, and icons. All the imperial tents and fur-

nishings had to be carried in duplicate since as soon as the Basileus halted in one place, his servants hurried ahead to the next one to set up camp and await his arrival. The progress of an army encumbered with such a train was of necessity extremely slow.

"We will stay here till winter if we wait for Alexius," said Godfrey, as they gathered for the tenth consecutive meeting of the council. The meeting was held outdoors and all knights participated.

"It is better to start even in wintertime if by then our strength is doubled by the Basileus' army."

"Do you honestly believe that he will come?" Raymond exclaimed with heat.

"Aye, he will, no doubt, but after we win the first victory, not before."

No decision was made. In the warm spring sun those of the crusaders who still were pious visited churches. Knights who had succumbed to the soft breath of the East lolled with their mistresses. The Greeks, afraid their visitors would stay another winter, tried tactfully to get them on their way.

Suddenly, dramatically, the dallying Latins were shocked into action. One of the imperial galleys supplying food to the camp of Peter the Hermit returned with a dreadful tale. All of the peasant crusaders were dead, slain by the Saracens.

The massacre took place near Nicaea, where Walter the Penniless had led Peter's army. Walter, encouraged by the success of the first looting expeditions against the local population, had attacked the Turks. He had seized the fortress of Zerigordon and slain its garrison. After that, proud to be the first crusader to open the war on the Saracens, he had brought the whole camp as far as Nicaea. There, unguarded and unprepared for defense, the thirty thousand still left to Peter were attacked by a detachment of Sultan Kılıj Arslan's army.

The slaughter went on for three days until the Saracens found no one was left alive. Peter, Brother Hyacinth, and Bartholomew the jolly cleric, were absent on a visit to a shrine in a distant village. On the way back they met a few who had escaped and these they brought to Byzantium. With horror the knights listened to their story.

No council was called; it was not necessary. The knights struck their tents and prepared to leave. Alexius ordered his galleys to ferry them to Asia. Alexius himself, on a gold-caparisoned horse with a high crown on his head, watched the departure. All over the city monastery bells pealed. The Patriarch came to bless the departing army. Adhemar stood on the Asiatic shore addressing his men as they landed. The narrows were overed with vessels as though a moving bridge spanned the waters. Nearby the troops of Tancred waited to welcome their friends. The crusade had left Europe.

It was May of the year 1097.

22.

The Continent of God

AN IMMENSE CEMETERY OF BONES MARKED THE PLACE OF PETER THE Hermit's armies last stop. For miles around, the ground was white with bones. Beasts of prey had dragged skulls, ribs, hips, and thigh bones all over the hills, ravines, and thickets. No one would be able to collect his own on that last day, the day of judgment when all would come to stand in the valley of Jehosephat. Jackals from all Bithymia and Phrygia had been feasting here for weeks. At night they were frightened away by the lumbering lions that approached with careless step, pawed the pile of corpses, then turned away from the stinking offal. Over the swarms of jackals circled flocks of vultures, their screeching cries audible for miles around. Even today, though the bones had long whitened, they still sat on hilltops, crowing and waiting for a new and unexpected prey to appear.

A pious Iman in a great turban passed by twisting a rosary in his hand. With contempt he turned his eyes away from the filthy bones of the infidel. May Allah never show them his mercy, he thought. He had punished them, all praise to Him. They had come here like a pack of rapacious wolves and had perished. They had learned how mighty the Prophet was, may His name be praised. It was said that new and even more numerous hordes of infidels were approaching from Byzantium, but they would perish like these. Allah was great!

From a distant trail, Sultan Kilij Arslan wrote to the Emir Mudjahid, son of Djubaira, commander of the garrison of the mighty city, Nicaea, girdled with triple walls and guarded by three hundred bastions:

"Allah is great! I have been told by Abdullah, son of Nadjiha, who heard it from Abul Hadjadja, son of Abbassa, that many *giours* have crossed the Bosphorus and are coming toward you. Their number is equal to that of sand in the sea, or of stars in the sky. These are the multitudes bent on our destruction of whose coming we have been foretold for the last two years. But what will their number avail them, since the unfaithful dogs know neither discipline nor the art of war? They are going to their doom as inevitably as those whom our sword guided by the hand of the Prophet, may His name be praised, have stricken down. Tell my beloved wife, Djurisha, that her heart may rest at peace. No danger can threaten her from the approaching locust. It will be smashed to bits against the ramparts of the city, even as a wave of the sea is smashed against a rock. Let me know when the locust has fled or when you have destroyed it completely to the glory of the Prophet. Allah be with you!"

The old Emir Mudjahid, son of Djubaira, read the letter with proper respect and devotion. He finished, kissed the seal with a loud smack, and stretched himself again on the silken-covered sofa to consider its contents. This word of the infidels' approach was not news to him. His own scouts had informed him of it long ago, and he grieved that those who came from *Rum,* as Europe was called, were such a paltry adversary. Defeating such foe would bring no fame, no glory. Ah! the glory of a Holy War! Nothing could surpass it in the sight of Allah. For had the prophet not said: "Allah loves those who battle in defense of the Koran in ranks as close as a structure joined with lead." And had he not also said: "Whoever fights in a Holy War, even for a time as short as that which elapses between one milking of the camels and the next, may be certain of Paradise."

Oh, would Allah but send a Holy War to gladden the hearts of the faithful! Would he likewise send an enemy for whom it would be worth while to bring forth from the bottom of one's soul that most beautiful of all gems called valor. Emir Mudjahid rose and stretched his arms beseechingly in the direction of Mecca. Then, reflecting that such a reward must first be earned, he did not return to his soft couch but sat down to the previously begun task of copying the Koran. With the exception of hunting, this was his favorite occupation; it took up most of his days. During his lifetime he had copied the Holy Book forty-six times—twice in pure gilt. Meritorious as such an achievement was, how little did it count compared to one stand in a Holy War!

Bracing his hand firmly on the wooden support he wrote slowly, tracing with a soft brush letters which looked like beautiful, complicated scrolls woven into ornamental borders.

"When the hour comes which must come

"Naught will belie its coming.

"The hour that shall raise and humble.

"When the earth will shake and grieve.

"And mountains scatter into dust.

"Some shall stand on the right and others on the left.

"Those that are on the right.

"What of those on the right?

"Among trailing morning-glories and wide acacia trees.

"And long cool shadows.

"And countless fruits and high cushions and beautiful maidens,
   they will enjoy a life of bliss.

"Those who are on the right.

"They shall hear no strife, no reproaches—
   only the words: peace—peace.

"And those on the left.

"What of those on the left?

"In the torrid wind and cauldron—in the pall of tarry smoke,
   in hunger and degradation.

"Shall live those who have wallowed in riches.

"And had not believed in the Prophet.

"Or said: when we die and turn to dust will we ever rise again?

"Of the tree of hell, Zakkum, they shall eat,
   those who have thus erred.

"And their bowels shall be set aflame.

"And they shall quench the blaze with boiling water.

"Lapping like thirsty camels.

"Such will be their feast on the day of judgment."

Tired at last, Emir Mudjahid put the brush away.

Such, too, would be the fate of the infidels who were now approaching Nicaea, he reflected. They believed, it seemed, that Christ was God. What an erroneous, blasphemous notion! Jesus Christ was no doubt a worthy prophet, but he was far from the Great Prophet Mohammed, and only Allah was God. Oh, may Iblis possess the infidels!

Emir Mudjahid called a eunuch, repeated the message the sultan had sent to his beloved wife, Djurisha, who was staying in Nicaea and ordered him to carry it to her.

The eunuch ran through the many halls of the palace. In the marble courts fountains were playing, water trickled and sparkled in the sun. In the halls, thanks to wooden, intricately wrought lattices fitted into the windows, reigned a refreshing cool dusk tinged with color from the cut-glass lanterns which were set in the carved beams.

Djurisha lay on a bed of cushions, as beautiful as Aisha, the beloved wife of Prince Hamdanida, Sultan of Aleppo, of whom her maidservants were singing now to the accompaniment of zithers.

"Handsome and brave was Hamdanida, master of Aleppo. The most handsome and bravest of all the Faithful. Three hundred wives he had yet loved but one. Who was his beloved? A Christian she was, a Greek. Once a captive, now the Sultan's wife! The foremost among wives.

"The other wives, two hundred and ninety-nine, hated this impure creature whom their master loved. Secretly they conspired to kill and destroy her. One would give her poison, another run her through with a dagger, a third would tie a silken string about her white neck. So they schemed, not knowing that all the while the Sultan was listening to them . . ."

The eunuch who was waiting for the song to end stirred impatiently. Djurisha noticed him and asked:

"What do you want?"

"Great is the name of Allah! Emir Nudjahid, son of Djubaira, sends you these words conveyed in a letter from our master, Sultan Kilij Arslan."

Djurisha leaped from her cushions and folding her arms across her chest, bent low, thus assuming the posture in which it behooves a wife to listen to her master's words.

"The great Sultan wrote: 'May your heart rest in peace though swarms of infidels should appear in the valley around the city. They will smash themselves against the ramparts even as a wave upon the rocks."

"My heart is full of peace and joy that my Lord should have remembered me," Djurisha returned.

As a reward for the glad tidings she took a fistful of dates from a silver tray and handed it to the messenger. Then, reclining once more on the cushions, she motioned her slave to continue the tale.

Bishop Adhemar sighed heavily and tears flowed down his face as he contemplated the vast cemetery of unburied bones.

The knights who surrounded him dismounted, overwhelmed by the sense of guilt; for it was they who were responsible for the death of these innocent wretches. They had not hastened enough and because, like children they had to give vent to every emotion they felt, they fell to their knees, accusing themselves at the tops of their voices and pounding their steel covered breasts with mailed fists. Grief and repentance soon turned into a thirst for revenge. They had lingered in Byzantium, forgetful of the Saracens, but they would not forget them now, nor waste another hour. "Onward!" they cried.

And onward they marched through the fertile valleys of Bythnia, their column a brown and gray snake moving slowly in the sunlight. Their drab clothing and somber armor seemed alien to the bright Oriental world they had entered.

23.

Nicaea

BEYOND NIKOMEDIA, THE SEA, WHICH UNTIL NOW COULD BE SEEN FROM every promontory, fled to the west. The trail of the army veered eastward to Helenopolis, completely destroyed in the course of the last wars between Greeks and Saracens. Here, the enormous mountains of Arganton, their peaks capped with snow, barred the crusaders' way. They would have to cross them, break their way somehow through the narrow gorge, blocked by rocks and overgrown with briars. So after crossing a river called *Drako,* the "Snake," by the Greeks and the "River of Forty Fords" by the infidels, the army set up camp in the river valley, and four thousand men armed with axes and stakes were sent ahead to cut the road, roll away the rocks, and cut the thorny bushes. On the rocky, steep walls of the gorge, they carved crosses to mark the trail. And because whatever they did, they did stoutly and mightily, these deeply gashed crosses would remain visible for hundreds of years, and save many a future pilgrim from losing his way. They talked as they worked and at the sound of the familiar speech, strange, ghost-like figures emerged from crevices and thorny thickets,—Walter the Penniless and a few of his companions.

When the massacres started, they had fallen to the ground, feigning death, and had not stirred though tier after tier of fresh corpses fell on top of them. Suffocated, they lost consciousness, revived for a moment only to faint anew and so on and so on for three days while the massacre lasted. Then in the dark of night they were brought around by a fresh breeze. Somewhere, hard by, they heard sounds of growling, lapping, crunching. Lions and jackals were dragging corpses away. The wounded could see the sky overhead and painfully they dragged themselves to a nearby thicket.

Jackals, tails between their legs, backed up a few steps and, licking their chops, watched them in wonder. That which just a moment before had been a corpse was now crawling in the thickets. The instinct of life suddenly awakened told the moribunds to hide, to crawl under the hard thorns, where even the lions could not get them, to lie flat, and hold their breath. And so they lay. They licked their wounds like beasts. In the daytime they dragged themselves to water and out into the fields. They picked fruits that grew low, chewed unripe melons or sucked green awns of wheat. At night they retired into the stronghold of iron-hard thorns which tore and wounded their emaciated bodies. Thus they had existed awaiting they knew not what, until at last they heard the sound of axes and of familiar speech. At first they were taken for ghosts, but later when they had told their story, they were tended and fed. At the request of the Bishop, Raymond St. Gilles made Walter a gift of a complete new attire and a sword which he, as of old, hung around his neck. But even when clad and fed, the gaunt giant no longer was the bold, dour Walter of former days. At confession, he admitted, sobbing, to the Bishop, that the responsibility for the death of so many thousands of fellow Christians gnawed at his heart and made his soul shrink. Not knowing what to do with himself, since he would not join the horseless men at arms, and the knights looked at him with scorn, he hung around the Bishop's tent where already another human wreck, less guilty, but equally hapless, was forever huddling in a corner. Peter the Hermit, was now completely out of his mind. *"Kukupetros,"* the droll name given him in Byzantium, supposedly by the Princess Anna herself, clung to him permanently, and well befitted his present spiritual state. Peter, the inspired orator of Clermont, the man of God, the leader of worshipping throngs, had ceased to exist. He was gone. All that remained was *Kukupetros,* a pitiful halfwit who saw Satan everywhere, even in a cup of water.

The sight of the demented wretch could not be pleasant to Walter.

"Why did God spare us?" he would ask the Bishop. "I wish I had died three times over! Why should I and this poor nitwit survive? Where is the justice of it? All those others who perished and we two who are to blame, who are responsible for their coming, go on living. What for?"

"To repent," Adhemar answered gravely.

Nicaea, the first enemy stronghold that the crusaders were to encounter on their way to Jerusalem, had been in the hands of the Moslems only for the past fourteen years. Its walls, first raised by the Romans, were later strengthened by the Byzantines in their usual grandiose manner. They encircled the city with a triple ring four leagues long, from the ramparts at frequent intervals sprang square or round bastions: massively heavy, they seemed to peer into the distance with their small peepholes, and of these there were three hundred and seventy. From one side the city was protected by a steep wooded mountain, from the other its walls fell straight into the Lake Askalon, vast as a sea, so that, like the Greek Aphrodite, the stronghold seemed to rise directly from the sapphire depths. The lake extended far to the west where only a narrow strip of land divided it from the deep Nicaean Bay and the Mediterranean. The city itself was entered by three gates. The southern one opened on the great thoroughfare which crossed the desert and led to Antioch. In the Roman fashion it consisted of three marble archways, covered with beautiful bas-reliefs depicting the legionnaires of Emperor Diocletian, armed with spears and shields. Close by the eastern gate which likewise had three arches ran the aqueduct, which supplied the city with spring water from the mountains. In case of damage to this aqueduct the city was forced to use the water from the lake, which though fresh, was unpalatable and smelled of fish. The third gate opening toward Byzantium was built of gray marble. Set over the central arch a terrible head of a snaky-haired Gorgon guarded its approaches; its eyes were white and sightless, but the snakes seemed to scan watchfully everyone who approached the gate.

Emir Mudjahid, son of Djubaira, the pious copyist of the Koran and commander of the Nicaean garrison, stood on the ramparts close to the gate and watched the approach of the countless ranks of infidels.

"By the sandals of the Prophet, dusty with the dust of pilgrimage! This is a Holy War. Allah is great!" he muttered, pleased at the sight. The approaching columns in no way resembled the predatory bands dispersed two months ago. This was, indeed, a worthy, well-armed, well-equipped enemy.

Djurisha, the favorite wife of Sultan Kilij Arslan, did not share this enthusiasm. She too had ordered herself to be carried on the rampart so she might see the approaching foe. Muscular black eunuchs, with golden bands on their wrists and ankles, carried her costly litter, which a flock of carefully veiled female slaves surrounded.

At the sight of the retinue, the Emir bowed low. Though the curtains of the Sedan chair were tightly drawn and nothing inside could be seen, he covered his eyes with the end of his turban so that no one might suspect him of the wish to look into the face of the woman who belonged to the sultan.

"Mudjahid, son of Djubaira," Djurisha said, her voice muffled by the curtains. "I want you to allay my fears. Our lord and ruler, may God protect his days, wrote that the approaching infidels would be smashed against the city walls like a wave on the rocks. Our lord and ruler knows whereof he speaks. Allah inspires every word he says. Nevertheless, I am frightened. Mudjahid, son of Djubaira, tell me, did our lord know the strength of the infidels when he wrote these words to me? Did he know how many of them were coming? I fear, Mudjahid, son of Djubaira, that it will be they who overwhelm us. I am afraid for myself, afraid, likewise, for my son, who is the apple of the eye of my lord and master."

"Allah is great," Mudjahid replied serenely.

At these words, Djurisha burst into tears and the old Emir, cursing inwardly the whole womankind, began to assure her that Allah would support the faithful and not the infidel; and that Nicaea was not a city like any other. No one could besiege it on the side of the lake. The infidels had neither vessels, nor sufficient strength to encircle the lake. "Our own vessels are well concealed in the canal behind the outer wall. Fear nothing, Djurisha!"

Djurisha sighed, and ordered her slaves to proceed. But whenever she looked the same sight met her eyes. Endless columns of armed men poured toward the city. On they swept from three sides like three mighty rivers. At the sight of the defenders standing on the walls they lifted their fists threateningly and shook their lances. The shout of "God wills it!" rolled over the ranks like thunder. It was accompanied by the thump of drums, a novelty acquired in Byzantium, where it in turn had been adopted from the Saracens themselves. Harshly, threateningly blared the wooden and silver horns, as amidst the martial din of shouts, drums, and horns, the army of the crusaders took up its positions. Godfrey and Baldwin set camps to the east of the city, the two Roberts, Tancred, and Stephen de Blois to the north, Raymond St. Gilles to the south, thus cutting the road through which reinforcements might come to the help of the besieged. Only from the lake the city was left unwatched since water itself would guard it from this side.

The mighty walls presaged a long and hard siege, so the Latin troops began to fortify their camps without losing time. Sods flew under the spades of ditch diggers, pastures in which the horses were to graze were fenced in. Whole detachments carried faggots, branches, and tree trunks. Within two days they had stripped all the surrounding hills of their green mantle of forests while the frightened birds and beasts fled far inland. The shores of the lake were strewn with withered branches and leaves and still the besiegers were short of wood. It took an immense amount of timber to surround with palisades three camps each large enough to hold a hundred thousand men. Soon the supply was exhausted. Nor was there enough of the brush to be tied into fences which would close the openings in the enclosures, and the good warriors did not feel like going far to look for it.

But if wood was scarce, there were plenty of bones, human bones. They shone, white wherever one looked . . . Sharp and strong, they would be just the thing with which to prop the fences.

The Normans were the first ones to load them on carts to be used in fortifications. Others at first recoiled at such desecration, saying that this was no way to treat Christian bones which ought to be buried in hallowed ground, not used for fences. The Provençals, always hostile to the Normans, went to the Bishop to complain.

The Bishop pondered long before he answered: "How do you know the sufferings of these unfortunates who must be now in purgatory will not be eased because at least their bones will help in the Holy Cause?"

Of course the Bishop was right. Why had no one thought of it before? And the same men who had gone to complain now began to pick assiduously the bones spread far and wide over the fields.

Independently of these preparations, from the ranks of the foremost knights upon the fields which separated the city from the camp, skirmishers rode out. Armed only with sword, lance, and shield they rode up to the very gates challenging the infidels. Nor did it take the Saracens long to take up the challenge. A postern in the side arch opened and a small bridge was thrown across the moat. One after another, Saracen warriors came riding out, clad in bright blue, yellow, and crimson silks, their wide sleeves billowing in the wind. Light, gilded plates covered their breasts and backs, brilliant-hued turbans enwrapped their helmets; they carried round shields on their left arms and sabres of the famed Damascan steel in their hands; they shone and glittered in the sun like gorgeous insects as they rode up to the Latins, their small beautiful horses stepping high and prancing. And so the tilting began, while from both sides hundreds of thousands of men looked on in breathless suspense. What indeed, would be the outcome of this encounter between agility and lightning speed on one hand and cumbersome, iron-clad might on the other? The iron men of the West were confident of their superiority. Their chargers wore chamfrons—sharp steel spikes on their foreheads, their chests were covered with steel, their rumps with iron-mesh caparisons. The deep narrow saddle with a high horn back and front protected the belly of the knight though at the same time it hampered his movements. In truth, once mounted a knight could bend neither forward nor back. He must sit stiffly with his legs stretched straight.

De Melun, one of the best skirmishers, snorted derisively at the sight of the pagans—why, they were mere striplings—and with lance at half tilt and visor raised as behooved at skirmish-time, he made straight for Ibrahim, son of Mudjahid.

The Saracen stood still staring at his assailant as though in wonder. He did not move. Under the hoofs of the French stallion, the earth shook and trembled. Surely the lance would pierce the unwary youth. But no! Even as the pale lips of the Emir, who stood on the ramparts uttered, "Allah is great!" Ibrahim leaped to the side. The lance ran through empty air. Carried away by the speed the knight could hardly stop his mount. At last he turned around and foaming with rage, charged again. Again he gathered speed, tilted his lance and . . . missed the nimble pagan. To make matters worse, Ibrahim's sharp javelin, thrown with an unerring hand, struck him painfully in the head, denting the plate of his helmet. Panting with passion, De Melun drove the butt of his lance into the earth and with both hands grabbed his sword, first spitting in his palms, not so much from fear that the hilt would slip as protection against pagan charms. Twirling his sword over his head, he approached now more slowly, watching carefully every move of his opponent. The air hissed under the impact of the heavy sword. The crooked saber of Ibrahim flashed in the sun. They met. The mighty sword came down with a whistle into the void—the flashing saber rattled ineffectually against the steel gorget and brassarts. This game could not go on indefinitely until both opponents were exhausted. De Melun fumed; never before had he met with such an adversary. He was so furious that when at a certain moment Ibrahim and his swift agile horse had once more leaped away and he, pursuing them at full speed, encountered another Saracen skirmisher, he swung his sword with the whole strength of impotent fury and cut the rider in two, cut him clear through like a tree in the forest. The trunk and head fell to the ground, while the quivering thighs still held the horse, spouting a fountain of blood. Shouts of anguish rose from the walls, shouts of indignation and glee from the ranks of the crusaders. Of indignation since it was not proper for a skirmisher to assail anyone until he had overcome his first opponent, of glee because the first to fall was a Saracen—a good omen for the future. Heedless of shouts but alert to what to him was most important, the squire of the Carpenter was already removing the corpse's armor and rounding up his horse.

"Allah is great," whispered Emir Mudjahid, as Ibrahim, the pride of his old eyes, turned upon De Melun again. Once more they closed in their deadly dance. The great sword clattered, the saber rapped sharply . . .

But just then the horns began to blare in the camps, calling the crusaders to Angelus. The skirmishers must leave the field. The day's work was done. On the pagan's side five men had fallen, on the Christian side three—two knights, Roger de Forez and Baldwin du Gand, and a squire. The first to fall, all honor to them, would be solemnly buried on the morrow.

"Allah is great," repeated Emir Mudjahid for the third time and quickly left the ramparts so he might touch (for it would not become him to embrace) his returning son. Aye, this indeed was a Holy War! The smooth mirror of the lake reflected the city walls and white clouds in the sky. On the balconies of the minarets stood muezzins, and bowing in the direction of Mecca called in singsong voices that Allah was God and there was none greater than He.

And from the crusaders' camps horns, bells, and the singing of a hundred thousand men proclaimed that the Christian God was one and there was none greater than He. Aye, God was one and there was none greater than He!

A month went by and still the situation continued unchanged, although the activity of the besiegers went on unabated. Time and again the knights would set up their all too short ladders against the walls, only to have the Moslems push them away with long perches and send them, climbing men and all, crashing on the heads of those below. So far the besiegers had only succeeded in filling the moats with dirt and brush and in completely destroying the surrounding countryside. Otherwise the fortress still stood as it had always stood within the triple ring of its walls, behind iron gates which neither fire nor axe would dent.

So until the siege towers were ready there was nothing else to do but to batter the walls with log rams and adz. And a thankless task it was. The Moslems showered the besiegers with rocks, scalding water, tar, and rags soaked in resin and set aflame. To protect themselves from these missiles the crusaders used a formation called "the turtles." Working in pairs, while one wielded the ram, the other held his shield raised to protect himself and his companion. To tell the truth, the scalding water thrown from such height cooled quickly in the air, nor could tar and burning rags set fire to armor and leather jerkins, so that the losses suffered by the crusaders did not exceed a thousand men. They were fairly safe provided they did not raise their faces, for whoever did that courted almost certain blindness.

Thus, with heads hidden under raised shields over which water splashed, and tar congealed in sticky pendents, the men-at-arms battered at the wall. Rubble fell, lime dust hung in the air like smoke. When the arms of those who held the shield grew numb, they changed around, the shield-bearers taking a turn at the rams. And again they would knock at the walls like so many woodpeckers.

But when at last they had penetrated deep into the masonry, so that the wall began to sway, the pagans started to drop on the heads of the diggers whole basketfuls of live snakes. Black and copper-colored, spotted and striped, small and large, they fell hissing among the men at arms and twined themselves about legs and arms. This was more than even the knights could bear. At the touch of reptiles, which in their minds were all one with Satan, they recoiled in disgust and horror. They who never retreated drew back in panic, leaping away from the walls and tearing off the hateful twine. They trampled the snakes beneath their feet and hacked at them with whatever they could grab, till a myriad segments writhed on the ground. The pagans howled in glee and pushed away the ladders, until now firmly held in place by the besiegers. Seeing the success of this new weapon they began to throw snakes more often in ever larger numbers. "Where did they get so many?

Was the city full of reptiles?" the knights often wondered. There was but one plausible explanation. Magic. The loathsome heathen priests who from the top of the minarets called Saracens to prayer, must doubtless turn city stones to snakes.

What was worse, the crusaders soon discovered that contrary to all knightly customs they must battle after sunset, after dark, like common robbers. Until now they had always fought with other Christian knights, abiding by the same rules. According to those rules, at the time of the Angelus the combatants left the field; the blaring of horns announced that the battle would recess until morning. This recess was faithfully kept by both sides, for the night was no fit time for honest strife. At night one might at best pursue thieves or chase after wenches; it was the time for conspiracy and betrayal, loathsome to any true knight.

Now, were the Saracens true knights or were they not? Brave they were indeed, none braver, though, in the Latins' eyes they were disgustingly sly and dishonest, for they did not abide by the rules of honest strife. Every night for a long time they had by means of ropes climbed down the walls and repaired the damage done by the diggers in the daytime, filling the breaches with rocks and brush, tamped with sand.

At first the besiegers, rushing back into action in the morning and seeing how little they had accomplished the previous day, were convinced that here as in the case of the snakes some magic was at work. Soon, however, Boemund's men espied the nightly sorties of the enemy. Startled and aggrieved by their discovery, the Latins decided to abandon their time-honored customs and to fight like the pagans, irrespective of the hour. The Bishop absolved them from responsibility and was the first one to encourage this course. From now on each unit would be divided into two parties, of which one would batter the walls during the day and the other keep watch at night. At the same time it was decided not to engage in skirmishes. No, not even on Sunday. Let the Saracens see in what contempt they held a foe who fought so unfairly.

No one was more perturbed by the latter decision than Sir William de Melun, who could not forgive himself for letting Ibrahim, son of Mudjahid, escape him unharmed. Vehemently, he assured everyone that he would not leave Nicaea until he had found and defeated him in single combat.

"And mind you, whoever starts to fight with him before I get my chance will answer for it to me," he threatened.

One day Elvira's pages came running after Raymond St. Gilles imploring to be released from the duty of carrying the fan and handkerchief of Her Ladyship and allowed to climb the walls in His Lordship's wake. In truth, in the last two years the pages had grown from small lads into stout youths, with long arms, big feet, and clumsy motions. They had long since outgrown their white-and-blue page garbs: the hose barely reached the knees, the long open sleeves had become too short, and hung as limply as rags. The boys felt ridiculous and craved a more manly employ, and Raymond would have gladly yielded to their pleas but Elvira would not even hear of it. What, she said. Did he want her to give up her usual retinue? What a preposterous idea!

As the time passed the heat became almost unbearable. The sun beat down with a fierceness they had never known before. The countryside stripped of forests had not even a bit of shade to offer and the knights began to regret that in their over-zealous haste they had cut all the trees. The logs they needed now for the construction of siege towers had to be hauled from a distance of several miles.

When at last the material was assembled a new difficulty arose. How were the towers to be built? There were no skilled carpenters in any of the camps, nothing but professional warriors. The carpenters had perished along with other artisans in the throngs of Peter the Hermit. Of course every knight knew full well that a siege tower had to be a stout log structure looking somewhat like a belfry, that on one side there ought to protrude a battering ram that would strike the wall with great force, that there had to be several floors on which archers, spearmen, and knights might stand, and that it all must be set on wheels which would permit the mighty wooden bastion to move along the walls. They knew all this but how was a siege tower to be built? How did one go about fitting the logs in place? In each camp, axes were knocking persistently but thus far the results were meager. The laboriously erected structures were clumsy, and turned over at any uneven spot, the ram would not work, or else the tower was so heavy that it sank in the ground and would not be moved at all.

And so, one day, heedless of the heat, Adhemar de Monteuil took Hugh de Vermandois, the Count d'Haineault, and several squires and went to the Greek camp to call on Butumitos. There were two reasons for this visit. The Bishop had been told that Butumitos was sick and wanted to see for himself whether that dignitary was actually ailing, or only pretending to be ill in order to stay away from the fighting. He also wanted to ask him for the loan of men skilled in the construction of siege towers.

The sun scorched the earth mercilessly. Grasshoppers buzzed in the parched, ash-gray grass and almost against his will the Bishop recalled how the same countryside had looked a month before. He felt a pang of unbearable sadness; for nothing but desolation remained, a land burned by the sun, stripped of its vegetation, and permeated with the stench of corpses which the besiegers threw in the lake to make the water undrinkable for the besieged. The attempt proved vain since Nicaea, like Byzantium, possessed ample reserves of water in its cisterns. Instead the corpses piled up into banks at the shore and poisoned the air and the water which the crusaders, not the pagans, had to breathe and drink.

"I must order that all these bodies be buried without fail," the Bishop told his companions. "This stench might verily bring on pestilence."

"Indeed, it might," D'Haineault assented absently. He was completely engrossed in his own troubles. He had begged the Bishop to take him along to the Greek camp in the hope that there, perhaps, he might learn something about Ida. She must have come to Byzantium, by now, or at least have sent some news. He was torn by an ever growing anxiety and as he rode now to the Greek camp he tried to comfort himself with the hope, vain and foolish as he knew it to be, that he might find Ida there. He told himself that perhaps she had arrived from Byzantium yesterday or even this very morning and had had no chance yet to let him know.

"Pestilence is sure to break out," Hugh chimed in with his usual unconcern. "But as for burying the corpses, I am afraid that our men will find it too much bother."

The Bishop did not reply, for the handsome sluggard was right. They would never consent to bury corpses, and pagan corpses at that. The order given by the Bishop would remain a pious wish, like so many others. Bitterness choked him at the thought of his title and responsibility backed by no authority whatsoever.

The area of waste and destruction ended abruptly at the confines of the Greek camp. Here, as of old, trees grew, and grass was green. Roped-off paths ran from tent to tent, from enclosure to paddock. All litter and refuse was promptly gathered and immediately burned or buried. Order reigned everywhere.

"Our lords could learn plenty from the Greeks," remarked the Bishop, looking about him with envy.

"That's what I always say," exclaimed Hugh enthusiastically. "Look at these comforts! Oh! the rascals know how to live."

"Yes," continued the Bishop, "but there's no telling whether there would be such order here were they like ourselves engaged in combat for the last four weeks."

"Very true. Will your Grace permit me to ride ahead?"

"Go ahead."

D'Haineault sped off at a gallop.

Butumitos was really sick. He was suffering from a fever, which was common in these parts. His face looked pinched and his skin was yellow, but the doctors believed that the ailment was now on the wane. He lay in his spacious and beautifully adorned tent. It was cool and breezy in there, thanks to two eagle wings attached to the ceiling and set in motion by a string pulled by a slave, and the gleaming white bedding looked so fresh that Hugh sighed with envy.

The Greek captain welcomed his guests affably, thanking them for coming. Slaves brought them soft seats, bowls of perfumed water in which to wash their hands, and wine tinkling with pieces of ice misty in opalescent glass goblets.

The hot and weary visitors took them in their hands with a keen sense of pleasure, though wondering at heart where the ice had come from. Meanwhile Butumitos expressed his surprise that the noble Latin lords should have refused his offer of Greek Fire. It would have helped them to start conflagrations within the city itself and thus weaken the courage and resistance of the besieged.

"We will see. We will see. Our knights are not used to this manner of weapon," replied the Bishop evasively. "There is, however, another favor we wish to ask of you: we lack men who know how to construct siege towers, and without siege towers we will not capture the city. So if you have such men will you let us have them? To us they will mean more than fire."

Butumitos stared thoughtfully at his own well-groomed fingernails, then glanced toward the corner of the tent where in an attitude of respectful expectation sat Pantopulos, famous constructor of war machines.

Should he or should he not ask him to come nearer, he wondered. After a moment's reflection he decided to wait. There was no hurry. No telling yet what turn the game he was playing might take.

"Unfortunately," he said aloud, "though I have run in my mind through all my men, I find none who could help you. But don't let that trouble you, Your Grace. I will send immediately to Byzantium asking for the foremost carpenters to be sent here at once."

"We will be greatly obliged," the Bishop assured him while his penetrating eyes scanned the other's face. Instinctively he had sensed his hesitation. What did it mean? If only one could see through these Greeks! The chilled wine was delightfully cool to the palate, the slowly moving wings stirred up a refreshing breeze, everything around was comfortable, soft, and yet so alien, strange, insincere . . .

Now the conversation turned to the Saracens, to their character and modes of warfare. The Bishop was always eager to collect information and Butumitos proved a learned and interesting informant. He told them that the name of "Saracens" was as loosely applied as that of "Agars." In reality the Moslems were a conglomeration of countless tribes, once unfriendly to each other, which Islam had combined into one and incited to set forth against the West.

"And what does Your Grace think of them as opponents? Brave, are they not?"

"Brave, yes, but terribly wily. We have just discovered that at night, stealthily, they were repairing the walls. So now we are going to watch them even after dark."

Butumitos was so astonished that he sat up in bed.

"What does Your Grace mean?" he asked. "Did you not watch them up to now?"

"We are accustomed to fight like true knights: only from sunrise to sunset."

Butumitos sank back and closed his eyes for a moment. Such simpleheartedness rendered him speechless.

"During the day we watched them closely, of course," continued the Bishop, a little nettled. "Now we will do the same at night. The orders are already issued. In the daytime not even a bird could fly through our lines . . . And this, my Lord, is not just a figure of speech but the honest truth, for when day before yesterday a pigeon flew out of the city our knights espied him at once."

Butumitos, his curiosity aroused, sat up once more.

"And what then?" he asked.

The Bishop did not understand the question.

"Nothing. It flew off into the wide world."

"Didn't they shoot it down?"

"No."

"Good God! How could they let it go? In which direction did it fly?"

"It was flying over our camp so it must have gone to the south. Why do you ask, my Lord? Can the direction of a pigeon's flight have any particular meaning?"

"Sometimes it might . . . So it flew southward? Tell me, Your Grace, do you anticipate the possibility of help coming to the stronghold? Kilij Arslan's wife and son are in Nicaea. He will, doubtless, hasten to their rescue. Are you ready for that?"

"Kilij Arslan, I was told, is a hundred leagues away. He can't possibly know what is going on here. And anyway there is no need for special preparations. When they come, God willing, we will defeat them. That is all. Our knights only pray to God for a battle."

For the third time Butumitos was overcome with wonder. No Greek had heard such words for a long, long time. Yet though he shared all the weaknesses and failings of his declining race, the old captain was a soldier. He could appreciate such spirit. From some dark recess of his memory arose the rankling recollection of a letter written by a Sultan to a Basileus who had dared refuse to pay tribute. The letter read:

"I have received your message, you unfaithful dog. You shall not hear my answer. You will see it."

The Basileus took fright and hastily sent the tribute. Butumitos thought now, not without bitterness, that these barbarians would have acted otherwise.

He shook his head and stretched his hand for the frozen peaches, inviting his guests to taste them, too.

"Oh, a man breathes differently here," said Hugh, biting into the fruit with relish.

"It is true that these parts abound in everything. One ought to take full advantage of it since a short way beyond Nicaea lies a most arduous stretch of journey."

"How far is it from here to Jerusalem?" asked the Bishop. He had asked this question countless times in the last few months and never yet had he been given a definite answer. Now, too, Butumitos began to inspect his fingernails with thoughtful attention. How was he to know whether these Latins were determined and persistent enough to be told the truth and still continue on their way? They might decide instead to return to Byzantium.

"Quite far," he said at last. "Still not so far that it can't be reached. The whole world is not so big that it cannot be encompassed."

"Still, no one has gone around it yet," retorted the Bishop. To them, too, the world had once seemed small, and only waiting to be measured in knightly stride. Only in the last two years had it grown so vast and strange.

"No one has gone around it yet," he repeated. "Besides, this is not what I was asking. What I want to know is how long it takes to get to Jerusalem?"

"It depends on how fast one travels."

"At the rate an army would march."

"There is marching and marching. Some fast, some slow."

The Bishop bit his lips and promised himself never to ask again. It was always the same story. Everyone he asked would wriggle like an eel, eluding an honest answer. Why? What was behind this general conspiracy? Was the Holy Land much nearer than the Latins reckoned, or was it much, much farther?

He rose to his feet and took leave of their host, much to the sorrow of Hugh, who would far rather have remained in the Greek camp for a few days and who suggested that they should at least await the arrival of the promised carpenters.

They rode off, with D'Haineault silent and gloomy, dragging behind. He had received no news of Ida. Butumitos' camp maintained constant communication with Byzantium and he had been told that no galleys either from France or Italy had arrived at the City Protected by God during the last few weeks. Neither had any noble lady, wife of a crusader, come by land. But in that case what on earth could have happened to Ida?

.In his tortured brain loomed visions of sea storms (but the sea was calm at this time of year), of pirates (impossible—they had all joined the holy crusade), of sickness; then again he was seized by fear that she had simply forgotten him or preferred to remain home with the child rather than to set out into such a distant world. The thought clutched his heart like a viper thrown from the walls. How was he to find out? Where to turn for news? and how was he to go on living in such incertitude?

In the main square, by the carved well, a throng of men surrounded a storyteller. Dark swarthy men, with black shining eyes, some in turbans, some bareheaded, some dressed in loose brilliant colored mantles, some in rags, still others in nothing more than a loin cloth. But all of them men. Women stole by at a distance, carrying pails of scalding water, or bunches of arrows toward the ramparts, but stop they dared not. Their faces were covered with thick, black-veils. So the Prophet had ordered. A woman must be still as the night, dark as the night, and invisible as the night; a woman must be removed from life, and looked upon as unclean. He is a fool who believes her; he is a fool who puts his trust in her; for women are deceitful. According to the Koran, a woman who stayed alone with a man, be it only for as long as it took an egg to boil, could be accused of unfaithfulness. So women must be locked up and carefully guarded.

Thus burdened with the Prophet's displeasure, the women of Nicaea dared not mingle with the crowd of listeners. They passed by, sighing regretfully. Ah, stories! That greatest joy of all people of the Orient! Lest he lose the thread of the tale a husband would stop beating his wife, and the executioner halt in mid-air the sword descending on the neck of the condemned. At the sound of a storyteller's voice, litter-bearers set down the litter from which a high dignitary, as interested as themselves, would lean out, and merchants stopped haggling or bargaining or noisily praising their goods. Ah! the wonderful tales! Everyone was ready to listen to them forever, even as that bloody Sultan had listened to the wise Scheherezade through one thousand and one nights!

With a sigh Emir Mudjahid tore himself away from the crowd surrounding the storyteller and walked off. Duty before pleasure. A Holy War, the dream of all his life, was on and the son of Djubaira must not forget it even for a moment. He went to the palace where important matters awaited the decision of the council.

The streets were noisy and crowded, so that slaves had to open a path before the emir and the shieks who accompanied him. The Musselmen lived in the streets, seeking the protection of a roof only when the sun beat too hard. They cooked in the streets, ate on the streets, prayed, quarreled, and bargained in the streets. Despite two months of siege, the city showed no sign of starvation or gloom; for galleys, as yet undiscovered by the Crusaders, brought food every night from the other shore of the lake.

As he ascended the marble stairs of the palace, the Emir looked up gratefully to heaven while his lips unconsciously repeated his favorite sura of the Koran: "I said to my soul, frightened at the sight of a numerous foe, 'Shame to you. Why are you frightened? Long life rarely clothes a man in the cloak of fame. The garb of longevity befits only a weak and cowardly heart. Happy is he who shall fall in battle in the fullness of his strength, and a hundredfold happier and more blessed he who shall fall in a Holy War. Life is but a deceitful treasure. Every night robs it. Every day decreases it. It is not worth sparing.'"

La illah el Allah, Mohammed rasul Allah! Praised be the Holy War, the joy of a knightly heart!

The beautiful hall built by the Byzantines and adorned by the Arabs was pleasantly cool, thanks to the fountain which played in its center. It was called the Hall of the Clocks, because of its famous double clock of which not even Byzantium could boast the like. The clock consisted of two gilded dials placed on opposite walls. The one on the left showed the hours of the night, that on the right the hours of the day. Each was provided with twelve openings. These served as doors for the hours. At every hour of the day from the proper door in the right-hand dial emerged a golden hawk and from his beak dropped golden balls which fell into a golden bowl below.

When night came, the golden hawk returned to his nest and the opposite dial began to function. One after another the openings of the hours lighted up, blinking the time. This beautiful clock had been sent to the Sultan by the Calif of Bagdad himself. The central wall, opposite the entrance, showed a huge mosaic map made according to a drawing prepared by Ibn Istakri, son of the famous Nadar of Bassora. Within its large circle it encompassed all the known world of these times. On the north it was bound by what was called the Sea of Darkness; on the south by a white blank which represented the lands uninhabited on account of heat; on the east, by the China Sea; and on the west by *Rum* or Europe. This included France, Germany, Poland, Russia, and England which was called *Anclitara*. The outlines of these countries were by no means exact and their respective size and proportions highly inaccurate, and none of the northern countries, Denmark, Norway, or

Sweden appeared on the chart. North Africa, however, Arabia, Asia Minor, and the whole shore of the Mediterranean were depicted with surprising exactness as were the Mediterranean islands: Sicily, Candia, and Cyprus. The Nile, the father-river of fertile Egypt, sprang from the great lakes which the descendents of the crusaders would not discover until six hundred years later.

The map as well as the dials of the clock were framed by the same ornamental design which covered the walls and ceilings of the palace. This design, rich and exquisitely beautiful though it was, was apt to weary the eye, for it never varied. Here in Nicaea, in Antioch, Damascus, Cairo, Fez, Alhambra, Granada, it was always the same. The aridity of Islam, which forbade the reproduction of living forms, whether human or animal, had destroyed the beautiful, varied Persian art which once flourished in these parts.

Next to the Clock Hall was the laboratory of Alchemy, where the learned Ibn Idjak spent his days. The Emir himself held him in great esteem and often inquired about his experiments. Alchemy, no less than geography, had attained among the Arabs a high level of which the rest of the world had not the slightest conception. Already a hundred years before the Crusaders' arrival, Arabian scientists had discovered pure alcohol, that spirit of wine also hidden in fruits and in grains, which, though a demon accursed by the Prophet, possessed an inestimable value in medicine. They had likewise discovered sulphuric acid and the basic principles of the transmutation of metals. They believed that each body in nature, be it alive or seemingly dead, solid, liquid, or gaseous, consisted of the same basic elements; only their composition and proportions varied. Hence, they reasoned, by splitting matter into infinitely fine particles and combining these anew one could create any new body at will. The Arabic axioms were to become the basis of all the future efforts of the medieval alchemists of Europe.

The fountain gurgled gently. Emir Mudjahid sat down on a leather hassock with a sense of satisfaction. The news which the Agha Sheik had brought him was good, very good indeed. The galleys which arrived last night with a fresh load of snakes had also brought word that the Sultan was hastening to the rescue, coming in great strength, bringing along with him all the tribes, once hostile to each other but now joining hands to fight the infidels. Allah was great!

"Has Agida found someone to interpret the infidels' writing?" the Emir inquired suddenly.

Agida, his private adviser, stepped hastily forward from behind the motionless rank of sheiks. Aye, he had found the man. He had brought the unfaithful dog with him. The wretch knew Greek as well as Arabian.

"Here he is."

He pushed forward a man shod in morocco slippers and clad in a long silk robe which must have been costly once but was now stained and frayed. The face like the clothes bore traces of former dignity and importance now abused and degraded. The man was an Armenian, and had been in the old days one of the leading merchants in town. Now he shook like a leaf and cast terrified glances about.

The Emir pulled out from his bosom a bit of soiled parchment tightly rolled and threw it at the interpreter's feet.

"Read!"

This was the missive which a few days before the Franks had tied to an arrow and shot over the walls. The origin of the letter, of which the Moslems knew nothing, was this. The numerous Christians who still lived in Nicaea had been from the beginning of the siege subject to severe persecutions on the part of the Saracens. Rumors of these persecutions had seeped through to the Latin camps, causing much indignation and fear for the fate that might yet befall these unfortunate fellow believers. The problem of how to protect them while the siege still went on had often been discussed at the baronial council. Then, one day, Butumitos, who on recovering from his fever had come to return the Bishop's call, suggested that a written warning be prepared telling the Saracens that if the Christians within the city were tormented, the Latins, once they entered, would put the entire population to the sword. Such warning written on a scrap of parchment, could be tied about an arrow and shot over the walls.

The idea met with general favor.

The Bishop alone showed some misgivings.

"Indeed, my Lord, you know the Saracens better than we do," he said. "Tell us in all sincerity. Are you sure that such a missive will bring the desired effect and not arouse the heathens to even greater wrath and make them more cruel to these unfortunate people?"

Butumitos glanced thoughtfully at the ceiling, then at his own pink nails. Why should he tell them what he really thought? The matter was simple enough: if the city was starved and expected to surrender, the letter might have some effect. But if, on the other hand, there was no hunger, and if in addition the garrison was expecting help from the Sultan, then the Christians of Nicaea would pay dearly for it. Oh! well . . . what did it matter? They had always been unbearably proud, these Nicaeans, curse the lot of them! At the time of the capture of the city fifteen years ago, the wealthy among them would not even help the Basileus, preferring to court favor of the Moslems. Mindful of that, they might now try to interfere in the subtle and shrewd game he, Butumitos, was playing . . .

"He who threatens shows strength and strength commands respect," he said sententiously. So it was decided to send the letter and now this same letter lay on the ground at the feet of the Armenian who unfolded it with trembling fingers.

"Read!" repeated the emir threateningly.

"I dare not, oh Mighty Ruler, guardian of the faithful!" moaned the interpreter.

"Read, I tell you."

"'A message from the good Christian knights to the unfaithful dogs,'" the Armenian began, stammering. The emir leaped to his feet grasping his yataghan, but quickly checked himself and calmly resumed his seat.

"'We surround the city in great strength and shall capture it before long with the help of God Who is on our side. If our Christian brethren now held under your cursed rule will have no complaint against your persecutions we shall show you our magnanimity and slay only your men, sparing the lives of your women and children. Should, however, a hair fall of their heads before we enter, we will not leave one of your seed alive. And so it will be, for the Might of Heaven is with us, and Satan, whom you worship, will not save you.'"

The Armenian dropped the letter and fell on his face before the emir.

"It is not my fault! It is not my fault!" he moaned. "Oh! Guardian of the Faithful, it is not my fault!"

"What else does it say?" asked the emir.

"That is all."

The emir turned to Agida. "Kill this dirty dog and throw his carcass out of the walls."

The interpreter, screaming with terror, was dragged out of the hall.

Emir Mudjahid's face remained impassive; it did not behoove a strong man to betray his feelings.

"*Bis M'illah el rahman el rahim,*" he said. "God is merciful; the barking of a miserable jackal cannot touch the faithful of the Prophet! Not one of these insolent cocks who now crow under our walls, shall escape alive. We shall leave them no room in this world, not even as much as there is on the back of a camel. As for the filthy dogs who have been obviously complaining, have them brought out on the ramparts and slain under the very eyes of the infidels. All of them. And let the younger women among them be laid out crosswise and raped even as we did at Mehten."

"Your will shall be done," answered the Agha Sheik with respectful approval. "Shall we round up the filthy dogs today?"

"Round them up today," the Emir answered after a moment's reflection. "But do not take them out on the ramparts nor kill them till our glorious Sultan, may the Prophet bless his days, draws near and the *Giours* are engaged in battle. Thus their attention will be drawn both ways and their purpose divided."

"Deep wisdom flows from your lips," exclaimed his listeners, smacking their lips in admiration.

The carpenters promised by Butumitos had not yet arrived though the galleys which brought food from Byzantium had made three trips since then. Butumitos swore he could not understand what caused the delay. Meanwhile, the clumsily constructed towers kept toppling over without causing any harm whatsoever to the besieged. So the laborious battering of the walls by pick-axe and ram had to go on, a task which was becoming more and more difficult in the ever increasing heat. Iron helmets and breast plates grew so hot in the sun that they sizzled at the touch of a drop of water. Yet it was impossible to remove them since stones continued to fly from the walls, thick as hail. Stubbornness and rage grew in the hearts of the weary warriors; they did not mean to parch and wither before this accursed fortress all summer long. They prayed for good carpenters and cursed the Greeks for their slowness.

Swennon, son of Olaf, the royal prince of Denmark, labored without cease. In him the passion of Scandinavian stubbornness was very much like that of the explosive Raymond St. Gilles, who continually stormed the walls on ladders too short and flimsy; all day long Swennon hacked at the walls with his axe, as though he were cutting wood in a Danish forest. He did not watch how others worked, but gaunt and blackened, he strained with all his might. The Danish knights followed the lead of their prince and nowhere was the breach in the walls as deep and threatening as at their tiny sector.

From Raymond's camp, Florine, accompanied by her duenna, hastened toward them, carrying lunch for her betrothed: cold wine and a beautiful golden melon. She had gone to much pains to obtain the melon, for it had to be brought from a good distance, where the countryside had not yet been destroyed. The two approaching feminine figures were soon noticed from the bastion and a hail of arrows whistled in their direction. Duenna Bonina, all a-tremble, begged fearfully that they move away from the walls, but Florine shook her head stubbornly. The blood of Burgundian lords knew no fear; nor was she going to waste her time by going by a round-about way; it had been a long time since she had seen her beloved.

By now, he too had noticed them and throwing his axe away he ran to meet them so that they would not come too close. With relief he removed his helmet. Underneath, his forehead was divided, half-tanned, half-white where the iron helmet shielded it from the sun. His hair was bleached and matted with perspiration, his eyes reddened from the dust and sun, his lips cracked. Florine eyed him sorrowfully. With her soft cool hands she gently caressed the face of her beloved as though seeking under this mask of toil the comeliness of former days. Then they drank from the same cup, but the wine so carefully cooled had grown warm on the way and was covered with foam. The melon now over-ripe was no longer palatable. Its delightful fragrance had changed into a sweetish, sickening odor; it had waited too long, but Swennon ate it with apparent relish in order to please Florine.

Then they both looked at each other in disappointment. They felt sorry about something, but neither knew what it was. Florine sighed; if only they could find a bit of shade, a tiny patch of turf where they could sit down and talk. But there was none. The sun smote them mercilessly, the sky seemed gray from the heat, the persistent nauseating odor of the dead hung in the air, and they knew not what to say. On the ramparts the vile Saracens were grimacing and shouting. The duenna panted like a blacksmith's bellows. Aggrieved, on the verge of tears, Florine prepared to depart.

24.

Sin or Learning

GODFREY OF BOUILLON HAD JUST ARRIVED AT THE BISHOP'S TO ATTEND THE council of the leaders. D'Esch, Du Bourg and De Montaigne, whom he had brought along, stood before the tent in the company of a group of Raymond's knights and eagerly questioned five Armenians who last night had fled from the city.

The conversation did not proceed easily since only one of the fugitives could speak some Latin. Groping for words, he told their story: "Seven of us let ourselves down from the walls, but two could not hold on to the rope. They fell and were killed on the spot. God in His mercy allowed us to descend without mishap, nor were we sighted from the top of the ramparts. The Moslems are rounding up all the Christians in the city and driving them to the market place. There they have kept them under guard for the last four days. They won't tell why. So we fled. We don't trust the heathen. Who knows what they intend to do?"

"No telling, indeed. And how about victuals? They must be short of them by now? No? And what about the city's wealth? Is it truly as rich as we were told?"

"Rich?" The fugitives smacked their lips. They could not find adequate words to describe the treasures of Nicaea. Verily it had once been the richest city of the Empire and the Arabs had added plenty to it since. The eyes of the listeners glistened. When the Basileus was putting gems into their hands they would not take them, but this was an altogether different matter. Wealth won from an enemy in honest combat brought not only profit but honor as well. After their return it would bear witness to the prowess of their arms, become the tangible record of past feats. Everyone, even the richest barons, coveted spoils. How much more, then did they mean to the impecunious warriors!

Here, for instance, was the graying, rotund Saint-Pierre de Luz, once

192

squire of Sir Roger de Foix, later belted in Clermont. He had resented
bitterly the poverty which forced him for so many years to serve one
whose rank was no more than equal to his own. He wanted now to leave
his son enough money so that the lad might not wait for the silver spurs
till his thatch turned silver, too. Deep in his heart he prayed to God that
whatever service he might render in the freeing of the Holy Sepulcher
be rewarded by a few earthly possessions, and with what eager attention
he listened now to the Armenians' tales—though not as eagerly, perhaps,
as did Lawrence, the shy little squire of Sir Gaston d'Armillac, whose
beloved brother, forced by want, had several years before given himself
up in bondage to the Bishop of Liege. He had signed a document declaring that of his own free will he had chosen to devote all his life to
the service of his new master. "And this agreement of mine," so read
the deed, "shall be binding to the end of my days, unless I pay Your
Grace 200 honest uncut dinars."

Two hundred dinars! Verily the good Bishop had set a high price
upon the youth! It was true that the lad was handsome, sturdy, a fast
worker, and handy with the arms. Besides, in these days it was of little
consequence to the two brothers whether the deed specified one, two, or
three hundred dinars. Either of these sums seemed equally out of reach.
But now—who could tell?

The group of knights who plied the Armenian with questions was
soon joined by Arnuld de Rohes, chaplain of Robert of Normandy, who
wanted to find out which were the most magnificent palaces in town
and where they were located. Scrupulously, he wrote it all down. He
was thinking not only of himself but also of his ever penniless, ever
debt-beset master, to whom in his own way he was deeply devoted. They
made a strange pair, these two: the reckless, thick-skulled Robert and
his wily, cool, level-headed chaplain, but they were inseparable. Robert
might fume and bridle under Arnuld's advice yet he never failed to heed
it. Arnuld, for his part, looked upon Robert as a stepping stone leading
to a higher goal. The ambition of the canny chaplain did not stop at a
mere bishopric. He felt enough ability in himself to reach all the way up
for a cardinal's hat. And from the hat to the papal tiara there was but a
step. The tiara and Peter's keys, one spiritual, the other temporal—
Arnuld cared nothing for the first, he would renounce it gladly so he
might strengthen his hold on the other, the one which meant that wonderful, magical thing—power.

For the time being the ambitious chaplain contented himself with keeping a watchful eye on the purse strings of the unpredictable Robert, and forever wrangled with him and his insolent courtiers. In his spare moments he found consolation in the company of two pretty girls, his nieces, he said, whom he had been obliged to bring along since the poor orphans had no other kin or friend to look after them.

The interview with the Armenians was broken by the approach of a new and unexpected group. Mounted on a bay mule and escorted by a handful of *warangs,* Butumitos' court physician arrived on the scene. The Greek captain had just heard that the noble Gontrane, sister-in-law of Duke Godfrey, was ailing and had dispatched him at once. The physician was attired in a dark loose robe and purple sandals; his sharp eyes peered from a face as wrinkled as that of an old crone. A large leather bag of medical supplies was strapped to his saddle.

"It's true that the wife of Duke Baldwin is ailing," said Konon de Montaigue. "And for that very reason the Duke is not here with us."

"How long has she been ailing?"

"Three weeks now."

"I should like to see her at once."

"I must first inform the Duke," said Konon reluctantly. With unconcealed regret he took leave of his companions, and, mounting his horse, rode off to the Lorraine camp. On the way he eyed the Greek suspiciously. All he had heard about the Byzantine physicians and how they cut up corpses came now to his mind. If that were true, how could one admit such a foul rascal to the bedside of an honest, high-born woman? Unable to contain his misgivings, he asked his companion directly. For a wonder the leech was not a bit abashed.

"To treat an ailment effectively," he replied, "one must have a thorough knowledge of the human body. And what other way is there to acquire it?"

Montaigue almost choked with indignation. Haughtily and contemptuously he gave the Greek his knightly opinion on the subject of cutting up human carcasses. There was but one proper way to treat sickness, he told him, and that was to confide it to the care of some great saint, even as it was done in the enlightened Christian countries of the West. Every city, nay, every village had its own patron saint, who cured some ailment or other. Thus, as every child knew, St. Gilles helped colics and ulcers; St. Mamert protected against hemorrhage, St. Guy cured convulsions; and St. Appolony, persistent toothache. After committing oneself into their care one could await confidently. One would be either cured or not, depending upon God's will.

The Greek listened absently while his eyes scanned the devastated barren hills.

"It's a wonder that all of you have not fallen sick in this air," he remarked suddenly.

"Air is the same everywhere," Konon muttered.

The physician gave him a sidelong look.

"Not so, my Lord. It often happens that in one locality people will live in health to an old ripe age while in another but a few miles away they will be ravaged by sickness without succor or end. There is a different air in the mountains and a different air in the valleys, different by the sea and still different, and most pernicious, in the marshes. That is why, when the great Arabian doctor, Ibn Razes, who lived a hundred years ago—for let us not forget it, the Arabs excel in medical lore as does no other nation in the world . . '. Indeed, they have means the secret of which we have not yet acquired, to remove the blindness called cataract from the eyes, they know how to make the flesh numb to pain so that a man can be cut to the quick while he sleeps peacefully knowing nothing of it. They know . . ."

"Any witch can do the same, since the Devil makes her insensible to pain."

"This is neither witchcraft nor magic, only science. But I forget what I started to say. So when the great Ibn Razes was to build a hospital in Bagdad, at the order of the Calif, he first hung hunks of raw meat and placed open vessels with water in various sections of the city. Three times daily he went to inspect them. And fancy, my Lord, in some spots it spoiled immediately, while in others it kept fresh much longer. He chose the spot where the meat was last to rot and the water to turn putrid and there he built the hospital, rightly saying that here the air must be the healthiest."

"Pure devilment, which only a schismatic could praise," burst Konon angrily. "Such pagan tricks lead straight to damnation."

"Damnation or salvation have nothing to do with knowledge which should be acquired from every possible source, even from the pagans."

Montaigue spat expressively, too angry to answer. They reached the camp in silence. The knight dismounted hastily and ran in search of

Baldwin, so he might warn him not to show his wife to the loathsome leech. The Greek sat on his bay mule waiting with philosophical calm.

Baldwin stood perplexed in his wife's tent scratching his head. Old Helgund sat in a corner mumbling prayer. The air was blue with the smoke of herbs and incense which they had been burning around the sick woman. Gontrane, parched with fever, lay motionless coughing and talking to herself incoherently. As far as Baldwin was concerned she was as bitter and hostile as ever; sickness had not mellowed her temper. Yet, whenever he or anyone else entered the tent, she would raise her head from the bolster and watch the entrance with flaming eyes, only to fall back again helpless and as if disappointed.

Now likewise at the sound of Konon's steps she sat up expectantly, then as she recognized the knight, her face puckered and she lay down again.

"What is the matter?" asked Baldwin, drawing closer.

"Nothing, nothing. Go away. Leave me alone, for Heaven's sake," she groaned.

Baldwin and Konon walked out of the tent with that poignant sense of relief one feels on leaving the chamber of one who is grievously sick and whom one cannot help. Montaigue in quick broken sentences related his conversation with the Greek.

"Do you think he would cure her?" asked Baldwin, thoughtfully.

"He would cure her without fail, since Satan can do anything. That is how he lures people, isn't it? But it would be mortal sin just the same. Think, my Lord, what would Duke Godfrey say?"

"Aye, you're right. But I will ask her anyway." He returned to the tent, greeted with an unfriendly look from Helgund, and bent over his sick wife.

"Gontrane! Gontrane! Listen to me: A Greek physician has just arrived. One of those filthy ones who cut corpses. He acquired his skill from the pagans. Verily a Devil's apprentice. He can cure flesh but he will kill the soul. Godfrey, no doubt, would not even hear of him. Do you want to see him?"

"Godfrey? Where is he?" cried Gontrane wildly, rousing herself from the pillows.

"Godfrey is in Raymond's camp. A Devil's servant came here. A Greek medic. Do you want to see him?" Baldwin explained patiently.

"No, I don't want him. I want no one. Leave me in peace," she retorted, angrily turning to the wall.

"She does not want him," Baldwin announced with relief, rejoining Konon who was waiting at the entrance. "Send the schismatic away. He can go back where he came from. Whatever turn things take for Gontrane is for God to decide. She needs no help from the Greek."

With unconcealed pleasure Montaigue announced the Duke's decision to the Greek. The physician showed no surprise; just bowed slightly, and prodded the mule with his heels. He had not yet left the camp when the air was rent by the shrill blare of horns. Men ran like mad to their horses, drums boomed, and from camp to camp swept the shout.

"Saracens! Saracens are coming!"

25.

Allah Akbar

WIDE SWEPT THE ARMY OF SULTAN KILIJ ARSLAN. HORDES OF WILD asses, horned antelopes, and desert rabbits fled before its hoofs, as they pressed swiftly ahead, loath to waste a single moment. A sacred fervor drove them on like fire. Holy War! Holy War! Woe to the infidels, glory to the faithful of the Prophet!

They came in great strength. There were ten regiments of cavalry alone, each regiment composed of five sections, each section numbering almost a thousand men. When they released their bows, arrows flew in a dark cloud like locusts on the wing. When they drew their curved sabers, a flash ran over the ranks like a sudden burst of lightning. They were all here; all the clans, all the tribes of Bithynia, Lydia, Phrygia. There were also dark-skinned Arabs from Nedjed, and light-skinned Arabs from the happy land of Yemen, and Bedouins of the desert in white or black coifs, held by a triple band. With their dark faces and vulture-like profiles, they looked at a distance like ravens.

The Sultan's horse was white as milk; its tail flowed down to the ground in a snowy cascade. On its rump it bore the sacred sign of Mohammed's fingers. The headstall was of pure gold; the breastband studded with a diamond star. Though not so richly adorned, all the other horses were beautiful, fleet, and high-bred. They knew only two paces: the walk and the gallop. When in gallop they stretched themselves and flew low over the ground like a shot sent from a bow. They were the love and pride of their masters' lives. To the Western knight, too, a horse meant more than any other possession; it was a mark of wealth, dignity, and rank. But to the Arab it meant even more: it was the great passion of his soul. For a horse an Arab warrior would give away his wife (that the soonest), his sons, his possessions, his very life. Had not the Prophet himself shown his love of horses? Did he ascend to the seventh heaven on the back of a camel, or on the back of an eagle, or on the back of a gazelle? Nay, the fiery charger, Borak, carried him up like a storm. No wonder that every one of his faithful held the noble beast in such high esteem.

At the head of each section rode a strident band composed of *shalshmays,* resembling oboes, of flutes, great drums, bells, and cymbals. But its shrill notes were drowned in the general uproar of voices. This was not a song but a measured choral recitation of the suras of the Koran. The Arabian tongue has a ringing, bell-like quality; the syllables *"jir," "jin"* and *"jan,"* drum on the ear like hail falling on brass. The sound intoxicated the marching hosts; it made them forget weariness, thirst, and hunger. These men of the free desert were enamoured of rhyme and rhythm. They loved it almost as much as they loved their freedom and their horses. When moved or roused they could not speak except in verse. In verse full of flowery metaphor the califs of Bagdad wrote their official documents. In improvised verse mourners wept their dead. In songs and verses, Arabian chronicles lived and survived. There was no higher honor than to possess a poet in one's family. And so now as they marched, the troops of Kilij Arslan raised their voices, reciting the rhyming suras which sang the praises of Allah, who gave them this Holy War:

"The angel Gabriel asked the Prophet: what is the essence of faith?

"Answered Mohammed: To profess that Allah is one and that I am his Prophet. To observe hours of prayer, to fast through the month of Radaman, and to make a pilgrimage to Mecca.

"The angel Gabriel knit his brows and asked again: What is the essence of faith? Answered Mohammed: To profess that Allah is one and that I am his Prophet. To fight in a Holy War against the unfaithful, to observe the hours of prayer. To fast through the month of Radaman, and to make a pilgrimage to Mecca.

"But the angel asked a third time: What is the essence of faith? Answered Mohammed: Oh, mighty Gabriel! To profess that Allah is one and I am his Prophet and to fight in a holy war against the infidels.

"And the angel brightened and said: I swear upon the night that comes and the dawn that bursts into blossom that you have spoken the truth, Mohammed."

* * * *

The Christian camps buzzed with feverish activity. In all haste squires brought horses to their masters and handed them their lances. The knights already mounted fell into formation called a *fence;* rank after rank, one unit behind the other. The city was on their right, the fortified camps behind them. The ranks stood deep. From the approaching cloud of pagans rose a loud, ringing *"La illah el Allah, Mohammed rasul Allah!"* Over the ranks of Crusaders ran the hard, curt: "God wills it! God wills it!"

Huge fists in iron guantlets twitched with joy as they grasped the shafts of the lances. A battle! At last! For two years they had wished, worked, prayed for it, and now it was here. God had willed it! God had led them, God would help them. He would strengthen every fist a hundredfold. He would arm them with might. God . . . God . . .

The force of faith taut as a bowstring quivered alike over the two armies. Two creeds were about to clash like two battering rams, like two clouds heavy with storm. The thunder born of their encounter would shake the earth; the whole world would hear it.

La illah el Allah, Mohammed rasul Allah!

God wills it! God wills it!

They met.

The Christian knights thrust like an iron wedge into the body of the Moslem army, trying to split it asunder and trample under their weight the bright silk-covered riders and their tiny, fleet mounts. They partly succeeded. The Arabs could not withstand the terrible impact of the charge. But since their tactics were different they were not alarmed. What Sultan Kilij Arslan wanted was precisely to let the enemy sink deep into his own ranks, then surround him, cut him off from the main body of the army and overwhelm him by sheer numbers. Let the steel wedge of assailants split into a hundred particles of battle; blind them with a storm of arrows. With a feigned flight force them to extend their lines, break their ranks, and then throw his reserves into the fray and sweep the unfaithful off their feet. Since the shots bounced off the iron plates, the Saracens began to aim at the horses. True that the chargers were likewise protected by iron breast-plates and headstalls and their rumps were covered with mail. But the Moslems aimed at the uncovered bellies and legs. When from the left wing the troops of Lorraine sallied forth to charge, with Godfrey at their head, his sword raised high, even before they reached the enemy lines the flanks of Godfrey's steed were bristling with arrows so that the bay stallion appeared like the winged charger Borak who had carried the Prophet to heaven. The brave animal ran a hundred steps, then fell suddenly on its nose. A squire in full gallop brought a fresh horse for the Duke. Other knights, too, had their horses slain under them and were forced to mount spare ones, cursing the Moslems for such a treacherous method of warfare.

At the head of his ranks Raymond St. Gilles fought like Roland himself. At his side Adhemar, the Bishop of Puy, sword in one hand, a cross in the other, had thrown the reins loose on the horn of his saddle. The wise old steed needed no lead. Behind the Bishop rode Peter, hunched in the saddle, half-crazed with fear, yet not even to himself would he admit that the uproar of battle, which intoxicated the knights and made their nostrils quiver, filled him with terror and robbed him of whatever remained of his courage and strength. Seeing his obvious fright they roared with laughter, and called to him to go back and hide among the women. But Peter would not go back. He must overcome his fear and fright. If he were killed, so much the better.

Right by his side Walter the Penniless swung his mighty sword. He was not afraid. Not Walter. The Bishop could safely put the reins down and pray and fight in turn, for Walter kept watch. Heedless of his own safety he guarded the leader. His terrible sword cut men in half, his mighty swing sent heads flying. Time and again an empty space opened about the Bishop. Aye, let the knights look. Let them see whether the despised bastard deserved a belt or not.

But who had time to look, when everyone had his hands full? De La Tour had just run his lance through his sixth opponent, lifted him from his saddle, let the body dangle on the lance, then with a 'mighty heave cast it, dripping with blood, at the enemy ranks. The Salviac de Viel twins fought shoulder to shoulder, each more concerned about the other than about himself. The Silesians, too, kept together, hacking obstinately as wood cutters might in their native forest. After spitting into their palms, they swung their broad-swords diagonally from the left as if wielding an axe. Some of their strokes would do credit to De Melun himself. So they fought shouting their family battle cries. Nagoditses and Osventas, Zavoras and Novinas. Only the Strzygonias fought in silence, for the battle cry of their clan was to be used only in the hour of mortal peril, when there was no help forthcoming from anywhere else.

But they did not fight any the less bravely for their silence. Though in a strange land and so far from Silesia, they fought as heartily as they

had at Krushvitsa or Kiev. Slashing methodically, precisely, keeping a
wary eye on the enemy lest they be separated and surrounded, they
moved irresistibly along with their squires at their backs.

Only for one moment did their arms falter and that was when from
the midst of pagan hosts emerged a group of camel-riders. The monstrous creatures sped forward craning their long necks, their unshapely
flattened hoofs that looked like wads of felt clopping on the ground.
Ugly mean lips spat at the horses, spraying them with stinking saliva.

"Mercy!" shouted the Babbler, aghast.

But the others promptly reassured him.

"Haven't you seen these ugly monsters in Byzantium? Beasts like
any other, they are. Stick them with the sword and you will see the
gore."

The old Anshelm de Ribeaumont seemed to have recovered the
strength of his long-lost youth, as he fought now, keeping a watchful eye
on Paul Engelram, his beloved ward. Let the youth battle with all the
mad recklessness of his age; the old man was guarding over him.

Godfrey of Bouillon fought with a strange, exalted, almost unearthly
expression on his face. As though he was engaging Satan himself in a
hand to hand combat. Between strokes, he lifted his eyes to heaven,
almost expecting to see there the Archangel Michael, likewise engaged in
battle. Though by nature not very strong, not to be compared with
De Melun, Walter the Penniless, or De La Tour, now, in this state of
strange exaltation he struck as hard as they. He chopped off arms and
ran his sword through torsos, convinced that he was striking at Evil
itself. He felt with satisfaction the bones of stricken enemies cracking
under his horse's hoofs.

Five hours they had been battling thus without break under a blazing
sun, in a heat so intense that the air shimmered and iron breastplates
burnt the flesh through leather jerkins, before the troops of the two
Roberts, Stephen de Blois, Hugh, and Boemund, who were guarding the
opposite side of the city, learned of the battle. In no time they fell into
ranks and in all haste set off toward the fray. But to get there proved
not easy. With the city on one side, their own fortified camps backed
against steep hills on the other, and the impassable lake in the west,
there remained only a narrow passage between the walls of the city and
the palisade of wooden stakes and human bones, through which they
could reach the battlefield. Into that passage from the western gate

sallied forth Ibrahim, son of Emir Mudjahid, at the head of three thousand horsemen to block the way. Unable either to enfold or to bypass the opponent, the Latin knights would have to stop and fight with Ibrahim, while in the meantime Kılıj Arslan might break through the Lorraine and Provençal ranks.

Always cool, Boemund did not rush into a battle, in which only the first lines fought while the rest milled about and cursed. Instead he climbed on one of the unfinished siege towers, which looked like a shapeless pile of logs and boards, from which he could command a much wider view. He saw that the Flandrians who fought with Ibrahim were holding up the whole march, while from the ramparts a hail of stones, javelins and spears fell upon the heads of the others. That sort of fighting could easily go on till sunset.

At a distance, on the other side of the city, a cloud of dust marked the spot where another battle was raging. The battle they had been dreaming of was being fought without the knights who stood here waiting idly.

Boemund hastily descended from the tower and withdrew his troops. He issued orders. In a trice his men had torn down the palisade and filled the moat. A moment later they sped across the camps, jumping over the ropes of the tents. Startled women and servants stared at them open-mouthed.

Soon they were breaking down the palisade on the opposite side, and rushing up the hill. Now down the steep slope; at last the way was clear. Horses galloped, their bellies almost touching the ground. Lances held at half tilt flashed impatiently. They had bypassed Ibrahim. Should they turn now and charge him from the rear or hasten to the other battlefield without losing a moment?

"By the blood of St. January," Tancred shouted suddenly in a voice choked with horror. "Look!"

They raised their visors and shaded their eyes with their palms: behind the screen of Ibrahim's cavalry terrible things were going on at the foot of the walls. The Saracens had dragged out from the city more than a thousand Armenians and were now massacring them calmly, deliberately, without haste. Men and women, old and young, adolescents and children. The victims, crazed with terror, squealed, thrashed wildly about, ran to and fro. But wherever they turned they met a wall of naked, sharp steel. Only the younger women were not killed at once.

Instead, the Saracens stripped them of their clothes, flung them on the ground, stretched out their hands and legs and tied them to pegs driven into the ground. They would remain that way. Let anyone who pleased dishonor them. Let them be eaten by ants. Let them be torn by jackals at night and by the vultures by day. This was Emir Mudjahid's answer to the empty threats of the Latins.

"Follow me," called Tancred, turning his horse around. But Boemund with an iron hand grabbed him by the arm.

"Stop. There is no time. What do you care about them? Those people are nothing to us."

"They are Christians!"

"They are schismatics. And we must hasten over there. If we tarry the Provençals will reap all the glory."

Relunctantly, his face pale from anger, Tancred gave in. Besides, Boemund was right. It was high time to reinforce Raymond's and Godfrey's host. After six hours of continuous battle in scorching heat, the knights' arms were growing numb, their breath came in gasps. Sweat and blood trickled from under the helmets, parched lips could no longer give voice.

But at this very hour Florine, who with others awaited the outcome of the battle sitting in Elvira's tent, suggested shyly that perhaps they ought to take water to their embattled men who, ever since morning, had been out there, under the scorching sun . . .

Elvira hesitated at first, but the others pounced upon the idea. Blanche was instantly ready to start; Elvira's maidens folded their hands in supplication, begging to be allowed to go, and at last the proud lady consented.

Then off they went, several scores of women running with pails, buckets, cups, and dippers. Carried away by their zeal they ignored all danger. What if the pagans captured them? What if they were shot at from the walls? They did not care. They would prove worthy of their men, prove that they had not come here in vain, that they were no hindrance to their husbands. And suppose they were to die? Did they not all come of good knightly stock? Now, they were in sight of the battlefield. The knights at first greeted them with suspicious wonder which soon turned to joyous gratitude. The warm turbid water tasted like nectar to their parched lips. They sipped slowly, savoring the invigorating moisture, trying to retain it on the tongue as long as pos-

sible. They did not drink much, mindful that many others were waiting.
A few swallows would do for the moment. And as they looked with
gratitude at the generous women, the good knights felt in their hearts a
growing desire to prove their own mettle before those feminine eyes.
Here was their chance . . . This was no conquest of a fortress of love,
no tourney in the lists . . . This was war . . . Let the good women
see how their knights fought. Let them marvel at their prowess. Nor
were the blushing women, greatly pleased with their idea, in a hurry to
depart. De La Tour came toward them leading Raymond, stunned by a
blow which had slipped off his helmet. The helmet withstood the shock
but the Count had fainted. Forgetting her wonted aloofness, Elvira sped
to him with water, and tender hands, eager to bring relief.

"My good, kind wife," Raymond mumbled, still dazed. For the first
time he was seeing her like this. Something was springing between
them, hitherto unknown, a common bond in the face of good and evil
fortune.

The battle still raged, dogged, cruel, fierce. The Normans and Flandrians had at last cut their way through Ibrahim's ranks and were
charging, with a tremendous clatter, into the flanks of the Moslem
army. The watchful Sultan, seeing this from a hillock on which he
stood, dispatched against them the last regiment which had so far stood
idle. They met the Normans headlong, ran through each other once,
then turned to strike again, but at that very instant the sky, which until
now had been a motionless pillar of heat, began to quiver and turn first
gray and then russet. A sudden gust of wind swept the battlefield sending clouds of dust swirling, blinding the eyes, swelling the burnooses
like sails, standing horses' tails and manes on end, pulling pennons taut
as string. It blew from the Christians toward the Arabs, from the north
to the south. Camels snorted and grunted, horses reared. Verily, Allah
was trying the faithful. Iblis had come to the infidels' aid.

The vulture-like Bedouins were the first to turn their mounts, and
the others followed. Once the signal of retreat was given nothing could
stop them. In vain did the Sultan threaten and call for a charge, in vain
did the sheiks intone suras of the Koran. In a world filled with storm
no one heard their voices. Before a rider thought of flight, his mount
had already turned with the wind. Amidst clouds of stinging, brown
dust the knights pursued the fleeing enemy. Ibrahim in despair gathered
what remained of his horsemen, turned the Christian flank and struck

blindly, struggling against the wind. But no sooner had he engaged the Frisians than Stephen de Blois charged at him from behind. Ibrahim's valor would avail him nothing; his men were surrounded, caught in an iron vise. Not one would escape alive.

Caught by the storm, Elvira, Blanche, Florine, and the rest of the women-folk lost in the general confusion did not know where to turn. Fearful, they crouched among the rocks like a flock of frightened quails. To find their way back to camp in this thick darkness which swept them from their feet and choked their breath was quite hopeless and they were alone. Elvira's pages had seized the arms and horses of the killed, and in their scanty droll attire dashed off after the knights. No doubt they would be punished for deserting thus my lady's fan and perfume, but it was no matter. They could restrain themselves no longer.

The battlefield was strewn with corpses. Piles of corpses appeared and disappeared in the flashes of daylight whenever there was a momentary break in the cloud of dust. There they lay all together: good knights and squires, servants and pagans, entwined in mortal embrace, for they had fought to the very last even on the ground. Horses and camels lay flat on their sides with intestines ripped out; some still steaming, others in cold, livid coils. Here and there were dismembered heads and arms, shapeless torsoes, and over the heads of the fear-stricken women, wings began to flap. Vultures were coming to the rocks where they would wait until morning. Their prize would not escape.

The sun, invisible behind the pall of dust, finally set and the wind suddenly subsided. So suddenly, in fact, that the body, used to opposing its impact, reeled for lack of support. The dust slowly settled. Far overhead a cool, sea-green sky appeared, in which presently a red moon would arise. Somewhere close by jackals began to howl. From the motionless corpses rose a creeping sense of terror. Huddled in a crevice of the rock, the women dared not leave their refuge. Lost in the desert storm, they had wandered far afield and were now on the other side of the city and they did not know which way to go. After the scorching heat of the day, the cold of the night pierced them to the marrow, and then there was that dread, that horrible dread.

A clatter of hoofs sounded at a distance. Some one was coming. Someone was calling their names. So it was their own, thank God!

It was Raymond St. Gilles, and along with him Swennon, De La Tour, D'Armillac, De Foix, and De Beaugency. Not finding the women on

their return to camp, they had searched for them, their hearts heavy
with apprehension. They were black from the exertion, hoarse, but
wonderfully pleased with the results of the battle.

"You must forgive those hobbledehoys of yours," said Raymond when
Elvira complained against her pages. "Egad! The lads fought prettily.
In truth, I have already promised to take them as squires . . . No gainsaying the victory is great. And all ours, too, since the Normans and the
Frisians did not arrive till the very end. Butumitos, the foul snake, did
not even budge, just stood there and waited to see how it would turn
out for us. Well, he shall see . . . We are going to send him three
thousand pagans' heads. The rest we will catapult into the city."

"How many of them fell altogether?" inquired the women curiously.

"Over six thousand, I'd say. Quite a few of our own, too. Come, now.
You had better mount, my ladies. We have a long way to go and it's
getting late."

The knights helped their women folks to climb on the mail-covered
croups of their mounts. Each knight took one and some took two, one in
front and one behind. The chargers were badly jaded, but if they rode
slowly enough, they would somehow plod their way back to camp.

"We must take a much longer way," Raymond explained to Elvira,
"so as not to pass by the Eastern Gate where those poor Armenian
women lie. It's dangerous to go that way and quite unseemly for you to
look."

"What Armenian women are you talking about?"

"Don't you know? Shortly before noon the pagans drove all the
Christians out of the city and slew them. At the same time they dishonored more than a hundred damsels, then just left them lying there,
still bound to pegs."

"Are they still alive?" asked Blanche, her eyes wide with horror.

"So the Danish prince says. It seems as though they were calling for
help when his men rode by."

"Then why doesn't someone set them free at once?"

"Set them free? And who would touch them? The pagans' seed is in
them. No Christian would go near the place."

"No doubt they are dead by now. The sand must have choked them,"
said Swennon, pressing tenderly the slender hands which Florine had
clasped around his waist.

"How dreadful, how dreadful," repeated Blanche, mounting De

Foix's horse. She pretended not to notice the horse that Raoul de Beaugency had brought for her.

The moon had by now risen high and turned from red to gold. The battlefield, so deathly still an hour ago, began to quicken with life. The living hovered among the dead; hosts of servants were cutting off the heads of the fallen foe. They were hurrying with the job, since at dawn the heads were to be cast over the walls of the city. They went about it briskly, efficiently, as back home they might have cut turnip greens on an autumn day. Sometimes in jest they tossed the heads at each other. Others loaded the awesome crop into big leather bags and dragged it into the camps. Still others collected weapons and stripped the corpses of their clothes, quarreling bitterly among themselves as each squire insisted that he could recognize the hand of his master in this or that stroke and claimed the prize on his behalf. Jackals yawned as they watched them from among the rocks. It was easier to devour stripped corpses but they were loath to wait.

Once back in camps, the knights threw themselves exhausted upon their pallets and instantly fell into deep slumber. Only Raoul de Beaugency could not find rest. He was overwrought and perturbed, for Blanche had roused his wrath. There had been times when she looked upon him kindly enough. Why would she not even glance his way, now? In addition he was tormented by the vision of the Armenian women whom he had glimpsed while riding by. They had shone so eerily white in the moonlight as they lay there like big, obscene spiders. An unnatural, irresistible desire to look at them once more would give him no peace, a cruel, shameful delight at the sight of torture. Anyone else would have been ashamed of such thoughts and would have banished them in fear and horror, but to Raoul it was all one; nothing could help or harm him any more. Damnation knows no degrees, any more than salvation. A damned man might go wherever he chose, do whatever he pleased. But he always belonged to Satan.

The moon shone with horrible brightness. Every shape was either black or white, and sharply defined. Head cutters and corpse robbers had left the battlefield and only the jackals remained. Like a thief, hiding in the shadows, the gloomy knight stole along the palisade from the top of which shone human skulls, the skulls of the crusaders from the army of Peter the Hermit. He was hastening toward the Eastern

Gate by which a thousand people had been murdered as a result of the warning sent at Butumitos' advice.

Here was the cursed spot, and here the piles of dead victims. And yonder—*they*, their naked bodies shining white as a witch's magic circle.

Raoul de Beaugency felt a cold shiver along his spine, not unmixed with desire, fear clutching at his throat, and above all else, horror of himself. Nevertheless, he continued on his way, drawing nearer to the crucified women. They lay half sunken in the sand which the wind had blown over them—nailed, stretched wide open . . . Upon the bosom of some the pagans had cut a derisive sign of the cross. Those lay still, their bellies black and bloated; merciful death had closed their eyes. But most of them were still alive, as betrayed by the convulsive quiver of their bodies and now and then a pitiful moan. Raoul stood amid them looking around with eyes that were not quite sane. It seemed to him at times that he himself was Satan, watching souls which had been delivered into his power. Suddenly he started: he heard approaching steps. Instinctively he jumped into the shadow and crouched on the ground. Thus hidden in the dark, he watched. Who was it? A slender figure in a dark cape, holding a vessel, no doubt with water. In the other hand something gleamed. A knife? The figure bent over each victim, sprayed water, cut the bonds. Or with a sure motion raised the hand and delivered a stroke which would end the torture. Unaware of being observed the figure drew quite near, and suddenly in the full light of the moon Raoul saw the face.

"Blanche! Blanche de Montbeliard!" he exclaimed, aghast.

Unable to check himself, he leaped from his hiding place and grabbed the hand in which she held the knife.

"What are you doing?" he asked in a whisper.

Recovering from her momentary fright she proudly tossed her head.

"Why ask? You saw for yourself."

"What are you doing?" he repeated uncertainly. He did not know what to do or how to judge this strange action of hers. His mind was completely muddled.

"Let me go," she said with distaste, trying to free her hand.

He only tightened his grip. At the touch of her slender, hot wrist, a wave of desire swept over him.

"I love you. I've loved you for years. Don't you know?" he whispered hoarsely.

She quivered with indignation. Such words in the face of what surrounded them were monstrous.

"Let me go," she repeated fiercely.

"Why do you drive me away? You would not mount my horse and I love you."

"Let go!"

"I won't!" he shouted angrily. Her obstinate resistance had roused him to fury. He felt a mad urge to tear the cape off her shoulders and lay her naked on the ground, even like those others. Now she was in his power, at his mercy! If he told where he met her, they would bury her alive, or burn her. He had seen her touch the violated women; she had gathered upon herself the evil spells of pagan seed. He alone was not afraid to touch her since nothing could harm him any more, but what would the others say?

She looked straight into his face, bold and challenging.

"Let me go immediately. What do you want?"

"Lie down," he growled.

She burst into malicious laughter.

"With you? Never!"

"I will tell everyone where I met you."

"Go ahead. Tell! I was setting these hapless creatures free. Those who barely breathed I killed so that they might not suffer any longer. Go, tell them. And I will ask you then: what were you doing here?"

He was taken aback but not for long.

"I was stalking you."

"That's a lie. You saw me but a moment ago."

"How will you prove it?"

"Let me go," she shouted angrily. "Let me go, I tell you. I have a knife—I am not afraid of you. No. You will not get me."

"They will burn you."

"They will burn us both."

With an unexpected agile twist she broke away from him and vanished in the night. He remained alone, disappointed and furious. His blood was in turmoil, but the motionless circle of women lured him no longer. What were they to him, those corpses with swollen abdomens, mutilated and disfigured? He wanted the other one, the warm and alive; he felt that he had to have her, even if both of them were to be burned afterwards as she had predicted.

* * * *

Emir Mudjahid, son of Djubaira, sat in his palace in the hall of the clocks. The golden hawk had just dropped six golden balls which rolled tinkling in the golden bowl when Aga-sheil accompanied by his *mooshirs* brought in the head of Ibrahim just thrown over the ramparts. The back of the skull had been crushed by the catapult but the face with the delicate, proud features was almost untouched. He had departed in glory, scorning the garb of long life, Emir Mudjahid's only child, the beloved Ibrahim.

"*Bia m'Illah el rahman el rahim,*" the Emir said firmly. "Thanks to the kindness and mercy of God, I am happy that my son has died in a Holy War. I am happy beyond words."

Those present bowed their heads in approval.

"Leave me awhile alone," pleaded the happy Emir in a low voice, as though ashamed.

They left, bowing deeply. Only the head of Ibrahim remained white as a sheet on the crimson cloth.

Emir Mudjahid took it carefully in his hands, a father's hands. The fountain murmured softly. And at once on the dead face glistening drops began to fall. From the fountain? No, it was Emir Mudjahid who cried—senile, impotent tears, unworthy of a devout follower of the Koran. May the Prophet forgive him his weakness.

* * * *

Bodies decomposed quickly in this white heat so that when the emissaries from the Latin camp dumped before Butumitos their bags of severed heads, the air turned sickeningly fetid. They were a ghastly sight, those blue and swollen heads. The cuts at the neck swarmed already with maggots, dripped with pus. Butumitos recoiled in horror but quickly mastered his feelings.

Sir William de Melun, who headed the Latin delegation, stepped forward proudly, his arms akimbo. "The good knights and Lords: the Count de Vermandois, the Dukes of Flanders and of Lorraine, the Count St. Gilles, and the Royal Prince of Denmark send to you, my Lord, this soldierly prize and ask you to send it on to the Basileus as a gift from the Latins. There are three thousand and more of these heads here. We have thrown as many into the city to frighten the heathen.

The heads belong to the warriors of Sultan Kılıj Arslan before whom Byzantium used to tremble."

"I will do immediately as your noble leaders wish," Butumitos assured them graciously. Speaking loudly and in Latin he issued orders that the bags be loaded in all haste on a galley which was to sail at once to Byzantium. Then in Greek he added:

"And mind, as soon as you are off shore, dump that horror into the sea and scrub the decks well with lye. Else we shall have pestilence on our hands. What savagery!"

Without betraying any of these feelings he turned to his guests, offered them rich gifts in the name of the emperor, plied them with frozen wine and sent them away with the assurance that the Basileus would be overjoyed. As soon as they were gone he called a war council, in which the leaders of the various units and Pantopulos, the skillful builder of towers, were to take part.

"Kılıj Arslan's forces are shattered," Butumitos announced with satisfaction. "That's all that matters. As you see, those six months of torment we went through with them in Byzantium have proved worth while. Now the problem is how to use the opportunity well. Nicaea must surrender. But it must surrender to us."

"Have they not sworn that they would not keep it?"

"Much good will it do us if they hand us back the city after they've looted, destroyed it, and slain the inhabitants. We don't want empty walls. Now, I think it is time to draw those fools' attention to the fact that galleys are supplying food to the city and that without the fleet's help they will never be able to starve it. And it is we who have the fleet. Pantopulos! You must go to them and build siege towers. You will discover the galleys."

"But they saw me here with you, Your Highness. They may recognize me and wonder why I did not come sooner," remarked Pantopulos.

"No, they won't, never fear. And if they do, it is up to you to think up some good excuse. You will go there tomorrow as the master builder sent from Byzantium."

26.

The Judgment of God

BESIDES THE BISHOP, WHO WAS TO PRESIDE, THE COURT WAS COMPOSED OF Raymond St. Gilles, Godfrey of Lorraine, the two Roberts, Chaplain Arnuld de Rohes, Canon Raymond d'Aguilers, Stephen de Blois, Hugh de Vermandois, and Archdeacon Alberon; all sat on a cloth-covered bench set in front of the tent. The accuser, Raoul de Beaugency, stood before them, the accused and her mother to one side, while a crowd of spectators, none but the foremost among knights, pressed closely around.

It was lucky that the Moslems within the city were busy at that moment with the burial of the heads of their own dead. The sing-song wails of their mourners could be heard even here. Otherwise they might have easily made a sortie and broken into the camp, unhindered. All minds, all attention was absorbed by this strange, incredible, dreadful trial which was about to begin.

Who would have expected that the good knight De Beaugency should ever accuse Lady Blanche de Montbeliard, daughter of the noble kindred of Salviac de Viel, of foul witchcraft? He had caught her, it seemed, touching the corpses of women defiled by the pagans. He saw her kill them, too, no doubt to take their blood for some devilish practices. It all seemed hard to believe, and yet the knight could not be lying. Besides, the accused did not even deny the charges. She only insisted that she did it not for the sake of witchcraft but out of pity. "For the love of our merciful Lord Jesus Christ." She said it boldly in front of everyone and looking straight into the judges' faces; she was neither afraid to pronounce the Most Holy Name, nor ashamed to drag it into so vile a crime.

The Bishop sat silent, hiding his eyes with one hand while the rest of the judges whispered among themselves, exchanging short remarks. The onlookers, however, did not spare loud comments.

"He has sold his soul to the Devil and now he dares accuse a good woman."

"Mind how she brought us water yesterday? And today they are trying her."

"Tut, tut! She is no better than that fellow De Beaugency. Remember how Montbeliard died?"

"Marry! That's right. She poisoned him!"

"A poisoner!"

"And remember how she said that the werewolf was nothing but a common dog?"

"She must have been in connivance with him."

"By the bones of St. Guy! She has been practising witchcraft for years, no doubt, and we held her in high esteem."

"A witch! A witch! Burn her!"

"To the stake! Burn her."

"Burn her! Burn the witch!"

Deathly pale and motionless, Blanche stood there and said nothing. Her face was set, her lips drawn in a thin line. But her mother, a small, stooped old lady, stepped forward, sobbing. "My Lords! Good knights!" she called to the judges. "For Christ's sake, believe me! She is no witch, my little love. No child could be kinder to her old mother . . . Ah! My poor, sweet darling. Never has God created a purer soul. They say here that she poisoned her husband. It's not true. Accuse me if you will. I did it! I gathered henbane and madwort by the light of the moon. I brewed the viper's venom. I! Not she!"

"I knew what you meant to do, Mother, and I did not interfere," Blanche retorted flatly.

"She admits it! She admits it herself!" shouted the crowd.

Adhemar de Monteuil raised his hand. How much did he know? How could he be certain? He simply could not believe that Blanche was a witch, and yet all about him shouts rose like thunder:

"Murderess! Witch!"

"Burn her. Burn her. To the stake."

Outstretched hands demanded that the crime be punished at once, but the Bishop did not intend to play Pilate. He would not wash his hands of the case.

"I am postponing the verdict until tomorrow," he announced in a firm voice. "The case is by no means simple. We must first ask God to give us understanding."

A general murmur greeted his words. What? The case was not simple? And what, pray, could be simpler! Was there not enough proof? If there was doubt, it concerned only one thing: would it not be better to burn the mother along with the daughter?

"I am postponing the verdict until tomorrow," repeated the Bishop, looking at his fellow-jurors. They assented. Raymond gladly, for he had always been fond of Blanche. Godfrey indifferently. He had grown strangely listless of late, thin and wasted as though grieved by some hidden torment. Baldwin listened to the Bishop's decision absently, for it meant nothing to him. Gontrane was very low and probably would not last more than three or four days. Because of that, Leone was becoming more and more demanding, insisting that she was with child. Bother the wench! he thought.

Hugh de Vermandois, who had been yawning with distaste, was glad to rise from his seat. Only Arnuld de Rohes shook his head disapprovingly.

"As you wish, my Lord. Nevertheless, I should think it would be better to close the case today. Such crimes should not be condoned even for a few hours. Evil deeds must be branded at once, else leniency becomes the partner of crime."

"Right, right," Alberon the Archdeacon chimed in, a worldly man and, like Hugh, always careful of his attire. He wrote beautiful verses in Latin and was reputed to be fond of the company of women, so he was eager now to show the sternness of his judgment. But the Bishop was adamant.

"I am postponing the verdict until tomorrow," he repeated for the third time. "The accused may return to their tent."

The assembly dispersed reluctantly. Raoul alone remained, bitterly disappointed. Throughout the whole trial he had watched Blanche, scanning her face for a sign of pleading or fright. If she had but once looked at him beseechingly he would have retracted everything; all his vindictiveness would have vanished, melted away. Indeed, he would have gladly risked his life to save her.

But Blanche had not looked his way. Not once. She did not see him, she did not even accuse him.

"No, they will never escape," thought the Bishop dejectedly, as he returned to his quarters. "There is no way out. The verdict will have to be given and everything is against her. Everything."

"What a fiendish case," he said half-aloud.

"Fiendish! Fiendish, indeed!" screeched a voice behind his back, so unexpected that Adhemar gave a start. It was Peter the Hermit talking from his customary hiding place behind the divan.

"A fiendish case," he repeated. "Of course it's all the Fiend's doing. The whole crusade. Fiendish."

"Be quiet. You know you are not allowed to speak in this way."

"And why not, Your Grace? Why shouldn't I? They all know about it. Everyone knows. We are all in the hands of Satan. Of the great, high, almighty Satan."

"Hush," shouted the Bishop angrily. "Hush, or you'll force me to try you too, you hapless wretch!"

"What do I care? I wanted to be killed in battle. No one killed me. What do I care whether I am tried or not?"

Raymond's personal squire lifted the flap of the tent.

"Your Grace," he announced, "the Greeks have sent a constructor of siege towers. He arrived from Byzantium yesterday, it seems."

"That's good news indeed," said the Bishop. "Let me have him here at once."

*   *   *   *

It was already dark outside when the old Lady Salviac de Viel entered Raoul's tent. He looked at her with derision, thinking, "So Blanche would not come to plead herself and sent her mother instead!" He motioned her to a stool. The old woman could hardly speak for the tears that choked her voice, but she neither cursed nor pleaded as Raoul had expected. She only reminded him that back in Toulouse they were the only ones who had not avoided him and she asked him why must he bring misfortune upon them now? Why was he so bent on hurting Blanche?

Tears trickled from her eyes in an unbroken stream. "And to think that once I had hoped that you two would marry some day . . . that I would yet rock your babes . . . And now you, sir, have done such a thing to my child."

"You thought that we would get married?" asked Raoul uneasily.

The old lady nodded her grief-stricken head. She did not dare to say it again, for she was suddenly assailed by a new fright. Perhaps her candor was a mistake? Perhaps the knight really believed that Blanche was a witch and would take offense at her matchmaking? And yet the life of her child was now in his hands.

"So you thought that we two would wed some day? Faith! I thought so myself . . . once."

"Mercy!" she whispered.

Clutching the arms of her stool she leaned forward, and asked with a whimper, "So it was out of love that you would have her tortured?"

He looked at her with blood-shot eyes.

"She would not have me . . . She hated me."

"So that was why? . . . Because she would not have you. Oh Jesus! Sweet Jesus."

"Beg as I would, she'd never give me a kind word. I was no better than a dog in her eyes."

"You are wrong, sir. She was always partial to you. To you and no one else."

He laughed bitterly.

"Partial to me, indeed! She hates me. I watched her today, watched her every instant. Had she but once looked at me as though I was a man, not a piece of chattel, I would have told the Bishop that it was all a lie, even though it is true."

"Is it true, then?"

"How can you ask? Would I lie against her? Of course it is true. I found her there, but I would retract everything if she would only look at me."

"And I will tell you this: she has loved you and none but you these many years. I watched her, I knew. But what did you do? You would take her high-handedly against her will. She is not that sort. She is proud, my Blanche. The astrologer told me that I was to bear a son, only something went amiss with the stars, but he was right. She has a manly heart, Blanche has, and a proud soul and she would make a fit mate for a knight. Yet you tried to force her. No wonder she turned bitter though she had loved you before."

"She had loved," repeated Raoul like an echo. "Loved me . . ." Something broke within him, something burst open. Tears welled up in his eyes. He felt like a pitiful wretch. He and Blanche. The unhappiest beings in the world. He and Blanche.

The old woman patted his arm without rancor. "Come, son. Perhaps all will turn out all right, yet. God be with you."

He drew back, saying with a shrill laugh, "God? The Devil is with me, not God."

"No son, you must not say such things. Quick, make the sign of the cross. Isn't God stronger than the Devil?"

Raoul blinked, struck by the truth of her words. Indeed, God was stronger than the Devil.

"I am going to the Bishop," he jumped up with sudden determination.

"God bless you, son. Go. I'll return to my little dove. I'll tell her."

They both hastened out into the dark going their separate ways. But Raoul did not find the Bishop in his tent; he was out visiting a sick knight. And Lady Salviac de Viel to her horror and dismay found guards posted in front of her quarters.

"By order of the Chaplain of the Duke of Normandy, no one is to go near the witch to-night."

*   *   *   *

D'Haineault circled around the tent of the newly arrived Greek, Pantopulos. The guards stationed at the entrance eyed him curiously, for the hour was late. The hour was late indeed, but D'Haineault had just learned of the arrival of the Greek engineer, and was unable to wait until morning. A man who had come from Byzantium yesterday might know something about Ida and it was absolutely imperative to see him this very night.

The light of an oil lamp seeped through the slits of the tent; the Greek was not yet asleep and the leader of the guards went in to announce the belated guest. While he waited for his return, D'Haineault slumped on a stone, mortally tired, weak with longing, choked by anxiety. Almost a year had passed without news of her. It was full summer now and she was to have come to Byzantium in early spring. What could have happened? What had delayed her? Where could she be? Every imaginable danger, every mishap, including, God forbid, betrayal, kept running through his harassed brain as he lay awake night after night.

His silver breastplate flashing, the leader of the guards returned and drew aside the flaps of the tent. D'Haineault entered, his heart pound-

ing against his ribs. Though the engineer had arrived only a few hours
before, the tent was completely set up and orderly, all the equipment
neatly arranged. The noble Pantopulos, himself, wrapped in a soft comfortable robe, sat at a folding camp table covered with strange drawings
and sketches. To the Count's infinite joy and relief he spoke Latin, as
well as did any other educated Byzantine. He greeted his guest graciously.

"You find me, sir, working on the plans for siege towers. I am trying
to ascertain which form would be the most suitable here. It all depends
upon the surface of the soil: sand requires one system of wheels and rock
a different one. I have just arrived and know not yet."

"I came here . . ." began D'Haineault, and broke off. His throat was
dry, perspiration stood out on his temples. The question he was about
to ask spun a thin thread of hope across the abyss of separation and he
feared to hear the words that might break it.

"I am surprised to hear that the stronghold shows no sign of being
ready to surrender despite the defeat inflicted upon the rescuing army,"
continued Pantopulos. "And after well nigh three months of siege, too.
Three months, isn't it?"

"Aye, three months," affirmed de Haineault absently.

"They must be starving by now. Aren't they?"

"I don't know."

"If there is no hunger, they must be getting supplies from outside."

"Impossible! How could they?"

"That I do not know, of course. I have just arrived. Perhaps by way
of the lake."

He looked attentively at the knight, to whom it suddenly occurred
that the face of the Greek seemed strangely familiar.

"I came to see you, sir, late as it is," he began, summoning all his
courage, "in order to ask you something. A matter that is most important
to me. Since you left Byzantium not so long ago, you must know, I
daresay, whether my wife, the Countess d'Haineault, has arrived there
on an Italian or French galley. I've been awaiting her since early spring."

"Countess d'Haineault," repeated the Greek thoughtfully. The knight
stared at him in expectation.

"She did not come," Pantopulos said firmly. "I am certain that she
did not. Many galleys came from the West for the John Mass fair but
none had a lady of mark on board."

"She has not arrived. She has not arrived," repeated D'Haineault several times. He clutched his head with both hands, took an abrupt leave of his host and rushed out into the moonlit night.

*   *   *   *

By the time the court had assembled, the square was packed tight with a crowd that had been waiting since dawn. Since all were here save the defendant, the mob was growing restless.

"Where is the witch? Where is the witch? To the stake with her!"

"Silence," shouted De La Tour threateningly at the behest of the Bishop. "Be quiet."

"Behold the impatience of the people in their noble desire to see justice done and the loathsome sin punished," Arnuld de Rohes said through his teeth.

"Aye, *vox populi, vox Dei,*" added Alberon sententiously.

Stephen de Blois turned toward them his bored, sceptical face.

"Fiddlesticks! All the mob wants is a spectacle. What does it care about justice? Not a fig!"

"Faith, my Lord! You must not say such things."

"Why not say it? Everyone thinks so, anyhow!"

"The witch! Where is the witch? To the stake!"

"Hush," De La Tour shouted again. "Before the defendant is brought in, the accuser wishes to make a new statement. So be quiet."

Silence fell. Raoul de Beaugency stepped out before the judges and said in a ringing voice:

"Your Grace and you, my noble lords! I, a dubbed knight, withdraw hereby the accusations I have so heedlessly cast yesterday upon the noble and virtuous Lady Blanche de Montbeliard, daughter of the good kindred of Salviac de Viel."

All gaped in astonishment, judges and spectators alike.

Silence. Then an uproar of voices:

"He recants! He retracts his accusations. What does he mean? Then he must have lied yesterday. Liar! Liar!"

"This is just what I expected," Arnuld railed. "Witchcraft! The mother of the witch went last night to see this knight. She plied him with some potation to deprive him of memory. And lo! here are the results."

Raoul smiled contemptuously.

"No one gave me anything. I am telling the truth, the honest truth now, not yesterday."

"He lied. A knight lied."

All at once those who only a moment before would drag Blanche to the stake turned against Raoul.

"True. I lied," admitted Raoul calmly. "Deal with me as you see fit."

"But why did you malign her thus?"

"Because she would not yield to me."

A murmur of horror ran through the crowd. Now they were all against him. They spat with contempt. Swords rattled. "Liar!" "Defamer!" came the cries.

"Wait," commanded the Bishop almost aghast. "Do you mean to say that she was not on the battlefield? That she did not touch corpses?"

"No, she was not. She touched no corpses. I made it all up."

"But, she admitted it herself yesterday, insisting only that it was compassion that had led her there."

True. Blanche had not denied the charge. Raoul, who had forgotten it, fell silent. Arnuld gloated.

"See? It's just as I told you. They've cast a spell over him. He says what he was told to say."

"Bring the defendant here," said the Bishop, sighing. The mystery which lurked under this strange affair filled him with dread. There was beneath its surface some quagmire which he found impossible to fathom. Where had it come from? What had wrought such change in these people, once so candid and forthright? What was happening to them all?

"Bring the defendant," he repeated.

Four squires set out. Lady Salviac de Viel hastened along with them; at last she would be able to kiss and comfort her darling. The Bishop rubbed his forehead with his palm, thinking that it was useless to seek the truth here.

"So you recant your accusation," he turned to Raoul.

"I recant."

"In that case it is bootless to pursue the trial."

"By your leave, Your Grace," the indignant Arnuld exclaimed. "When demoniac practices are involved, the withdrawal of accusations does not dismiss the case."

"You are too prone to tax as satanic practices what is likely nothing more than a lovers' quarrel. Neither of them was under oath."

"To me Satan's hand is plain as day in all of it. I said so yesterday."

"You are a stern judge, sir."

"Indeed we are stern. And no wonder! Such things do not happen among us Normans."

Livid with rage, Raymond rose to his feet.

"That will do! We've had enough of Norman lip. To hear you talk one might think all Normans were saints!"

"Saints? Who is a saint?" snorted Omer de Guillebaut unexpectedly. "The Norman women perhaps? Faith! they are whores, one and all! It's they . . ."

Laughter rose all around. Arnuld glared.

"In the name of the Duke, I command you to close your mouth," he hissed into the ear of the knight. Sir Omer fell silent and looked about sheepishly.

"Sit down and be quiet," said Robert.

Omer sat down.

"Well now we have heard the truth about the Norman women," observed Stephen impartially, smiling a little, for no one liked Arnuld. But the chaplain would not be routed.

"Women are the same everywhere," he retorted blandly. "Never, though, have I met a Norman knight who would speak this way today and that tomorrow, or deal in slander."

"That's because you Normans speak falsely every day."

"What did you say?" bellowed Robert of Normandy, leaping from his seat.

"I said nothing but the honest truth. We know you well, you church robbers, you stealers of relics."

"Hold your tongue!"

"Nay! That I will not. This shaveling here has taunted us long enough. And who is speaking? Did you not loot Nantes, Chartres, Rouen? Did not men flee before you all over France to save holy relics from falling into your hands?"

Robert stood panting with rage, then, suddenly, burst into laughter and sat down pacified.

"Anyway, you admit that they fled before us."

Raymond bit his lips, vexed. He had spoken rashly. Now, it was too late. Words once spoken could never be unsaid. He shrugged his shoulders with assumed unconcern.

"Aye, they fled, not knowing in those days that Normans are in no haste when it comes to battle."

"As to that we shall see . . . yet."

"We saw it already three days ago. At the time of the battle with Kilij Arslan."

"We came as hastily as we could, and, mind, it was only then that the Saracens fled . . ."

"Oh, merciful heaven! So it was you who won the battle?"

"Certainly! Who else?"

"To arms! To arms! Toulouse! Toulouse!"

"Normans! Normans!"

"Jerusalem!" shouted the Bishop, rushing to separate them. Again even as he had done so many times before, he pleaded, cursed, coaxed, forbade, and reminded them of the Holy Sepulcher. Good God, were they going to fight now—after such a gallant victory over the infidels? What disgrace! And what would the Greeks say?

This last argument proved effective. Raymond and Robert subsided and resumed their seats. The Lord of Toulouse struck his chest with his fist: "I will let them be this once but I swear to God that as soon as we leave Nicaea I will go my own way. I'll have nothing to do with these slanderers."

"Nor will we with you. Just wait till we move from Nicaea."

"First take it, my Lords! First take it!"

"We will, never fear . . . In the name of God! What happened now?"

A crowd of people was coming running from the Montbeliard quarters. They shouted and waved their arms.

"Dead! She is dead!"

"Stabbed herself."

"Must have done it during the night; she is stone cold by now."

"Who? Who?"

"Why, the witch, of course. Blanche."

The court rose at once and hastened to the spot: Bishop Adhemar, the barons, the three priests, and Raoul.

"And the old lady said that God was stronger than Satan. Yet who proved the stronger? Ah! it's plain enough."

Plain and true. There had been no mistake. Blanche de Montbeliard was dead. She lay on her divan half twisted from the effort of driving into her breast the knife which she still clutched in her cold hand. She lay with wide, staring eyes, her mouth half open though mute. When her mother bent over her, two flies flew buzzing out of it.

"God have mercy on the unhappy creature," said the Bishop of Puy.

"So she ended her sinful life with the vilest of all crimes—suicide," Arnuld de Rohes commented dryly.

Old Lady de Viel lay in a heap across the divan, clasping in her arms the body of her daughter. She neither heard nor understood what was said all around her. But Raoul wheeled about threateningly.

"Have I not told you before that Blanche de Montbeliard was innocent, a noble, virtuous woman whom I have defamed? I won't have anyone malign her memory now. If she stabbed herself it was because she could not bear the infamy unjustly cast upon her."

"And what are you, in that case, my good sir?" sneered the chaplain.

"I? I am damned to hell," muttered Raoul. "Besides, as I told you before, you may do with me whatever you see fit. Here I am."

"What punishment do you demand, Madam, for the slanderer of your daughter?" asked the Bishop. But Madam Salviac de Viel did not hear him. So, tearing her away from the body, they lifted her to her feet and repeated the question again. She shook her head distractedly.

"Punishment?" she mumbled. "Punishment for Raoul? No . . . None."

Then suddenly as if recalling something she drew herself up, her eyes flashing.

"It is he who would not allow me to see her last night that I want punished! All alone she was, my dove, my poor darling. Ah, may God strike down the knave whose doing it was. Aye, may his eyes rot. May he die like a dog without Christian ministration and his soul never know peace! May the hollow ground give up his body! Oh, may Satan take him to Hell alive!"

"Hush, hush, my good woman. You must not talk in this wise. So you demand no punishment for the knight De Beaugency?"

"No . . . I always thought that these two would marry. That I would live to see their babes. Ah! my darling! My poor darling!"

They departed, leaving the mother to her sorrow. The court resumed its seats, and the Bishop arose to announce the verdict.

"In the name of our Lord Jesus Christ. In all fairness and to the best of our judgment this is what we found and announce hereby with regard to this case. The knight De Beaugency has retracted his accusations against Lady Blanche de Montbeliard. Nevertheless, before we advised her of it she took her own life. Thus, in turn, the knight De Beaugency stands accused of having heedlessly brought about the death of a good and innocent woman. We have asked the mother of the deceased what punishment she would have meted out to him? She said that she wanted none. Therefore, since the law says that where there is no accuser there is no trial, the case is closed."

"Stop! We demand punishment," announced the two brothers Salviac de Viel, speaking in one voice, and stepping simultaneously out of the throng. They were greeted by a hum of disapproval. Where had they been hiding yesterday? Why had they not stood by their kinswoman nor offered to testify either for or against her? Look at them! Yesterday they had kept out of the way hoping that people would forget that they were blood relations to a witch, and now they came forward claiming kinsmen rights!

The Constable of Clermont and his twin stood perplexed, shifting from one foot to the other. It was true enough that yesterday when the whole camp buzzed with the scandal and everyone said that Blanche was without doubt a witch they preferred to keep to themselves and avoid attention. But today it was another matter. They were both good men at heart, and the last events filled them with grief and shame. They wanted to make up for yesterday's neglect, and both were incensed at De Beaugency.

"We demand punishment," they repeated sullenly.

"Do with me as you wish," said Raoul. "It is my fault."

"Wait," said Adhemar. "The lie has not been proved. Your niece killed herself and you seek vengeance, but it has not been proved that the knight spoke untruthfully.

"He has admitted lying, in that he says he did not see her touch the defiled women. But yesterday she admitted to the court that she had done so.

"It is a complicated case, but before the knight can be punished for lying it must be proved by the Judgment of God that he is or is not a liar. Therefore I order that you two accusers meet the accused, one at a time, in single combat."

The brothers were puzzled and unsure. They did not understand the Bishop's reasoning and they knew Raoul was a fine swordsman. He would probably defeat them. But there was nothing now to do but go ahead with the test.

While squires measured and fenced off the field of combat, the Bishop sprinkled holy water on the weapons and heads of the opponents. Then the knights went to their tents to prepare for the encounter.

In a short time the brothers appeared. The horn sounded for the first summons: "In the name of God come forward!" Raoul did not appear. In his tent he sat steeped in despair. If he went forth he knew he would kill the two brothers. The Devil would see to it. Blanche would be proclaimed a witch, and her body would be thrown in the lake. Was he to wrong her once more? And yet to refuse to fight meant infamy. As far as the other knights were concerned he would cease to exist. No one would come near him, no one would address him. No one would even revile him; he would be below their contempt. Beads of perspiration stood out on Raoul's brow.

The horn sounded again: "In the name of God come forward!" The square was packed. The crowd waited tensely. For the third time the horn sounded, a long, mournful, compelling moan. A deathlike stillness fell over the field.

At last a single voice was heard. It was Adhemar proclaiming that the Judgment of God would not take place since the accused had failed to appear, thus admitting his guilt.

*   *   *   *

Swennon found Florine sitting on the parched grass.

"Have you heard of the decision of the barons?" he said. "When they leave here they will march separately, each with his army. You and I will no longer be together."

"We will be together," Florine said. "We shall be married."

Swennon looked happy. "Then the vow will be ended?" he said.

"We shall keep the vow," Florine said. "We shall be man and wife but we shall live as brother and sister."

Swennon drew back in horror. "This is madness," he said. "It will never do. It is one thing to be betrothed, another to be married. We cannot keep the oath under such conditions."

"We must," she said. "We must marry and keep the oath. We must go together to Jerusalem."

Swennon sucked in his breath. "This is foolish talk," he said. "It is sinful and useless. You are an innocent, foolish babe. Nothing but evil can come from such a twisting of nature."

He got up and walked hurriedly away.

* * * *

The building of the siege towers was proceeding apace now. There would be three of them: one large with four stories and two smaller three-storied ones. The large tower could hold a hundred men. The bridge thrown from the top locked fast so that it was almost impossible to throw it back. The defenders would have to chop it up first which would not be easy, either, since the bridge was reinforced with iron bolts. The Latin knights, weary of three months of hopeless hacking at the walls, used to come in droves to see how the construction was progressing. When would it be possible at last to open the assault?

"In two weeks—so the Greek told Count Raymond yesterday," De La Tour informed the Silesians who had come with him.

"Two more weeks! We will parch like this grass from this waiting."

"The Greek also told something else. He said that during the night while he lay sleepless because of the stench (the fastidious ninny!), he heard something splashing on the lake. He suspects that the pagans are stealthily bringing food to the city at night."

"Nonsense," laughed Glovach. "Where would they keep their galleys?"

"That's just what the Count said. You can't see a gate or an entrance to the water, but the Greek would not give in. He said that there may be an entrance, but so concealed that it is impossible to see it."

"Devil take it all! It might be true!"

"Don't evoke the Fiend's name! There is enough evil prowling about here as it is. Still, if the Greek were right I'd never forgive myself. What a bunch of fools we'd have been! Why not go and take a look at night?"

"Go, look, you won't see a thing. There can't be any galleys. If there were we would have spied them long ago."

"I don't know. Here is the Greek himself coming toward us."

"The vile louse! Just like all of them."

"Hush! He understands everything."

Pantopulos, who had sighted them from a distance, approached with a gracious smile which they did not return. "The vile louse," as D'Armillac had said. They were ready to admit and even to admire his skill in constructing war machines, but otherwise he was as repugnant to them as Strategos Argyros, Butumitos, Tatikios, Euforbenos Kalatos, and the Basileus himself. Their minds could not perceive differences existing between men of another race; whatever opinion they had of them, they generalized without qualification. To them all Greeks were alike, the same motions of well-cared hands, the same insincere smile; they were all the same.

"Our work will be soon done, now," Pantopulos assured the knights. "And the storming can begin. But did you notice, my Lords, what is going on on the lake? Last night again I heard something splashing."

"We were just talking about it. I wonder how we could find out?"

"How?" Pantopulos smiled imperceptibly. "It seems to me the best way would be to build a barge, steal out on the water one evening and lay in wait until morning."

"You're right. As I love God, you're right."

"We have boards a-plenty and we'll show the carpenters how to go about it. By tomorrow night the boat will be ready. And a good night for an ambush, since the moon won't rise till after midnight."

"It will do no harm to have a look," conceded De Foix. "And the boat will come handy for fishing too. To tell the truth we could have used one long ago only somehow it never occurred to us."

"Does anything ever occur to you? I wonder . . ." thought Pantopulos, bidding the knights goodbye.

*   *   *   *

Pantopulos kept his word. By the next day, a light barge, still somewhat sticky from tar, had been launched, ready for use. Seven knights, De La Tour, De Foix, De Luz, D'Armillac, Imbram, Yashek Zavora, and Novina embarked. Rowed by six servants, they glided silently. The night was dark and moonless; the lake lay still, a dull, steel surface, stretching before them without end. Close by rose the mass of the city, the dim outlines of bastions and crenelated ramparts looming darkly against the black sky. Unlike the other sides of the city where the fires of the watch shone brightly at frequent intervals, not one light gleamed on the lake side. Darkness and silence lay everywhere as though the city were dead.

"They keep no watch here, whatsoever," remarked Imbram. "Not a bad idea the Greek scoundrel had when he counselled this boat. Why couldn't we build great rafts, steal up to the walls at night and strike from this side?"

"Look. There is a light." It shone with an even flame like a lantern.

"They have just lit it. Could they have spotted us already?"

"Let us get closer to the walls."

Warily they moved into the shadows of the walls, then stopped and waited. At the end of an hour the boat began to rock slightly in the wind, which had died down at sunset, but had now begun to rise again and rippled the lake. Small waves struck at the bottom of the boat like the drumming of hasty fingers and the knights shivered to think that it was perhaps the dead thrown into the lake who were knocking thus from the water. But they stood bravely at their post and waited for what they hardly knew.

"Did you hear?" whispered Novina, cocking his woodman's ear.

"Aye. Something is knocking."

"And splashing—something is moving on the water."

They grew silent, turning all eyes and ears. The night was dark, but not so dark that they could not see the passing galley. It seemed to have sprung out of the wall and it glided noiselessly right by them. Either it moved by sails alone or else its oars were wielded so skillfully under water that not a splash could be heard. Only the quick lapping of the tiny waves at the hull. There was no light aboard; it moved like a phantom.

"The Greek wizard was—"

"Be quiet. Here comes another."

"And a third! A fourth!"

Four. They sailed by and vanished. The knights waited a long time but no more came and they decided to turn back.

"And to think that they have been sailing in and out like that every night while we stood on the shore," said Imbram, shaking his head wonderingly.

"The miserable, crafty pagans."

"The Greek found them out because he is no better than they are themselves. But how were we who are used to honest battle to come to think of it?"

"One thing surprises me," remarked the hitherto silent De La Tour.

"How could the Greek hear the splashing from the shore? We stood right by and we hardly heard anything?"

"Ah, the Greeks. They have tricks for everything."

*   *   *   *

The news brought by the knights created a sensation at the council of the barons. All previous happenings: the quarrel between Raymond St. Gilles and Robert of Normandy; the recent mysterious case of Blanche de Montbeliard and Raoul Beaugency; Florine's surprising request that Raymond on behalf of her absent father give her permission to wed in "white nuptials" the royal prince of Denmark and that the Bishop perform the ceremony—all were temporarily forgotten.

For once Pantopulos was invited to join in the council. No one liked him, but after all it was he who had discovered the infidels' ruse. Boemund looked at him with envy. "How could I fail to think of it before?" he mused. "Boemund, my friend, you have proven a fool, no better than the rest of them. What imbecility to leave the lake unguarded! It took a Greek to point it out with his finger."

"It's a pity we let it happen," said the Bishop wisely. "But instead of fretting, let us decide how we can close the fortress on the side of the lake. We shall need vessels. Should we build them? What should we do?"

"To be sure, I could build the necessary vessels," said Pantopulos hesitantly. "But it would be a long job. It is one thing to build a light barge and quite another matter to build a war galley. If I may offer my opinion I think it would be wiser to ask the Honorable Butumitos to transport our galleys from the sea to the lake. The Honorable Butumitos will no doubt agree, since no consideration can outweigh with him the holy end of the expedition."

"Hm . . . it might be a good idea."

"If your Grace desires, I can advise the Honorable Butumitos of your Grace's wish."

"A wish is not yet a decision. For the present we can only thank you for your kind offer. And we will call you, sir, as soon as we resolve the matter."

They wanted to discuss it freely without him; Pantopulos took the hint and left immediately. Once outside he stopped for a moment. Boemund lifted the flap of the tent to see if the Greek was not eavesdropping. They eyed each other, both equally cool and polite, and Pantopulos walked away, unabashed. He was satisfied; everything so far had gone as smoothly as he could wish.

At the council everyone began to speak at once.

"What? Are we to ask the Greeks for help? Never."

"And let them say that without their aid we could not have done anything."

"Better wait here a year than ask the Greeks' help."

"I see no shame in it," said the Bishop. "The Greeks are our allies. Unpleasant as it is to ask for help, the welfare of the cause is more important. Our goal is not Nicaea but Jerusalem. Why should we care about the glory of one victory when the true glory still lies ahead?"

"Well spoken, indeed," said Boemund. "But before we resort to the Greeks' aid, we ought first to make the round of the lake. It is a pity we neglected to do it so far. Such an inspection will readily disclose where the pagan galleys are landing, where they have their warehouses and docks. Perhaps we can make an ambush and destroy the galleys? Perhaps the shore can be reached only in a few spots and if we post guards there we can accomplish as much as a fleet might? My nephew and I shall start today, taking a thousand men along. I trust that the noble council will consent to wait for our return before Pantapulos is sent to the Greeks."

"Certainly we shall wait," the Bishop assured him.

"I will go with you," exclaimed Hugh de Vermandois, welcoming a chance to get away from the desolation surrounding the camp. The proposal was accepted without one dissenting voice. Such unanimity was rare, indeed, but the barons were ready to agree to anything that would delay the necessity of asking help from the Greeks.

*   *   *   *

After living for the last three months in the scorched, treeless desert, which they themselves had sown around the fortresses, Boemund and his men greeted with delight the shade and fresh scent of the woods. Their eyes fed greedily on the greenness which began at a distance of four hours' ride from the camp. Sunny patches lay on the ground like golden quivering discs and antelopes and wild goats, following their own secret trails, came down to the lake to drink; hares and quail scurried from under the horses' hoofs. Weary of long idleness, falcons flapped their wings on the fists of falconers, screamed and struggled to rise, and time and again Tancred ordered them released. Let them have their fling! The knights stretched their bones, weary from endless standing about under the loathsome walls and at the top of their voices they intoned an old Italian battle song. They did not try to conceal themselves. Indeed, they would have welcomed an encounter with the Saracens. What could be more beautiful than a battle fought on green turf in the shade of trees? But there were no Saracens about; the retreating Kilij Arslan had taken with him all the tribes. What remained of the local population had fled to the other side of the lake, and they wandered three, four, five days, burning fires at night and building thorn fences to keep lions at bay, without meeting another human being. Finally they reached the spot where only a narrow strip of land separated the lake from the sea. They rode hastily up the nearest hill and looked out across the beloved Mediterranean, their own native sea. The Italo-Normans loved it with a double passion: the fierce love of the Vikings and the soft tenderness of the southerners, for whom the sea represents the most beautiful dreams. It was their true fatherland, a beloved road to power and glory. The sea!

It rose high to the sky like a dark sapphire cloud. A fresh breeze blew from it, a breeze like none other, tasting of salt and freedom.

They were standing in the middle of the isthmus. Behind them, on the lake, there was no sign of life. Neither vessels nor docks. If there were any they must have been well hidden somewhere on the southern side.

"Look! There are galleys right by the shore," pointed Tancred.

And so there were. Quite close to where the group of knights stood on the hill, almost at their feet, in fact, a flotilla of vessels rode at anchor, with masts tilted and folded sails, black ships, ugly as crows, and on the shore were a cluster of campfires. Whose ships were they? Not Greeks since the ships were not painted and no labarum shone on board. Not Saracens since there was no green flag. Not Genoese, for their galleys could be easily recognized from a distance.

"Pirates! Pirates! My pirates!" shouted Hugh de Vermandois in glee. "I recognize them. It's Guynemere."

"What manner of pirates?" asked Boemund curiously.

"Why, crusaders like ourselves though true rascals. I came with them, only the Genoese would not let them into Byzantium. God sends them to us! You'll see! We will not have to ask for Butumitos' help after all."

"Are you certain, my Lord, that these are the ones you knew?" asked Boemund doubtfully.

"We can find out at once. Let us shout all together, but loudly, 'God wills it.' They will answer immediately, you'll see. They are crusaders, too."

A mighty shout of: "God wills it. *Dio li volt*," thundered from the hillock.

"Dio li volt!" came the answer from the fires below. The men who stood by them began to turn about, looking up.

"You see?" said Hugh. "It is Guynemere. He has ten vessels, just what we need. Let us go to him."

Without waiting for an answer he pushed his horse downhill and made straight for the shore, waving his hand to the pirates. They recognized him at once as the rich loafer they had taken to Byzantium. Boemund and Tancred followed more slowly, but on seeing Guynemere their suspicions vanished. He was cruel of face, bold of eye, and dark of skin, but he wore a knightly, gold-studded belt around his jerkin and a short sword hung from it.

"Guynemere of Boulogne, a true sea knight," he said by way of introducing himself. "They call me king of the pirates. The Genoese have put a prize of a hundred ducats on my head. Many a vessel have I sunk but never have I lifted my sword against a dubbed knight."

Boemund looked curiously at Guynemere's men. They were lean as hawks, with sharp teeth and rapacious eyes, yet they stood respectfully at a distance and remained in orderly rank.

"The heathen keep galleys concealed in Nicaea," said Hugh. "They sail at night across the lake and bring back provisions. We have no vessels and cannot stop them. The Greeks want to help us by moving their fleet to the lake but . . ."

"May hell swallow the Greeks!" said Guynemere. "Say no more. Give me three hundred men and we will move our galleys to the lake immediately."

"I will give you a thousand men," said Hugh.

"So much the better," said Guynemere. "Let them start cutting trees at once for the causeway. The whole isthmus from the sea to the lake must be laid with logs. I will show you where to get them. Meanwhile my men will dismantle the galleys."

As he talked he moved. Instantly the shore was astir with feverish activity. The knights rode off to order their men to work. Soon axes were swinging and freshly cut logs were rolling into place on the isthmus. By dusk the causeway was almost finished.

By noon the next day the galleys were moving over the isthmus. By night the last one had slipped into the lake. Quickly Guynemere's men rigged them. On each Tancred posted some of his own men. He himself sailed with Guynemere. Under a new moon they set forth.

Before long the galleys of the heathen appeared. The pirates closed in. Bulwarks collided, frames creaked, prows reared like frightened horses. Quickly and deftly the pirates went to work with their knightly allies. In the dark, blood flowed quickly; the wounded were pushed into the water.

Guynemere, listening to the groans and cries, heard a feminine scream rise above the tumult on the galley he had boarded. Going below he entered a cabin and found a woman, crazed with fear, trying to avoid the knife of a black eunuch. The eunuch was trying to do his duty—his mistress must not fall into the hands of the Christians while alive. Guynemere struck the man with his mace and felled him.

"Stop yelling," he said to the woman. "He is gone. Not that it will help you much, but at least you will have some frolic before you die."

She was, he discovered, the Sultana Djurisha, wife of Kilij Arslan. Her small son was in an adjoining cabin. Guynemere locked the woman in and went on deck where Tancred and his men still fought.

"Don't kill the oarsmen," Tancred shouted. "There might be Christian prisoners among them."

In a short time the carnage was complete. Back on his own galley Guynemere shouted orders: "Set the sail! The wind is rising; it will carry us straight to the camps. Take the pagan galleys in tow. We will divide the prize ashore."

When they had landed and it was day, Guynemere asked Tancred what portion of the loot he wanted.

"None," said Tancred. "I have no claim on it."

"What about the woman?" Guynemere said.

Some of his men brought the sultana before Tancred and tore the veil from her face. They were about to strip her when Tancred stopped them.

"Let her be," he said. "No need of that."

He looked at the uncovered face and blushed in spite of himself. The woman was incredibly beautiful—soft eyes, a skin of rose and snow, a heart-shaped painted mouth. But these things were not what stirred him. It was the fact that the sultana was the essence of womanhood, the incarnation of sex, that struck him. She was something without a will, sinless and irresponsible, unlike the coarse, stout-hearted Latin wives or the learned, refined Greek courtesans who meddled in masculine affairs. She was just a woman, a slave, and the sight of her brought but one thought to mind—pleasure of the flesh. She was a perfect instrument of love, an ideal vessel for passion. To give pleasure was all she knew. Her one and only duty was to be sweet in the loving embrace of a man, yielding to every one of his desires.

This was so apparent, so plain, that Tancred instantly knew two things. He must not be near her himself, and he must not allow the pirates to have their way with her.

"Since she is the Sultan's wife," he said to Guynemere, "she must not be touched until the barons have decided what is to be done with her. Until then she will remain in my camp and under the guard of my men."

Guynemere smiled and nodded. Tancred took the woman and her son and went to his camp. Boemund agreed with his nephew's decision.

"You are right," he said, "but our barons will not see it that way. To them she will be just another pagan woman and they will not protect her. I suggest that you keep her yourself."

Tancred blushed. "No," he said. "I will not do that. It just doesn't seem right."

"Then send her to Butumitos. He will be glad to have her as a hostage." He smiled. "You won't see much of her then."

"I never want to see her again!" said Tancred angrily.

But Butumitos was glad to receive the sultana and paid the pirates a handsome ransom for her. He was disturbed that the crusaders were on the lake, however. They would cut off supplies to the city and soon the garrison would be starving. Pantopulos was delaying the siege towers but even so Nicaea might eventually surrender to the Latins.

Butumitos sent for one of his aides. "Signal the fortress that we want them to send a messenger here at once," he said. "How is the task of erecting the siege towers going?"

"It awaits only your word to be completed."

"It must wait until I reach an understanding with Emir Mudjahid. Send the signal."

*   *   *   *

The wedding of Swennon, son of Olaf, and Florine, daughter of Philip, took place on the eve of the great assault. In the chapel-tent which the Basileus had given to the Bishop still back in Byzantium, all the barons stood in a body. Outside, a host of knights pressed and craned their necks. Oh! how differently they would have celebrated these nuptials back home at the bride's ancestral castle. From all over Burgandy folks would have come riding, bringing gifts, to pay homage. A hundred boards set in the field, a hundred barrels of wine, continually replenished, a hundred oxen, a hundred hogs, a hundred sheep killed every day. A hundred bridesmaids in white and gold in the bride's train. A hundred musicians, a hundred booming bells. And flowers . . . flowers everywhere, sweet-scented, brilliant, an endless sea of bloom, as though all the Burgundian orchards, vineyards, meadows, and groves had come to meet at the ducal court.

It was these flowers that Florine missed most as she walked now towards the chapel tent, surrounded by her maids-in-waiting. Oh! could she but have some here! She wore a tiny green wreath upon her long, fair hair, but what a pitiful little wreath it was! Myrtle or rue were not to be found, and who could tell whether the leaves from which her wreath was woven had not come from some tree inauspicious to wedlock, if they might not bring childlessness or domestic strife? Count St. Gilles had sent his men that morning to the distant woods to cut and bring some green sprays and they had returned at noon with this weak foliage already withered in the August heat, its branches curled, its leaves shrivelled; what remained fresh was scarcely enough to make the wreath.

Swennon waited for his betrothed, dressed in a short crimson kirtle, cut open at the sides, and trimmed with white. Over the crimson tunic he wore a belt of silver links with his sword attached. A golden band on his head proclaimed his royal descent. The youth's face was handsome but pale and haggard; and he was without joy as he led his bride to the altar. Behind him stood his Danish knights, in helms adorned with aurochs' horns, wolves' heads, or bear fangs, their fair faces honest and simple. They looked around with disbelief and wonder. By the old Gods of the Sea! What manner of nuptials were this? they thought. No white coif to be pinned on the bride's head, no bridal bed to lead the young couple to—what was the use of such espousals? They kept their counsel, however, since it was not for them to judge, and as best they could they concealed their grief; it was not so that they had pictured their prince's wedding.

Indeed, few of those present understood what the young couple was about. The Bishop, who knew, had advised them to reconsider their decision. "The idea, itself, is pious and praiseworthy indeed," he had said, "but it will be hard to carry out, human nature and flesh being what it is. In all sincerity, I advise you to wait. It is a hundred times better not to take a vow than to break it afterwards."

"God bless you," sighed the Bishop, as amidst solemn silence he now tied the hands of the young couple with a stole, while the assembled knights raised their right palms to bear witness that Swennon, son of Olaf, and Florine, daughter of Philip, were truly wed.

The marriage rites were finished, but the young couple did not rise from their knees. They were ready to take another vow. The Bishop brought forth the Gospel. Both laid their fingers on it, Swennon trembling, Florine steady and masterful, and they spoke simultaneously: "For the love of Our Sweet Lord Jesus Christ, we swear, that though wed we shall live in chastity until the Lord's Sepulcher is set free. So help us God. We swear not to enter the nuptial bed nor to embrace each other until we reach a liberated Jerusalem. Amen."

"Amen," repeated all.

The cortege left the chapel tent amidst a din of oboes, horns, and drums, and Raymond St. Gilles invited all present to join in the feast which, in the absence of the parents of the bride, he had prepared at his camp. Bards were waiting; there would be music and song.

"I shall welcome you with a glad heart," he repeated and all knew that he was speaking sincerely. "Make merry and be of good cheer for good luck to the newlyweds, and for good fortune in tomorrow's battle."

So they trooped to the tables, and drank wine; but the conversation languished. Swennon and Florine sat side by side silently, and the others were thinking about the morrow. Who would survive that great day? Who would cover himself with glory? Only one thing was certain: tomorrow evening the stronghold would be theirs.

*   *   *   *

And indeed, before dawn, the body of the army began to move toward the walls. Though profusely greased, the wheels of the siege towers squeaked lugubriously under the weight of hundreds of armed men. Nevertheless the giant machines moved smoothly enough, pushed from inside by men seated on the lowest platform. All around pressed a crowd of unmounted knights, and servants carrying ladders, ropes and hooks. Hands quivered impatiently, eyes glared.

Baldwin of Lorraine had just led his own men out of the camp, when old Helgund, breathless and perspiring, came running and clutched at his mantle.

"What do you want?" he hissed angrily. He hated the loathsome hag. Besides, what an ill omen! Why! It was common knowledge: let a woman clutch at a knight going to battle and he was bewitched for the rest of the day.

"What do you want?" he repeated harshly.

"Lady Gontrane is calling you, my Lord. She wants to tell you something."

"Me?" he cried astounded, for Gontrane had been lying unconscious as though in the throes of death for the last few days, so that a priest had administered extreme unction.

"She has regained consciousness and keeps calling for you," said Helgund. "But hurry, my Lord, for she is terribly weak."

She was overcome by tears. Her grief was sincere for after Gontrane's death, her lot at Baldwin's court would be a sad one. Baldwin sighed and turned back, leaving Konon de Montaigue in command.

Gontrane was indeed conscious with the consciousness of the last flicker of life.

"Baldwin," she whispered in a barely perceptible voice. "I don't want to die here. I am frightened."

"Why should you die?" asked Baldwin uncertainly. "Perhaps you will get better yet."

"Listen, a Greek physician came here once . . . didn't he? You said so."

"Yes, he did."

"Send for him. Send quickly. Let him cure me. I am afraid to die here."

Baldwin opened his eyes wide.

"You want me to send for the physician now?" he repeated. "But look here! That's quite impossible. We are about to storm the ramparts. Besides, the Greek's camp is a long way off. It will be all over with you

long before he could get here. Whatever put such ideas into your head?
Why, the man is the Devil's own donzel. Whatever he knows he learned
on corpses. It would be mortal sin to call him. You admitted it yourself."

She understood nothing of what he said, only kept repeating in a
pitiful voice:

"Send for the Greek. Send for the Greek. I am afraid to die here."

"I cannot send for him," he tried to explain, much perturbed. "Think
what would people say? You have already received the last rites and you
have no need for a leech."

She looked at him sharply and said strongly, "You don't want to bring
him."

"I cannot bring him."

"You don't want to. You don't want to," she repeated. "You would
like to see me dead so that you might lie with that wench of yours to
your heart's content. You don't want to. You don't want to!" Anger
gave her strength and her eyes shone in a face that was already almost
cadaverous. Her fingers played convulsively upon the coverlet.

"I will curse you if you don't send immediately," she groaned. "You
understand? I will curse you. Send at once! I want to live."

"Very well! Very well!" muttered Baldwin and ran out of the tent
in despair.

He found Godfrey already dressed in his armor, his shield hanging
from his neck.

"Come to her," pleaded Baldwin. "Come. She must not die in anger or
else she will never find peace in her grave, nor leave us any, either. She
will keep returning. And yet how can I bring that miserable leech to
see her?"

"Is it as bad as that with her?" asked Godfrey, staring straight ahead.

"She will give up the ghost any moment now. Do come. She always
listened to you. Come, speak to her. Let her die in peace. Did I tell you
she is cursing me?"

"How can I go?" Godfrey said softly and Baldwin was suddenly
struck by the change in his brother's face, by a sudden aging. "How can
I go?" he repeated, "when already we ought to be starting for the walls?"

"I will take your place. I turned my men over to Montaigue. Do go."

"All right," said Godfrey with sudden determination. He pulled the
thong of his shield over his head and threw the shield to his squire. Before the tent of his sister-in-law he hesitated a moment, crossed himself,

and entered. She recognized him at once and a shadow of a smile flitted over her sunken face as she raised her hand a few inches in greeting. Godfrey seated himself carefully on the edge of the divan.

"Don't be wroth with Baldwin, Gontrane, because he would not send for the physician. You must think of God."

"I need no one now that you are here," she whispered.

He lowered his head in confusion, not knowing what to answer. Gontrane went on, gasping painfully between words:

"Did Baldwin send you here?"

"Yes."

"Would you not have come of your own?"

"No."

She closed her eyes as if he had struck her.

"I've been ailing so many weeks," she complained. "And you never—asked—nor came to see me."

"Ever since you fell sick, night after night, I prayed for you from dusk to dawn," he replied in a low voice.

"What good are your prayers to me? You would have prayed for anyone else even as you did for me."

"I prayed for you, and for myself."

She glanced up questioningly, not understanding. Avidly she watched his bent head, the bright tow of his beard, the gaunt outline of his cheek. Suddenly with an effort she stretched her palm toward him and said in a clear, solemn whisper: "Godfrey, I am about to die. Lying here on my death bed I shall ask you something. Upon your knightly honor tell me the truth: Did you ever love me or not?"

He turned white as a sheet. In the same solemn voice he replied:

"I loved you, Gontrane, from the moment I set my eyes upon you until now that I am at your death bed. I never loved any other woman but you."

Overcome, she closed her eyes. From under the sunken lids big, rapid tears began to flow. "Why didn't you tell me?" she whispered with bitter reproach.

"I vowed chastity."

"What for?"

The question startled him.

"What do you mean: what for? Is there anything more pleasing to God than chastity?"

"Then why didn't you retire to a monastery? Why did you remain in the world? Do you think that it pleased God that you should lose my soul? I was good and I turned wicked. Wicked as the Fiend himself. I am doomed forever."

"You are not doomed. Not after you've been shriven and received the Holy Ointment."

"Oh! yes, I am doomed. Even now I think more about you than about God. Why, oh, why did you do it? Why did you never tell? Not a word?"

"How could I tell? I had to guard you from sin. And believe me, it was harder for me than it was for you."

She wanted to laugh but could not. "How do you know for whom it was harder? All my life! All my life! Oh God!"

"Still we avoided sin," he said by way of comfort.

"You avoided it by pushing me into it. And Baldwin? What did he do to deserve this?"

He raised his head, about to answer, but suddenly fell silent. Baldwin had returned to the tent, feverish and excited. He glanced at his wife almost absentmindedly. "Well, Gontrane," he asked, "did Godfrey convince you?"

She gave him a strained smile.

"Forgive me, Baldwin, for all the wrong I've done to you. Your life with me was no bed of roses. Pray, forgive . . ."

"I have nothing to forgive you," he replied, startled. He meant it. He felt no ill-will toward his dying wife.

"Thank God," he added, "that you feel no wrath towards me. Helgund is on her way here. And we, Godfrey, must be off. There is something wrong in the camp. Horns are blowing."

"To the storm!" cried Godfrey, rising to his feet.

"Nay, not to storm. To council. The Bishop's messengers just passed by a moment ago. They must be delaying again. Come, let's hurry."

With a convulsive grasp of her hand, Gontrane clutched Godfrey's jerkin.

"Don't go," she whispered half consciously. "Stay here awhile. It won't be long, now. Remember I will never see you again."

He staggered, trying vainly to break away from her clenched fingers.

"I must go. God be with you, dearest. I ought not to say that . . . I must go. It is my duty, Gontrane, my duty."

"Can't you forget your duty this once! For my whole life! Just that short, little while. Stay!"

Baldwin stared at them with round eyes, completely baffled.

"I will stay," Godfrey said meekly. Beads of perspiration stood out on his forehead. He sat down again on the divan.

Gontrane's face grew smoother, softer, gentle. The lids closed over the eyes and she seemed completely changed.

Suddenly Konon de Montaigue burst into the tent.

"My lords!" he shouted. "For the love of God come! The city has surrendered to Butumitos! The Greeks entered it at night, in secret, while we slept! The Greek labarium is already flying on the walls. They won't let our men in. Chariots with Greek Fire are posted at the gates. They say that Nicaea is theirs and we can go on our way!"

"By the passion of Christ," roared Baldwin and rushed out of the tent with Montaigue at his heels. Godfrey rose to his feet. Gently, tenderly he loosened the fingers of Gontrane from his mantle, folded her palms on her chest, bent over her in farewell, and made the sign of the cross. It seemed to him that her lips quivered, that she whispered yet, "Godfrey."

"God have her in His care!" There was no time to look back. He ran out from the tent, mounted his horse, and caught up with Baldwin and Montaigue. Others surged up on every hand. Hugh and Stephen de Blois galloped by.

"*Graeca fides!*" the latter called to Godfrey. "*Graeca fides!* They made fools of us again!"

"Surely, we will not let them get away with it," Baldwin snarled. "We must storm the walls at once."

"I promised her to stay. What if she awakens once more and doesn't find me there?" thought Godfrey, following the others.

Raymond St. Gilles stood by the Bishop livid with rage, tugging at the neck-band of his jerkin.

"I know nothing of it! I know nothing of it! I am going to storm at once, and damn the schismatics!"

"It shouldn't be done without the Council's consent," the Bishop said. "Wait, my Lord, till they all gather."

"No need waiting! I shall attack no matter what they decide. I won't let the Greeks get away with it! I won't!"

"Nor will I," Baldwin shouted.

Boemund, Tancred, and the two Roberts arrived simultaneously. They all knew already what had happened, and their hands shook with rage.

"Attack! Attack! Storm the walls!" bellowed Tancred.

But Godfred still wondered sadly. "Did she ever find out that I left her, or did she die happy and at peace?"

◇◇

BOOK THREE

27.

Dorylaeum

THE RIVER SAKKARA SWEPT LAZILY ALONG ITS SLIMY BED. ON ITS BANKS shone innumerable campfires built of dry dung, and by their meager, smoky, evil-smelling flame, knights and servants huddled, the knights by the larger, the servants and the usual camp rabble by the smaller ones.

Of the total number of the huge army, the knights constituted but a fraction, the rest was made up of squires, donzels, lute-players, ostlers, falconers, men at arms, the numberless tail of a great army.

Amidst those regular servants there had seeped in a large number of vagabonds from the ranks of Peter the Hermit, who had remained in Byzantium to roam and pillage the suburbs after the main body of the peasant army had been removed to Civitot. Many had been caught and summarily disposed of by the *nyctoparkos;* quite a few, however, had survived and joined the regular army. This rabble stole anything it could lay its hands on, dressed in rags stripped from the corpses on the battlefield, lived on scraps from the masters' tables, and in battle stood up to the enemy with fierce and cruel bravery, caring not what they fought for. They had but one dream: to amass some wealth and to go home rich and free.

Among these throngs who sat now in the heart of Asia Minor, huddling around dung fires, among these men with plebeian, oftentimes ludicrous names and no patrimony, of whom the priests said, though not very loud, that they had an immortal soul, though neither the lords nor they, themselves, believed it, there began to awaken after these long wanderings new ideas and new feelings.

What once seemed the natural order of things, as unalterable as birth and death itself, began to be tinged with doubt. Vague, unacknowledged doubt to be sure, but doubt just the same. Thus, it was hitherto taken for granted that the servant was born to obey and the lord to rule. The lot of one was to be a serf, of another to be the master. As a fish lives in water, so the knave must live in stench, toil, and bondage, and as the eagle soars toward the sun, so the knight would fly toward fame, fortune, and glorious adventure. Right or wrong, that's how it was. And that was how it always would be. One could not change fate.

Now, however, after two years of wandering across the world, this simple belief was beginning to crack. Already, once before, old Blaise, a garrulous drunkard from the retinue of the Count de Blois, had loudly announced by the fire that if all the servants left them, the lord knights would be forced to groom the horses themselves. Aye, they would have to, since there were no other servants to be found here. And what of it? It wouldn't kill them, either!

"Hush!"

"You'll only bring on trouble," others tried to restrain him, looking around anxiously.

"Why should I hush? Isn't a knight a man, same as I? Was he not born of a woman, even as I was? Only that his mother lay in a bed and mine by the pig-sty."

"Sinful talk," others shook their heads. And even old Blaise, once sober, hardly believed what he had so brashly proclaimed, but the seeds of his words remained and sprouted. Resentment was born, and in time turned to hatred. Why was it that in the old days they did not feel that hatred? The reason was simple enough. Look at winter! Winter is fierce, winter is cruel, particularly cruel to the poor wretches who have neither roof nor warm food to fight it with. Yet who would think of cursing winter or rebelling against it? Winter must be. Everyone knows that. One must suffer, one has to put up with it; so people bear it with patience. But just think what would happen if some wizard or, still better, some saint proclaimed that there need not be a winter, that it can be driven away! How everyone would fall on it then! How all the old pains and grudges would be suddenly remembered: the cold, and the hunger, the frost-bitten feet, and numb hands. How everyone would shout, "Down with winter! Down with winter!"

The knights, too, were slowly becoming aware of the change. Almost unawares they showed more forbearance, more friendliness to their men. They were beginning to realize that should a lazy donzel take it into his head to abandon them and hide in another camp, or go over to the Greeks or heathens, the position of his master would be sorry, indeed. Just as old Blaise had said in his cups, the knight and the squire would then be forced to water and groom horses, to cook the food, clean the harness, and bother about a thousand things of which a nobleman knew nothing. And so, mailed fists, once so prone to blows, were checked time and again.

Alas! No servant felt the slightest gratitude for this unwonted kindness. The knaves understood the motives that lay behind it far better than the knights themselves and they scoffed at it behind the masters' backs.

"We must go on serving them for the time being," declared Klimek, an old crony of Blaise, "otherwise we would get no grub. Nor do we know the way. But you just wait till we get out of this God-forsaken wasteland!"

"Right you are. Once we get out . . ."

"If we ever get out," sighed someone, "looks as though the devil lured us here to our death."

"That's so. We seem to be going off further and further. No telling if a body will ever see the old country again."

"Oh! Lord, don't say . . ."

"Come, man. You whimper as though it was all cakes and mead back there. Has the brand peeled off your back, or what?"

"You fools! Who wants to go back?"

"How then? Would you as soon stay here?"

"Here!" Klimek, Blaise and several others laughed scornfully at the idea. No one in his right mind would choose to remain in this wilderness. But between the heathen desert and the domain of the baron there stretched the entire wide world, across which they had wandered for the last two years, the vastness of which they had trodden with their own feet. There were in that world fertile lands where life would be easy and sweet. "Once we get to these parts we will all band together and found a duchy of our own where we shall be lords and masters!"

Thus spoke Klimek and, carried away by his own words, he sprang to his feet. The others stared at him in horrified silence.

So they talked, squatting on the hard sun-baked ground and shivering with cold, for the paltry fires gave practically no heat. Somewhat more profuse, for they were reinforced with wood, were the fires of the lords burning nearby. Around them, too, buzzed a constant hum of loud voices, time and again rising to the pitch of a quarrel. The recent Greek betrayal, the necessity of leaving Nicaea empty-handed, after wasting there so much time and effort, the harassing march amidst the heat and draught of the desert, had left the knights as irascible as bees at swarming time. The summer-parched Phrygia which they were crossing now was not a true desert, nevertheless to the western knights the march seemed unbearably arduous. All day long a brown cloud of choking dust enveloped the marching troops, wells were scarce and insufficient, and the dry brooks, called *wadi,* yieded nothing but stones. Wistfully they recalled the profuse morning dews, the drenching showers spouting from big-bellied clouds, and they wondered whether they would ever see them again.

The knights chafed and fumed and did not know on whom to vent their ill tempers. Ever fiercer quarrels flared up around the fires and life in the camp became almost unbearable.

On nearby hillocks other fires could be seen—those of the Normans who, as agreed upon at Nicaea, were pursuing their own course.

The Bishop had opposed this division as best he could, but to no avail. "It would be wise, indeed, to take two separate trails," he had argued, "for it will be easier to find water, and two will go hungry where there is food for one. But we must constantly keep in touch to prevent our falling into a trap."

But they would not even listen to these sensible words. They maintained no contact, no communication of any sort. We will have nothing to do with these double-faced deceivers, said Raymond's men. And the Normans for their part maintained that life would be sweet indeed, once they were rid of the black-faced garlic-eaters. They would meet only, God willing, in Jerusalem. And who would get there first was yet to be seen.

So they had parted. The Provençals and the troops of the Dukes of Lorraine took to the right; the Normans, the Flandrians, and the troops of Boemund, Stephen de Blois, and Hugh, to the left. They drew several leagues apart and meant to widen the gap still more. For the present both armies were camping on the banks of the Sakkara river, blessing its scanty, muddy waters. Actually, they ought to have made a longer halt to give both men and horses a breathing spell, but the leaders in each camp trembled lest the other army should start to march ahead of them, and reach Jerusalem or engage the Saracens sooner than they and this fear induced them to leave the river after one night's halt.

Pagans, so far, were nowhere in sight. The few wretched villages they encountered stood deserted, their stone houses, with their flat roofs and low doorways, gaping vacantly at the passing troops, their inhabitants fled.

The country was growing more and more desolate, the heat more and more oppressive. The flat, scorched plain stretched endlessly; no-where did a green patch betray the presence of water. The Provençals and the Normans had been wandering across it already for three days. The Provençals had had better luck than the Normans; for they had encountered on their trail a large settlement, Lenkas, and from its abundant wells were able to renew the supply of water which they carried in leather pouches, strapped to the saddles. The Normans found no water whatsoever and on the third day of the march after draining the last few drops of tepid liquid that stank of hide, they plodded on staggering from heat and weariness.

Far away, on the horizon a mountain range loomed blue. The sight braced them some. The Armenian guide assured Arnuld, the chaplain of the Norman Robert, that from the mountains sprang a river which in its upper course must have no doubt retained some water. Before evening there would be water, they said to one another; there would be shade and fodder! And they marched on more quickly.

And, in truth, the gray boulder-strewn bed of the stream that they had been following for the last two days began to turn dark with moisture. The hounds, released from their leashes, ran ahead, yelping joyfully and sniffing the none too distant water. Then the gravel at the bottom of the dry *wadi* became wet. Men grabbed it by the fistful and pressed it to their lips and parched faces. The ranks broke up. Everyone scrambled to reach the water before others had turned it into a muddy puddle. The mountains seemed quite near, now.

"They are called *Dogorganhi* or 'Gorgons,'" the Armenian informed the chaplain. "This stream the pagans call *Sareh-Su,* which means 'Yellow-Water,' and the valley from which it flows is called 'Dorylaeum.'

There's a village of that name, too. Dorylaeum—that's in Greek; in the heathen tongue it's *Ineu-Su,* or the 'Caves,' for the mountains all around here are honey-combed with caves burrowed by demons that they call *Djins.* In some of them the people bury their dead, in others they dwell themselves. Look, my Lord, you can see them from here."

They reined in and scanned the mountains, shading their eyes with their palms, for the sun was already beginning to set. But the caves were not to be seen; an even low forest covered the mountain slopes.

"What singular woods!" Arnuld observed. "What can it be—brush-wood?" He glanced at the guide and suddenly broke off—the other seemed aghast.

"No . . . no wood grows there," he muttered and began to tremble.

"Then what can it be?"

"I don't know."

"It's an army! The Saracens!" the chaplain shouted after straining his eyes awhile. "I am not mistaken! Saracens! Your Highness!" He rushed to Robert's side. "Sound the battle horns! The enemy is close by!"

"The Saracens! The Saracens!" the shout ran over the ranks. Tumult broke out. The hoarse blare of the trumpets added to the din. Those who had drunk their fill ran to take up their posts. But by the river bank a block of thirsty men and horses barred the way.

"It is not right to start battle in the evening. Let's wait till morning!" cried some. And, indeed, at home it would never have occurred to anyone to go into strife at nightfall when the Angelus was about to ring, but the Moslems would not wait. They meant to take advantage of the confusion that had broken out among the Latins, and had already started down the hills. The forest had suddenly sprung to life; the entire valley, as well as the mountains, seemed to quicken and move under the surge of the swarming throngs. Countless they seemed, as though they had gathered here from all over the earth, or, wrought by *Djins'* magic, had sprung from the caves, from the bowels of the mountains. Over their heads floated a forest of standards and above the standards rose the shout of *"Allah akbar!"* flung from three hundred thousand throats.

It was Kilij Arslan who had collected all Islam and strategically backed by the mountains awaited the *Giours* here, eager to avenge the defeat of Nicaea.

"La, illah el Allah, Mohammed rasul Allah."

Then they came, moving to the charge, rolling down the mountain slopes, pouring out of ravines, sweeping on faster and faster. They moved with incredible precision, spread in a semicircle, in the shape of a new moon whose two prongs were turned against the Latins. These prongs were the flanks of Kilij Arslan's army which would circle and strangle the *giours!*

But now the three bodies of Western warriors promptly fell into deep ranks deployed into a long line of defense. In the middle, a little ahead of the others and pointing straight at the center of the Moslem crescent stood Robert of Normandy and Stephen de Blois; on the right, Boemund and Tancred; on the left, Robert of Flanders, Swennon, and the Count of Vermandois.

Now they closed on each other and the sound of clashing arms, of swords ringing upon shields, rose towards the mountains and returned, carried back by the echo.

Only a few of the Western knights had time to water their mounts or catch a few drops of the longed-for liquid into the hollow of their helmets. But never mind. Now that they are about to join battle with the entire might of the Moslem, who would think of thirst?

But as unpredictable Fate would have it, victory or defeat, whichever was to be their lot, was still far away. Dusk had already fallen on the slopes and was rapidly sweeping down into the valley. Soon the moon would rise and to fight by moonlight would be an evil omen and a sin. And first in the growing murk, then in complete darkness they fought, until at last, unable to distinguish friend from foe, they stopped and stood motionless, as they would stand until morning, without dismounting, eating, or drinking, never letting go of their arms, the sword raised at dusk waiting to fall at sunrise.

Boemund was issuing orders. Unasked, he had from the very beginning of the battle assumed command of all forces; for everyone knew that where skillful and determined leadership was required none save Raymond St. Gilles could compare with the Duke of Tarentum. And so, at Boemund's orders the servants and men at arms were now setting up a fortified camp. Backed against the river, it would protect the rear of the army. Four deep, they lined up wagons from which horses had been unhitched and bound them with chains. Women, children, the sick, and the weak, in fact, all who might impede the battle, would be placed inside the enclosure out of harm's way. Boemund's orders issued with great speed were carried out as swiftly. Driven at a gallop, colliding in the darkness, the carts were brought together, the horses unhitched. Servants, drivers, ostlers, worked madly, and before dawn the quadruple ring of wagons, hitched and bound by ropes and chains into an impregnable stronghold, manned by shield-bearers and axe-men, was ready—even the tents of the noble ladies were pitched.

Amidst the fever of expectation, the sleepless night went swiftly by. The murk soon became suffused with silvery paleness and from behind the hillock on th left leaped two long brilliant rays; then, suddenly, as though ejected from a catapult, the sun shot out in a fierce red ball. At once every object assumed a purple hue, every shape became outlined with a flaming aureola. *"Ave Maria Stella,"* the knights intoned in a mighty chorus.

"La illah al Allah, Mohammed rasul Allah!"

As though at a signal, fighting broke loose along the entire valley and its din reverberated from the mountains. From the very onset, the battle assumed the highest pitch of impetus and fierceness. The Moslems tried their usual tactics, endeavoring to lure the enemy by a feigned retreat, then surround and cut him off from his base, but the Latin knights had learned at Nicaea to see through those pagan tricks. Checking their own zeal, they closely held their ranks; even the impetuous William de Melun did not rush out after the fleeing foe. Arrows which wrapped their heads in a whistling buzzing cloud were no great threat provided one shielded one's eyes properly. They were very dangerous to the unarmored servants but bounced off the iron plates of the masters. And in hand-to-hand fighting the Western knights had the advantage of their tremendous strength. Standing now as though rooted to the ground they fought with the most intense fervor, chopping right and left like so many woodcutters. Strange woodcutters, indeed, that did not move forward but let the forest come to them ever thicker and thicker. Piles of bodies rose around them and they looked with clear unblinking eyes at the swarms of enemy that pressed upon them from every side, so that at times the mighty Norman army seemed like an island lost in a Moslem sea. But this could not be prolonged indefinitely; there were limits to the endurance of the muscles of even the strongest man. A time would come when the numb hand would drop the sword.

This was what Sultan Kilij Arslan was counting on. He admired the fierce bravery of the Franks, but, confident in the strength of his own forces which outnumbered them three to one, he calmly awaited the outcome. *Allah akbar!* Praised be the Prophet, he thought, who after trying his faithful so sorely at Nicaea was sending them now the chance of such a beautiful contest! Blessed be his name! Here at Dorylaeum the defeat of Nicaea would be at last avenged!

Meanwhile Arnuld, the chaplain, fidgeted in the Norman encampment. "No gainsaying," he thought, "the situation is bad. Very bad, indeed. Our forces will never be able to hold out. The Moslems are rested and have been awaiting us in a cool spot. Even now their regiments not engaged in battle stand in the shade of the hills. And we? We arrived more dead than alive, exhausted by a three days' march without water. Only a few had had a chance to drink and to water their horses before the battle began. All night long they stood in readiness, neither sleeping nor eating. And the battle is now being fought in an open field, in the full blaze of the sun. How much longer will they endure?"

Not without difficulty Arnuld slipped between the hitched wagon and made his way through the ranks of infantry and horsemen. He caught his master by the stirrup.

"Excellency—perhaps it would be possible to slip through to Raymond," he faltered. "Let him strike from the rear!"

"Never!" snorted the Curthose wrathfully, "and I'll kill you like a dog if you mention it again. Ask their help, indeed! How they would gloat!"

"We would not be asking their help by giving them a chance to crush the heathen might."

"I'll kill you like a dog, I said. Frightened already, are you?"

Arnuld withdrew without another word and returned to camp. In the center of the enclosure there rose a small promontory commanding the view of the entire battlefield, a place already occupied by a group of women who anxiously watched the surge of the battle. Arnuld posted himself in their midst, scanning the field anxiously. The female babble annoyed him—it interfered with his thinking. Of all the women present only Florine and Willibald kept their peace. The others whimpered, complained, prayed, exclaimed shrilly over the prowess of their own men or cursed the pagans. Their incessant clamor drowned out the din of battle.

Trying to ignore the noise, Arnuld pondered. At the very best our men would be able to hold out until the evening. At the very best. Aye, there was no time to waste. "I'll kill you like a dog," Robert had said—

the fool! Let him die, if he had a mind to, others preferred to live. Who would heed him, anyway? But where to look for the others? How far away could they be?

Arnuld summoned four squires, choosing the brightest he could find. Squires, not knights, since he did not want to waste time arguing with each whether or not to call the Provençals. Aye! Five would be enough: four squires and he, Arnuld. And they would take five spare horses.

They watered the mounts from leather bags and hastily unhitching the wagons to let them through, they made their way through the ring of infantry. The men at arms raised no objections. The chaplain of the Norman prince was a familiar figure; they knew that he was the right hand of his master. If only the Moslems would not spy out their departure and send pursuers after them!

Either they did not notice or could not get across the river. Anyhow, they did not follow, and now the five men and ten horses flew across the scorched desert. Upon their speed hinged the salvation of the entire army. "For God's sake, hurry," cried Arnuld. "Hurry!"

Yes—but where?

By St. Maxenus—where? For the last three days, neither of the two armies had known what was happening to the other; all contact had been lost. The Provençals might have halted on their way, they might have turned east or, on the contrary, they could have hastened their march and be by now south of Dorylaeum: who could guess how far away they were? Half a day journey, one day or two?

Cursing the stupidity of the barons, Arnuld headed straight east. There was no time to ponder. Speed was all that mattered. They tore ahead, faster and faster, the hooves of their horses thundering across the plain.

The battle continued unabated. Minute after minute passed, each measured by the fall of a cleaving sword. Hours passed, each tolled by the pulses that pounded in aching skulls. The air stood motionless like a pillar of fire and in the parched mouths the blackened tongues clung to the palates.

The women confined in their fortified enclosure sensed the peril of the situation. Anxiety drove them from place to place. They would have gladly done something, helped in some way. If only they could have carried water to their men as the wives of the Provençal knights had done at Nicaea! But they could not get through that mighty cordon of wagons.

Florine sat alone in her tent. Her thin girlish arms clasped around her knees, she moodily stared into space and her ardent blood rebelled at this enforced passive role that was a woman's lot. Could she but stand by Swennon, now, battling side by side with him, and even perish with him if their fate were to be sealed today. At last reluctantly she turned her head; Duenna Bonina had just entered the tent.

Bonina was weeping. Tears streamed down her good-natured fat face. "Holy martyrs!" she moaned. "It's dreadful! The Armenian guide, the one who speaks a little Latin, has just been to see Lady Gwenon. He says that the Saracens will spare no woman. They slay them all at once. All but the ones who are uncommonly beautiful and beautifully dressed, and they take these to their harem for their foul use. What is to become of us, my dove? Holy patron of Burgundy, save us! What is to become of us?"

Florine shrugged her shoulders disdainfully. Didn't Bonina know that women of her blood did not fall into the enemy's hands? She, too, could perish by her own hand when the time came.

"My dove, my dove!" sobbed the duenna. She clutched her head in desperation and fell to her knees to pray, only finally to spring up and run back to the tent of the Lady Gwenon in hope of finding further news.

There was no news, but all the women were still there. The Armenian guide for the tenth time repeated in broken Latin, aiding himself with gestures, that old hags like this one (he pointed at Bonina, thereby deeply wounding the good lady) would have their throat slashed, while young and comely ones like this one (he glanced at Gwenon, who smiled pleasantly) would be taken to share their captor's bed. Saying this he twisted his face into a false smile of compassion. He wasn't afraid for himself; when the crucial moment came, he intended to don the turban he carried in his pocket and to greet the conquerors with a profession of faith in the teachings of the Prophet.

Bowing deeply, he asked the noble ladies to permit their unworthy servant to depart. He promised to let them hear at once of any new developments, then slipped out of the tent. Left alone, the women sighed and moaned at the thought of dying. It was easy enough for knights to look recklessly into the eyes of death while they themselves dealt it out to others. But how could such fortitude be expected of women sitting helplessly in their tents like birds caught in a trap who wonder when their captor will come and wring their necks? Knowing that their doom was inescapable, they died a hundred deaths, till at last the torment became unbearable, the waiting turned into mad despair, and their whole beings rebelled at the thought of death.

They wept and wrung their hands. And as they wrung them they became conscious of their round white arms and all at once were overcome with grief for their own youth and beauty, for their flesh that was to become the prey of worms. No, no, they could not die! they cried. They huddled together and hiding their heads in each others' shoulders, they wept and begged God's mercy. They implored Him to spare their lives, to let them blossom and ripen, and mellow and wither in peace. It seemed to them that they knew nothing of life and yet Fate was bidding them to die.

Florine, who sat alone in her tent, caressing proudly the gilded hilt of her dagger, also wanted to live. Her whole life lay before her, as yet not begun. But she, the heiress of the proud lords of Burgundy, came from a stock in which women were their men's peers, and unlike the other women, she thought now only of how to die as became her rank.

Apart from her, only Willibald, the wife of Omer de Guillebaut, neither wept nor moaned. With dull resignation she awaited whatever Fate might bring. Surely, she thought, death could not be worse than the life that had filled her with bitterness and shame. For years now deep in her soul she had only one longing: to see Omer no more! If the only avenue of escape led through the gates of death then let death come and welcome!

Watching from the hill, one need not be a knight wise in the ways of war to see that the defeat of the Latins was nearly completed. The cruel sun was sinking at last, but that blessed relief had come too late. The resistance of the Latin knights was weakening visibly. They still lifted their arms and continued to fight, but they did so as though in a trance, moving automatically, almost unconsciously. Only one thing mattered to them now: to fall sword in hand. And they fell in ever greater numbers; the Moslems pressed more and more fiercely. The forest was at last beginning to envelop the woodcutters.

It was then that Sultan Kılıj Arslan, who had been closely watching the situation, decided that the time for the final charge had come. Four cavalry regiments, who until then had been waiting in the valley, now moved at full gallop into action, and sweeping in a wide circle fell like vultures on the weakened right wing of the Norman army. *Allah Akbar! Allah Akbar!* They broke through the cavalry. They were fighting with the infantry, breaking the chain-linked wagons. A few more minutes and the camp would be captured, and the enemy at the rear of the knights!

Screaming, the women fled from the hill. Huddled in the tents they squealed in an agony of terror. It availed them nothing to have thought all day of the approaching end. Now that the dreaded hour was at hand, the mind instead of accepting it with resignation, rebelled more than ever in a frenzy of fear.

At once Lady Alberta jumped up, and with lips pressed tight, saying nothing, she threw off the white coif which exposed only a narrow triangle of her face, cast off the stiff fringed kirtle which denoted the wife of a noble, tore off four petticoats and her coarse linen shift, and stood shivering and naked, smoothing with her hands the red marks impressed on the flesh by the strings of her skirts. The other women stared at her stupefied, then suddenly grasping the meaning of what she was doing they quickly followed her example. Frantically they threw off the heavy Latin attire which made it impossible to tell whether a woman was young or old, straight or crooked, fair or ugly. Let the Saracens see them as they really were. Let them take them to their harems to be dishonored, abused, enslaved—no matter—as long as they did not kill them. Anything but death!

Willibald looked on with scandalized astonishment, then quietly walked out of the tent. She would not follow their example, not that she was not afraid of work or slavery—but to fall into the hands of another man? All she asked for was to die quickly and without much pain.

Moving like a sleep-walker with stealthy, hesitant steps, Bonina crept into the tent where Florine sat staring into space. The head of the old duenna shook queerly, as though in perplexity.

"Is it time?" asked Florine in a flat voice, clutching the hilt of her dagger.

But the duenna did not answer. She neither heard nor saw her charge. Trembling feverishly, she undid the front of her gown, exposing a yellow wrinkled neck and withered flat breasts; she opened a vanity box and began to rouge her cheeks.

"They say," she mumbled, "that they won't kill . . . those . . . who . . ."

Florine looked at her in astonishment. "What are you doing? What is the meaning of this?" she called peremptorily. The duenna suddenly sobered, dropped the rouge and fell sobbing to the ground. From the outside came screams, moans, the clatter of hoofs, and the clang of arms. The battle was now raging inside the camp, right by the tents. In a moment the pagans would rush in. In a moment . . . Oh, Lord!

*　　*　　*　　*

Raymond St. Gilles tore like mad way ahead of his men. Now and then he turned back toward them and with angry, desperate motions urged them to greater speed. "Make haste, you fools! Must you creep like turtles!"

The detachment that he led consisted of a thousand men mounted on horses that had been specially picked of the fastest and the strongest. Nevertheless, to the impatient Count it seemed that they dragged along like oxen. The rest of the army under the command of the Bishop and Godfrey followed in their tracks speeding as best they could. But in spite of every effort they were still several hours behind.

Horses groaned with strain, sweat flooded the eyes of the riders. And even as the Moslems striking on the right flank burst into the camp, and were about to strike the rear of the army and smash it completely, Raymond St. Gilles fell upon them from the right. He swooped down like a hurricane, like a desert wind, like a thunderbolt, striking so suddenly, and with such force that he cut through the ring of Moslem cavalry, reached the Norman ranks, turned about and struck again.

"God wills it! Take heart, Normans! Toulouse! Toulouse! Take heart, Normans!" As though their hearts had ever been faint. Nevertheless, this call coming from the throat of rivals revived the senses like the lash of a whip, goading men into passion, prodding the flesh to superhuman effort. Men who a moment before could hardly lift their swords, now seized with fury, threw themselves into the fray. Through the break between the wagons, Normans and Danes rushed into the camp, at the heels of the Saracens. They fought like mad in the narrow enclosure, pressing the Saracens back, killing, pushing, hurling them out beyond the ring of carts.

While some were still wiping out the foe, others leaped off their horses, overcome with anxiety over the fate of their wives. How long had the Saracens been roaming the camp? What had happened to the women? Where were they? The knight, Le Grand, followed by others rushed into the nearest tent to stop dead in his tracks, aghast. On the benches by the walls lay naked women, their cheeks painted, their hands and breasts bedecked with jewels. And right opposite the entrance was Gwenon Le Grand. With a coy half-smile on her fear-twisted face, she rose from her couch invitingly, then with a terrified scream fell back and hid her head in her hands. She had recognized her husband. The others sprang up with squeals and crouching close to the ground feverishly began to don their recently discarded clothes. The knights looked on in brooding silence, for they could not conceive why they had found their women stripped as though in the bath house.

"Who told you to take your clothes off?" asked Le Grand sternly.

The women remained silent, overcome with shame. The comely Marguerite du Grai had snatched by mistake the shift belonging to Placide de Berneville who was much smaller and thinner than herself. With her head and arms stuck in its narrow opening, she wiggled helplessly, her face and shoulders hidden by the cloth, her buttocks aquiver with effort, exposed to the sight of her husband and the rest of the knights. Others wrapped in shifts, petticoats, whatever they could lay their hands on, crouched with chattering teeth.

"Who told you to strip?" Le Grand and De Regnier continued to ask.

Omer de Guillebaut who had pushed his way into the tent burst into venomous laughter. His loathing of women made him for the moment especially clear-sighted. "Who told them?" he repeated. "Why, they stripped of their own accord to dazzle the pagans, the filthy bitches!"

Gwenon burst into loud sobs, Marguerite followed suit. And, indeed, this weeping sounded like an admission. The knights were overcome with inconceivable shame. To these stout-hearted men who had fought all day long like heroes, like Oliver or Roland himself, it suddenly seemed as though an abyss had opened at their feet. They dared not peer into it lest the sight drive them stark mad. Their wives, their own wives . . .

"Whores!" foamed Omer de Guillebaut.

Du Grai vigorously rubbed his eyes as though he had just awakened from sleep and called: "Hey, my Lords! They are fighting out there without us!"

"Right!" All breathed with relief and left in a body, eager to get away.

Omer, however, ran first to his tent. He wanted to catch Willibald in her naked shamelessness. He had not the slightest doubt that this was how he would find her. Was she not woman even as those others? Women were all the same. Under his outward fury there lurked a malicious triumphant joy at the thought that he alone had proved right, that he alone had seen through the perfidy of women.

Contrary to his expectations, Willibald was not awaiting the victors stripped to the skin. Fully dressed, and swathed up to the eyes in her coif she sat as usual in the corner of her tent, and lifted upon her husband eyes full of pitiful surprise. Omer? Was he alive? So neither he nor she had been killed, the pagans had not come, and everything would be as of old.

"Bitch! Lecher! Wench!" roared Omer. "So you stripped like the rest?"

"I am not stripped," answered Willibald.

But Omer would not see the obvious. "You did strip!" he repeated stubbornly. "Ready and waiting for the pagan lust. You filthy beast! You trollop!"

He shook his fist over her and stamped his feet in rage. At once anger and rebellion rose in the weary and defenseless woman. She had had enough! More than enough. What did he want of her now? She must get rid of this accursed tormenter. Get rid at any cost.

"You are disappointed to see your husband come instead of a pagan," Omer hissed tauntingly. "I saw the glance you gave me, you cursed carrion! You would rather see a pagan."

"I would," she cried defiantly.

"What?" Omer, dumbfounded, drew back a step.

In her something broke, something burst loose. She rose to her feet. "I would," she repeated breathlessly. "I hate you, fool. You wanton, I loathe you. I despise you. May God punish you for all the wrongs I've suffered. Yes! I would rather live with a serf, with a servant, with a pagan! Anyone but you. Yes! With a pagan! Do you hear me!"

"You . . . you . . ." Beside himself with rage Omer ran her through with his sword. Without a sound Willibald fell to the ground; she died quickly and without pain. Without a glance at the corpse Omer walked out, his calm restored. He could go and fight now. He had destroyed the wanton! The viper—he thought—at last she had shown her true face. But how well he had known womankind.

Dead tired, spattered with his own and other people's blood, Swennon burst into the tent of his wife. Florine stood in the middle, motionless and stiff as a statue. No! She had not taken off the white coif which she tied now over her maidenly, unshorn tresses nor had she opened her kirtle. Not Florine! She stared at him blindly as though she did not know who it was.

"Florine, it is I! Florine!"

"I was about to stab myself," she whispered, showing a stiletto held in a tightly clenched fist. And suddenly freed from the inhuman strain under which she had labored for the past six hours she fell on her husband's breast and burst into childish sobs. She wept from exhaustion, and also from joy that they were both alive and that she need not die. Swennon clasped her in his arms and held her tight, his heart flooded with tenderness and love. He raised her pale face toward his own and lightly kissed her tear-stained cheeks. She was the soul of his soul, his dearest friend, his best companion, his most beloved treasure.

But at that very instant Florine stiffened and slipped out from his arms, remote, almost hostile.

"You vowed not to kiss me," she told him reproachfully.

"Damn the vow!" Swennon clapped on the helmet which he had discarded a moment before and ran furiously out of the tent.

The battle seemed to be starting all over again. The arrival of help had not settled the issue in favor of the crusaders. The Saracens did not intend to relinquish a victory that had been so nearly theirs. They had recovered from the shock of Raymond's unexpected attack and were again attacking fiercely. Evening approached, the second evening of unabating strife.

But before darkness had had time to settle over the world, there came a new thunder of hooves, a clatter of arms, and the first detachments led by Godfrey and Baldwin plunged into the battle. The two opposing sides mingled, tangled. Each had the enemy in back, in front, and on either side. In this turmoil one could hardly tell friend from foe. Lest they be

lost in the press Latins summoned each other with the battle cries of
their clans.

The Silesian knights had arrived with the first of Raymond St. Gilles'
detachments and were fighting the pagans with a bravery that excited
the admiration of their companions.

Vaguely they felt that they carried on their shoulders the honor and
good name of their country, and the feeling doubled and tripled their
strength, lent perfect unity to their effort. They were twelve, they fought
as one. And though that day each of the Western knights was too busy
to pay much heed to anyone else and though there were none but brave
men here so that it was not easy to shine forth among them, word would
soon spread throughout the Norman and Provençal armies of the valor
of the Polish knights.

But it is not easy to think at the same time of winning fame and pre-
serving life. Determined to win the first, the knights forgot the latter.
Recklessly pressing ahead, they soon found themselves cut off from the
rest. In spite of all efforts they were pushed toward the ravine. In vain
did they throw themselves about like fish in a net, slashing blindly, and
cutting the foe down with terrible strokes. For each one killed ten new
ones sprang up. They were completely surrounded. Already Nogodits
had tumbled off his horse. Ludbor Osventa was dead. Novina the
Babbler, spattering blood, slumped over his horse's neck. In a trice the
rest would likewise fall.

Glovach turned around to look at his brothers. They were still alive,
still fighting, their faces stony, the cheeks sunken from exertion, the
eyes covered with mist. All three would perish here, not one would
return home, to the old Silesian manor, not one would cross again the
sacred thresholds of their home.

"At least one must go back," thought Glovach, warding off the thrusts
of a black-faced assailant. One at least must be spared. But how, unless,
he thought, I should call *Her?*

The very thought froze the marrow of his bones. Call *Her,* the mysterious guardian of his kin? His father had told him on his deathbed that
she must be called whenever their line was threatened with extinction,
but that whoever called her must die.

"I have to," Glovach thought. "The time has come when I have to."

His teeth chattered with fear, yet it was up to him, the eldest, to call.
He stood up in his stirrups and looked about; all hell seemed to have

broken loose around him. Snorting, grunting, howling men had discarded broken swords and axes, and were now clawing each other with naked fists. As though bewitched and doomed to battle like this for the rest of eternity, they fought on and on. The moon shone from on high. ' And somewhere, infinitely far away, there still was a native land and home.

"If I must, I must." With a sudden determination Vitoslav Strzygonia, called Glovach, turned to his brothers, Zbylut and Imbram: "I shall call Her! Lower your visors and don't look!"

And raising his head to the sky, in a strange, awesome voice he called three times:

"Stshiga! Stshiga! Stshiga!"

She came. At once, gliding through the affrighted air she swooped down. And right here in the heart of the Asiatic desert they saw her, the Slav vampire, with her double row of teeth in a corpse-like head, her clawing fingers, deadly gray shroud, and bald skull. Instantly she was sitting on the neck of the nearest pagan, sinking her teeth through the steel into the flesh. Then she moved to the next one, then a third, a fourth. At once an empty space opened around the fighters; the road was free. Cold sweat flowed from the foreheads of the Polish knights. With the stubs of their broken swords they continued to strike out, unaware that they were striking at a void. They had but one thought: they must not raise their heads, nor look around. They must not see her again.

Nay, they would not see her. She was gone. In the spot where the death shroud had been, only moonlight glimmered now. Could it have been only a fancy? But no, she must have been there for who else would have cut the path through?

Deathly pale and shaken by their awesome experience the Silesian knights rejoined the Toulousians, and battled on. But Glovach's palm had lost its strength. As though overcome by weakness, he limply raised and lowered his sword. Already twice Zbylut had saved him from certain death.

"Don't," Glovach mumbled. "Don't, it was I who called, so now I must die."

And at that very moment failing to parry a Saracen spear, he fell heavily to the ground.

When over fifty thousand of the Sultan's warriors had died the hero's death, so beloved by the Prophet, and the Angel Gabriel had carried their souls to Paradise, where among the festoons of morning glories and wide-spread acacia trees, amidst long shades and soft cushions, and the young and beautiful maidens they would enjoy every kind of bliss, the brave Sultan Kılıj Arslan, suddenly aghast, retreated into the hills, leaving behind a rich camp full of provisions, fodder, horses, and every manner of wealth.

Whereupon Raymond and Tancred, without even throwing off the armor which by now stuck to the flesh, remounted their men on the freshly captured horses and raced off in pursuit of the fleeing foe. Though the Saracen horses were too small for the heavy Western knights, they were well rested, fleet of foot, and used to mountains. They soon overtook the rear guard of the fleeing pagans and riding close upon their heels forced them to ever greater haste. It did not occur to the Sultan that men who had fought for a day and a half could be pursuing him now. Convinced that the Latins had received new reinforcements, he did not even try to oppose them.

Meanwhile in the moon-drenched valley on the banks of the river, from which everyone could now drink to his heart's content, the Bishop gave thanks to the Lord of the Heavenly Hosts, who had granted them victory. All dismounted. Swaying on their stiff legs they discarded their helmets and bared their heads. The leaders advanced toward each other, their unarmed palms extended, once more pledging friendship and alliance. At the same time they exchanged thanks, the Provençals thanking the Normans because they did them the honor of asking them to join in such a glorious strife; Normans thanking Provençals because they had come to their help. Both sides were vying in mutual courtesy.

When morning came they began to reckon their losses. They were staggering. Twenty thousand of the foremost knights had perished in the strife. Dead were D'Armillac and Saint-Pierre de Luz, Du Grai, Wilfred Guillebaut, brother of Omer, De Hauteville and Humphrey Scaboioso, a nephew of Boemund. Konon de Montaigue was wounded, Godfrey, however, escaped without a scratch as though to confirm the well-known truth that death flees those who seek it. Dead, too, were the Hungarian Zupan Geza, Sukki de Szuka, and his companion Gyor Bakocz, four Polish knights, and Raoul de Beaugency. The latter had kept away from the rest, fighting single-handed. He was found dead, bristling with arrows like St. Sebastian, since, God knows why, he had gone into the battle without a breastplate. Indeed, since his disgrace, he wore neither belt nor spurs. All about him was a field of bodies. It was decided at first to throw him among the servants, to be buried in a mass grave, but the Bishop objected. He ordered that the hapless knight be restored to honor and given a decent burial. So they dressed him in his armor with silver belt and spurs before they laid him in the earth.

28.

The Death of a Good Knight

CUSTOM REQUIRED THAT A DYING KNIGHT BE LAID ON A BED OF PEA-VINE spread over with a death shroud. But here in Asia there was no pea-vine, and Glovach, whom his brothers had carried away from the battlefield, lay on the bare earth with nothing but his mantle beneath his head. They had placed under his shoulders and on his chest a fistful of dirt, a bit of their own native soil, which before departing each of them had picked from under the threshold of the ancestral manor and carried with him, hidden in his bosom. Thus Glovach was resting on his own soil and despite the distance, the bond between him and the ghosts of his forefathers remained unbroken. This at least was some comfort—thought the Strzygonias and the two Zavoras who shared their friend's grief as though they were blood brothers; for, otherwise, how many things were lacking, things which would protect Glovach's soul and help it on its last journey after it left the body! They dared not talk about it since by talking they might draw attention of the deities to these very omissions which, though due to circumstances and not neglect or oversight, could easily prejudice the nether powers against the dying man.

But they thought of it constantly and trembled lest their inability to provide all that was needed and proper for the dying should bring ill-luck upon the entire kin. Just as they had no pea-vine, so they also lacked millet, the cereal which was dedicated to the goddesses of Fate and which, mixed with cooked barley and honey, should have stood for three days at the feet of the dying man. They could not bake buck-wheat cakes. Nor could they place on the breast of the knight eggs upon which a special black-and-white design had been traced in wax, this design without beginning or end, representing eternity, the circle of life that closes behind every man. They also lacked herbs to burn around

265

the moribund and with which to rub his body. Some herbs had healing properties and could retain the soul within the body, while others insured a light death, but where was one to find them in this foreign land; and they dared not use the stalks which grew by the river since they knew nothing of their properties.

Whatever was in their power, however, they did with the utmost care. A bowl of water with beech charcoal floating in it (they had burned the saddlebow of Glovach's saddle which they knew was made of beechwood), stood by his head so that the fleeing soul might have something in which to wash itself. They had brought to the tent the sick man's horse, his good Silesian steed, and, sensing death, it had neighed. Then they had removed a horseshoe from one of the animal's forefeet and had drawn it over the chest, back, and abdomen of the sick man. Before the tent they built a small stack of wood which they had taken great pains to collect. When Glovach expired, they would set the wood on fire, and carry his corpse over the flames to drive the evil spirits away, and at the same time to show that they would burn their brother on the pyre as was done in days of yore, with horse, servants, and chattel—indeed, they would begrudge him nothing—were it not that the true God, Lord Jesus, was mighty wroth and threatened the soul with eternal damnation if instead of being buried in the ground the body were allowed to be consumed by flames. They lit a taper which De La Tour had brought and since there was nothing more they could do they seated themselves on the ground by his side and bared their heads as custom demanded. Glovach lay motionless with eyes closed and mouth open. His fingers groped about, raking the ground. There was a rattle in his throat, the wheezing breath escaped laboriously, at moments stopping altogether. This, they knew, was the soul wrestling with the flesh which was loath to let it go.

They averted their eyes in order not to make the struggle harder and tried to fix their minds on the dying man's virtues. They thought how good and true a knight Vitoslav Strzygonia had always been, how he never broke any of the knightly tenets nor failed in his duties, how strong he was, and wise and steadfast. No wonder the goddesses of Fate had always treated him with due consideration. Still at one time he must have erred in some way and brought upon himself the wrath of the gods; that was why he had no son.

With heartfelt gratitude they recalled that it was he who had saved the lives of all of them when he called *Her* whose name none dared mention now.

Zbylut held the lighted taper close to the Headman's hand. Yellow streams of wax flowed on their two hands, sealing them together. Yashek Zavora was singing in a mournful voice a snatch from a song half remembered from the funeral of his own father, the old Prybovoy Zavora, for whom the Abbot Guido himself had celebrated exequies.

> Oh my grief, my untold sorrow,
> I know naught about tomorrow,
> Where, oh where, will my first night be
> As from my body the soul will flee.

This, since he remembered no more and knew no other prayer, he repeated over and over again.

My God, thought the others, if that was what the Abbot told them to sing, even though old Zavora had died in his own manor only a furlong away from the burial ground in which all his forefathers lay, what would become of Glovach who was dying in this remote wilderness? How would he ever find his way?

The breathing of the sick man was becoming increasingly difficult; beads of cold sweat stood out on his sunken cheeks and forehead.

"Zb-zb-zb-zbylut, g-g-give the c-candle to Imko," said Zavora the Mumbler. "P-p-perhaps he has a l-lighter h-h-hand. Will m-make the dying easier."

Imbram drew closer to his brother and reached out for the candle. Zbylut looked at him askance. "Good!" he remarked. "A weeper is just what we need."

Imbram turned red as a beet and hung his head low. It was true, that he was crying. He was ashamed of these unmanly tears but unable to check them. An unbearable pain clutched at his heart and throat; he could almost see the vast emptiness into which Glovach's soul was about to depart and which soon would swallow both Zbylut and himself. Oh, how far they were from all that was familiar, beloved, their own. Distance and strangeness, difficult enough to bear in life, became a hundredfold heavier at the moment of death.

The Mumbler was right when he said that Imko's hand might prove lighter than Zbylut's for now Glovach opened his eyes and looked about, completely conscious. They poured some of the charcoaled water into his mouth. He swallowed and for a while his breathing became easier; his lips moved; he was trying to speak.

The four knights bent over him, holding their breath. In the beam of light which fell through the opening, flies buzzed monotonously. Glovach was speaking. Here and there they were able to catch a word.

"Zbylut . . . the eldest . . . love him . . . like a father . . . dominus. . . . Imko . . . will you obey him?"

"On my knightly honor I will, Vitoslav," said Imbram with feeling. He did not call his brother by his nickname, Glovach, but by his real exalted name.

"Zbylut, will you love him?"

"I will," muttered the latter, averting his head. The breath of the sick man became wheezy and raspy again. He now opened, now closed his glazed and already unseeing eyes.

"Don't forget the helmet," he said almost clearly.

"We won't forget," all four answered. How could they forget? The helmet under the arm, the belt girding the loins, the sword at the side, this was how a knight was buried. Otherwise he must come back in quest of those objects and would be sure to seek revenge on his careless kinsmen.

They thought he had expired, but he opened his eyes again. Last earthly thoughts still kept breaking, dissolving, flaring up, then flickering out again. Reassured as to the matter of his brothers and the helmet, he suddenly grew anxious lest they forget to break the pot over the threshold. Bogucha would know just what kind to prepare. Where was Bogucha anyway? Ah, yes, she was not here, nor was there any threshold. The threshold was back home, and home was far, far away. Home . . . Home where Imko's little son was. The tiny babe . . . Aye, even though all three of them perished, the line would still go on since that little one was there.

And with what remained of his waning consciousness, with his last earthly thought he smiled at the picture of that distant nephew of his, the tiny green twig on which hung the hopes of the line. He smiled at the infant who on his small feet must be toddling now between mother and aunt . . . prattling his childish carefree babble. A shoot from which some day the old trunk would grow once more.

He moved his stiffening fingers. And though his brothers did not understand what he wanted, he in his mind was raising his hands and blessing the little one. He blessed him in the name of the Lord Jesus Christ, and of all the old deities of the forest. He blessed him in the name of the ghosts of his forefathers that dwelled in the table board and the carved beam of his ancestral manor. And he invoked for the child the protection of sprites that lived under his threshold, and to those that hid in the granary, all the powers of earth, water, and air, of this world and of the beyond.

And with this blessing and smile, he died.

For a long time the knights sat motionless and silent, afraid to touch and startle the soul which was floating over their heads. They could almost hear it flutter in the hot noon silence as it soared high like a dove that tries to find the right direction. May God help it on its way!

At last after well over an hour they rose to their feet, moving slowly, deliberately, with ritualistic solemnity. They put a gold piece in the dead man's hand and with two more covered his eyes. At the entrance to the tent they placed an axe and a broom. Between these Imbram carefully spread the dirt from the little bag he carried in his bosom. Each cut a strand of his hair and laid it on the dead man's heart under the vest as proof of grief and also to show their trust in their brother, who through the possession of the hair would hold them completely in his power, yet would never use that power save for their good.

They laid the deceased on a previously prepared bier and carried him out of the tent. At the entrance they lowered the body and three times let it touch the earth spread by Imbram so that the dead man might take leave of his own native soil and home. Outside the stack of wood was burning. They carried the corpse over it, stopping for a moment to make sure that the evil ghosts were properly driven away. As they moved on, both Imbram and Zbylut turned their heads at the same time and glanced back. Smoke from the fire was drifting in the direction of the tent. They lowered their heads and said nothing, for it was an evil omen. It meant that someone else in the family would soon die. "He or I?" they both wondered.

Imbram picked up the earth from the threshold and carefully replaced it in his bag. Glovach's remains were placed in the biggest of the tents where already rested the bodies of Nagodits, the elder Osventa, and Novina the Babbler, silent for the first time in his life. By these four dead knights those that remained of the Silesian group sat in wake three days and three nights, never leaving the tent, not speaking, eating, nor drinking. In the sweltering heat bodies decomposed quickly and already by the second day the stench in the tent was almost unbearable. Hunger gnawed at their entrails, thirst burned their throats. But they bore it all for the sake of the dead who had been good knights and must be properly honored. After three days they left the tent half-poisoned, looking like corpses themselves and reeling on their feet. Famished as they were they could not eat: food made them vomit. It was not till several hours later that they had sufficiently recovered to lift the four stretchers and carry them to a cave, which the servants had in the meantime found, cleaned, and prepared. Here the dead were laid to rest, each with spare clothes, arms, saddle, bridle, and some food by his side. Then the knights blocked with great stones the opening of the cave, thus sealing the grave for good and ever. No lion could budge the boulders they had rolled up, no jackals would sneak in. The dead would rest in peace. Using their battle axes they cut a cross in the rock over the entrance, and underneath it the crests of Strzygonia, Osventa, Novina, and Nogodits, four good Silesian kin strayed in the heart of Asia Minor.

There was no more need for silence. The dead had received their due, and now the living could return to life. Zbylut with a wry smile edged up to Imbram.

"So on your knightly honor you promised to obey me?"

"So I did," Imbram admitted.

"Then you will have to make obeisance before me, too, did you know that?"

"I can make obeisance before you, brother."

Zbylut, a little startled, looked closely into the absent eyes of his younger brother.

"Oh, I was only jesting," he said and walked away. The other knights had already left. They were in a hurry to return to their camp duties which they had neglected for the past three days. Imbram remained alone at the mouth of the cave. Unlike the others he was in no hurry to go back. He had sprung so far away from life and had clung so fast and so wholeheartedly to the hereafter, that it seemed strange to him to return to go on living as before. He tried to recall his beloved wife, but she had become so that now he had to make an effort to recall how she looked. How Ofka looked! After merely two years!

What made it even worse was his deep conviction that she was still waiting for him with the same devotion and longing. From Yuletide to

THE DEATH OF A GOOD KNIGHT

Yuletide, year after year. She knew nothing about him, had no idea in which direction to turn her longing, from where to expect him. In the deep of night she repeated her little incantation, begging the Morning Star's help. She could not understand what had become of him. She would come out to the crossroads and wait; every time she heard hoof-beats, she would think it was he and be ready to stretch her arms and call his name. And all the while he was at the end of the world, in a land so distant that not even Abbot Guido knew where it was.

The trial of the shameless wives was to begin in an hour, and Bishop Adhemar thought of the prospect with growing distaste. He had hoped until now that the Norman lords would balk at the prospect of having the disgraceful affair aired before the whole army, and would settle the matter in private. But Robert Curthose, egged on by Arnuld, demanded a wide publicity for the case.

It devolved upon the Bishop to render a verdict, and now, in his tent he prayed ardently for the enlightenment of grace, for that Divine flash that puts all problems in their proper place and makes a man's mind swift, lucid, and unerring. Only with the help of grace, he felt, would he be able to inspire the barons with the need of mercy and move them to leniency. Without it, he felt empty, unconvincing, doubtful, and dejected.

But grace would not come. Instead Arnuld appeared to announce that they were all ready and waiting in the camp square.

"Mark my word, no good will come of this trial," Adhemar turned to him petulantly, "Could not your nobles settle the matter in private, each with his own wife? This is bound to cause new trouble between the Provençals and yourselves, and the fault will be yours, Chaplain."

"Mine?" Arnuld exclaimed with candid surprise.

'Don't you remember how at the time of Blanche's de Montbeliard trial you kept badgering the Provençals about their women till at last you had them almost up in arms? I wonder what made you do it?"

"Oh! My deep loathing of sin. The sin of concupiscence in particular," sighed the chaplain, raising his eyes towards heaven.

"Sin ought to be hated but men should not be taunted. I fear that the Provençals will pay you back in kind to-day."

But the chaplain would not be daunted.

"We care nothing what others, and the Provençals in particular, may say about us," he retorted spiritedly. "We brand evil wherever we find it, even when it happens amongst our own kin. There are more than five hundred noble ladies in the Italian and Norman camps. Of these only fourteen have disgraced themselves. They must be severely punished for the sake of those many virtuous women whom no evil gossip has ever touched. I have here with me two nieces of mine, two God-fearing orphans who live in nun-like seclusion. What would they think were they to see that the vilest crimes go unpunished?"

Adhemar cast him a piercing glance? What was in the man's mind? Why this great show of piety and virtue? There had been ugly rumors concerning these God-fearing nieces. It was said that Arnuld had picked one up on his way through Italy and that he had bought the other in Byzantium. Actually, no one had ever seen the two women. Perhaps it was all low, common slander. Still, the bishop did not trust the pious chaplain.

"Let us go and open the trial since you insist," he said with a sigh and rose to his feet, "Anyhow, I will ask for mercy."

"And we shall demand the harshest sentence. According to the law they ought to be flogged, stripped of all clothing and driven out never to return."

"Driven out into the desert? You might as well put them to death."

"Yes. We could do that. Bury them alive as is done with husband-slayers," agreed the chaplain.

Meanwhile Elvira's tent was crowded; the ladies of the camp flocked together to talk; they could not remain alone. What would be the judgment on their sisters? Yesterday, when the news of the Norman women's disgraceful behavior had first spread through the camps, they had all agreed that no punishment was harsh enough for such cowards and harlots, but today their mood had changed.

They were thinking of what happened to Willibald, who had done no wrong; they were thinking of Blanche, guiltless and dead by her own hand. They were thinking of the Greek women they had seen in Byzantium, free, educated, mixing in the affairs of men, having as many children as they pleased. Timorously, as if afraid of their own thoughts, they began to speak of their unfortunate position as Latin women. Elvira joined them; women were poor wretches at the mercy of men from birth to death, she said. Quickly the others agreed with her; they talked vehemently of their misery, bound to a father or husband or brother from one end of life to the other, without hope or honor or distinction.

The trial had begun. In the corner where they stood the fourteen culprits huddled together. They were changed beyond recognition, yellow with grief and dark with anguish. Sackcloth hung from their shivering bodies. Since the time of their discovery they had been shunned by everyone; their own serving maids had reviled them. What dire punishment would the judges invent now? And why did everyone take their guilt for granted? They knew not themselves how it all had happened. They had been horribly frightened all day long, and no one came to give them a little heart. They had thought that their husbands had long since fallen, and at last they had gone stark mad with fright. But they had not meant to do wrong.

In the name of the fourteen husbands who stood silent and motionless Arnuld repeated the accusation and asserted the guilt. The women were wantons. They should be stripped, branded, flogged, and driven into the desert, declared lepers in the sight of man. A Christian, seeing them, was to kill them as he would mad dogs.

Desperate sobs tore from the terrified women. Some fell to their knees, others wrung their hands whimpering like children. Their husbands, watching them, wished it had all been settled with a good beating. But it was too late, now. They could only hope that the barons would show mercy.

From the battlefield the breeze wafted the stench of decomposing corpses.

The Bishop's voice shook with pity as he rose to defend the accused.

"Human justice will only resemble divine justice when as its weapon it uses forgiveness," Adhemar said in answer to Arnuld. "The punishment as foreseen by the law is far too harsh in this case. Let the accusers recall what faithful and brave companions they had until now in these same women who stand here accused. Let them remember what hardship they have borne, what courage they have shown. They did not break faith. They succumbed to weariness, heat, uncertainty, fear, but not to concupiscence. They are right when they say they did not know what they were doing. How can we punish them so harshly? My Lords, I ask mercy."

"There is no forgiveness for sin," Arnuld said.

"There is forgiveness for far greater sins than these," Adhemar said.

"My Lords, let every one of us ponder and pray, after which each shall voice his opinion. May God enlighten us. In the name of the Father, the Son, and the Holy Ghost."

All crossed themselves. Silence fell, broken only by the weeping of the accused women and by the cries of vultures busily circling over the battlefield. The knights tried to think, but cerebration was foreign to them. Thoughts wandered. Robert of Normandy had no need to think, anyway; his chaplain had told him to demand a harsh sentence. The fourteen husbands dared not think for fear that they might weaken in their stand.

Boemund cared nothing for whatever fate might befall the whimpering little fools. His mind was made up; he would side with the majority. What interested him right now was what made Arnuld take such an inexorable stand? Horror of sin, indeed . . . Beomund, who in Byzantium had often met the Norman chaplain in places where no cleric ought to have been, knew what to think of such lofty reasons. The man was full of cunning. This was worth keeping in mind. He might prove useful in the future.

Tancred tried hard to think of the defendants but instead Djurisha, the lovely sultaness, kept rising before his eyes. The very thought of her made him blush. He remembered how she had screamed, and hid her face in her hands when the pirates had torn off her veil. Could it be that she, a pagan, had more dignity than these Christian ladies? No. It probably never occurred to her that she could be spared. They were all alike. Afraid of death like children. And like children they should not be punished too harshly.

D'Haineault sat with his head propped on a lean hand. He should be concentrating on the trial and the verdict, yet here he was thinking of Ida. Why did he love her so? He loved everything about her, down to the tiny wrinkles on her temples and that proud little fold in the corner of her mouth which had etched itself so deeply during the early part of her life that it never quite disappeared, not even when he kissed her. Ida was as essential to his life as food and air. He would have any time let himself to be torn limb by limb rather than doubt her honor, her virtue, her unfaltering faithfulness. Faithfulness? They never even mentioned it, it seemed so obvious, so natural, so much part of their love. Did any other woman, save Ida, exist for him? Could another man exist for her? And yet, now, after a year of separation he was no longer so certain. Ida, after all, was but a woman. A woman like these fourteen here, subject to the same weakness, unable to answer for what she felt and did. She might have even forgotten!

With grim pleasure he prodded his own wound, telling himself that this was, no doubt, what had happened. Dreading the journey, Ida must have remained at home. While he withered in anxiety and longing, she lived peacefully in the old castle and, who knows, perhaps even welcomed swains.

Suddenly, grief and fury swept over him with such force that had the Bishop in that instant asked him for his verdict the gentle D'Haineault would have sent the women to their doom.

Godfrey of Lorraine was steeped in prayer. His answer was ready: mercy. Nevertheless he continued to pray so he might not hear the sobs of the accused women which reminded him all too vividly of that other woman who was also afraid to die. The woman whose memory haunted him day and night. She had told him that he had lost her soul. Had then his entire life, a life of self-discipline and denial been wrong?

Baldwin pensively tugged at his moustache. His usual cheerfulness had deserted him of late. The last words exchanged between Godfrey and his late wife kept preying upon his mind. He ruminated them going over the whole scene over and over again, and still they made no sense. How did it all come about? Gontrane was afraid to die, and had asked for the Greek leech. Not knowing how to cope with her Baldwin had ran to Godfrey to ask his help, and Godfrey came and calmed Gontrane. So far everything was clear, but what happened afterwards? Why was Godfrey so pale and confused when he, Baldwin, returned? What was the meaning of Gontrane's words: "For my whole life . . . just that short while," and Godfrey's "It's a sin, dearest . . ."? Dearest? Gontrane? The more Baldwin thought of it the more convinced he became that these two must have shared a secret of which he, the husband, knew nothing. The realization filled him with bitterness and fury. All his life he had looked up to his brother with admiration and respect. He had trusted him blindly. And now . . .

The Bishop rose to his feet and asked if the Lord Barons had made up their minds. All nodded assent. "They should be punished according to law," said Robert of Normandy curtly and with complete indifference.

"They should be punished according to law," repeated Arnuld.

The rest said nothing. They were in no hurry to reveal what they thought. The Bishop cast them an apprehensive glance for whoever ventured to speak up first, now, would be sure to decide the issue. Those whose minds were not made up were certain to follow his lead.

At once, to everybody's surprise, Robert of Flanders rose to his feet. His courage and probity were proverbial but so was his taciturnity. Women were no concern of his; he had left his own wife, a placid Flandrian, at home, and all through the campaign lived in chastity. That was perhaps why he was the only one of these present who at the Bishop's behest had only thought of the defendants, and not of some particular woman.

He spoke slowly, stammering a little at first and frowning with concentration for he was not sure of his ability to put his thoughts into words.

"These women have acted disgracefully and no good knight would share his bed with such a wife," he said. "But that is not the point. They have taken the cross. They have taken the oath. The Holy Father honored the oath from women as he did from men. We cannot then be the means by which that oath is broken. Let them live alone, doing penance, having nothing to do with their husbands. But let them remain with us. When we are returned home each husband will then be free to drive out his wife as a wanton. But out here these women bear the cross as we do."

The knights were thunderstruck. Women of the cross? Female warriors of Christ? What did a woman's vow matter?

Argument broke out like a field fire among the barons. Arnuld, dismayed, saw that the simple Robert, speaking what he honestly thought, had turned the argument from punishment to something else—whether or not the women were actually bearers of the cross. His own point suddenly was lost and he knew it. All that mattered now was whether the women were crusaders or whether they were not.

"They are!" said Raymond, and gradually the others began to agree with him, though Omer kept shouting, "Away with them! Punish them!" Arnuld, moving to take advantage of the turn in the situation, whispered to Robert of Normandy and then went to the fourteen husbands, speaking quietly. Then Robert of Normandy rose and said that the barons sided with the noble lord of Flanders and that the fourteen husbands had agreed to suspend sentence until they returned home,

giving their wives a chance to fulfill their vows and declaring themselves satisfied with a church penance, preferably a heavy one.

As Adhemar rose to pronounce the sentence the women burst into
loud cries of prayer. Before the Bishop could speak, however, Elvira's
squire came into the circle, bowed, and said he brought a message from
the ladies.

"Don't bother us now," said Raymond. "This is no court of love. We
are dealing with serious matters."

"The ladies send you this message," the squire said. "The Lady Elvira
and those gathered with her have commanded me to tell you that they
do not wish the women before you today to be put to death. They beseech Your Grace and you, my Lords, to spare their lives. They say . . ."

He was interrupted by laughter. Suddenly with the tension gone the
knights were in a mood to receive buffoonery. A message from the
ladies asking mercy! That was a wondrous joke. Women sending a
herald, women expressing an opinion.

Even the Bishop was nonplussed. "Go back," he said, "and tell the
ladies the court has already ruled mercifully and the women are not to
be punished by death. Tell them also that their request could not in any
way influence the decision of the court."

The squire bowed and left, taking the rebuff to his mistress. Raymond
stared after him in anger. What was Elvira up to? How dared she hu-
miliate him!

29.

The Desert

COULD IT BE TRUE OR WAS IT A DREAM HALF REMEMBERED FROM ANOTHER life that there was a time, long, long ago, when lying abed at night one heard the monotonous splash of rain, and the rain trickling along the walls? Drops rapped at the copper plates. Long ropes of the downpour, swift rivulets gurgling in the gutters fell, splattered. The drenched earth smelled like a freshly cut loaf of bread. Low clouds crowded the heavens, lazily clung to the tower of the castle, leisurely spread their gray fleece on the hillocks, all the while spouting water . . . water.

There were no rain, no clouds, no water in this God-forsaken desert through which the crusaders now wandered. The desert surrounded them like a formidable, vast, ever-changing sea.

A week, nine days, ten days, two weeks had gone by and they were still plodding through the sun-scorched waste. They had taken enough water to last them three days. It had not occurred to them that any desert could stretch any wider, and now they crawled along in the white-hot air, a half-dead host. The snake of the great army stretched endlessly, like a gigantic bridge thrown across the desert. The head was still edging slowly on, the rear remained still and would move no more. An ever-growing number of corpses marked the trail of martyrdom and death. Horses, cattle, dogs, falcons, children, women, squires, and knights, fell by the wayside never to rise again.

Those who still could keep on their feet staggered on with the blind steps of flagellants, their eyes wild, their mouths dry as a bone.

In whispers they raved of spring water, of rain . . .

In the sunken face of Bishop Adhemar only the eyes still remained alive. With a supreme effort of will he tried to control his thoughts and keep track of what went on about him. He felt that cost what it may, he must till the very last stay conscious and aware of his responsibility.

His responsibility! When he thought of it, his own torment vanished from sight, became an insignificant detail. He, the leader, had not properly inquired about the route. He had learned nothing of what the lands that lay ahead of them were like. Like the other knights he had allowed himself to be carried away by pride and his dislike of the Greeks and had made no effort to force the latter to give him clear and precise information. He did not press that old fox Butumitos. Meeting with his evasive answers, he had fallen silent and asked no more.

Now it was too late. They must get across or perish. There was no retreat. He had thought about retreat himself back in Byzantium, in an hour of weakness . . . or . . . O! God, was it presentiment? From Byzantium retreat was still possible. From Nicaea, too. Now no more.

But a while ago he was still so confident, so serene, so certain that they would reach their goal. He had rejoiced like a child, wept with bliss as all the while fate had been preparing the trap which would swallow them all. Already then it lay in wait for those who were now falling, twisted and blackened from thirst, or who lay dead with faces upturned toward the merciless sun. Every day their number grew. The desert seemed endless, or else they had lost their way and were wandering in circles led by Satan.

Satan and Death. This no doubt must be their domain in which they could revel to their heart's content. And suddenly the Princeps Mendacii, the Prince of Deceit and Darkness, who once in a blessed hour of Grace had seemed to the Bishop but a pitiful shadow, began to grow, to spread till his ominous wings had darkened the world.

It took the Israelites forty years of wandering to cross the desert. But then whenever Moses who led them struck a rock with his rod, water would spring forth. "If I were holy and strong," thought Adhemar. "If my faith were so simple and firm that no doubt ever touched it, this arid soil would likewise obey my command. If I were a saint. . . .

"But I am not a saint. Yet, I must answer for what is happening to them. I am responsible . . . O, merciful God!"

He walked slower and slower, leaning on a staff surmounted by a cross. Ahead of him four camels were being led. The saddle-packs of three were already empty, only one still carried two bags of water. The camels came from the captured camp of Kilij Arslan, so did the water bags. The knights wanted to abandon both, they could see no possible use for them. They had enough bags and saddle-packs of their own, and as for these outlandish beasts, why take them? No knight would ever disgrace himself by mounting one; even a squire would be ashamed to do so. Nevertheless, the Bishop took four camels and filled eight bags with water. What was left of it was all the water they now had. And unlike horses the camels continued to stay on their feet so that men looked at the hardy beasts with ever increasing respect. They looked jaded, of course, their humps grew flabby and almost disappeared, their lips hung down even uglier than usual and their small half-closed eyes took on an expression of long-suffering misery. But they still walked, still paddled along on their long sinewy legs, while most of the horses had already fallen. Now and again one of the faithful beautiful chargers would stumble, groan, and with its black dead tongue hanging from a wide open mouth fall down heavily on his head. The knight hastily dragged himself out of the saddle, stood awhile swaying on his feeble legs, then moved on on foot, leaving his shield and lance behind. Only the helmet on his head, only the breastplate, only the belt that hung loose on the emaciated hips, only the sword on which he tried to brace himself while walking. Oh, how heavy were those scorching iron plates, that seemed to suck from the flesh whatever remained of its moisture, how hard to lift the mighty sword meant for a strong arm full of vigor and not for a weary ghost. As long as he lived, however, no knight would part with his coat of mail, his belt, and his sword. If his bones were to shine white in the desert let them rattle in the faithful armor with the sword beside. Let the stars from above see that here lay a knight and not a common knave.

Most of the women, especially those who were with child, had already remained behind. Leone, though more dead than alive, still dragged along clutching at Baldwin's arm. Her face had assumed a strange likeness to Gontrane's just before she died and Baldwin looked at her with pity mingled with revulsion and dread. Which one was she? This or the other one? Not that it really mattered. A few hours hence he too would fall. Once down he would stir no more.

Lamenting voicelessly in mute despair, mothers carried infants born during the journey. There were none others here. Most of the babes had already sunk into wakeless sleep by the dry maternal breasts. Some, however, still gasped for breath, opening wide their tiny thirsty mouths, like fish taken out of water. Their thin little bodies looked like skeletons. Now and then a mother would silently lay a tiny corpse into a cradle

dug in the sand, and seat herself by the side to watch over it forever.
Others unable to part with either infants or life stalked along with the
small bodies clasped in their arms. And as they walked they moaned an
eerie lullaby of death and despair. It was to the mothers and children
who still remained alive that the Bishop doled out a few drops of water
every morning and every night. It was for them that he saved the bags
carried by the camels. Down in his heart he often thought that he was
acting unwisely, that it would be better to save instead the strongest men
who had a chance to survive. These poor things would perish anyway,
in spite of his help, and even if they did not, they were of no real use to
the crusade. Squandering water in this way was certainly not wise. But
the instinct of chivalry, still stronger than anything else, made it imperative to save first of all those who were the weakest and the most
defenseless . . . the women and the children. So to them went the
thimbleful of tepid foul-smelling water. To them alone. Unaware of
their own heroism, the knights did not rebel—as yet . . .

For the first time since the campaign began, Elvira had left her chair;
there was no one to carry it. The chair remained where it was abandoned
on a sandy dune and shone from afar like the ark. The proud lady
walked without a word by her husband's side. Both reeled like drunk-
ards but she did not remove from her head the high coif from which
the faded, dusty veil floated down her back, and his hand still lay as
before on the hilt of his sword.

Florine did not complain, either. She walked, the ghost of her own
lovely self, beside the ghost of the Danish prince. This morning after
the Bishop had distributed the usual ration of water, less than you can
hold in your palm, Florine returned to Swennon and threw her arms
around his neck, seeking his mouth with hers. Before he knew what she
was about she had let trickle between his lips the water she held in her
mouth. He choked on it, then, overcome with grief for her and for
himself, broke down and sobbed.

Afterwards she put her head on his shoulder and they walked on,
trying not to see the corpses of those who had gone ahead of them but
had already fallen. Some among them had summoned the last of their
strength to pull their mantles over their heads, shyly concealing their
death-contorted faces from the eyes of the curious. They lay still and
calm, forms without features. Others had had no strength to do so, or
perhaps in the agony of death no longer cared whether anyone saw them

or not. Their eyes shone white in gray parched faces. A few were still alive, and gazed at the marching throngs with horrible indifference, feeling that they were already on the other side.

Stumbling on every unevenness of ground, D'Haineault for the first time in two years was thanking God that Ida had not come. It was better to know that she had forgotten him, that she loved another, than to watch her die. Praised be the Lord that she was not here. Alone he could bear everything and face death without misgivings.

The two brothers Stephen and Paul Salviac de Viel, twin shadows with eyes sunk deep in their sockets, walked along in a daze, supporting each other. They had kept only one sword between them and carried it by turns. When time came when their tottering legs would refuse to carry them any farther they would lie down side by side, with their two palms on the hilt of their single sword.

Stephen said: "Brother, back home you had everything a man's heart can desire. You held a high office and men looked upon you with respect. For my sake you left it all, only to perish in this God-forsaken land."

"I regret it not, brother," Paul assured him.

"Brother, back home you had a good wife and children sound as apples. I will never forgive myself that you left it all for me."

"Not for you, brother. Both you and I abandoned all we had for the love of our Lord. It would be a sin to regret it."

But Stephen would not be comforted.

"I went for the sake of Christ. You went for my sake. I know that and it grieves me."

"Grieve not, brother. You and I will die in the same hour and that is as it should be, since we are twins. You are dearer to my heart than either wife or children, for were we not as one even in our mother's womb? I could not live one hour longer than you."

Haggard and thinner than ever, Blaise was saying to Klimek: "So here you are, you and your dukedom! Mind how you used to wag that silly tongue of yours? Though in a way it all came out as you would have it. Are we not all equals now? Look at the barons. They are walking and dying, same as we are. Even faster for that matter, since we have none of those heavy plates to carry. So here comes the end . . . and equality."

The gray mule, whose pelt the women of Auvergne used to pluck as a holy relic and who until now had stoutly kept up with the Crusade, lay dead by the wayside. As gray as the mule, his long hood dangling down to his heels, Peter the Hermit still dragged along. Curiously enough, despite the torment he felt better, saner than before. His men were slain by the Saracens, the Bishop's, he thought, not without satisfaction, by the desert. It all came to the same. No doubt the thing was preordained. It had not been his fault. No, he was not to blame.

Imbram and Zbylut dragged themselves along swaying on their feet. Both were thinking of the smoke that had drifted back toward the tent; it must have meant that both of them would die. Nor did it occur to them to lean on each other like the two Salviacs de Viel. Behind them stalked the two Zavoras, Novina, and the youngest Osventa. Only these six remained of their band. The middle one of the Osventa brothers, who was always bemoaning his ill luck, remained by the wayside with the old complaint still on his lips. So did Moymir Stiborovits, the trusted friend and companion of the late King Boleslas.

Less fortunate than the four who fell at Dorylaeum, these two received no burial, no water for the soul to wash in, no fistful of native soil on the chest, no coals, no fire, no axe, no food, no prayer, not even a compassionate thought.

Arnuld de Rohes was more spry and looked better than the others, thanks to a large jug of holy water preserved for exorcism, which remained in his care. Fearful that someone might profane the hallowed liquid, the chaplain assumed personal care of the jug and used it properly. With complacent scorn he thought of the Bishop. What a fool the man was! With two whole bags of water still in his possession, he doled it out most unnecessarily to women and children who, the sooner they died the better. He, himself, did not drink at all. You could see at a glance that he would not last more than a few hours. Was this the way for a leader to act? And when the Bishop died, who would become the spiritual leader of the Crusade? Who, indeed? Surely not Alberon, nor the Canons Raymond d' Aguilers, or Foucher de Chartres. The choice was obvious—Arnuld, himself.

But would there be anyone left to lead? It suddenly occurred to the wily chaplain that all might perish leaving him alone with his jug of holy water, the last survivor doomed to a lonely death in this wide desert.

Brother Hyacinth, the copyist of holy books, and Bartholomew, the once merry cleric of Marseilles, walked along holding each other's hand. Gray, shriveled, tiny, looking more like gnomes than men, they peered

about them with pained wonder. Was it possible that God should try
men like this? Before and behind them stalked endless rows of spectres
as gray and parched as themselves, spectres who in the agony of thirst
were trying to drink their own urine.

After that nothing remained but blood. The mount of the knight De
Beauregard, one of the few surviving horses, went down under the
rider. The knight whipped out his misericord and swiftly cut the vein
in the animal's neck. The dark thick gore spurted heavily, almost reluctantly. Greedily the knight put his mouth to it. He sucked. At once
someone grabbed him from behind. Enraged, De Beauregard turned
about grim and threatening. De Melun stood behind him.

"Away." He shoved the rightful owner aside and put his own mouth
to the wound of the animal.

"It's mine . . . Let me . . ." mumbled Beauregard in despair. He
seized De Melun by the middle and tried to pull him away. The heavy
palm of the giant came down like a hammer on his head and without a
sound he fell between the stiff legs of his horse. De Melun sucked and
sucked. At last he rose with a sigh. In his cadaverous face the blood-
smeared lips shone red like those of a vampire. He walked away reeling
and stumbling. He felt no relief. In the first moment, while the warm
bubbling liquid was filling his mouth, he had an impression of drinking.
But the sensation was only momentary. The blood had not quenched
his thirst.

Trembling with impatience, the squire of the knight De Beauregard
waited for De Melun to depart. Now he, in turn, clung to the horse's
neck. But the blood had already coagulated into a black, sticky mass.
Whereupon the man flung himself on his own master, who still lay
dazed by De Melun's mighty blow, cut a vein on his neck and drank.
While drinking he looked about uneasily to see if anyone was approaching. He feared not punishment, but that others would take the corpse
away from him.

For an example is soon followed. Only a few hours before, the dying
sank peacefully to the ground and no one even gave them a glance. Now
since the news spread throughout the ranks that one could quench thirst
with blood, no sooner did a man go down, and often even before, the
stronger threw themselves upon him, slashing with knives, fighting with
each other over his half-dead body. They quickly found out that it was
better to suck from those who were still alive because the blood did not

clot so fast. From then on screams were constantly bursting from ranks suddenly turned into a host of vampires.

De Melun summoned all his strength to catch up with the van of the column. For some time he had been obsessed by the thought of water which the camels carried on their backs.

De Melun had never denied his flesh and his flesh had become his master; there was none as miserable as he. His huge bones, huge muscles, huge veins demanded, craved, screamed for water.

The two bags were almost unguarded. Only Walter the Penniless walked by the camel's side. Dry as a bone he stalked rattling with his sword which still hung from his neck. There was no one else about. It simply never occurred to anyone that any of the knights might lay hand on what belonged to the weakest.

Red circles danced before De Melun's eyes. Red as the blood which he had just drunk. They danced in the desert, they whirled in the air. Red circles appeared on the bags. In the bags which held water . . .

All at once De Melun fell upon the unsuspecting Walter. Once they were equally strong, now they were equally weak and they both went down. But De Melun rose first and grabbed the bag. The precious fluid swished softly inside. If he were to die a hundred times he would not surrender it now. With feverish fingers he untied the neck of the bag, lifted it to his mouth and began to drink. His cheeks swelled. He stopped, vomited blood and water, gasped, hiccoughed and drank again. At last he lowered the bag, glared challengingly at those present and at Walter who with an effort was rising to his feet.

"I'm full," he announced.

No one said a word. Hugh de Vermandois approached. The once handsome and frivolous count was changed beyond recognition. His eyes shone wildly in his dirty hirsute face, his armor rattled over his dry lanky frame.

"De Melun, leave that alone. Have you gone mad?" he said harshly.

"Let me be, you fool," De Melun replied.

"You always were a rascal. Return the bag and come along."

"Let me be, you fool," repeated the giant. His voice was already more vigorous. His bloodshot eyes glared at them boldly. He was strong once more. He waited.

"I am full," he said again and walked off, hugging the bag with both hands. For a few steps Hugh dragged in his wake. He was torn between

a righteous indignation at the ignoble action of his companion and a
faint hope that perhaps De Melun might let him have a drink from the
stolen bag. Just a tiny sip. Since he had already taken it, anyway.

But would it be right? Would it be seemly? Poor Hugh, shook his
head miserably. No, it would not be right. He sank heavily to the
ground, staring sadly after the departing ruffian. Let him drink it all
himself. Not for nothing was one a knight and a royal prince.

"What can I do for them?" thought the Bishop. "The end is at hand
and it is worse than the worst expectations. The final, the ultimate end:
degradation. For, surely it does not matter that a man dies, but only how
he dies. If we are all to perish here, let us at least perish like Knights of
the Cross and not like murderous beasts."

"Brethren," the Bishop spoke with an effort. "Why are you weakening? Did you not back in Clermont willingly offer your lives to Our
Lord? God chose to take those lives in a manner different from what
you expected, not on the battlefield but here in the desert. But this makes
us no less Christ's own warriors and each of us who falls here has won
the same merit as though he had fallen at the Holy Sepulcher. Do not
withdraw now that which you offered to God! Perhaps Jerusalem cannot be taken in any other way save by a legion of ghosts! Perhaps our
souls will go straight into battle with the infidels! Perhaps dead we will
more easily achieve our end than alive. Have confidence in the God that
accepted your oath!

"We are not a desperate herd caught in a trap, but true Christian
knights out to conquer evil. The desert is as much our foe as the pagans
were. So fight it! Fight to the last, do not succumb! If we cannot
conquer, we shall fall without regret. God wills it!"

"God wills it!" called voices from all sides. Those standing near the
Bishop relayed his speech to those more distant, and he, fortified by his
own words, added, "Who is still strong enough to mount a camel?"

Four stepped forward though swaying on their feet; the emaciated,
ash-gray Tancred; Konon de Montaigue who with his big jutting-out
nose more than ever resembled a vulture, and was even weaker than the
others, having been wounded at Dorylaeum; Wilfred d'Esch; and De
La Tour.

"Mount," Adhemar urged them. "You need feel no shame, since the
salvation of all hangs in the balance. The camels can still move at a

brisk pace. Drive ahead as fast as you can. You might find water. If you do, you will come back and bring us the news."

Until now no Latin ever sat on the hump of one of these monstrous creatures. How, they wondered, was one to climb on it? Unless, of course, the ugly beast happened to lie down as they were doing now. Even so, the four knights, scarcely able to lift their stiff legs, found it hard to mount. At last they were in saddle. The others poked and shouted, till they had goaded the camels into rising. They moved off slowly at first, then at a run. Finally they vanished from sight.

"Come! We will follow them," called the Bishop. "Take heart! I feel that God will yet show us His mercy. Onward, onward. Do not give up. We may be near our goal."

Onward! Onward! Hold on to your life! Don't let it slip you, grasp it like a sword! The Bishop was right: the desert was Satan's ally, one had to fight it as one fought the pagan, to the last, to the bitter end!

And so the column of spectres moved on. Every hour was an eternity. Despite superhuman efforts to remain alive, men continued to fall. The sun sank slowly but no one paid any attention to it. They had long before lost track of time. Day or night were all the same to them. Presently pain turned into numbness. Only the Bishop still strained his eyes. He felt that something would happen, was already happening. God had seen the act of good will and trust and was about to answer.

The Bishop was right. At once, starting at the van a tremendous clamor rose through the moribund crowd. Mounted on a camel a rider had appeared on the horizon and was racing toward them. Konon de Montaigue, waving his arms madly, swaying to right and left, pulled up, and slipped from the camel before the beast had time to kneel down. In a strangled voice he whispered: "There's water . . . nearby!" And fell to the ground. They raised him, but he slipped limply through their hands. The man who had brought them glad tidings was dying of thirst himself. For the good knight, after sighting from a distance the well from which the others were already drinking, had not gone on but had turned back at once to fortify his companions with the news.

With trembling hands the Bishop sprinkled the face of the messenger with the water from the last and only bag, while through the ghostly ranks of the bloody-lipped, parched, half-dead madmen a mighty roar thundered like the horn of Gabriel.

"Water is near! Water!"

30.

Incidents of the March

FROM ICONIUM TO HERAKLEA THE LAND WAS FREE OF SARACENS. AT THE news of the crusaders' approach they had vanished. Marching across the fertile countryside, the Latin army, though whittled to half its former size, built back its strength quickly. The autumn harvest was abundant and equipment was available for almost every need. Only horses were difficult to find, and these the knights required before they could continue their march in earnest. They forayed constantly in search of them.

Tancred was the most zealous of the searchers, but eventually he tired of the almost fruitless business and began to look longingly at the peaks of the Taurus Mountains which rose in front of the camp, towering halfway to the sky. On an impulse he took a thousand men and set out to cross the range to the valleys and seashore on the other side. There lay thickly settled cities and rich towns, waiting to be conquered.

It was a difficult crossing. The cliffs were high and the way treacherous. For long hours the knights proceeded carefully with clouds drifting below their feet. Then they glimpsed the valleys and the waves of the sea and descended to them, filled with joy. They were convinced that they were the first of the Latins to reach this far on the journey.

They went first to the city of Tarsus, home of the great St. Paul. It lay about three hours' journey from the sea, surrounded by walls dating to the time of the Roman Caesars. Beyond the walls minarets shot up from Moslem mosques and as Tancred and his men descended into the valley they heard a muezzim calling the faithful to prayer. Piously they recited the Angelus to drown out the sound of the pagan voices.

When night came they did not start fires or pitch tents. A patrol of a hundred men under Marco di Santa Leone prepared to start at dawn to look for crossings along the river Cydnus. The remainder made ready to storm Tarsus. All night they felled trees and prepared storm ladders.

The sound of their axes seemed to echo an extraordinarily long way off.

By dawn the ladders were ready and when the sun rose they raced for the walls, horns blaring, mouths shouting, "God wills it!"

From the ramparts, defenders poured hot water and tar on them, threw stones, and pushed the ladders away from the walls. The assailants clung to the walls like cats. They sent hissing coils of rope over the battlements, fastening the ends to ladders. The Moslems cut the ropes. A few Christians reached the walls but were instantly killed.

"What shall we do if we are not in before evening?" said Tancred. "We can't retreat. Perhaps we should try from another side."

Suddenly a commotion broke out from among the Moslems. Their attention seemed to turn in another direction. Some left the walls, and at last Tancred was able to gain a foothold. Quickly his knights established a position on the walls, then descended and ran to open the gate, shouting "God wills it!"

Their voices were echoed, echoed so clearly that they turned toward the sound. Through the streets Moslems were fleeing in terror. Behind them came Latin knights. Tancred's men stared at them with open mouths. Who were they? What had happened?

The strange incident was soon explained. Tancred had not been the only one to cross the mountains. Baldwin of Lorraine had been imbued with the same idea. He had crossed with five thousand men and had been storming the city from another side. The two armies had been helping each other unawares.

Neither Baldwin nor Tancred was happy about the situation. When the fighting was ended they sat down to discuss a division of the spoils. Baldwin, irritated and disgusted with his luck, demanded a five-to-one distribution in his favor, pointing out that he had five thousand men to Tancred's one thousand. Tancred shouted that numbers had nothing to do with the taking of a walled town, since at the most a few men did the fighting that mattered while the rest held the ladders and waited. He suggested that they count the dead and make this the basis of the decision. Baldwin refused, clinging to his original assertion.

"Godfrey would divide it evenly," said Tancred, looking at Baldwin with suspicion and distaste.

This was all that was needed to settle Baldwin stubbornly in his decision. Since the scene he had witnessed at the deathbed of his wife, qualms about his brother had rankled desperately within him. He had worshipped Godfrey and followed his leadership without question. The loss of his wife was nothing; the loss of his idol was a blow he could not sustain.

"We shall divide it five to one," he said coldly.

"Then keep it all," said Tancred.

He got up, called to his men, mounted and led them out of the city and away. Baldwin watched them go without happiness. His act was not right, he knew, but he seemed unable to do anything about it. He was in a constant state of anger, petulance, and irritability these days. When darkness came and the gates were closed, Marco di Santa Leone came knocking with his patrol, expecting to find Tancred in the city. Baldwin refused to let the men in.

"We're in danger," said Marco. "The country is full of Saracens. Already twenty of my men have been picked off. We are tired."

Baldwin was adamant. Again he knew he was acting wrongly; again he was unable to control the contrary will that forced him to act in defiance of all the rules of knightly behavior. Marco and his men rode away into the night. Next morning they were found massacred a mile from the city. Immediately Baldwin rounded up the horses he had captured and returned over the mountains.

News of his unfairness to Tancred and his inhospitality to Marco had preceded him. Adhemar questioned him; Godfrey denounced him.

"Something is wrong with you," said Godfrey. "Something has changed you. What is it?"

"It is you," said Baldwin. "I thought you a saint. It seems you are not. What was there between you and my wife?"

Godfrey stared at him in amazement. "Gontrane?" he said. "I have never had anything to do with any woman, much less with your wife." But he said it with an effort.

"Can you swear on your knightly honor that there was nothing between you and Gontrane?" said Baldwin.

Godfrey stared at him. In his over-scrupulousness, in his complete honesty, he was not certain that something had not existed between himself and Gontrane, some subtle bond that somehow affected the physical union between her and his brother, perhaps causing it to be an unhappy one. He hesitated.

"So you can't swear," said Baldwin bitterly.

"I must explain," said Godfrey. "I must examine this with you. . . ."

"In that case I shall wait for your explanation before I explain anything of my conduct to you," said Baldwin. Then he walked out and went to his own tent.

For days he brooded, while the barons shunned him and many of his own knights went over to Godfrey. He could not resume his faith in his brother; neither could he countenance the way in which he had acted toward Tancred and Marco. In desperation he called together the remainder of his forces, broke camp, and set off by himself, not knowing where he was going or what he intended to do. He was leaving the main camp, so he said, to proceed by himself. He did not intend to return.

Once more he crossed the Taurus Mountains; then he went on to the banks of the Euphrates. There he pitched camp by the great, half-dried river, uncertain what to do next. While he wondered, emissaries of Abba Thoros, the Christian ruler of Edessa, came to him. They desired, they said, to ask him to defend their city from the Saracens and to settle in it and be its prince. Baldwin was flabbergasted.

The city of Edessa lay in a part of Mesopotamia which although surrounded by the Moslems had not yet fallen to them. Admirably placed between the Tigris and Euphrates rivers, in a fertile country and with splendid defense weapons, it had staved off the flood of Islam during the fourteen years which had passed since the Arabs and Turks had taken Jerusalem, Antioch, and all of Asia Minor up to Nicodemia. Now, however, the situation was becoming increasingly desperate. Resistance was more and more difficult. The fact that Edessa had not fallen during the last year was due largely to the concern of the Moslems with the Latin invasion. The Latins, so the people of Edessa believed, were the greatest warriors in the world. Since they were Christian they were obviously meant as the salvation of Edessa. Now that Baldwin had come into their country it seemed the providence of God.

The emissaries were Syrians. They wore mantles and turbans somewhat like those of the Moslems, but large gold and silver crosses hung on their breasts. They explained to Baldwin how they had been able to hold out by the valor of their Ethiopian soldiers, all Christians, and how now in his old age Abba Thoros wished to hand on his city to a Christian who could preserve its freedom.

"Our abba wishes to adopt you as his son and heir," the emissaries said, "so that after him you may succeed to the throne and be our king. We have brought a document stating this."

Baldwin was staggered. He had dreamed of carving for himself a kingdom somewhere in the world, but he had not actually supposed that it would be accomplished. At home he had nothing; Godfrey had sold their possessions, their lands, and their privileges to gather money for the crusade. Now here, after he had disgraced himself with his own people, suddenly a kingdom was placed before him, dropped in his lap.

"Accept it," whispered Leone. She was big with child now and pestered Baldwin constantly to marry her.

"Accept it," Baldwin's inner self whispered to him. But the thing was so incredible that his reasoning mind could not accept it.

"Go before me to Edessa," he said to the emissaries. "I shall follow you there and make my decision when I have arrived."

The city received him as its prince and emancipator. The abba, a man not far from death, begged him to accept the kingship. Still dazed, unable to believe his good fortune, Baldwin gave his assent. In a few days the ceremony was performed and the outcast Latin found himself king of a Christian city richer and stronger than any of the feudal fiefs in Europe. He married Leone, fought the Saracens, and soothed his conscience with the thought that he was only putting off his journey to Jerusalem.

Meanwhile Tancred continued to roam the coast in search of horses. In Mamister he ran unexpectedly into Guynemere of Boulogne whose flotilla lay at anchor in the bay. The king of pirates greeted him heartily.

"I thought that you had all perished in the desert," he told the young knight, "And that we alone were left to carry on the fight. Made me feel like that Good Thief to whom Our Lord promised Paradise. Well, I am mighty glad to see you. We will continue to sail close to the shore following your progress, and any time you need our help just light a beacon on one of the coastal hills. We will watch out for it. And how," he asked unexpectedly, "is that Sultaness Your Honor took at Nicaea?"

"I sent her back to the Greek camp," Tancred replied stiffly while his face turned red as it always did whenever Djurisha was mentioned.

"Ah? What a pity! So she proved unworthy after all?"

"I don't know what you mean, Sir Guynemere. I sent the sultaness to the Greeks right away, and never saw her again."

"Is that so? Well, well . . . Who would have thought of that."

The old rascal was obviously making fun of him, and Tancred was sorely tempted to slap his face. Guynemere, however, knew when to stop.

"Seems that our galleys have special luck that way," he continued blandly, "for this time, too, we brought a noble lady with us, the wife of one of your barons. His name is Gaston d'Haineault, I think."

"What? Ida of Montferrand is here?" exclaimed Tancred, "Her husband has been expecting her for over a year."

"She started on her way last winter but robbers incited by Jews captured her and held for ransom. She was sailing on a Genoese galley when we met her, so she moved over aboard one of our vessels."

"Why?" Tancred asked naively.

"Just a feminine whim, no doubt. Though, to tell the truth we had grappled the Genoese galley pretty thoroughly and it was taking in water like a torn sieve. The Genoese went to the bottom along with their vessel but, of course, ladies deserve special considerations. And when she told me she was a crusader's wife, I assured her that we, too, were true crusaders, and promised to take her to her husband. So I brought her here. I have been waiting for the last two weeks for someone from your camp to appear. I am mighty glad it was Your Honor who happened along since from past experience I know that I can safely entrust the lady's virtue into your hands. Would Your Honor care to meet her, now? My boat and oarsmen are at your disposal."

There was a mischievous twinkle in the pirate's eyes but Tancred was too engrossed in the news of Ida's arrival to notice the barb. The woman, he had heard, was something of an Isolde. She and Gaston had long been in love, but each had been married, he to a shrew and she to a man for whom she did not care. Her husband died and Gaston went to Rome to beg the Pope to free him from his unhappy marriage. His plea was refused. He then disappeared and all the efforts of his wife to find him were in vain. When she died he reappeared and soon he and Ida were married. They had lived together only a short time when the call came at Clermont.

Now, with understandable curiosity, Tancred gazed at the woman who was leaning toward him over the bulwark of the ship. Tall and slim she stood poised as though about to fly to the small craft. Perhaps at this distance she took him for her husband? When he leaped on deck she stiffened a little and drew back.

"But she is quite old!" thought Tancred disappointed. Much older than Isolde. A tired face framed in a white coif tightly drawn under the chin. Dressed plainly, with almost nun-like simplicity. Big eyes with heavy bluish lids. He followed her to the cabin which proved to be a dark low closet, with badly scarred walls. A narrow couch, a table, and a stool made up all the furniture.

"Pray be seated, Sir, and tell me the news. I am anxious to hear it. Do you know my husband, Count Gaston d'Haineault? Is he in good health?" Outwardly she was composed but her hands trembled. She seated herself on the edge of the couch and motioned the knight to the stool. Through the open door of the cabin came a flood of bright noon light.

"Indeed, I know the Count d'Haineault," answered Tancred. "He is well though he has grown thin and grey worrying over you, Madam."

She smiled in shy embarrassment, nodding her averted face, and Tancred, to whom a moment before she had seemed old, suddenly understood all the follies committed for this woman.

"I could not come earlier," she said after a pause. Her voice was low-pitched and pleasant though somewhat throaty. "I left a year ago as we had agreed, on a galley which carried thirty knights who had likewise taken the cross and were on their way to join you. I thought that sailing with them would prove the easiest way to reach you but as it happened it turned out otherwise."

"Guynemere told me that bandits bribed by Jews assailed you but I could not believe it."

"It is true though. All the Jews are dead set against the crusade and hinder it in any way they can. They spend large sums of money to hire galleys and bandits to stop those who would follow you. They held us in captivity for half a year demanding such a ransom that no one could raise it. At last I ordered my castle sold, and bought my freedom."

"You sold Montferrand?" Tancred asked surprised.

"What else could I do?" She smiled in her peculiar way.

"Yes, but a family castle . . ."

"I thought of my husband who was waiting for me." Ida replied simply.

"Montferrand sold for a ransom to robbers," repeated Tancred aghast.

"The boldness of those vermin! We will settle with them when we return."

"When we return," she echoed, "How long do you think it will be before we reach Jerusalem and return, Sir Knight?"

The question caught him unprepared. He admitted that none of them knew how far they still were from Jerusalem. But, surely, they could not be far now. They had already been travelling for a year.

"The Genoese with whom we were sailing when the pirates fell upon us said that it was still terribly far, that the distance you have covered is a mere trifle to what is to come. They said—pray forgive me for repeating their words: 'If the crusaders take Antioch then we shall believe that they can reach Jerusalem. But no one will ever capture Antioch for that's beyond human power.'"

"But not God's," said Tancred, bristling. "The Genoese don't know what they are talking about. They said the same thing about Nicaea and yet Nicaea fell. True—they will never take Antioch with their galleys but we will!"

She smiled at his youthful confidence and promptly returned to that which concerned her most.

"How can I get from here to my husband?"

"You must come with me. God willing, within two weeks I will be back in camp."

"Two weeks!" she exclaimed. "Could I not get there sooner? How far is it?"

"Just beyond these mountains," he pointed at the blue peaks. She drank them in with avid eyes.

"I could give you, Madam, a few men to take you there but I fear it would not be safe. Saracen bands roam the coast freely, made bold by the knowledge that our army is on the other side of the mountains. Only three days ago they surrounded and wiped out completely a patrol of mine. Only one servant escaped to bring me the news."

He flushed darkly with anger and grief at the recollection of Marco di Santa Leone and the circumstances under which he had perished. Unable to contain himself he related the whole incident to Ida, in a voice that quivered with indignation. She listened horrified.

"Lord!" she whispered. "To think that such things can happen amongst you . . . That Baldwin must be a fiend. And I have looked upon you as saints."

"Indeed, no one else has thus far done anything as ignoble as Baldwin," Tancred affirmed. "But Lord!—we are no saints! There is no end of quarrels, squabbles and common human sins."

This seemed to sadden her.

"Half a year I spent locked up in a small chamber," she told him. "Not knowing where I was or in whose hands I had fallen or whether I would ever be set free again. I knew that none of my kin would come to my help since they all thought that I had rejoined my husband in Byzantium. Days dragged so . . . I had only one occupation, one comfort, to think about you, about the crusaders. I saw you marching your eyes fixed upon the Holy Goal. In my ears rang your cry: "God wills it!" I prayed not only to be united with my husband but also to be part of that holy throng."

She stopped suddenly embarrassed by her own ardor.

"Please, forgive me Sir Knight, for speaking so much but this is the first time in a year that I speak with someone other than a merchant or a bandit."

"I would gladly listen to you forever," Tancred assured her, "Only it shames me that you should have conceived so lofty an idea of us. We are no holy throng. Each one of us is but a man, and you know what men are."

"I know," she sighed. "And yet don't you think that even to be a mere man is a difficult and wonderful thing?"

He did not understand. What did she mean? Every man was a man even as a horse was a horse, and a dog—a dog. How could a man be anything else or stop being a man? What a strange woman Ida was. She spoke in riddles. And yet there was something simple and straightforward about her, too. She looked the speaker straight in the eyes without a trace of bashfulness or coyness. Like a man. And it occurred to Tancred that here was a woman with whom one could talk as though with an equal and yet so much more pleasantly than with a comrade.

He awoke from his reverie much embarrassed for she had been speaking and lost in his thoughts he had missed what she was saying.

"About my journey," she explained with an indulgent smile. "I would like to leave at once. Would you give me a few men, Sir Tancred?"

"I am afraid a misshap may befall you," he replied, hesitantly. "I could not spare more than twelve horsemen and in case of attack . . ."

"No one will attack us. Please, Sir Knight. You look like a kindly man. Don't detain me," she pleaded.

Should he let her go or not? Or should he, perhaps, return sooner himself? The Saracens might capture her. Besides, if they were to journey together there would be plenty of time to talk more fully of these matters that seemed incomprehensible and yet—perhaps—quite comprehensible, too. He had already taken a few horses—they would have to do. He was about to tell Ida of his decision when in a hot wave of suspicion it occurred to him that what prompted him was not so much his concern for her safety as his own desire to journey by her side. The thought horrified him. Good Lord! Another man's wife! No, no. Let her go as soon as possible.

He rose and a little stiffly, in an almost formal voice said:

"Go, Madam, since you so desire. I shall give you four knights, as many squires and a few servants. I will chose a good horse for you. You can start any time, even to-morrow."

She did. But when two weeks later Tancred returned to camp Ida was not there. Five anxious days went by. Then, one morning a bedraggled grievously wounded man appeared in bishop Adhemar's tent. He was one of the four knights whom Tancred had appointed to escort Ida. The others had died fighting a detachment of Saracens who had come upon them after they had crossed the mountains. Ida had tried to kill herself but had been taken alive before she could plunge the dagger into her breast. Tancred and d'Haineault dashed off in pursuit. But to no avail. All trace of Ida had vanished. The incident roused the knights as had the news of the massacre of Peter's men. Once more they set off on the march, crossing the mountains and heading toward Antioch.

31.

Antioch

THE PEAKS OF ANTI-TAURUS, HOW LONG WOULD THE GRANDCHILDREN AND great grandchildren of the crusaders recall that dreaded name! How deep would it impress itself upon the memories of the wanderers themselves. Those who had survived the desert and the battles froze with fear as they hung now suspended between heaven and an abyss that seemed to reach to the bowels of the earth. Clinging to the rocky ledges, they could not believe that any living mortal had ever passed this way before them, and perhaps they were not mistaken. Farther to the east or more to the west there were better crossing places, not so wild, where old Roman roads once led to Antioch, but the crusaders knew nothing of them. They would not believe their guides and refused to take a more roundabout way. Straight ahead! Why waste time? What were mountains to them? Had they not crossed the Alps and the Balkans?

And so they made their way along the sky-high trail accessible only to eagles, along a ridge so narrow that they could not place both feet side by side. Once they had entered it there was no retreat. The path was barely perceptible. Fallen stones, rocky bridges, overhanging cliffs and shelves constantly barred the way so that men had to hang their swords from their necks and claw the bluff with their fingers. One glance underfoot was enough to cause vertigo and a fall. Horses tumbled heavily into the the chasm, beating the air with their hoofs. Some of them had been strung together with ropes; these fell in rows one behind the other. Those which still remained braced their hoofs against the rock, snorted, and backed. And as they backed they pushed off those that came behind. The newly won chattel, tents, kettles, arms, and supplies, fell like hail into the yawning depths.

In the mountains of Anti-Taurus, renamed the Devil's Mountains by the chroniclers of the expedition, the army of crusaders crumbled like sheaves under a flail, a flail swung by death. The great body of the army shrank, yet it still moved on, it still existed, and after days of wandering it descended into the valleys, once more horseless, decimated, spent, exhausted by sleeplessness, mountain sickness, and hunger, yet still undaunted.

Then they stopped to rest in the valley of Marash, which was as beautiful and abundant as a rich harvest. There was nothing half-way about this Asia Minor, nothing tame, mediocre, ordinary. Either there was abundance, teeming with all lures and delight of the earth, or deadly desert and wild rocky bluffs. A land of extremes.

No wonder that the people believed that this was the site of Eden. Just one step and from the fabulous garden of plenty, our sinful parents, Adam and Eve, stumbled into the God-forsaken desert where only thistles and burrs grew. Just one step . . . across the line traced by the Archangel's sword.

Along the valley of Marash, so different from the wilderness they had just traversed that men gazed about them uncertain that they were really awake, the army headed for Antioch. The long-awaited city loomed before them unexpectedly, not further than an hour's journey away. Surrounding hills had hidden it from sight. Stopping in their tracks the Latins stared in silence at the City of the Apostles. Some knelt in the dust and crossed themselves, praising God aloud. It seemed to them that they could already see the Holy Land, that they were at its very gates. Antioch . . . The first city met thus far of which they knew from the Gospels.

The day was the twentieth of October; in the year of Our Lord 1097, the third year since the Crusade began.

* * * *

In Antioch Emir Yagi-Sian had assembled thirty thousand troops, gathered large stores of food and supplies, closed the gates; and there he was waiting.

Three hundred and sixty bastions defended the walls of the stronghold. The walls themselves were smooth, thick, enormous, like cliffs. On the southern side, from the Gate of St. Paul to the Gate of St. George, a distance of two miles, there was not a single break, not a gate or a postern. Nothing but a blind naked wall climbing higher and higher over the rocks, jutting out from slopes of Mount Pierius, Mount Silpius, and the steep peak of Cassius which from three sides protected the city. Only an eagle could have flown into the city this way. It was impossible to put ladders against the walls or roll up siege towers.

Within the enclosure of these formidable walls loomed four steep hills fortified like bastions. On the highest and most inaccessible peak rose the Citadel, a mighty, fortified castle which from its lofty heights dominated the whole city. It was here that the masters of Antioch resided and it was from this stronghold which commanded the entire valley of the Orontes that they held in check the city's rich burghers and its ever-restive rabble.

On the northern side the walls were protected by the bend of the Orontes River and from the Sea Gate to the Bridge Gate, the walls of the city seemed to spring from the water. Further down where the river swerved away from the walls the space between the two was taken up by the summer residences of rich Antiochans. An incredible wealth of flowers cascaded in terraces down to the river. Multicolored petals rained upon the water; roses everywhere, for this was the birthplace of roses. In the evening the rippling surface reflected countless lights that brought to mind the Byzantine nights, and from the houses, hidden by blooming shrubs, came the strains of music and song. On each palace hung an ikon or a cross until lately concealed from the eyes of the Mohammedans, now prominently displayed, so that the Latins could tell at a glance that those who dwelled here were Christians like themselves.

As a rule, at the first rains heralding the onset of winter, the occupants of the beautiful gardens deserted their palaces for their city homes. Not so this year. The Moslems, goaded by the approach of the Latins, had begun to treat the Armenians and Syrians, whom they suspected of sympathy for the invaders, with open hostility. For fear of even worse persecutions all who could do so fled to the suburbs, so that now as the troops approached, through the latticed windows of the *ginecea* peered big brown eyes, painted lips smiling invitingly. Let the fathers and mothers pray locked in their chambers, let them weep and shiver with fear of what the oncoming war might bring; the maidens did not care. Besides, the women of Antioch believed that no matter what went on in the world, a man still remained a man and a woman a woman and there were no circumstances under which the two could not spend a few pleasant moments together.

The Orontes was spanned by a great stone bridge called the Bronze

Bridge, built long ago by the Romans, with an entrance guarded by two enormous towers sheathed with bronze plates. Facing it and bolted fast, rose the Bridge Gate. To its left were the Sea Gate and the Gate of St. George. To the right the Dog's Gate and the Gate of St. Paul the Apostle. That was all. Despite the enormity of the city, which ranked third largest in the world (next to Rome and Alexandria), there were no other gates. But if the gates were few, the churches were many, three hundred and eighty of them, each with a gilded roof, all now turned into mosques. So the Christians, deprived of their own temple, went to pray on the nearby hill called *Djebal-Seman*, the Mountain of Simon, where a weather-beaten stone pillar stood, from which once St. Simon Stylite used to preach. It was here that the stern, unrelenting preacher had stood year after year, oblivious of sun and winter rains, overgrown with moss while still alive until he looked more like a statue than a living man, parched and withered like a leaf. His eyes which knew no sleep were forever fixed upon the city from which came the breath of selfishness, worldliness, and lust. ·

Ever since the city had been taken by the infidels the pillar of the austere Saint had become an altar before which the penitents of Antioch knelt and prayed. And the relentless Stylite, looking down from heaven, might have well rejoiced at this contrition and grief, if, ah, if only they had changed Antioch in any way. But what did it avail that people came in droves to cry and pray at Mount Djebal-Seman when they still persisted in their old sins, when the old iniquities continued to thrive under the reign of the Crescent even as they had under the reign of the Cross? Concupiscence was as strong as ever. Repentant women bedecked with relics returned from the mount straight into their lover's bed, and every true Antiochian still showed more concern for worldly beauty and pleasure than for the salvation of his soul. Even St. Paul the Apostle himself must have long since relinquished his guardianship over the wicked city.

Sybaritism, flowing from abundance and ease of life, prevailed not only among the inhabitants themselves but engulfed likewise every newcomer who came to rule the land. Greeks, Mussulmen—all had succumbed to it. Now it was the Latins' turn.

*   *   *   *

Opposite the gate of St. Paul rose low treeless hillocks. It was here that Boemund pitched his camp. To his right in the valley facing the

Dog's Gate the two Roberts, Hugh, and Stephen de Blois took up their stand. Raymond St. Gilles commanded the whole distance from the Dog's Gate to the Bridge Gate and Godfrey of Bouillon kept watch over the sector from the Bridge Gate to the Sea Gate and beyond. Only the Gate of St. George remained unguarded since there was no possibility of pitching a camp there. It was decided that various units would guard it by turns.

So far no one interfered with their pitching of camps and the digging of fortifications. Yagi-Sian calmly awaited the arrival of reinforcements promised from Bagdad, Persia, and Egypt. The whole of Islam was on its way here to crush the infidels, and it was bootless to begin the battle until they drew near. And so the ramparts remained empty. The very smoothness, height, and immensity of the walls were protection enough. One had only to glance at the mighty scarps and the rounded hips of the tower, to realize the fruitlessness of hacking or hewing the way it was done at Nicaea; a woodpecker trying to tear down a church steeple would not have been more silly.

There could be no doubt that the Moslems watching through the shooting holes saw all that went on outside. Nevertheless they did not appear, answered no calls and challenges, sent out no skirmishers. This indifference filled the barons with cocksureness and confirmed their belief that the pagans were quaking with fear. But Bishop Adhemar was worried. He knew from experience that there was nothing worse for the crusading army than a long wait in one spot, and, judging by the present tactics of the Saracens, the wait this time might be long indeed. One could have sworn that the city was dead.

It was not dead, though, because when one day a band of knights ventured close to the walls to abuse the name of the Prophet and to knock with their lances at the gate, a ball of Greek Fire burst forth from an invisible embrasure flowed down in a thousand flaming tongues among the riders, searing the horses, who went mad with fright. The rancor of the knights rose to unprecedented heights.

"We must begin to build siege towers at once," called Raymond St. Gilles at the barons' council. "Thank God we have carpenters who know how that rascal, Pantopulos, did it."

"Alas! We have very few carpenters," broke in the Bishop. "It seems that they either withered in the desert or perished in the mountains. I

ordered the horns blown to summon them to work. Thus far only four
have appeared . . ."

"These four will teach others. The important thing is to begin."

"We need about ten battle towers, very high ones. About twice as high
as those at Nicaea."

"The work will take a lot of time."

"It will," nodded the Bishop. "So, before we begin, let us consider
other things, too. We have plenty of food now. There is an abundance
of grain everywhere, plenty of fodder, wine, and olives. The place teems
with cattle, sheep, and goats. We must take good care of all this so that
it will last. Right now the waste is appalling. I saw with my own eyes as
I rode through the encampments how the grooms bed the horses belly-
deep in straw, though the weather is still warm, and give them so much
fodder for the night that no horse could eat more than a half of it. The
rest is trampled and destroyed. And the same goes for food. When cattle
are slaughtered, good pieces of meat are tossed to the dogs because men
no longer find them to their taste. Servants throw groats at each other
for a jest. Bread lies about everywhere, sinfully wasted. This cannot go
on. We have too much today, in a month there may not be enough."

"Not enough?" they repeated incredulously. "Surely Your Grace must
not have seen how much there is. Never fear. There will be enough for
all."

"For how long?"

"For as long as the siege lasts."

"And none can tell how long that will be. At Nicaea we lost more
than eight weeks, and what was Nicaea compared to Antioch?'"

"Oh! That was because at Nicaea we didn't know how to lay a siege."

"And still we know very little. So we better gather, reckon up and
measure all the supplies we can find in the vicinity, and store them in
warehouses. Then, we can issue them to each encampment according
to its needs."

They laughed at this monkish providence. The man looked like a
knight and lo! the cloth stuck out all over him. "Reckon up. Gather—
Oh, yes! We will come to Your Grace to get a measure of flour or a lamp
of oil."

The Bishop remained unmoved by these jibes.

"Not you, my Lords, will come for that, but a steward appointed from each camp. He will come once a week with carts and men and take whatever each camp needs."

"Right," said Boemund, Stephen, and Robert of Flanders simultaneously. But the rest would not listen. Even the usually indifferent Godfrey made a wry face. It looked as though they were getting ready to remain here a year, while he was determined to be in Bethlehem by Christmas.

"I hope we will not come to regret it bitterly some day," warned the Bishop. "You scoff at laying up supplies, my Lords, but even that is not enough. Now that the harvest is gathered we ought to see to it that the fields are tilled and sowed. The native population has fled into the mountains. If we cannot bring them back we should do it ourselves."

The knights' gaiety reached a new peak at this unexpected proposal. Fancy them plowing and sowing in wartime! And in a foreign land to boot! Plowing and sowing. Had anyone ever heard of such a thing?

"I hope we won't come to rue our neglect," repeated the Bishop doggedly.

32.

The Blue Dress

THE RAINY SEASON WAS FAST APPROACHING AND STILL THE SITUATION OF the besiegers and the besieged remained unchanged. No one in the Christian camp any more expected to celebrate Christmas in Bethlehem, but only hoped that they might spend Easter at the Holy Sepulcher.

Although the winter of Antioch was in no way as severe as the winters of France, Auvergne, Lorraine, or Silesia, men grew languid and heavy with sleep. One was tempted to curl up into a ball, dig oneself into the ground, and go to sleep like those wise beasts of the forest, the bear, the badger, and the thorny hedgehog, or at least to stay by the fire forgetting all cares and listening to the storytellers' yarns.

In any other country, in any other circumstances, the Bishop would not have reproved this desire for rest; he would have found it natural and wholesome. But not here, not in Antioch. The Bishop had seen clearly that what Byzantium had started Antioch was about to complete. The luxury of everyday existence, the lewd insistence of women, the very refinements of life proved too strong a poison for these simple, harsh, unprepared men.

The enormous stronghold stood as before. The building of siege towers progressed very slowly; the carpenters were unskilled and lacked saws, axes, nails, and all manner of tools, which had been left in the desert or lost in the mountain pass. The knights chafed at the delay, but none of the warriors would think of lending a hand or helping with advice. Weeks passed. It occurred to the Bishop to abandon the siege, by-pass Antioch and press on to the south, but the barons opposed the suggestion with rare unanimity; and perhaps this time they were right. To leave the enemy in the rear was not only dangerous but contrary to all good knightly principles.

The only noteworthy success with which the crusaders met at this

305

time was, strange to say, connected with the Gate of St. George. Noticing several times imprints of horse-hoofs upon the soft ground, and horse and camel manure strewn on the highway which led to the gate, the Bishop began to suspect that the Saracens were using it to bring in help or supplies. He spoke about it to the barons who denied vigorously any such possibility, insisting that the gate was vigilantly guarded. Nevertheless, shortly before Martinmas, servants who had gone fishing in the stream came running to the camp with shouts that a long line of carts was entering the fortress from the side of the ravine. The men of the Duke of Lorraine had left and the Flandrians had not yet arrived. The pagans apparently had been only waiting for this chance. A long line of heavily laden camels and donkeys was entering the gate, passing at the entrance a throng of veiled women who, it seemed, were being sent from the city to the south in order to save food for the defenders. Raymond St. Gilles and Tancred, each at the head of several hundred men, were the first to pounce upon them, while from the fortress sprang a strong unit of Moslem cavalry. The gate banged closed behind them. And so in the tight confines of the entrance to the ravine a battle began, the more fierce and bloody since there was no room to deploy the troops in battle array. Men trod on each other fighting in tiers and layers; the women trampled by horses, screamed to high heaven. The Moslem unit was completely wiped out. Most of the women perished under the horses' hoofs, only a few climbed the cliffs of the ravine and scattered in the mountains. From the ramparts spears fell like hail, arrows flew in droves, Greek Fire spurted, too, but in the heat of battle almost no one noticed it. Still drunk with fighting, the knights in a mad scramble stormed the gate, pounding at it with rocks, logs, anything they could lay their hands on, but the brass portals did not even budge.

The unexpected clash sobered the knights and awakened them to the need of vigilance. As it turned out the enemy was neither as fearful nor as impotent as his crouching behind the walls had led them to believe. But the guarding of the gate even when the hours of watch were strictly enforced proved difficult because of the terrain itself. Frequent downpours had turned the ravine into a roaring river. Drenched to the skin the warriors complained and hid under rocks. So it was decided to interrupt the building of siege towers for a time, and let all the carpenters work at a wooden bastion that was to stand on a rock right opposite the gate. The bastion was to consist of a great, squat, four-storied tower

considerably wider at the base than at the top, surmounted by a crenelated platform from which watch would be kept, and two lean-to sheds
which were to house men and horses. The entrance to the tower and the
lean-tos was protected from enemy shots by a stockade of stout posts
planted upright in the ground. Since the ground was rocky, these were
reinforced by stones piled inside and out. In order to save time the Crusaders did not bother to hew the stones but used instead gravestones
brought from a nearby Moslem cemetery. Set up edgewise they made
excellent props for the stockade, but the pagans, seeing from the walls
this desecration of their dead, howled with rage and tried though in vain
to reach the builders with their arrows. Time and again they opened the
gate for sorties, sprayed the unfinished structure with Greek Fire and
scattered the workmen. But each time knights, who were now constantly
on guard, fell upon them like a storm, so that not once did any of the
raiders return to the city alive, particularly as the Moslems were afraid to
open the gates to the survivors. Nevertheless, because of the confined
space, each sally meant a complete destruction of the work already done.
It began to look as though the bastion would never be finished. At
last the Latins, losing all patience, summoned the strength of a thousand arms and piled high against the gate rocks so heavy and great that
no human power could open the portals from inside. From then on the
pagans' attempts at interference was reduced to ineffectual shooting,
stone-flinging and flame-throwing, from the walls. Indeed, they still
tried sallies through the Bridge Gate. The latter, however, was carefully
guarded and two weeks later the bastion was ready. It was clumsy and
gloomy but solid and roomy enough. According to an old custom followed in their native lands the Latins covered the entire structure with
hides, which, drenched as they were by the constant rains, would protect
it from catching fire. The bastion was named *Malhommerie*, "The Watch
Tower Against Evil Men," and Tancred took permanent command of it.

And so after two months of siege thoughtlessly wasted, the fortress
was at last really closed and cut off from the outside world.

The barons rejoiced, convinced that the fall of Antioch was now close
at hand, but the Bishop was not so sanguine. He fretted over the waste
of provender, and once more brought up the matter of tilling the surrounding fields.

The barons shrugged their shoulders and told him to go ahead if he
liked. They would have nothing to do with it.

So Adhemar de Monteuil sowed on his own. He gathered all his men and set Walter the Penniless to oversee their work. The gaunt giant with the sword dangling from his neck was too blindly devoted to the Bishop ever to object to his orders, so he strode obediently through the fields, watching the work of ox drivers. Stooped and dressed in a short jerkin he looked from a distance exactly like a stork. The Bishop came now and then to give him heart and to see for himself how the work was progressing. In truth, he came more often than was necessary, for the sight of work on the soil drew him irresistibly, soothed, and restored his spirits.

During one of these visits, Adhemar met Imbram. The youngest Strzygonia was breaking a new horse and never failed to stop off to watch the plowing. Like the Bishop he felt an unconscious and deep respect for the soil, for that earth from which God had created the human race, for that dust to which all living creatures would return.

They stopped side by side, watching in silence. Adhemar spoke first. "The knights scoff at me, for tilling another's land, but I still say it's good to sow, even though we are not certain who will gather in the harvest. Can we be sure of reaping when we sow our own? Sowing is a good thing of itself, a divine endeavor. Our Lord was pleased to call himself a sower. Yes. Sow wind and you will reap storm but sow grain and you will reap blessings. I am glad I sowed this, though I pray to God that we never need to use this harvest."

Imbram listened attentively, understanding not so much the words as the thought behind them. It appealed to something fundamental within him. For a long time now he had been sorely missing the life on the soil, that was why he had stopped to watch and that was why, a few days later, carefully concealing the fact from Zbylut and the rest of his companions, he selected a likely piece of land bordered on one side by the lake and on the other by an olive grove, and ordered his men to plow it.

But later, when he came to watch their work, he was outraged by the crooked furrows and the obvious indifference of the men to their work. He gave his servant his horse to hold and grabbed the plow himself. Ah! The joy of it! He drew a deep breath. A ridge of rich shiny sticky loam falling slowly to one side, the long furrow ripping open the soil, the fertile soil the same as that back home. The warm closeness of the eternal mother earth enveloped him. He felt that he was doing the thing which, long as he had been deprived of it, was to him most natural and real in the world, and the thought startled him. Could it be that at heart he was more a husbandman than a knight? Which did he enjoy more· a battle or plowing and sowing? Deep in his soul he had to admit that it was the latter. He felt with delight his feet sink into the soft loam as he called out to the oxen, "Haw!" Looking at their strong rumps, he could have sworn that he was back home plowing the newly cleared field by the forest.

The smell of the earth, always and everywhere the same, carried him back to his native land, evoked fancies as real as life itself. Look, the evening is near; mists drift over the stubble field, and from the forest comes Ofka, singing, "Oy dana, da dana, oy dana! da dana, oy dana, da dana!" Soon she will be here; she carries a full bark-basket of blackberries. Striding slowly, his palms pressing the handles of the plow firmly, Imbram awaits his beloved.

"Make haste, my darling, make haste! How handsomely you've dressed today. Isn't that the fine blue gown brought from Kiev in the days of the late king, the gown they said was woven in Byzantium by the clever Greeks? The last time you wore it, you and I were receiving gift-bearers at the christening of the babe, and now you wear it to the woods? Is it not too fine for that? Won't the long fringes catch on the heather, get wet with dew? Oh! Never mind the fringe, come quickly, my darling! We will be soon driving the oxen home." From beneath the white kerchief peers the beloved face. Without looking, Imbram can see the deep-set blue eyes, the straight, narrow sensitive nose, the tiny, childish mouth, ever ready to laugh or cry, the slenderness of the neck as fragile as a flower stalk. Ah! you beloved, winsome form, what a joy to see you after so many years, the same as you always were! To watch in your face the same play of shadows, colors, of mobile little quivers that make these eyes, this mouth, this face the dearest in the world.

Suddenly he awoke. Still dazed by the vividness of the dream, for a moment he could not remember where he was. Near by flowed a strange river. Beyond loomed a city, an enemy city which knights were besieging, knights of whom he was one. Here were oxen, a plow, a field, but where was Ofka . . . ? God Almighty! Of the whole dream only Ofka had been real and she was here, right here! The fringed dress shone blue only a few steps ahead of him. He was about to run to her to grasp her hands when he saw his error. The dress was the same, absolutely the same, but the white kerchief was tied differently, and under the kerchief the face

was different, too, darker, and longer. Big, black eyes, timorous movements, she stepped up to Imbram saying something he could not understand. He did not look up at her, but stared only at the dress.

"I think this woman wants your Lordship to follow her," his servant
said in a low voice.

The lad was right. This was exactly what the woman wanted; her cat-
like, inviting motions made it plain enough, as she pointed to a bushy
plume of trees behind which shone a white house. But still Imbram
stared at her wildly. Only a moment before she had been Ofka, his
beloved wife, and now nothing remained but the blue dress.

The woman must have been of base condition and sent by someone
else because, after pointing to the road ahead, she fell back respectfully
half a step behind him, and Imbram, who did not want to lose sight of
Ofka's dress, had to look back constantly. They entered the grove of
olive trees, sycamores, fig trees, and trees bearing fiery red pomegranates.
Rain-beaten morning-glories dangled from the branches like tangled
snakes. In front of the house, built in a half-Byzantine, half-Arabian
style, shone a pool tiled with marble, in the center of which a fountain
splashed. From the thicket came the strident screams of a peacock. They
passed through a beautifully carved door and entered a square inner
courtyard. Overhead in the typical fashion of Antioch stretched a multicolored silken canopy which covered the whole yard. Sifted through it,
the sunlight fell in colored patches. And now from a bench strewn with
cushions slowly rose a woman dressed in a white robe, slit high on the
sides. Her eyes were lengthened with paint as far as her temples, her
lips were carmine, and her hair was wrapped in foamy gauze. She smiled
warmly at her guest.

The blue dress had vanished and Imbram looked about for her, lost
and confused. A different slave girl brought in a tray with two cups of
wine and, with a smile, the Syrian woman handed him one. He drank
it clumsily, ungracefully, cleared his throat and spat. She looked at him
curiously, obviously disappointed.

"I saw you working from a distance, Sire Knight, and thought that
you must be tired, and in need of refreshment," she said in Greek. "My
husband was taken as hostage by the pagans, and I incessantly tremble
for his life. Oh! when will you free us at last?"

He did not understand a word. Although he had been now and again
hearing Greek for almost a year and understood a good many words,

this time he did not even try to grasp her meaning, for still he expected the dream to vanish at any moment. So far the only thing that mattered was the blue dress and he looked about for it anxiously. His hostess noticed that he wanted something and, not knowing what it was, led him from the courtyard into the hall. The walls of the hall were lined with porcelain of azure blue, the holy color which was supposed to guard against evil spells. The ceiling was wooden and marvelously carved and the floor was covered with a mosaic depicting water rippled by the wind, with the sand of the bottom, and fish swimming among long, floating seaweeds that showed through its clear depth.

Talking incessantly, the lady seated him by her side on a low sofa full of soft shiny cushions. She asked if it were true that the Latin knights were forbidden to love women, and were their women more beautiful than women here? And was it true that they had been wandering so long, and did they like it here in Antioch? And would they defeat the pagans? And had they only one wife or many? She spoke vivaciously, using her lovely hands to illustrate what she meant, but he only stared at her with dull, unfriendly eyes giving the impression of a perfect simpleton and a boor. Suddenly he gave a start and seemed to come to life. Out in the courtyard he had caught a glimpse of Ofka's blue dress. He pointed with his hand and asked loudly and clearly who the woman was. His words were as meaningless to his hostess as her previous talk had been to him but she understood the look and the gesture.

"Leah," she murmured with distaste. A flash of pained, scornful surprise froze her face. She turned her head away and shrugged her shoulders.

But Imbram did not care. What did it matter what anyone thought of him? All this was not real, anyway, it was just a dream. He rose and walked out into the courtyard, headed straight for the blue dress. Dismayed, not knowing what he wanted, the girl fled into the garden and he ran after her. In the garden the peacock screamed again—rain was in the air. Imbram overtook Leah on the other side of the pool and seized her brutally by the arm. Immediately, and with the force of a blow, he remembered that it was the third year now that he had remained faithful to his wife, the third year that he had lived like a monk, and he shook with a sudden access of desire. The woman with Ofka's dress and figure and the face of a stranger gave him a sidelong glance, a throng of emotions crossing her face. There was fear in it, and embarrassment, and satisfaction that she should be preferred to her mistress, and surprise, and submission. Fear won, for she wondered what would her mistress say? It was true that, mortally offended, she had not deigned to follow the man who had scorned her—she would not see. But there were other eyes ever ready to spy, and suppose the mistress ordered that the nostrils of the brash slave be torn or her breasts cut off? No, no! Nimbly she freed herself and ran away. Imbram stood a long time motionless rubbing his brow. What had come over him? How terribly he wanted this woman. Yet she was not Ofka, did not even look like Ofka. . . . Only the dress was the same.

"Let us go," he said to his servant, who had followed him with his horse. He mounted his horse and rode slowly away. He had forgotten about the plowing and the men still working in the field. Suddenly the knight reined in his horse. There was something blue at the fringe of the forest. Was it water? Was it a dress? He leaped to the ground and Sobek caught the reins.

"Wait here for me," he told the lad in a choked voice.

33.

Brother Against Brother

ADHEMAR DE MONTEUIL AT THE REQUEST OF SWENNON RODE OVER TO the Danish camp for a heart-to-heart talk with Florine. The royal prince of Denmark had often complained to the Bishop about his marital life.

"Truly it would be better if we never saw each other at all," he told him. "I would rather we were separated than forced to live in such torment. We fell in love at first glance, but soon we shall come to hate each other. Perhaps some day we shall free the Holy Sepulcher; perhaps we shall return to our land. How are we to live then? How will there ever be understanding between us when now we do nothing but bicker and fight? I am as a foe to her and she—as a stranger to me. And yet we love each other."

"I will speak to her," promised Adhemar, and now he rode somewhat morosely to pay the promised call. It struck him how much older Florine looked, how greatly she had changed. Her somber, set face reminded him rather of Blanche de Montbeliard. There was something tense about her, a stubborn, ever-watchful defiance. Upon the first words of the Bishop she burst out in a flood of bitter complaint against her husband. The man was a savage, he gave her no peace day or night, always reproaching, always lamenting. Could he not wait in peace as she was doing? Did he think it was not hard for her, too? And yet she waited. She would keep her vow.

"You don't know men, my child," sighed the Bishop. "You know nothing of life. I am worried lest you two should fall into a greater sin. Why spoil your lives? You vowed like two ignorant children. I will release you. I have the power to do so, and God will free you from your ill-advised vow."

She shook her head in protest without opening her tightly closed

313

lips. No, no! the heiress of Burgundy did not withdraw her pledged word. She did not want to be released from her oath. She said that she would hold out, and hold out she would.

The Bishop looked at her quizzically. "I fear, my child," he said slowly, "that you are prompted more by pride than by your love of Our Lord and an honest desire to honor the Holy Sepulcher. It is out of pride, not out of piety, that you refuse to accept the release which I am offering you. Beware, for this is a grave sin."

Florine burst into tears and wept with bitter grief. After the Bishop left, Swennon found her still weeping, and his heart melted at the sight. He could not bear to see her cry. He longed to take her in his arms, soothe, and comfort her grief. Only a moment before he had been praying ardently, offering God his troubles and begging Him for the strength to endure, and he returned now strengthened and at peace—ready to resume his burden. He bent over Florine, that beloved girl-wife of his. Truly, he wanted nothing of her, just to put his arms about her like a brother, just to say a few kind words and hear the same in return. He asked no more.

But Florine pushed him rudely away and called for her duenna, the foolish old Bonina. Now Swennon forgot all his good resolutions, and once more a long bitter quarrel broke out between them, full of gall, resentment, and undeserved reproaches.

"You shall yet live to regret your stubbornness," shouted Swennon. "Would to God that you don't lose your soul and mine! You have no heart! In the desert you gave me water though I did not ask, but now that I am begging and craving for love you have no pity at all."

"And yet even now I would gladly give my life for you," she replied in a whisper.

"I don't want your life. I want you! You are mine. The Bishop said that he will set us free."

"But I will not set myself free."

"Oh! Lord! What am I to do?" groaned Swennon. "Do you want me to go to the Syrian women like all the others?"

"Go!" Florine said. "If a wench can take my place—go! But mind— thereafter I will neither know nor see you."

"It will be your fault, not mine."

"My fault? My fault that you cannot keep your vow?"

"God, oh God!" cried Swennon in despair. He shut himself up in his tent, refused to eat, and would see no one, not even his own knights. He lay tossing on the couch, worried, furious, feverish. How could he explain to this wicked, stubborn, childish, beloved Florine of his what went on within him? How could he tell her that he could stand it in the desert, in the mountains, on the march, but not here. Not in Antioch. In this accursed valley the very air was heavy with lust. With the exception of the Bishop, Godfrey, and a few of the old and sick, none could resist the lure. Pagan magic, people said, and they were right. It was magic.

"I want to speak to you," said Zbylut to his brother in a voice that boded no good. "Why do you close your tent and post that fool, Sobek, by it? What have you there?"

"That's no concern of yours," Imbram answered bluntly. In the last few days he had grown hard, bold, altogether different.

"I am your senior. I have a right to ask."

"Aye, I was to obey you and you were to love me. And I would have obeyed you, too, if you had—"

"Loved you?" snorted Zbylut. "You will never live to see the day! What am I to love you for? For the wrong you did me?"

Imbram, sincerely astonished, opened wide his blue eyes.

"I wronged you? When?"

"Much you know, you half wit," snarled Zbylut. "Answer my question. Why do you keep your tent closed?"

"That's my business, not yours. The tent is mine."

"You think I don't know? You fool! You took in a wench. A wench!"

"Since you know why do you ask?"

"You took a wench. You—! How did you dare?"

Imbram folded his arms and looked at his brother with assumed calm.

"What do you care? Do I forbid you to take one, too?"

"Shut up!" fumed Zbylut. "You know well what I mean. You have a wife at home. How dare you go wenching here? For shame!"

"Leave my wife out of this," answered Imbram coldly in a strange, unfamiliar voice. He was not going to justify himself before anyone, least of all before Zbylut. He would never admit and to tell the truth he could not have explained even if he wanted—that the wench he kept in his tent had in some strange way merged in his mind with Ofka. If he fell in love with her it was only because he loved Ofka. He had not even looked at the beautiful Syrian temptress but had followed this one because she wore a dress that was Ofka's.

He would admit none of this. Mastering his feeling he said in a blandly detached voice: "So I have a concubine. She came to me herself while I was out in the fields. I had a mind to take her, so I did. Now what do you want?"

"Chase her out at once. This very minute!"

"I will not!"

"I order you to. I—your senior!"

"Your orders be damned! I'll do as I please."

Livid with rage, Zbylut leaped forward like a wildcat, but before he could clutch Imbram's throat the latter caught him by the middle and lifted him off his feet. Imbram was the stronger of the two but Zbylut was more agile. They dragged each other back and forth like two wild oxen, eyes bloodshot with hate. Mutual enmity, pent up too long, flared up suddenly like a consuming flame. They longed to kill, to crush each other's bones in mortal embrace. Sobek, terrified, ran for Zavora the Mumbler, who was the oldest of their group.

"Hey, there," called the Mumbler, seizing Zbylut's jerkin in an iron grasp. "Have you g-g-gone mad? Swallowed m-m-madwort or what? Aren't you ash-sh-ashamed?"

Reluctantly they let go of each other, but the eyes still held fast, filled with hate.

"What are you f-f-fighting about?" asked Zavora sternly.

"Zbylut is wroth that I took a wench to my tent," Imbram burst out. "What business is it of his? I don't look into what he does."

"I keep no wench even though I have no wife," replied Zbylut in a surly voice, wiping the sweat from his forehead with a palm still trembling with rage. "Why must this rogue bring lechery into our camp?"

"Osventa, too, h-h-has been keeping one f-for about t-t-t-two weeks," said the Mumbler placatingly.

"I will not have it!"

"I am not asking your leave."

"You knave!" shouted Zbylut in a few fit of fury. They leaped at each other again but the Mumbler stepped between them, now really wroth.

"S-s-stop it or I'll thrash you," he bellowed. "Are you not ash-sh-ashamed of the s-s-servants? Knights forsooth! Ough!"

They drew apart growling and bristling like dogs.

"T-t-t-tell m-me straight what this is all about," Zavora demanded.

"I told you; it's because I took a wench to my tent."

"D-d-did Z-zbylut want her too?"

"No," roared Zbylut. "No, I don't want any schismatic whore, though I am free and he has a wife. It's his wife I am concerned about."

"B-b-but why? Imbram's woman is no kin of yours?" marveled the Mumbler, completely at a loss as to what it was all about.

Zbylut looked at them both as though he had been stunned. He hissed passionately: "Much you know! May the ground swallow both of you." He kicked the servant, overturned a pail of water, and dashed out of the tent.

"G-g-gone clear out of his h-h-head," decided Zavora. "M-must have wanted that S-s-syrian woman hims-s-self. It is a S-syrian woman, isn't it?"

"Yes."

"A g-g-good thing that she is n-not a p-p-pagan. S-some have t-t-taken p-pagans. Those who s-s-scattered through the m-mountains. That's b-b-bad. They cast spells."

Imbram said nothing. He breathed heavily like a man rescued from drowning. The rage which was foreign to his nature had exhausted him. He never knew he could fly into such passion. Honestly, he could have choked Zbylut. What was that nonsense that he, Imbram, had wronged his brother? It was Zbylut who always wronged and abused him.

It was already dark outside when he entered his tent. Sobek, released at last from a wearisome watch, ran happily to the horses, while at the sound of her master's steps, Leah rose from the ground, bowing low. She was a slave, accustomed to work and abuse, so she did not mind the confinement which gave her a chance to rest. She had plenty to eat and no one beat her. All this filled her heart with gratitude for the unknown knight whom her mistress had called for herself but who, instead, chose her, a poor slave. This feminine triumph was the great, the most important event of her life. No wonder that she was quite sincere when she clasped him passionately.

But Imbram's thoughts were more involved. He knew by now that Leah was not Ofka but a Syrian slave who had only worn a dress like Ofka's. Perhaps there was magic in that dress and then perhaps there was not. How could he tell? All Imbram knew was that he no longer could live without Leah. He was ashamed to go to her in the daytime but as the evening approached he awaited with ever-growing impatience the coming of the night. And once night came there was no more room for a thought of Ofka.

One night, when exhausted by passion as he had never been by battle Imbram lay steeped in deep slumber, he was awakened by a slight clicking sound. He half-opened a sleepy eye then closed it again before the glare of a burning rush-light. A gigantic shadow of Leah wavered on the walls. What was she doing? Why had she lit the rush? Pretending to be still asleep Imbram watched her from under his half-closed eye lids. Presently she turned around and he almost shouted with horror.

In one hand she held scissors; in the other a strand of straight, flaxen hair. His own hair! Now, she held him in her power, she could cast upon him any spell she pleased. She could bring death upon him, or infirmity, or sickness, deprive him of virility, take away his memory. She had just cut it off; it was the click of the scissors that had awakened him.

Terrified by the discovery he lay motionless while thoughts raced through his head. A witch . . . Where was his sword . . . ? He must kill her, kill her at once before the spell began to work . . . But how could he? How could he hack up the flesh which afforded his own body such infinite delight? "I still have time, the sword is right here," he re-assured himself and continued to peer. Still holding his hair Leah raised the scissors and cut a lock of her own hair from above her left temple. Then she mingled the two locks carefully together weaving them hair by hair, black into fair. Imbram sighed with relief. She was mingling the hair so it must be a love charm. She wished him no harm, only tried to bind him to herself.

But even so he must not let her complete her spell, for if the magic worked he, Imbram, would forget Ofka, and only Leah would remain. He must kill the sorceress. Kill her now: . . . There still was time.

And yet he hesitated.

Ah! If he only had some hope of returning? But was it possible to retrace that endless chain of events, marches, perils, lands, deserts and mountains? No, he would never go back to the old Silesian manor, never see Ofka or his little son. So why kill Leah? Why extinguish that tiny glimmer of happiness he had known in all these years of exile?

Let the charm work. He would not interfere.

With the feeling that he was burying Ofka and himself he watched the slave girl go about her magic. She twisted the hair into an artful ring and whispering some incantation burned it over the rush-light, all the while holding her hand cupped under it to catch the ashes. Three times she sprinkled the fine dust over the bed never ceasing her mysterious whisperings. The acrid smell of burned hair filled the tent. Leah's shadow stood on the wall behind her, huge as though impressed with the importance of the rite. Finally she put out the light and with infinite caution crept back into bed. Suddenly, violently, Imbram seized her slender hot body and pressed it to himself. Leah grew rigid with fright. Had he seen her? She was quickly reassured. He had seen nothing. He wanted nothing save her.

34.

Ostoy

IMBRAM HAD LOST HIS GOOD NATURE. IN LEAH HE HAD EXPECTED TO FORGET Ofka; but the memory of Ofka remained strong and harassed him day and night. Yet he could not remain away from Leah. Zbylut and he did not speak.

Yashek Zavora looked on his friend's troubles with sympathy, but he was unable to do anything. Imbram avoided him as he did everyone else. To Yashek it did not matter that Imbram had a mistress. Everyone had a wench, some two or three. It was not a thing to question; eventually the women would return to the fields or the servant quarters; meanwhile what was there to bother about?

One night Yashek intercepted Imbram and insisted that they take a walk together. "Let's see what the pagans are doing on the walls," he said.

"Why?" said Imbram. "It is night. We cannot see."

"There is a moon," said Yashek.

They walked beyond the camp and looked toward Antioch. The walls seemed untouched, peaceful, and secure.

"Not a dent," said Imbram bitterly.

"Imko," said Yashek, "what has happened to you? You and I were good friends. We had no secrets. Now you will not talk to me."

"I am talking to you now," said Imbram.

"It is that wench," said Yashek. "She has bewitched you. But do not let that stand between us. What does a woman matter?"

"She has bewitched me?" said Imbram. "Perhaps she has. Perhaps she has changed me."

Suddenly he wanted to tell Yashek everything. "Listen," he said, then.

He stopped and stared ahead of him, where a turbanless Moslem had risen from a ditch. Yashek looked also and drew his sword.

320

"In the name of Christ, tell me who you are," the man said suddenly. He spoke in Polish.

Imbram and Yashek gasped. They were seeing a ghost. They made the sign of the cross and backed away.

"I am not a ghost," the man said. "But a mortal man even as you are, and a good Christian knight. Wait and hear me."

"Who—who are you?" Imbram managed to say.

"I am Ostoy, son of Gnyev," said the man, "of the good kin of Yast-shembiets."

"Christ's passion!" said Yashek. "What are you doing here?"

"I escaped from the city. I have been a captive there for more than two years. I would have escaped sooner had I known there were good Polish knights with the Franks."

"Ostoy, son of Gnyev," Imbram repeated. Of course! They had heard at the Breslau Council that Shechek had sold into slavery the heir to the house of Gnyev. No one believed that it was really true, that Shechek would dare to do such a thing. But here he was, the victim himself.

"I escaped last night," Ostoy said, "but I was afraid to make myself known in these pagan clothes and without a cross—they took mine away. I cannot speak Latin and so I was afraid if I gave myself up I would be killed before I could make my identity known. So I lay here in this ditch. And then, as if by a miracle, I heard Polish spoken—my native tongue."

"You must come at once to the camp," said Yashek. "The barons will want to speak with you, and you will want to speak with the other Polish knights. You will become one of us."

They walked hurriedly, Ostoy explaining that he could have escaped at any time, since he was not carefully watched. At the camp the other Polish knights were dumb with consternation, then eager with hospitality. They fed Ostoy, dressed him in knightly clothing, and poured a stream of questions at him. He answered volubly, ate with appetite, and begged for news of the homeland. They gave him what they had— old to them but new, most of it, to him. When he was well fed and properly dressed, Imbram and Yashek took him to the barons. Adhemar, Raymond, and Robert of Normandy questioned him. Imbram acted as interpreter.

"Have they much food?" the Bishop asked.

"Plenty," said Ostoy. "They have set aside large stores of dried and smoked meat. It is enough for six months. The army is fed on rations. The populace feeds itself. Those who had not much put by will soon be hungry."

"Then they can hold out for six months?"

"Yes, but they expect reinforcements from the Emir of Mosul, called Kerbogha. He will bring a hundred thousand men. Others are coming from Aleppo, and Arabs from the clan of Kilab. Kılıj Arslan is also on his way, the same man you defeated at Nicaea and Dorylaeum. When all these are arrived the garrison expects that you will be wiped out."

"How does the garrison know these troops are coming?" asked Raymond.

"By carrier pigeons," said Ostoy.

The knights stared at him. "By what?" Raymond asked.

"By carrier pigeons," Ostoy repeated. "They tie messages to the legs of the pigeons and turn the birds loose. They fly home. In Kerbogha's camp are many pigeons whose home is Antioch. In Antioch are many pigeons belonging to Kerbogha. It is a simple thing. I have tended these birds myself. They will fly home if released, that is all—a message tied to their legs goes with them."

"He speaks the truth," said Adhemar. "I recall that we saw a pigeon flying from Nicaea. Later Butumitos marveled that our archers had not shot it down."

"There is much to be learned from these devils," said Raymond. "But tell me, knight, how did you, a prisoner, learn all this?"

"Most of it I got from Firus, a Greek renegade who renounced his faith on the promise of the pagans that he would be made a sheik. They did not do it and he is very bitter. At night I stood with him while he guarded the tower. He told me I could escape whenever I pleased."

Suddenly Boemund, who had joined the group, pushed forward. "What tower does this Firus guard?" he asked.

"It is on the south side, near the gate of St. George. It is called the tower of the Three Sisters. Firus guards it, as I said, and he and Yagi-Sian hate each other."

Boemund's eyes flickered. "He and Yagi-Sian hate each other?"

"Yagi-Sian is a Turk, fierce and bloodthirsty. He despises Firus for being a Greek and calls him an infidel dog. Firus would give his soul for revenge, but what can he do? Firus is small and a coward besides. Yagi-Sian is a giant."

Boemund nodded, his eyes almost closed.

The arrival of Ostoy stirred the camp into action and talk. The siege was again discussed with hope, though what Ostoy had contributed to this hope was not known. Next day the escaped prisoner rode around the walls with the Polish knights and some of the barons, pointing out sections of the city and particularly the tower of the Three Sisters. They paused when they reached it and stared up at its curved walls, closed except for a slit near the top, a slit through which a man could barely squeeze.

"So this is it," said Boemund. He noticed that the terrain rose here, bringing the top of the tower a little closer to those on the ground.

"I would risk my soul to see it destroyed," said Ostoy.

"Then listen to me," said Boemund quickly. He whispered in Ostoy's ear. The prisoner frowned and muttered.

"Betrayal is a foul business," he said.

"Vengeance is worth it," said Boemund.

35.

The Legend Is Born

THE GILDED IMPERIAL GALLEYS MOVED IN AN EVEN LINE; OARSMEN chained to benches struck the water rhythmically with the blades of their long oars. The noble Tatikios, proconsul of the Western Provinces of the Holy Empire, was on his way from Byzantium to Alexandretta, the port that was closest to Antioch, to see with his own eyes whether it was true that the Latins stood before the city walls. From these iron louts one could expect almost anything and once they got this far, perhaps they might even capture the long-deplored pearl of the empire, the key to the Orient, Antioch. In any event it was best to be at hand to take full advantage of a possible victory.

As soon as the galleys moored at Alexandretta, Tatikios informed the Bishop that he had brought a missive from the Holy Father. Boemund, acting as emissary for the entire knighthood, came promptly to fetch it and was received by Tatikios with royal splendor on board his vessel.

The two chieftains greeted each other with great civility, protesting their joy at this unexpected encounter.

"I trust," said the Duke of Tarentum, "that Basileus Alexius is in good health."

"Aye, the Most Enlightened, Most Pious Basileus, may God protect his days, is well and will soon be here."

"These, indeed, are happy tidings. And how is the noble Butumitos, our old companion?"

"The noble Butumitos governs Nicaea. He, too, is well."

"It so happened that we left Nicaea without being able to bid him a fitting farewell."

"He regretted this deeply," Tatikios assured him, blandly.

Now that the first amenities had been exchanged, the talk could en-

THE LEGEND IS BORN

ter into more practical channels, but neither of the two wanted to be first to reveal his mind.

A pause issued of which Messer Luigi Chiaco, a Genoese merchant also present on board, promptly availed himself. He was immensely rich, the possessor of many galleys, warehouses in fifteen ports, his own troops and look-out posts, his own counters for the exchange of money. The volume of his transactions exceeded that of many a great kingdom and he was always the first to arrive on the heels of every conqueror. He had come with Tatikios now and would like to know from whom, in the spring, he might buy Antiochan silks.

He came to the point immediately. Commerce, straight trade, had no need of circumlocutions.

"Does Your Honor count on the possibility of capturing Antioch?"

Boemund considered him haughtily. "Possibility? We have a certainty," he let fall, with disdain.

"Certainty." Both Tatikios and Messer Luigi started at the words. "A certainty? When, how soon?"

"I could not tell you that. It does not depend on us."

"On what then is this certainty founded?"

"On the righteousness of the Holy Cause which God shall second even as He has done in the past."

Their faces fell. Chiaco snapped his fingers with annoyance. "For a merchant such certainty is not worth a farthing."

"What a pity!" said Boemund coldly. "For me it is quite enough."

"And yet until now nothing has been done," exclaimed Tatikios. "So far as we know the fortress has only lately been closed from outside. For over two months the Agars came and went as they pleased, bringing reinforcements and supplies."

Boemund made no reply, but sat there enigmatic and indifferent. He praised the wine. Water splashed against the sides of the galley.

"We would like to help you," resumed Tatikios. "That was why we came."

"Thanks for your good intentions, but we need no help."

"You need no help," repeated Tatikios, astounded.

"No. None whatsoever."

"Pantopulos is here with us! He has brought skillful workers with him. He will help build the towers."

"Many thanks, but our carpenters can do it themselves."

"But they have not built one so far. They have no idea how to go about it."

"It is remarkable how well informed Your Honor is about our affairs. But rest easy. Things are not so bad. Our carpenters blundered at first, then lost several weeks building the *Malhommerie*. Now that they have set to work in earnest, however, the building will progress without a hitch."

"So you don't want any help," repeated Tatikios in wonder. He had not expected this. He had come convinced that as soon as he arrived, the Latins would beseech him for builders and supplies. "How do you stand on supplies?" he asked aloud.

"Not too well," admitted Boemund easily. "Providence is not among the virtues of which our knights can boast."

"But in that case are you not afraid of starvation?"

"Before it comes to starvation we will be inside Antioch."

"May God grant it! Far be it from me to dampen your ardor, but it seems that help for the besieged is on the way!"

"We know about that. The Emir Kerbogha is coming from Mosul and Atabek Tohteguin from Aleppo. Before they arrive the city will be in our hands."

The Greek dignitary fell from one astonishment into another. The Latins knew everything and asked no aid! He wondered what had come over them.

"I trust that the noble knights have not forgotten their oath?" he asked suddenly with harsh imperiousness.

"We forget nothing. Nicaea, either."

Tatikios grew slightly confused.

"The noble Butumitos blundered. He misunderstood the orders of the Most Enlightened, the Most Pious Basileus, may God bless his days."

"Has he met with fit punishment?"

"So far, no. The senate has yet to consider the case. It was all an error. Besides, this has no bearing on the oath."

"I wonder. And anyhow, I will tell you in all candor that how well we recall the oath depends largely upon me."

"Oh, so?"

Tatikios screwed up his eyes. Then it was all a matter of price. The Duke of Tarentum wanted something, but what? Despite all efforts and shrewd questioning he refused to be drawn out and was preparing to leave. With much reverence he put away the papal missive and bidding farewell to his host inquired again about the health of the Autocrator, the Empress Irene, who was so like a rose, of that winsome young successor to the throne, John Porphyrogenitus, and of the Imperial Princess Anna.

"She had a magnificent betrothal," remarked Messer Luigi Chiaco who had grown tired of saying nothing.

Tatikios glared at him. Boemund turned quickly around.

"Ah," he said. "So she was betrothed? When I saw her last winter she seemed still very young, ripe in mind but not in years."

"And for that very reason what was celebrated was not a betrothal but an understanding—of no consequence," explained Tatikios, visibly confused.

"Would Your Honor mind speaking more plainly? Was there a betrothal or not?"

"Well, there was but it was not final."

"With whom?"

"With the noble Nicefor Brennios."

"I recall seeing him at the court. He seemed somewhat advanced in years. But if Princess Anna deigned choose him, he must have great merits indeed," said Boemund, seemingly unperturbed, and bidding his host farewell departed for the shore.

Aboard the galley Tatikios was bitterly chiding the Genoese merchant for his loquacity. "Who asked you, Messer Luigi? Who asked you anything? This piece of advice given at such an inopportune moment may cost us dearly."

"I had no idea. How could I suspect?" Chiaco tried to justify himself.

"A merchant should stick to measures and weights and keep out of conversation. Upon my word, Messer Luigi, you deserve to be cast into the sea. I should like to see you in Guynemere's hands . . ."

"I am in despair, Your Honor. However, I'd venture to say that the Duke seemed to attach little weight to the news."

"So much the worse, Messer Luigi, so much the worse. I know the man well."

Tatikios was right. Boemund was fuming with rage as his men, who awaited him on the beach, soon found out to their grief. On the way back to camp he sped like mad, yanking his horse's head and spurring it so savagely that blood trickled to the ground. They had betrothed

Anna! They betrothed her and wanted to keep it from him. Were it not for that merchant fellow he would not have known it even now. The blackguards! They purposely bespoke her so young and to the first man that happened along so that they might send him, Boemund, away empty-handed the moment they no longer needed him. But the Basileus, may the devil take his soul, had overreached himself this time. He could have had a powerful ally, now he would have a powerful foe. An implacable foe! He was no more likely to see Antioch now than to glimpse his own ear. Antioch would be captured but not for him . . . And he would tremble before its new master more than he ever had before the pagans! He would try to ingratiate himself, then, but it would be too late. Ah! He would be sorry for it yet.

When he appeared before Adhemar, Boemund cried angrily, "These Greeks are scoundrels, traitors, and crooks! They merely wait to see what shall befall us. But help they will give none!"

"Not even a master-builder?" asked the Bishop, disappointed.

"Neither master-builder, nor carpenters, nor food, nor anything . . . The vipers! I argued and haggled till I well nigh drew my sword. Only a fool would go there again to implore the good grace of the almighty Basileus."

"We would not think of it," answered the Bishop with heat. "To tell the truth, though, I cannot understand such politics. Surely, it would be to their advantage to aid us in every way. If we capture the city, it will be theirs."

"They do not believe that we can take it, and it almost seems that they are in connivance with the pagans."

"Anything is possible with the Greeks," sighed the Bishop. "Well, we will have to do our best unaided, save by Our Lord. And what of the letter from the Holy Father they said they had brought?" And when it was given to him, he reverently kissed the seal of the Fisherman that hung, large, heavy, and intact on its silk cord. Then he bade good-bye to Boemund, telling him to come to the evening council, and carefully unfolded the sheets. There were two letters: one in beautiful, illuminated script, containing apostolic blessings for "our beloved son—*dilecto filio*," and all the good, God-beloved knights, to be read in public. The other longer, written in a fine, modest hand, was addressed to Adhemar alone.

"My brother and friend," it began.

"The tidings of your doings which reach us here fill our hearts with

joy that no word can express. I would I might describe to you all that is
happening in these parts, but I know not that I can. A quill is a refrac-
tory instument. The changes here are many and range wide, and blessed
changes they are! You who press forward with your eye fixed on the
Holy Goal can know nothing of them, but believe me, my brother, you
would not recognize Europe today. Your Holy Sacrifice has already left
its mark, is already bearing fruits that will not perish. They are visible
in every walk of life. Peace and order reign everywhere. With so many
barons away, fights and continuous wars have ceased altogether. All the
fields are tilled and, like ants tracking from an ant-hill, merchants and
savants have followed in your path. You have blazed the trail and
shown the way. Where once only the Genoese dared go, and that by sea,
now large bands of merchants travel by land to Byzantium and even
beyond. They bring many wondrous things hitherto unknown. Glass,
fine steel, sweet preserved fruit, paper better than parchment, silk cloth
thin as mist which they call in Arabian 'gauze' and about which our
women-folk rave. They bring Greek books which our learned monks
translate, marvelling at the wisdom contained therein. There are strange
things in them that fill one with wonder, such as that the earth is round.
Assuming its round shape, they explain all the phenomena of day and
night, of winter and summer, in a manner which is admittedly simple and
convincing. Our savants who, as you know, still hold that the sun shines
upon Purgatory at night and that the earth rests on water, and water
rests on a slab of rock which in turn is supported by the Four Evange-
lists, laugh at this, but I feel that there is a great deal of truth in this new
knowledge. Nor is there anything in it contrary to the Faith, and therefore inacceptable to a Christian. Even greater news has come to us in
the field of philosophy. You recall, my son, that Aristotle, son of Nico-
machos? Verily, you and I have been brought up on him. Fancy that
the *Organon* is but a small part of his vast system of philosophy, astounding beyond conception. All his works have been brought here and
are being translated into Latin. I have not read them so far, but I was
told by Brother Sylvester, one of the copyists, about some of the parts.
It gives an entirely new outlook on the world. Already in the monasteries they talk of little else but this ancient wisdom so long unknown.
The physicians likewise are benefitting greatly, thanks to the many herbs
and medical secrets brought from the East. The merchants ride out
freely, for the castles stand empty and no one levies tolls on the highways

and there are also fewer bandits about, since most of them have followed
you, lured by the tales of Greek wealth. Trade flourishes and towns are
thriving and waxing rich; villages and hamlets too have grown more
prosperous and laborers are valued because they are scarce. If a thrall
runs away from his master, the new lord will not send him back; indeed,
he will keep him, being short of field hands himself. So the lords for
their own good take better care of their serfs. Truthfully, such order,
peace and prosperity was not seen in Europe since the days of the
Caesars. But all this is nothing, my son, compared to the spiritual change
that has come over the world. Hearing of your greatness, devotion, and
pious zeal, every Christian strives to show himself worthy of you, and,
great or small, all talk only of those who went to the rescue of Christ.
We know more about you than you suppose. Pilgrims who have followed your trail bring more and more news of your deeds, and no tale is
more avidly listened to than theirs. Beloved brother, do you remember
your fears and doubts and do you realize the glory into which they have
turned now?

"Though far away, I can easily guess how those brave deeds of yours
whose mere reflection was enough to transform an old and rotten world
must have affected your souls. How you walk in the light of Divine
Grace! God bless you, beloved soldiers of Christ! Thanks to your val-
iance, a decayed strife-torn world has found a new life. From the distant
trails that you have blazed, a fresh spirit wafts upon us all. Young ardent
hearts tremble with eagerness to follow in your steps. People pray to you
as though you were saints."

"Hey, hey! There is a fight on! The Normans fight our men!"
shouted a squire, thrusting his flushed face into the tent's opening. Before the Bishop had time to recognize him, he was gone, shouting the
warning as he ran. Adhemar folded the letter with a sigh and hastened
out to the camp square. Shouts of "Toulouse! Toulouse!" rang out from
every direction. Riders dashed by, fastening the clasps of their helmets.
Adhemar jumped on his horse and galloped after them. At the entrance
to the camp he found Raymond standing in the midst of his knights
and livid with rage. Facing him, raving and ranting, stood Omer de
Guillebaut, with De Regnier, Le Grand, De Berneville, several squires,
and a crowd of rabble behind. All faces were swollen with fury and
wine. Adhemar soon discovered that Omer de Guillebaut, in his insane
hatred of womankind, had proposed that all women be held in a

stockade, as in a nunnery, away from the camp. Raymond St. Gilles, who considered this an insult directed against his own wife, Elvira, was calling for revenge, and now, at the height of his fury, with blows about to be struck in spite of anything the Bishop could do, while Raymond was shouting, "I'll kill him! I'll kill him!" he dropped his sword and fell heavily to the ground. Blood had rushed to his head, flooding the brain, bursting the veins in his temples.

Forgetting all else, the knights of Provence rushed to his side and, somewhat sobered, the Normans retreated hastily; no one paying them any more heed. The good knights lifted their liege lord, removing his helmet and breastplate. Someone threw water on the seemingly lifeless head; others ran for a physician. They brought a Syrian Jew who opened the vein, but the black, thick blood would not at first flow, and only after a while did it begin to spurt. By and by the face lost its bluish tinge, and warily, as though he were a child, the warriors carried the unconscious man to his tent and left him there in the care of his wife.

Boemund and Tancred were on their way to the Bishop's tent where the council was to be held. They knew nothing as yet of what had happened in the camp and Boemund was lost in thought.

"Look here, my lad," he said to Tancred. "You are the only one of us who did not swear allegiance to the Basileus."

"True, I did not," admitted the young knight proudly.

"And luckily, too. It will come in handy now. Listen! I have found a way to gain possession of Antioch. It will be mine, and no one else's. I will give it to you, or rather we shall seize it together. Antioch will be yours. Yours and mine, for you are still too young to govern alone."

Tancred stared at him stupefied.

"What do you mean? Why should it be ours? What about the others?"

"The others? They will proceed on their way. I told you already that they will not capture Antioch. Only you and I will."

"That cannot be."

"But I assure you that I have a way."

"It's not that . . . It's the betrayal of our companions I have in mind. We set out together. We do everything together. There is no need to give Antioch to the Basileus, of course. I took no oath. I can, as you say, keep the city, but only to share it with the others."

"And why share it?" Boemund asked. "Everyone should think of himself."

"Not I. I will not do it."

There was a note of finality in the young man's voice and Boemund shrugged his shoulders with vexation. "You are more stupid than I thought. No use talking of it now."

They rode on in silence. "There will be an uproar," thought Boemund. "But they will come around to it once want stares them in the face and that will not be long."

The council was stormy. There was much to discuss: the arrival of the Greeks and their refusal of help, the blessings sent by the Holy Father that was to be read, the outrageous act of Omer de Guillebaut. So all the barons were gathered. Even Raymond St. Gilles, though pale as death and still reeling on his feet, had ordered himself brought in. He wanted to be present so he might demand an apology from Robert for the way Omer had insulted him.

Adhemar sided with him, denouncing in stern words the whole scheme of driving womenfolks out of the camp.

"I abstain as a rule from meddling in your affairs," he said. "But I was horrified to hear of what the Normans have done. Noblemen's wives and serving wenches, the virtuous and the unchaste, all locked together? Shame upon the husband who consented to such outrage. And who, pray, tends to the need of those poor creatures? Who sees that they are provided with food and drink or how they live there? No, it's a wicked shame, and I trust that the Duke of Normandy will revoke it forthwith."

Robert looked perplexed and let Arnuld speak for him. "The idea itself is not bad," said the chaplain. "The good knight Sir Omer de Guillebaut acted wrongly, no doubt, insofar as he went on his own to the Provençal camp. Let us not forget, however, that he was prompted by his love of virtue and his dislike of sin."

Raymond staggered to his feet.

"I will not have that cur, Omer, called a good knight," he said with an effort. "I demand his head."

"We see no reason for that," Arnuld retorted. "Sir Omer has already been admonished."

"I demand his head," Raymond insisted. "He insulted my wife, the royal princess of Castille."

"Surely he could not have! He did not even see the countess."

"Because I did not allow the rascal to set foot in my camp. He wanted to lead her away with the others. My wife! Lady Elvira!" He lifted both his hands to his throat for anger was beginning to choke him once more.

"Easy, my Lords!" Adhemar intervened. "I trust that you can settle the matter between you. The guilty will be punished, no doubt, though perhaps not as severely as the Count St. Gilles demands. For the present, let us turn to more pressing matters. The Duke of Tarentum is just back from Alexandretta where he went to see the Greek captain, Tatikios. Let him tell us of the tidings he brings from there."

"As your Grace says," assented Stephen de Blois. "Nonetheless, may I first ask one question: Are both nieces of the Norman chaplain locked up with the others?"

Arnuld de Rohes squirmed.

"My nieces are poor, God-fearing orphans and are above suspicion."

"No doubt, no doubt. All I ask is, are they locked up?"

"No," admitted Arnuld.

"That is all I wanted to know," said Stephen, smiling.

"Let us postpone the matter until later," insisted the Bishop again. "Will the Duke of Tarentum speak up now?"

Boemund stepped forward briskly. He repeated at length what he had already told the Bishop. The Greeks refused all help. The Basileus in person was on his way to Asia Minor, but only to exact another oath from them.

The news was greeted with indignant puffs. Swords rattled. So the accursed Greek would take their oath again, they said to one another. Now, after the Nicaea betrayal, indeed! But Boemund went on speaking, not of the Greeks, but of the present sad position of the crusaders themselves. He spared no efforts to depict it in the darkest colors; he spoke of the impossibility of building towers, of the threatening hunger (what remained of supplies would barely see them through the next two months), of the approach of Kerbogha with tremendous reinforcements. Truly, never before had the crusading troops found themselves in such desperate straits. "We're in bad shape, my Lords!" he concluded. "We have gone through many a peril but I fear we shall not escape alive this time."

The Bishop gazed at the speaker thoughtfully, wondering what purpose he had in disheartening the men and creating such an atmosphere of gloom? Whatever his purpose was, he was well on his way to its achievement. Though no one was hungry and all had been before in worse straits than these, they sat staring at the ground, forlorn and sombre, almost ready to quit.

"We must not become unduly disheartened," he said aloud. "God has led us thus far and He will lead us farther. We did not perish in the desert; why should we perish now? It's wise, indeed, to anticipate peril, but only to ward it off, not to weaken spirits."

"I am not striving to weaken spirits," Boemund rejoined, "I am merely seeing things as they are. Why deceive ourselves? Let the others say if I am right."

He looked at Stephen de Blois who nodded his head.

"What you say is true, no doubt, but you only point out the dark side of things," the Bishop argued. "And that, I think, is bootless unless you have a remedy to offer."

"And what if I do?" asked Boemund.

They all gaped at him, dumbfounded. Then, "Come man!" they shouted. "What do you mean? For heaven's sake, speak up!"

Boemund rose to his feet.

"If," he announced solemnly, "all the knighthood gathered here and you, your Grace, consent that Antioch and all the lands that go with it shall be exclusively mine, we will be inside the city within a week."

There was a moment of stupefied silence. Then a great storm of protest broke out, everyone shouting at once, startled and indignant. It was nothing short of betrayal, they cried—no good knight would act in this way.

"We took the oath," called Godfrey. "We must hand Antioch over to the Basileus."

"The devil take the Basileus. We owe him nothing. It was he who broke faith first at Nicaea."

"That does not release us from our pledge."

"Never mind the Basileus," yelled Robert Curthose. "But why should Antioch fall to one man? We are all equal here. We will not consent!"

"No! Never!"

"Is it true that you have a way to capture the city?" asked the Bishop, looking at Boemund in awe.

"I have. But only if Antioch will be mine," answered Boemund calmly.

"Do you care nothing for the common cause and the success of the Holy Expedition?"

"And do the others care? If they did, they would consent to my proposal and gladly go their way."

"We will never consent," they shouted in chorus.

Raymond St. Gilles forgot his recent illness and thundered louder than all the others! "I will not have it! We will either stick to our oath or each take his share. We won't allow anything else."

Tancred feverishly pushed his way to his uncle's side. "Kinsman," he implored. "You must be jesting. Don't you see that the welfare of us all and the rescue of the Holy Sepulcher are at stake? You took the oath, too."

"Keep out of this," Boemund shoved him roughly aside. He looked darkly and coldly at the screaming throng. He wanted to speak but his voice was lost in the din. Finally he leaped on the table. "Listen!" he called. "You say I care nothing about the Holy Sepulcher. And what about you? How much do you care? You would like to take the city yourselves, but, remember, I have a way to gain possession of Antioch. You have none. So it stands to reason that it should be mine and not yours."

"Over our dead bodies! No! Never!"

"Perjurer!"

"You will yet come to me begging for it. The food will give out shortly. The camps are already full of rottenness. Even today the daughter of Alphonse the Great was to be dragged out like a common whore. What will things be like two months hence?"

"Shut up!" shouted Raymond. "I can take care of Lady Elvira myself. We will never consent. I do not need Antioch and I do not crave it, but I will not have it captured by some scheme unworthy of a knight. Besides, we all took the oath."

"Tancred did not."

"I will have nothing to do with it. It's either all or none," objected Tancred, an angry flush mounting to his cheeks.

"Either all or none," repeated Raymond. Suddenly he turned white, swayed, and slumped to the ground. As though through a thick fog he still heard the voice of the Duke of Tarentum saying:

"You will come to beg me yet."

The relapse suffered by Count St. Gilles was more serious than his previous fit. Not only did he lose consciousness this time but his left arm

and left leg were touched by palsy. The physician shook his head helplessly and counselled that a Greek leech be brought from Alexandretta.
The Bishop thought it wise, but neither Elvira nor Raymond's faithful
companions gathered by his bedside would hear of it.

It was late evening when, after administering the Holy Sacraments to
the sick man, Adhemar de Monteuil returned to his own quarters harassed and weary, oppressed by dark thoughts. If Raymond were to die,
the loss to the crusade would be irreparable. Though hasty and uncontrollable, the Count St. Gilles was a true and just man and a leader of
rare ability, and his death would leave a gap that no other knight could
fill.

Then there was Boemund's shameless demand, the madcap incident
provoked by the Normans, and to top it all, the endless headaches in
connection with the general state of affairs. The Bishop admitted in his
heart that Boemund had not exaggerated when he depicted their position. They were in a dire predicament, indeed. "God have mercy
upon us!"

He sighed deeply, and opening the wooden chest, took out Urban's
unfinished letter. Where was he when he was interrupted? —Here—

"People pray to you as though you were saints. All would imitate you.
All want to love Christ even as you do. Morals have improved, faith
burns high. Time and again we hear of the miracles that happen among
you.

"Oh! How I envy you, beloved brother."

Adhemar de Monteuil stopped reading, his hand dropped limply to
his lap. "Oh! Brother Urban," he thought, "if you knew! If you only
knew!"

What if I wrote in all sincerity and told you that nothing of what you
think of us is true, that nothing even remotely resembles the truth, that
the army of crusaders is a nest of rascality, corruption, hate, greed, madness, and terror, that the holy crusade is one living hell?

But, he thought, no evil tree can bear good fruit, nor a good one—evil.
The changes in Europe of which Urban wrote were the fruit of the
crusade. The fruit was undoubtedly good; therefore the crusade itself
could not be evil. As he sat there, oppressed though he was by a thousand troubles, he felt suddenly a glimmer of hope.

"I shall not write at all," he decided.

36.

The Tower of Three Sisters

SHUDDERING WITH REPUGNANCE, OSTOY DONNED HIS OLD SLAVE'S GARB. The servants had been told to burn the rags some seven months ago, but at the last minute they had felt loath to do so, for, after all, they were clothes. So they had put the outfit away. And it was a good thing, too, for the rags had proved useful on several occasions. Now for the last time the knight was donning them again.

It was a dark, moonless night and the wall under which he and Boemund stood could not be distinguished from the dark sky above. Only a small gleaming window, high in the tower, shone like a star. They had come here not like good knights, who battle openly in the daylight, but like thieves, hiding in the dark. But neither cared; one was prompted by vengefulness, the other by greed.

Ostoy, cupping his hands to his mouth, gave a short, throaty call in Arabic. Then they waited in silence.

As they stood thus, gazing up, Ostoy felt the old wave of hate sweeping over him. In the course of daily life he hardly remembered those two years of captivity; the thought that he had ever ceased to be a free knight seemed like an evil dream. But the moment he pulled on the rags of slavery, the memory returned. His back ached, the whip hissed. Firus' daughter had brought him food in a bowl as though he were a dog, and once an agha in passing spat into his food and he, being hungry, ate it withal. Ignoble memories that he could neither drive, nor tear, nor wipe away, clung to him like lice cling to want. Not even a tenfold blood retribution would rid him of the nightmare. Everything that had been witness to his shame must be destroyed, the walls as well as the people, those who spat and those who pitied. Only then would he be able to tell himself that it had never occurred.

The tower remained silent, the narrow rectangle of the window empty. Ostoy called again a little louder.

This time he was heard. A head obstructed the light.

"Who calls?" a voice asked in Arabic.

"It's I, Amin, escaped from the _giours_. In the name of Allah, let down a line!"

"Are you alone?"

"Aye! But they are on my trail. I can hear them coming. A line in the name of the Prophet!"

There was a moment of silence and then a line fell from the tower, strong, heavy, coiling like a snake. Then a bow appeared in the window. Someone was watching closely to see that the climber was really alone.

Ostoy seized the rope and climbed hastily. He soon reached the small window and disappeared.

The Duke of Tarentum sighed in relief and lay down on the ground to await his return.

Ostoy was gone a long time, and while he waited, Boemund stretched and yawned in the grass. He yawned not because he was sleepy, but from general debility caused by hunger. All went hungry in the camps now. All about them a fabulous May rioted and bloomed and they had nothing to eat. Neither grain nor wine nor olives, nor meat. Whatever livestock there had been, even cats and dogs, had been eaten long ago. Fish in the lake were scarce and it was becoming more and more difficult to catch anything. Even the hides which covered the walls of _Malhommerie_ had been stripped off and devoured. The troops were ravaged by hunger, fever, and hungry, dropsy men died in ever-increasing numbers. And there were those who could scarcely wait for men to die to steal the corpses, so they might roast and eat them. In the desert they drank their companion's blood and now they devoured his flesh. Those who could not bring themselves to do it ate tree bark and weeds. Since they knew not which were edible and which were not, cases of poisoning were frequent.

The horses fared better, for there was plenty of grass. If only men could eat grass like horses! They could have, it is true, eaten their faithful mounts, but no knight would ever do such a thing. Verily, they would sooner have killed and eaten their servants than touched their precious chargers.

Famine drove all else out of their minds. Gone were the days when under these same walls they had gone mad with lust and could talk and think of nothing but women. The Syrian women had long since left for Alexandretta, thence to the south to lands as yet untouched by war. Saracen captives had died or been chased from the camp so that they need not be fed. Paramours, like Imbram's Leah or Osventa's concubine, had run away as soon as hunger appeared. Those who still remained loitered about, haggard and slovenly, seeking edible plants and ready to sell themselves for a bit of food to takers who grew increasingly rare.

The position of the crusaders was desperate indeed. They had arrived on the first of October and it was now the last day of May. In all that time the real siege of the stronghold had not progressed at all. It was senseless to begin with less than ten towers and so far only four had been somehow put together. The workmen, weak with hunger, were scarcely able to work, and the only consolation of the knights lay in the hope that the supplies in the fortress were likewise running low and there was no further news of the approach of Emir Kerbogha.

The position of the crusaders could hardly be worse, Boemund, lying in the grass, told himself, not without satisfaction. Indeed, had things not been so bad he would not have accomplished his end. Their Lord-ships the barons had to be immersed in trouble up to their ears before they agreed to his demands.

Why was Ostoy gone so long? he wondered. Boemund stretched, peered anxiously at the sky to see if it was not growing lighter, and then once more returned to his recollections of last winter's events.

So the foreign women had fled or had been chased away, and only Gouffier de la Tour kept his sweetheart, who proved more faithful than any of the others. All through the autumn and the first half of winter he had fed her raw meat. Then in mid-February he brought her to the camp. Since he had told his friends beforehand that they would at last meet his paramour, they awaited her arrival with a curiosity that turned to fright when De La Tour appeared leading a handsome full-grown lioness. Undaunted by the presence of a gaping crowd she walked with silent, elastic, menacing steps, now and then flashing at the onlookers a yellow eye which sent a tingle down their spines. She rubbed her side against the thigh of the knight with the familiarity and confidence of a cat, and De La Tour pressed his face against her tawny muzzle with its thorny tongue and twin rows of formidable white teeth, and assured everybody that Sarah was the gentlest creature in the world, who, unless provoked, would never harm anyone. Only then he told his amazed companions how, soon after their arrival at Antioch, he had, while hunting, come in a clearing upon a lioness—this very one—engaged in mortal combat with a huge snake. The snake had coiled itself around her body and was seeking to pin her to a tree. The beast, already half strangled, groaned.

"The reptile was so vile," said De La Tour, "that I could not stand the sight, but leaped forward and slashed with my sword where the head joined the body. The loathsome thing fell away like a dead stick, but the lioness, too, was well-nigh done for. I brought her some water in my helmet and she drank. The next day I came to see how she fared. She had not moved. Her legs were broken. So I began to feed her and water her. It was more than four months before she recovered and by that time we grew so fond of each other that she would not leave me."

That was in February. About that time Ostoy, standing at the foot of the walls, overheard a conversation about a rescue party that was on its way and expected at any time. It was not Kerbogha, against whom several tribes had rebelled, but Emir Rodoan of Aleppo and the Emir Sokman ibn Ortok, both bringing considerable forces along. Thanks to this information the Latins were able to lay in wait for them in a spot where the Orontes flowed only about a thousand paces from the lake. It was Ostoy, too, who pointed out and counselled to use this particular spot. Wedged between the two bodies of water, the Saracens could neither deploy their ranks nor follow their favorite encircling tactics. The battle that issued raged long, furious, and unrelenting. Not once since the Martinmas skirmish had the knights a chance to cross arms with the pagans, though they saw them day after day safe and jeering on the walls. Here at last was a chance to give vent to their pent-up hate. The victory was complete. Rodoan fell, Ibn Ortok fled with whatever remained of his men. The Latins returned to the camp bringing with them more than a hundred carts filed with cut-off heads which were promptly catapulted into the city. Let the pagans rejoice at their reinforcements.

They also brought food, but not nearly as much of it as they had brought heads, since Ortok had somehow managed to dump the largest part of his trains into the lake. After a few days, hunger returned once

more. Overhead passed flights of storks and swallows returning to the
north, a sight that stirred the heart, awakening grief and longing. Trees
burst into flower, spring bloomed all around, sweet and enchanting, but
what was the good of spring when there was nothing to eat? In vain did
the knights roam farther and farther afield in search of food. The country had been completely ravaged. Crowds stood around the Bishop's field
avidly watching the rippling wheat, first green, then bleaching, ripening.
But one field amounted to nothing. Imbram's unsown field was now
overgrown with weeds, and Adhemar's wheat had been stolen before
it was ripe, the soft, swollen grain, carelessly ground, giving colic to the
impatient thieves.

Toward the end of May two men, unable to stand the constant press
of hunger, deserted the camp and set out for Alexandretta. One of them
was Peter the Hermit, now completely out of his mind. The incessant search for food set up in his dim mind memories of the march
through Hungary and the crossing of the Sava; what remained of his
courage was stripped away. With him went Hugh's friend, Sir William
de Melun. "The Carpenter," a brave knight in battle, in the face of
privation became an irresponsible brute.

No one cared about Peter. But that De Melun, a belted knight should
desert the ranks . . . ?

Tancred, riding out with some of his men, overtook the two and
brought them back. With disgust he dragged them into the Bishop's
tent. Peter wept brokenly. De Melun lay on the floor, staring at the
gathered barons with hate.

"How could you do it?" Hugh moaned. "How could you run away?"

"Give me food," growled the giant. "Since you have brought me back,
give me food. That is all I want."

The knights looked at him in horror. Yet who could tell if De Melun's
ignoble deed would not find imitators? Perhaps it would be wiser to
take Beomund's offer.

When the deserters had been taken away they discussed the matter
and voted. Boemund's plan was accepted. Only Raymond St. Gilles did
not concur. He was ill in his tent and knew nothing of the proceedings.

"Then you swear on your knightly honor that the city shall be mine?"
said Boemund.

"On our knightly honor we will leave you the city."

They were sure he meant to capture it by some foul means, but the sight of De Melun had so dispirited them that they were ready to agree to anything. Anyhow, it would be Boemund's sin.

The next night Boemund sent Ostoy to the tower to meet Firus and bring him for a meeting. Lying on the grass in the dark, fighting the pains of hunger, he felt uneasy. Everything depended on one man, Firus. Suppose he faltered, or was discovered. And why did Tancred shun his uncle, the only man truly aware of the difficulties of the crusade, the only one dealing with those difficulties realistically? In a few years —all depending on Firus—Boemund would be as powerful as the Basileus himself, and Tancred would be his captain and perhaps his heir.

But if Firus did not come? What would Boemund's companions think of him? He would perish, even as they would, in the trap he had himself prepared.

Then, a rustle. Someone was coming. The Polish knight would not betray him, but Firus might. These might be his men come to seize the *Giour* who dared urge him to betray his own side. Tomorrow Boemund's head would be stuck on the ramparts.

Should he strike out in the dark? He held the dagger ready. Two figures loomed in the murk close before him, Ostoya and another man, shorter, wearing a big turban, the renegade Greek, Firus. Ostoy, who had by now picked up enough Latin to converse freely with Boemund, translated their short broken words in a low whisper.

"The command of the stronghold in return for letting you in. Are these the terms?" asked the Greek.

"Yes. But only if it is done at once. Day after tomorrow."

"Good. I am on watch that night. Then I shall have command of the whole fortress. The Citadel, too?"

"Yes."

"What pledge am I to have?"

"Pledge? Is not my princely word enough? It's I who ask what kind of surety you give me?"

"My honor."

"The honor of a renegade? Fine honor. Give me a pledge, otherwise tomorrow we will announce under the walls that you offered to open the gate."

Firus looked at him aghast. "But that's madness."

"Let us not squabble. Why waste time? I demand a pledge, a warrant."

"I must go back," whispered Firus. "They will soon be changing guards; they might miss me. Night after next, as soon as it turns dark I will drop a ladder from the window."

"I will not let you go till I have your pledge."

Firus looked about desperately. "What can I give you? I have nothing with me."

"Send your son. Send Isaac," said Ostoy sternly.

Boemund pounced on the suggestion. "Send your son."

"He is away."

"He is not," Ostoy contradicted him flatly. "He is asleep at home. You can send him here."

"We will wait," added Boemund. "If within an hour your son is not here, before noon tomorrow we shall announce your betrayal. You will perish, and so will all your kin."

"My son—will he be safe?"

"That is up to you."

"Oh, Lord! I must go. But what of me? Me? What assurance have I?" mumbled Firus walking toward the wall.

"My word."

They watched him climb the rope. Ostoy began to pull off his disguise. Boemund stopped him hastily.

"Why? Suppose you have to go up there again?"

"If I go I will go sword in hand like a knight. Nothing will make me take up these rags again. Nothing! I have had enough."

"Once the wine is drawn it must be drunk," muttered Boemund angrily. Nevertheless he let the knight change into his own clothes. They waited.

"How far does Firus live from the tower?"

"No more than a hundred steps."

A hundred steps. He would have to waken his son, throw some perfunctory excuse to the boy's mother, send out the soldiers from the tower, tell the boy to go climb down. All this could not take very long.

Nevertheless, it did take time. They waited; birds twittered in the shrubs. Soon now the darkness would no longer conceal them.

Psst! Psst! Here he comes. Something dark moved down the wall, softly slipped to the ground and waited motionless.

"Will you recognize him, sir knight? Firus might have sent some one else," asked Boemund, hastening toward the still form. Ostoy nodded his head without a word. He knew the whole family. The young lad, wrapped in a dark cloak, trembled with fear and disturbed sleep. The warmth of the bed still clung to him. He was slight and lithe, looking more like a girl than a boy. He had been born in Christianity, but when his father had changed his faith, he had been circumcized and his name changed from Isaac to Abdulla.

Boemund and Ostoy led him hastily away. The lad recognized Ostoy, and taking heart, huddled confidently against his arm. Like all that reminded him of his captivity, Isaac-Abdulla was loathsome to him and Ostoy had to restrain his impulse to cast him away. He looked to much like his sister who out of pity threw him uneaten crumbs from her family's table.

Boemund was addressing the leaders. Save for Count Raymond of Toulouse, they were all assembled once more.

"My Lords, even as I said, tomorrow night Antioch will be ours. Meanwhile, let each of you take half his men. We must set out forthwith in the direction of Aleppo."

"Against whom?"

"You shall see. It's the way it has to be. We will leave, horns blaring, standards flying, so that the city cannot help but notice our departure. Let those who remain drag the siege towers toward the Dog's Gate and St. Paul's Gate. No others. Just the Dog's and St. Paul's. They can shout and burn fires as though they were preparing for an assault."

The troops marched all day vainly asking where and against whom they were going. Before evening Boemund called a short halt to feed the horses. Men did not eat. Now, Boemund said, the horses would remain here with the ostlers, while the knights, the spearmen, and the axemen would proceed on foot through the mountains, and circle the city, bypassing the peaks of Silpius and Cassius. Tomorrow by dusk, they must be close to the Bridge Gate.

"Then why take the roundabout way through the mountains? Why did we leave the camp at all? Weren't we only an arrow shot from the Bridge Gate?"

"That's the way it has to be," said Boemund. "Wait till tomorrow and you will know why."

The upper chamber in the Tower of Three Sisters was dark and small. The tower itself was wide, but since the walls were six feet thick, little space remained inside. The room had only one small window, set so close to the clay floor that one had to lie down in order to peer out.

On the stairs outside the door, three janizaries stood guard and Firus sat alone inside. Ever since last night when he had told Isaac-Abdulla to slip down the rope he had been beside himself with anxiety and fear. If he failed to hand the tower over to the Latins, they would kill his son. He waited impatiently, first for the customary inspection of the guards by the shiek, then for dusk, then for the signal. At last dusk came. The inspection of the guards was over. Now for the signal. Outside the window an owl hooted three times, and he knew the Latins were there at the foot of the tower, waiting.

The little chamber contained a couch, a stool, and a pitcher of water. Wedged between the stones of the walls was a row of pegs from which hung clothes, sheepskins with which Firus covered himself on cold nights, and an old cloak. From behind these rags Firus pulled out a tightly rolled leather ladder. Looking about fearfully, he lay down on the ground and carefully fastened it to the hooks driven into the wall just outside the window. The ladder fell down with a rustle. Firus gave a soft whistle. He dared not whistle louder though he was not sure that they saw the ladder in the dark.

But they did. There were half a score of them. Boemund, Ostoy, Eberard du Puiset, Renard de Toul, and several others. Their eyes had grown used to the dark. They saw the ladder as it slid along the wall, swayed right and left, then came to a standstill.

The ladder was too short. It did not reach the ground. It would take a strong leap to reach the lowest rung. Boemund looked questioningly at his companions. Who would be the first? He saw that none of them were in any hurry. Had this been an attack in the bright daylight they would have pushed and jostled to get there first, heedless of certain death. What held them back was the feeling that here was something secret, stealthy, unworthy of a knight. This blind tower, the silence, the ladder hanging in the darkness, the bright bit of window behind which there was no telling what might lie in ambush—all these caused them to waver and look around though there was no time to be lost.

"Then I shall go first," said Boemund with studied calmness. "When I give the signal from the window, follow. But mind: not before."

"It's dark. We might not see the sign."

"I shall call softly, 'San Gennaro and Amalfi!' When you hear that come up at once." He caught the end of the thong and with a heave pulled himself up and began to climb. His sword kept getting in his way, banging against the wall. Hanging on precariously by one hand, he slipped it to his back. There, though it still hampered his movements, it did not make so much noise. He climbed higher. Damn! What a weak ladder! he thought. It stretched like dough; it would never hold several men at once.

He reached the window and thrust his head and shoulders through the narrow opening. Now he was completely helpless. The man whose legs were right before his eyes could chop off his head. He could order him seized and trussed. It all depended on whether he was or was not the father of the lad whom Ostoy guarded below.

Fortunately, he was. It was Firus, pale and with drops of sweat standing out on his forehead.

"Quick! . . . Quick! Where are the others?"

"I will summon them right away," said Boemund, who had guessed from the gesture what the other meant. He was about to lean out of the window and call, when Firus clutched his arm. Someone was ascending the stairs of the tower. Hastily, the Greek pushed Boemund against the wall where hung the sheepskins and clothes. He hid the knight behind them. As an additional precaution he threw a roll of blankets from the couch on the ground to hide Boemund's feet and moved over the stool. The door opened. In came a slight, withered little man, Firus' brother.

"What do you want?" asked the captain of the watch. His teeth chattering, he knelt on the ground and pretended to peer out.

The newcomer sat on the stool. If he leaned back his shoulder blades would touch Boemund's belly.

"Anisa sent me," he said. "She never stops crying for the lad. It's night and he is not back yet. She told me to see if he was here with you."

"He is not here but I have already told her that she can rest easy. I know where the lad is. He will be home tomorrow." (Here Firus spat furtively over his shoulder; who could tell if Isaac-Abdulla would be home tomorrow?)

"She would know where he is now. What have you done with him? Come, tell me."

"Leave me alone. Go and tell Anisa that no harm will come to the boy. Tell her to stop worrying."

"She will, if you tell her in all candor where he is."

"I had to send him off."

"Where?"

Firus wiped the sweat from his forehead. Here, every second counted, and the man would not budge. The Latin knights had to get in, leave the tower, run all the way to the Bridge Gate, for the Gate of St. George was blocked with stones, and open it . . . And all that before the guards changed.

His brother settled himself more comfortably on the stool.

"No use returning to Anisa without the boy," he announced. "The woman is a fiend. She has already roused the whole neighborhood."

"Take my advice and go back anyway. I would prefer you did not remain."

"Why?"

"Yagi-Sian might come. He often makes a round of the walls at this hour."

"What if he does see me? We can tell him we are keeping watch together."

"Go, I tell you!"

"First explain why," the guest persisted. No, he would not leave. The disappearance of the lad, Firus' troubled face, his obvious anxiety, his insistence that his brother should leave when in the past they had spent whole nights here together—it all looked mighty suspicious, though what it might be he had no idea.

Firus took his courage in both hands.

"Be it so. I will tell you. I am still a Christian at heart. My conscience will not let me alone."

"Your conscience!" snorted his brother. "You old rascal."

"You may believe it or not," said Firus with dignity. "Nevertheless it's so. My conscience is awakened. And I feel we should help the Latins."

His brother started from the stool.

"What?" he shouted in a shrill voice. "What? And perhaps you sent the lad to them too? Are you out of your wits? I will not have it! The Latins are worse than pagans. Don't you dare even think of it. This—"

"Be still!"

"I will not. I will not have it!"

"For God's sake! Hush, and begone!"

"No."

"Then die!" Firus cried hysterically and struck out wildly with his dagger. The little man had barely time in which to start up in horror before his throat was laid open and he sank to the floor, drowning in his own blood.

Firus sobbed. He had killed his brother so that he might save his son . . . The duke could come out—but now heavy steps clattered on the stairs. Yagi-Sian, it was Yagi-Sian, with whose coming Firus had tried to frighten his brother, but whom he really did not expect at all. The guards on the stairs were already calling: *Allah akbar!* and in a moment Yagi-Sian entered the chamber. Because of the lack of space the two sheiks who accompanied him remained at the door.

"A giant of a man," Ostoy had said of the commander of the stronghold, and a giant he was indeed. Eagle feathers stuck out of his helmet; his coat-of-mail was wrought of thick steel mesh. He had a drooping, black mustache, expressive eyes, and a proud and stern cast of features.

Boemund looked at the Turk through a gap in the clothes. Yagi-Sian was so close to him that he held his breath lest the other should feel it. Even so, if the Turk moved he was bound to touch him. What should he do? Forestall him and leap out, sword in hand, so he might perish while attacking or go on waiting and let himself be captured hiding under the Greek's rags? He cursed all his unlucky stars.

The huge Turk stared in surprise at the corpse.

"Who is this man?" Firus could not control his trembling. He was as pale as the dead man. He bowed to the ground, touching his hands to his forehead.

"*La illah el Allah, Mohammed rasul Allah!* He is my brother."

"Your brother? How did he perish?"

"I killed him with my own hands. He urged me to betray."

"If so, he died a just death." Yagi-Sian looked hesitantly at the body. One could put no trust in the words of an unfaithful dog, and the corpse was forever silent. No one would ever learn what had happened here. Well . . . they might have quarreled over something else. Otherwise all seemed in order in the tower.

And yet he lingered on. There was something in the air, that awoke his apprehension. Yagi-Sian was a soldier, and even as a horse will sense ghosts, so a soldier senses treason. Yagi-Sian smelled treason in the tower of Three Sisters and decided then and there that the next day he would put someone else in the Greek Firus' place.

Without another word he turned to leave. Firus bowed again to the floor. *Allah akbar!* The Sheiks followed the commander and their steps died on the stairs.

Down below the knights were full of misgivings. The short summer night was on the wane. An hour had passed since the duke had vanished in the window and he gave no sign of life. The ladder hung invitingly. Should they climb? He had told them to wait until he called. Should they climb or wait?

Isaac looked at them uncomprehendingly.

"It looks as though I'll have to kill you," Ostoy told him in Polish. His voice was a strange mixture of relief, repugnance, and pity.

"Shall we climb?" debated the knights. There seemed to be no doubt that they had been betrayed. The pagans had strangled the duke and were now lying in wait for the others.

But at that very instant they leaped to their feet. From above they heard a voice, soft but clear. "San Gennaro and Amalfi!"

They hurled themselves forward. Ostoy, letting go of Isaac, was the first to reach the ladder. He climbed like a cat. Behind him came De Toul. Then Du Puiset and the others, but half way up the ladder broke. Those who came behind fell heavily to the ground, breaking ribs, legs. Only Ostoy and De Toul remained, already at the window.

"Make haste! Make haste!" urged Firus, shaking as in ague. The corpse of his brother lay on the ground already stripped of clothes.

"Where are the others? Where are the others?" Boemund asked feverishly.

One glance through the window was enough to explain their absence. There was no time to look for another ladder. Three would have to suffice. Originally Boemund had planned to massacre the unsuspecting garrison of the tower and rush out, sword in hand, making for the bridge. He reckoned that before the startled pagans had time to recover, some of the knights, at least, would have reached the gates and flung the portals open. Now that there were only three of them the plan would have to be changed. And so in all haste Boemund put on the clothes of the dead man over his armor, replacing his helmet with a turban; Ostoy took a cloak from the wall; De Toul wrapped himself in a sheepskin, and all three concealed their swords under their garments. Then, treading with firm, calm steps they walked out of the chamber and descended the stairs. The guards stared after them with the dull gaze of men whose business was not to think but to stand and watch the entrance to the tower. They had no doubt but that the strangers had entered with the emir, may God protect his days.

The knights reached the bottom of the stairs. They walked briskly through the rapidly thinning darkness toward the Bridge Gate. Yagi-Sian had just passed and the sentries still remained bent in humble salute, with their palms to their forehead. *Allah akbar!* No one paid heed to the three knights, taking them for the belated escort of the emir. They walked faster and faster. The night was almost over. The first rays of light would reveal the troops hidden by the gates and ruin the whole scheme. Almost running they reached the gate. Two guardsmen looked at them unsuspectingly. Leaping like a tiger Boemund fell on one, Ostoy on the other. Before the Arabs had time to call "Allah" they had them by the throat. Daggers struck to the heart. De Toul and Firus were already removing the bars. Two other guardsmen, hitherto concealed in the shadows, sprang now on the knights. The sound of struggling and cursing brought down the sheik from the top of the tower. He clambered down much wroth. Again the Turks were fighting with the Arabs, he thought; he was sick of these eternal fights. But at once, half way down, the sound of a falling bar struck at his very heart. Gripped by horror, he ran like mad, nor was he the only one. The enormous portals would not open either fast nor noiselessly; the heavy locks rattled; and at the sound of the clatter, white-turbaned figures darted from every direction, but before they could prevent it a mighty heave from outside pushed the gate open, and the cry of "God wills it!" rang out.

Through the gate which no power could close now, a surge of Latins poured, spread, overflowed the city. And so the battle began, cruel, more murderous than any fought so far. It raged everywhere at once: in the narrow passages that ran under the walls, in the streets, alleys, inside the houses, and on the rooftops. Dead bodies rose in piles, banks, ramparts. Blood flowed in streams over the stones, the ground turned into a reddish bog. As the work of slaughter went on in the western part of the city, Ostoy, taking advantage of his disguise, broke across to the Dog's Gate. There he cast off both turban and the renegade's cloak, pulled out his sword, and thus, once more in the guise of a good knight, appeared before the startled eyes of the watch. They had heard the din on the other side of the stronghold but had no idea what went on there. Nevertheless, they promptly fell upon the unexpected assailant. But there was no stopping Ostoy. The knight went mad; he hacked, slashed, struck as though he had the strength of ten. He cut them down and opened the gate.

"God wills it!" came a thunder of voices from outside. They swept in like a river with Raymond St. Gilles at their head. The Moslems, taken unawares from two sides, began to give way. The morning shone bright upon the victory of the crusaders. The battle still went on in a hundred points, but Yagi-Sian, with a handful of soldiers, had retreated to the rocky Citadel where he would have to be besieged separately. Left without its leader, the garrison knew not which way to turn. The crusaders continued to cut them down without respite. Prisoners? What for? And anyhow no one asked for quarter. The white turbans fell to the ground in silence, praised be the Prophet who allows men to fall in a Holy War, and tries the faithful ere he raises them in glory.

Before evening came the crusaders were the masters of the city, even as Boemund had promised. Antioch, the almost impregnable, had fallen.

37.

The Snare in the Victory

THE WEALTH OF ANTIOCH RIVALED THAT OF BYZANTIUM. IT WAS SPRIN-
kled with palaces and decorated with gold. Fortunes in silk, porcelain, jewels, and works of art were stacked in treasure rooms throughout
the town. But one thing was lacking; there was no food.

Ostoy led the knights to the warehouses, but they were found to be
almost empty. Yagi-Sian had been down to his last resources. He could
not have held out for more than a few additional weeks.

What remained of salted meat, olives, flour, corn, and wine, was
quickly used up. The crusaders had been fasting for months, now they
feasted. Their stomachs, shrunk by hunger, refused to hold much, but
they paid no heed to this limitation. They ate until they vomited, then
ate more.

The odor of roasted meat and spilled wine mixed with the smell of
blood which covered everything and with the stench of decaying bodies.
The crusaders had no time to dig graves for pagans. Soon they would be
on their way to Jerusalem. The road was open.

Boemund looked on the feasting with distaste. Already the owner's
instinct was strong in him; it was his city that was being looted and he
did not like it.

"The bodies should be removed and buried and the city cleaned," he
said. But nobody paid any attention to him.

"Look after it yourself," said one of the knights. "You came by it
easily enough; you can spend a little time taking care of it. Tomorrow
we leave for Jerusalem."

But the next day things were different. When dawn lighted the hills
it shone on a forest of standards and flags. Moving down on Antioch
was a Turkish army of one hundred thousand men, the long awaited
forces of Kerbogha, the Emir of Mosul. Quickly the crusaders rounded

up their horses and drove them into the city. The siege towers were burned and one by one the gates were closed.

In the tower of St. Paul, Adhemar, Raymond, Boemund, and Robert of Normandy stood watching the preparations. Up the steps came Stephen de Blois.

"Why are you bringing everything in?" he asked. "Surely you don't intend to lock yourselves up in this city? You will starve. There is nothing to eat."

"What else can we do?" asked the Bishop.

"Leave while there is still time. Go to Alexandretta. Withdraw into the mountains, to Tarsus and Adana. Don't remain here. It is madness. There is nothing to be gained but death—certain, inglorious, bootless death!"

"We will not flee," said Raymond calmly. The others agreed with him. Stephen turned and went down the steps. Outside the tower he mounted his horse and raced for the gate of St. George. Seeing him go, Hugh de Vermandois whispered to his friend, De Melun, "You cannot bear to go hungry. You had better go with him."

The giant shook his head. He was full of food and now he thought that he would as soon die of starvation as of a sword thrust in battle.

Stephen reached Alexandretta and went to Philomenium, where Alexius waited with his armies and his court. He had been there for several months, watching to see what turn events would take. The crusaders had acted as if they did not know of his presence, and he had repaid them in kind. Now he received Stephen coldly. The crusaders had turned Antioch over to Boemund. They had broken their oath to him. What did they think to gain by it? God would punish them.

"He is already doing so," said Stephen. "Kerbogha stands outside Antioch now. Inside the city there is no food. The Latins have not a chance. I am no coward but neither am I a fool. I shall return to Byzantium with you and go back home. I have had enough. Three years is as long as a sensible man should spend in the midst of half wits. I suffered willingly as long as there was hope of attaining our goal."

"You are right," added Alexius. "The whole thing was sheer folly."

"There is food for ten days," said Stephen. "After that there is nothing. Kerbogha will not let a man out of the city alive."

Alexius nodded and smiled. "The crusade is over," he said. "We shall return to Byzantium."

BOOK IV

38.

The Mission of Peter the Hermit

IT WAS WITH SELF-PITY THE CRUSADERS RECALLED HOW ONCE THEY HAD looked upon their final months before the walls of Antioch as the direst extremity of poverty and hunger, for today in retrospect they discerned in those days the tilting horn of plenty. How could they, now but gaunt scarecrows reeling through the city streets, ever have regarded their stay outside the walls a time of destitution? Despite their immediate trials, many opportunities had been theirs to pursue: hunting, fishing, the search for edible roots and herbs. Dry stalks had been theirs to suck. There had been green fruit on the trees! What matter that the food thus garnered was poor and insufficient? Time did not linger so long as a man had his traps to visit, his lines to tend, and so long as the trails through the mountains held hope of an occasional wild goat or hare.

But today? There was nothing whatever to eat! No man could devour gold or chew on marble. For, ironically, how rich in gold each man now was! From grand seigneur to the humblest camp follower, all now were loaded down with priceless loot, their purses bulging with Syrian coin, their quarters heaped high with cloth of gold. Squire Laurentius had seized gold thrice enough to release his brother from captivity. Blaise, Klimek, and all the other men-at-arms were each in possession of far more money and jewels and raiment than ever had been the property of the great ones who ruled their clans. But to what good end? The

looted treasure was no longer of any value. Not a crumb was to be had
for the whole of it. A string of pearls could not be exchanged for so
little as a handful of peas or beans.

These inseparable companions, Brother Hyacinthus, the pious scrib-
bler, and Peter Bartholomew, the once gay seminarian from Marseilles,
had undertaken, in a spirit of wry jest, to robe themselves in kingly
garb. Brother Hyacinthus had swathed himself in the loose folds of a
silken material tinted a dreamy peach, Bartholomew in a fabric holding
bright stars against a background of sapphire night. As he lay there,
weak with hunger, and slowly raised his hand, the material flowing
from his shoulder appeared to him like the heaven to which his soul
was already ascending.

Silence lay over the city. Yagi-Sian, marking the silence with satisfaction, awaited his moment of vengeance.

To Peter Bartholomew, as he lay there by the wall and gazed at the
folds of his mantle, came many a flitting impression. People, real and
imaginary passed before his eye. Reality was shot through with the stuff
of dreams. Roger de Foix had passed but a moment before, and now.
Who was this? Ho, never a man! No, here more likely was a vision of
his patron saint, the Apostle Bartholomew! Aye, that was just who it
was! And small wonder there, considering that Peter could not but believe himself already at Heaven's threshold! Indeed, he had come to
Heaven's gate, for all his sinful nature, probably as a reward for having
taken the cross and died for Christ; for, properly speaking, was he not
already dead? Everywhere these stars . . . this heavenly blue? Behold!
There indeed was the Apostle Bartholomew! And behind him walked
all the other Apostles! Peter, John, Thaddeus, Philip, Andrew, James
. . . Fascinated, Peter Bartholomew tried to kneel, but he could not.
Then suddenly his vision cleared. Those were not Apostles, they were
knights! They were walking slowly along in their broad cloaks. Into
Peter's ears seeped odds and ends of their remarks.

"My lance, 'twould slip from my grasp in battle . . ."

"Battle? Hah! It will never come to that—never!"

"Then why should the Bishop be calling us to council before the
altar?"

". . . can hold neither sword nor lance. Ho, then I shall break my
sword as did Roland his Duranal! For a man's sword is no plaything
for the infidel to toy with! A man's sword is sacred . . . holy . . ."

They were gone, and Peter Bartholomew could no longer be certain whether they had been knights or Apostles. What had they been saying? There had been mention of a council before the great altar. He closed his eyes. But then the procession returned, this time the saints! For could he not see through them? They were transparent and luminous. Even through closed eyes he could see them, circling the city. Oh, never the city—this was Heaven! And, as the procession withdrew, it was Andrew who was last in line, and it was Andrew who turned and smiled at him. Why Andrew? Bartholomew wondered.

The Bishop's original plan, which had led him to shut himself up together with his army within the fortress city, had been to leap out upon the enemy and engage him in grand battle. In order to execute this plan, however, it would be necessary to effect a sudden sortie, to lead at least a third of his fighting men out through the gate in a surprise attack. But this plan had been proved impossible, for the eye of the Saracen was fixed upon the city both day and night. Were ever a gate to be opened before the first lines of assault should manage to pass through, the infidels would be upon them, would surround them, would force them back and crowd into the city behind them!

What then? Were they to meet their doom, one by one, slowly starving to death, without ever having an opportunity to raise a hand against the evil destiny which had caught them in this trap? Adhemar de Monteuil, for one, was of too keen and brisk a mind to submit without a struggle, and it was to examine a further proposal that he had summoned his nobles to solemn council in the cathedral.

Within the church the stifling heat of the city had not fully penetrated. There, too, the miasmic stench of corpses rotting under the walls, when tempered by the fragrance of incense, was not so overpowering. In the glimmer of light filtering through the prisms of the windows, the assembled nobles would have appeared to a mind far less feverish than Bartholomew's to be a gathering of phantoms.

The Bishop was suggesting the dispatch of an envoy to Emir Kerbogha of Mosul with a request to do battle. Let the infidel withdraw and permit the Latin forces to emerge from the city. Thereafter, they would engage as honorable fighting men. Or, should the emir prefer, they would offer him a single combat, leader against leader, or picked groups from each encampment, the result of such a meeting to decide the final issue. Here was a course of action often chosen by warriors of noble blood.

The starving knights showed sudden signs of life. Yes, here was a spirited notion! The only thing was, it must be put forward while there were men still strong enough to lift a sword!

At length, Ostoy spoke up. "A worthy suggestion, Your Excellency!" he approved. "The Saracens are a warlike people and should accept the challenge. But who is to be our envoy? I know the devils well. They have no respect for envoys. The man accepting the mission exposes himself to their indignities. Were the Saracens satisfied only to kill! But they are always likely to indulge in insult and injury. Their way is to drive a man naked around the walls, to flog and castrate their victim. All would depend upon the emir's fancy, and there is no telling what notion might fly into his head. I am prepared at this moment to descend the wall and there be cut to pieces, Your Excellency—my life is not the matter that most concerns me, I vow—but I should still decline to be our envoy. For I have eaten enough of disgrace, Your Excellency! I know too well the taste of that!"

There was silence following this warning. And it was certain that no belted knight would volunteer to carry the petition. Each man was ready to die, no man to be disgraced.

"Then might we not dispatch a letter?" the Bishop suggested.

Letter? Aye, that might do well. But how were they to dispatch it? The men of the Cross possessed no charmed birds, no pigeons. Despite Ostoy's explanation, the knights still clung to their belief that carrier pigeons were birds upon which a magic spell had been cast.

"We might bind our missive to a stone," someone suggested, "and cast it forth by sling."

"Aye, so—but would there be one amongst the infidels who might manage to read it?"

"As well that as know what an envoy is saying!"

"Not so! Because for the spoken word they can always find some renegade Greek with a fairish ear for Latin. But with writing, the matter is worse—for our characters are not like the Greek or the marks of the filthy infidel!"

"That may all be, but still we may try. The Canon d'Aguilers will compose such a missive tomorrow!"

With this decision they parted. The Bishop dragged himself labori-

ously back to his tent. There he collapsed into a chair and held his head
in his hands. Hunger was wrestling with his bowels, but a hundred
times more painful were the thoughts assaulting his brain. Why had
God forsaken the crusaders? Count Stephen de Blois had done the
sensible thing. The others should have listened to his counsel and followed suit; they should never have deluded themselves that aid would
come from Heaven!

On the morrow they would hurl a missive from the wall. But there
was small reason for fond hopes to be raised by that. In all likelihood the
communication would fall unnoticed; if seen, it might never find its
way to the emir. Even so, it might never be read. A spoken message
would offer more certainty, but no one was willing to go.

"No one will carry our message!" The Bishop uttered the words half
aloud. There was a rustle over in the corner where Peter the Hermit
had his bed. Slowly his small, hunched figure dragged itself across the
floor to clutch at the Bishop's knees. "I will go, Your Excellency!" Peter
whined.

"Go? Go where? What is it you want?" the Bishop asked absently.

"I was in the Cathedral, Your Excellency! I heard! And I will carry
your message to Kerbogha. I can speak or take him your missive."

Adhemar fastened his gaze upon him. "You!" he murmured. "You
would go!"

"Yes, Your Excellency! Why not? Pray, let me serve you, at least at
the end!"

"I shall mention this to the barons at once," said the Bishop. Then,
with a hasty gesture, he bent over Peter and kissed him warmly on the
cheek. "Brother Peter!" he breathed. "Our good brother!"

Ostoy mounted the wall and shouted loudly in Arabic that a Latin
envoy was leaving the city with an urgent message for Emir Kerbogha
of Mosul. Would Moslem guards be so kind as to conduct him safely to
their chief!

Peter was preparing to leave. He was not afraid to die, nor did he
tremble at the thought of indignity. He had no occasion to fear for his
lordly honor as did the belted knights, but he was pleased to be able thus
to sacrifice himself.

A narrow wicket in the wall slammed shut behind him. The noise
awakened a forgotten echo in his soul, an expanding recollection of the

power which had once possessed him, at the time when he had been arousing the masses at Clermont, a power which he had felt as a great pain in his breast. Memory of that glorious occasion, when vast crowds of people had clung to his words and women had brought him goats' milk and olive oil, was now awakening in the brain of this poor, degraded buffoon and was inspiring him to go forth to accomplish a deed which even the knights of the Cross cowered and shrank to contemplate. Here was the very Peter whom Walter the Penniless had kicked with contempt, whom Tancred had slung like carrion before the Bishop's tent, whom every man in the camp roared with ribald laughter to behold, and whose life was one of trembling in the shadow of an imaginary demon—and what was he doing now? He was marching forth in hero's boots to face a mighty enemy! He had risen from the dust; he was a man reborn! He straightened his small withered body as he trudged forward.

From the walls the eyes of many a knight followed him admiringly. The Bishop blessed him with the sign of the Cross.

Extravagantly rich and elegant was the camp of Emir Kerbogha of Mosul. Its stores were piled far and wide and the tents of the emirs were a riot of color, for twenty-six Moslem tribes were united beneath Kerbogha's standard. From Persia and Media and the lands of ancient Babylonia these allied warriors had come, and from Damascus and Tripoli and Jerusalem. The brave Kilij Arslan, twice beaten by the Latins and burning for revenge, was there with his host, as was the doughty Ahmed ibn Meruan, lord of all Palestine. Chafing under the high command of the Emir of Mosul, Ahmed was unable for the life of him to understand why a wise and illustrious Calif had preferred Kerbogha's prestige to his own in appointing a commander-in-chief; he was deeply aggrieved by the Calif's choice and harbored in the depths of his soul a solemn hope that Kerbogha might fail in his undertaking.

The task, however, was fulfilling itself. The Latins were as good as finished. It was quite enough for the Saracen hosts to stand idly by and wait for the besieged Christians to perish from starvation. Yagi-Sian, himself surrounded in the citadel, was in daily communication with Kerbogha's force by means of an underground tunnel. Supplies were reaching him by the tunnel, and he sent back with the porters full information concerning the deterioration of the Christian ranks. The crusaders had formerly been a noisy lot who had indulged in much ruffianly shouting in the streets. Today, Yagi-Sian could report, all shouting had ceased. There was silence, and there was no mistaking the meaning of that!

Kerbogha's pavilion, for its size and sumptuousness, stood out among the tents of the lesser chiefs, like a mighty castle supported on bamboo frames. Four turrets rose above its billowing roof, and within were many halls and chambers connected by sweeping corridors in which, it was said, two thousand people could gather. The walls were draped with cloth of gold, aglitter with precious stones, the floors well covered with costly rugs and carpets.

The Emir Kerbogha, dressed in a coat of golden mail encrusted with countless gems, was seated on a throne which in splendor rivaled that of the Basileus. Surrounding him were the chieftains of the twenty-six nations, a scene of blazing glory to which Peter the Hermit, led by two contemptuous sheiks, was admitted.

Now here was indeed a strange thing: the more of wealth and grandeur he saw about him, the less grotesque this pauper in his tattered rags appeared to himself. In the course of his brief journey from the beleaguered city to the palatial headquarters of the foe, Peter had so grown in his own esteem that he was no longer able to recognize himself as the tatterdemalion he really was.

"Here is the envoy dispatched by the Franks!" cried an agha-sheik, prostrating himself before Kerbogha.

Explosions of indignant laughter greeted this announcement. Here was hardly the type of man the Moslem chiefs had assembled in state to receive. Was this shriveled mongrel to be accepted as a knightly envoy? From behind the throne an interpreter appeared, a Syrian who had acquired Latin from the Genoese.

"I have come to you as envoy of our leader, the Holy Bishop Adhemar de Monteuil!" said Peter proudly. "I am to speak his message to you!"

"Is your bishop an old beggar like yourself?" the emir shouted derisively.

There was no answer.

Kerbogha, too, remained silent. Narrowing his somewhat slanting eyes, he endeavored to fathom the reasons lying behind the enemy's choice of such a messenger. He had heard much from Kilij Arslan con-

cerning the courage and pride of the Franks. The Latins he had encountered while trying vainly to retake Edessa had been a spanking
crew, tall, hard and proud, worthy opponents of those who followed
the Prophet, as all who had encountered them could attest. Were not
the besieged of Antioch men of the same blood? How then could they
have chosen to send such a wretched dervish as this for an emissary?
A dark flush spread over the face of the emir as suddenly he thought to
detect a hidden insult. "Could they find none better than you in the
Latin army to send?" he asked at length.

"Properly speaking, O Emir," Peter proudly but courteously replied,
"none meaner than I was to be found. I am more wretched than the least
of our fighting men."

"Then why did they choose you?" Kerbogha's narrow nostrils
quivered.

"Our knights refused to come, for fear of torture and outrage. In our
camp they fear that more than death."

Kerbogha relaxed, calmed by the thought that the Franks were in
truth at his mercy and knew it. "And you are not afraid?" he smiled.

"I? No!"

The emir raised three fingers to his chin, leaned his head gently
forward upon them and studied the wizened figure standing so stiffly
before him. At length, with a patronizing arching of his brows, he
asked: "Well, what message have you brought from your people? Come,
man, speak up!"

"Our leaders are minded to request you, O Emir, to withdraw your
forces so that our fighting men may be free to leave the city and meet
you in open battle. We would fight you as men of honor, leaving the
decision to God. Or, so say our leaders, if the Emir is unwilling to grant
this, he might agree to select a number of his stoutest warriors who
would meet with an equal number of our own in single combat for
possession of the city. This is what they have commanded me to say
to you."

"Nothing more?" The emir blew on his fingers.

"Nothing more! Our men would meet yours in fair battle."

"Allah be praised!" said Kerbogha, leaning forward and showing his
white teeth in a sardonic smile. "Your people are dying from starvation,
and they would do well to plead for mercy and never for battle! Pray,
with whom would I meet in combat?" The emir leaned back on his

throne. "There is not one amongst you still man enough to hold a sword in his fist! You are dying by hundreds each day! I know your situation!"

Suddenly reminded of something, he clapped his hands and spoke to the agha-sheik who hurried from the chamber. There was a brief pause, then all eyes followed Kerbogha's to a passageway from which four half-naked slaves soon emerged with an enormous tray heaped high with food. Balancing the tray on their heads, they approached the throne and knelt before the emir. With a flourish, he bade them set the tray before him.

"I repeat, your people are starving by hundreds at this very moment!" said Kerbogha, digging into the mountain of lamb and rice with the full of his hand and beginning, with much champing of jaws and smacking of lips, to dine.

"My people seek honorable battle!" said Peter grimly, casting not so much as a glance at the rich food which Kerbogha was so thoroughly enjoying. Fervently he offered up a silent prayer. He prayed that the Lord might spare him from revealing his hunger in any way, that he might not betray, by so much as a swallow the saliva gathering in his mouth, the weakness of his flesh, for was he not here as the representative of the crusaders? Whatever these people might be led to think of him, that would they think of all Franks.

Somewhat disappointed in the effect of his unholy show, the Saracen chief took a handful of meat and casually tossed it to the dogs which, being already overfed, were slow to arise and sniff at it. One piece fell at Peter's feet.

But Peter stirred not a muscle.

Kerbogha stared. Then, drawing up a fistful of rice, he offered it to Peter with a magnanimous gesture. "Here, take and eat!" he said.

"I am not hungry," Peter replied quietly.

"Not hungry!" Kerbogha and his chiefs burst into roars of laughter. "Not hungry!"

"I am not hungry," Peter repeated. "I am wasting from a voluntary fast, such as is observed by certain of our people. Do not your own dervishes also observe such fasts?"

Kerbogha started. "What know you of our dervishes?" he inquired.

"I saw many of them whilst in Jerusalem."

"You have been in Jerusalem?" Kerbogha's wonder grew. Had this wretched creature been that far abroad? Had he penetrated the Holy

City of the Prophet David, the Prophet Elija, the Prophet Jesus, all three of whom had proclaimed to the world the coming of the greatest of all and the only true prophet, Mohammed? Had he entered Jerusalem and lived to return? Impossible!

"I have been in Jerusalem," Peter stubbornly maintained. "I have seen with my own eyes the infamy committed by your people in the holy places. My heart grew sick within me. And when I returned, I announced to the Christian world what I had seen. And the people rose in arms, and together we came here."

Kerbogha and all his assembled chiefs stared at Peter incredulously. "So it was you!" Kerbogha shouted. "It was you who caused the Franks to desert their homeland and come here?"

"I was the cause of their coming!"

The emir had suspected this man of being a sorcerer; he was now convinced. That was the real reason why he had been selected to come! Very well, then, they must be rid of him as soon as possible. He stirred on the throne, as though prepared to end the interview.

"The Emir will accept our offer of battle?" asked Peter, standing his ground.

"The offer of starvelings who, like yourself, are observing a 'voluntary fast!'"

"Our knights are both able and fit," said Peter calmly.

"Fit? In the manner of these weapons of theirs, I take it! Here, bring me those splendid weapons which were found!"

A slave ran up to him and placed at his feet the stump of a broken lance and a light sword, both well eaten with rust.

"Your weapons picked up near your camp!" Kerbogha laughed scornfully. "There is indeed a sword worthy of your grasp!"

Peter glanced at the objects the Emir was exhibiting. "Those are not our weapons," he quietly remarked. He could see that the lance was of archaic design and that the other trophy was quite unlike a Latin sword. "They are not ours," he repeated. "Surely the Emir must be able to see for himself that these weapons have been lying in the ground for many years!"

"Not yours? What a pity! They match your own person so perfectly! Here, have them as a gift from me, so that you will be the better equipped to do battle against us!"

"Then the Emir is accepting our offer of battle?"

"No! By the holy stone of Kaaba, no!" Kerbogha roared. "Listen to me, you Latin dervish! Hear my answer which brims with benevolent mercy! I hold you all in the palm of my hand, remember that! that! Now then, if your princes together with their entire armies, will deny their own incompetent God who was powerless to prevent his own suffering on the Cross, and if, after doing so, they will recognize the faith of the Prophet Mohammed, then I shall be happy to leave the city in their hands, to make peace and send gifts and food and women and whatever else they may lack! All this I shall do in the name of Allah, since the Koran bids us love all followers of the one true faith! Now take that message back to your leaders and have them speedily benefit from this charity of mine before it will change into anger! And take your weapons with you!" He flung the sword and lance head at Peter's feet.

"Our leaders are begging the Emir not for peace but for battle!"

"And death is what they shall have! Death and nothing else! Let their filthy clans perish! Now get out of my sight! At once, do you hear? Begone, before I lose all patience!"

With no sign of haste, Peter picked up the lance head—the property of some unknown pilgrim—and the sword corroded with rust. Then with dignity, he returned to the city.

In a few simple words he reported to the Bishop and the barons the outcome of his mission.

"So! Then it was all in vain!" sighed Adhemar. "Hope melts into disappointment. What iron have you there?"

"Some old relics dug up from some ancient camp site by the people of Kerbogha. He sent them back with me, saying they were ours, only in order to deride us. He said such weapons match our condition! I took both pieces, thinking that perhaps God would punish him for thus scoffing at misfortune."

"There was no reason to take them!" snorted Raymond. "Throw that scrap away!"

Obediently Peter put it by and retired to his corner. Brother Hyacinthus was lying there, on fire to hear what had happened.

"He offered me food. You know? Food!" Peter reported to his friend, prepared to omit no detail in relating his experience. "He held a whole fistful under my nose. Roasted meat and rice! His fingers were dripping with grease!"

Brother Hyacinthus choked with desire. "Then what?" he asked, swallowing hard. "Did you eat?"

"Nay," sighed Peter. "I told him I had no hunger." His will, which he had proudly strained to maintain during the last few hours, relaxed and fell away. He hid his face and wept. "I told him I had no hunger!" he sobbed, "No hunger—no hunger!"

Brother Hyacinthus regarded him with amazement and admiration. "Said you that, forsooth?"

Peter lifted his tearful face and nodded.

"Do the Bishop and the others know—?"

"Nay. I did not tell them that."

"Why not?"

Peter was silent, unable to explain. Perhaps he had been afraid of being disbelieved. Surely they would have accused him of boasting. For had he not but recently fled the camp because of his hunger? How might he have proven to them that he was speaking the truth—especially since the high-born are forever prone to doubt the word of the lowly? Moreover, the affair had concerned himself alone and had had nothing to do with his duties as an envoy.

39.

A Sign from Heaven

THE LAST OF THE HORSES HAD BEEN DEVOURED . . . ALL LEATHER HAD been eaten . . . boots, jerkins, belts . . . the bark from the trees, even the grass had been taken. Within the city walls nothing remained except earth, stone, marble, gold . . .

Of the roving bands of children, those flocks of small gypsy-like vagabonds deprived of home and sheltered existence, not one was left. Only a few of the women were still alive. Serving-folk, men-at-arms, squires —even the belted knights—all were dying like flies. All social distinction had vanished, as once it had in the past—in the desert, when they had encountered the disaster of thirst. In matters of death and burial all men were equal.

Diminishing numbers of the living fed on the corpses of the increasing dead. A few with utter indifference, others with abhorrence and dread. But hunger can conquer both. A man can grow used to anything.

And as starvation stalked the city, the weakened flesh, no longer aware of the pangs of hunger, gradually became too frail to hold the fancy, and all manner of hallucinations tortured the mind. Images of saints and of the redeemed would flit before the wasted eye, together with foul impressions of all the monsters of hell.

Some ran away, aye, fleeing the morgue into which the city had been transformed. Here and there, they would be found, sliding down ropes at night from the walls, only to fall into enemy hands and perish before they could so much as cry out to the Saviour. They were seeking certain death in preference to enduring the pains of further starvation. *"Furtivii Funambuli,"* the knights called them, satisfied that among these deserters were none from the belted order.

Their satisfaction was short-lived, however, for 'twas not long before the great knight, William de Melun, was seen scrambling over the wall. *Furtivus Funambulus*—even one of the elect! In vain had Hugh of Vermandois given him well-nigh everything he had been able to obtain for himself in the way of food and, never leaving his side, had begged his friend not to bring shame upon himself. In vain had other knights striven to restrain him. "Hands off me, louts!" De Melun had screamed. "Perhaps they'll feed before they kill!" Then, felling one of his comrades with a swing of his fist, he had slid down from the wall. From the campfires of the enemy he had caught the scent of food, and straight for that bewitching fragrance he had bolted.

Three days later his head, wearing a Moslem turban, was paraded about the walls on the tip of a Saracen lance, while enemy warriors capered and shouted that such were all Latin knights—men who would deny their God for the sake of their bellies!

The incident had a bad effect upon the morale of the people. In the eyes of the populace the halo that had graced the heads of the high-born had, during the past three years, been wearing pretty thin, and now—with this—it melted away completely. To hatred was now added contempt.

Peter the Hermit, Brother Hyacinthus, and Peter Bartholomew were discussing the situation as they lay beneath a sunshade in the courtyard of a palace. Flies, importunate gray flies, were buzzing about unceasingly, alighting on their eyes and mouths. The fountain no longer played, and it was therefore no longer possible to cool one's face in its mist; for the Saracen had closed off the secret aqueduct which had led water underground from the hills into the city. The remaining water supply, contained in cisterns, was already perilously low.

"St. Sylverius Day—the twentieth day of June!" Brother Hyacinthus was saying, as he flicked at the flies. "The eighteenth day of our hunger here in the city! I wonder if anyone will live to see July!"

"Doubtful!"

"Antioch! Who would have thought us all doomed to die here without ever a sight of the Holy Sepulcher?"

"The Lord Jesus must have turned against us, deserting us thus in our need!"

"And has he not had good cause, after all our wickedness?"

"O, yes, yes. It was Sodom and Gomorrah all over again! What's that you're saying there, Bartholomew?"

The young cleric opened his unconscious eyes. "I have not spoken."

"Yes, you did! You spoke!"

"No! But if I did, it's only that I always have such visions, my tongue cannot stay still. Sometimes my hunger speaks . . . They walk, they scold, they are angry . . ."

"Who? What is this you are saying?"

Peter and the good brother crossed themselves and peered about uneasily.

"Be not afraid! Not evil spirits—Apostles!"

"Apostles?" The other two bared their heads respectfully.

"O, one time I saw the Lord Jesus, but from afar and once only. The others visit me oftener. St. Andrew the Apostle, he is usually the one who comes. He is small and dark. Looks a mite like our Bishop. When I close my eyes, he is here . . . commanding . . . commanding!"

"Commanding what? Come, come, speak up!" His friends became excited.

"Stay, stay, I don't know! Just let me try to remember . . . Oh, everything gets so mixed up in my head! . . . Ah, now I have it! We are to dig in the Cathedral . . . before the main altar . . . to find the Holy Lance . . ."

"Holy Lance?" repeated Peter in a quavering voice. "Tell us, Brother —might it be the spear that pierced the side of Our Lord, Jesus Christ?"

"That's it!" Bartholomew was quick to declare. "That's it! . . . The same! And when we dig and find it . . ."

"Then we shall be victorious!" they all shouted exaltedly.

"And St. Andrew the Apostle spoke that to you, Bartholomew?"

"Yes, Yes! He did! When I close my eyes, I see him. And he commands me go and dig . . . And scolds me for not going directly!"

"Why have you not told this to the Bishop?"

"The Bishop! How could I go to him? He would laugh! All men would laugh! That the Apostle could find none better to choose and had picked such a one as I! . . . That is what they would say, and rightly so! For who am I? But dust, but wretched dust! . . . For have I not wenched and drunk and brawled? I should not dare!"

"The lowliest are often chosen by God, Bartholomew! cried Brother

Hyacinthus. "And do we not already have an example? How low is our own Brother Peter! And did he not put by the infidel's food, the while one of our great belted knights was willing to sell his God for victuals! The Bishop must be told!"

"You can go if you like—but you'll be laughed at."

"So be it! Now hear me, Brother Bartholomew—it might be that they'd put you under oath. Will you swear it was just as you've said?"

Bartholomew struggled to smile. "Swear? Aye, I'd take a hundred oaths."

Within a few hours later, Peter Bartholomew was in the Bishop's presence, whither Peter the Hermit had taken him.

"How do you know it is St. Andrew?" the Bishop inquired cautiously.

Bartholomew hesitated. "That I cannot answer," he admitted. "First I saw them all together. In single file they were walking . . . And all around were stars, as though they were in Paradise. They were walking in the order of their wisdom—Peter, John, Thaddeus, Philip—my own patron saint, Bartholomew, walking along at the head. St. Andrew came last of all the Apostles. The first time I saw him, he turned and looked at me . . . Looked at me and smiled . . . Now he always comes to me and speaks."

"By what token did you recognize him?"

"How can I say? Perhaps I told myself it was he—or perhaps I was told by another . . . I can't remember now."

"Very well, then, let us assume that it is indeed St. Andrew the Apostle who speaks to you. What is he trying to tell you?"

"He wants me to tell Your Excellency that if we dig before the main altar in the Cathedral, we shall find the Holy Lance, which pierced the side of our Saviour. 'By that you will conquer the infidel!' he keeps repeating to me the moment I close my eyes."

"But why should he appear to *you?*"

"That I know not either, Your Excellency," Bartholomew replied with such sincere astonishment that Adhemar at once had faith in him. "It was a matter of surprise to myself—for who am I but a common ignorant sinner here among so many grand priests?"

"Will you give your oath that all you say is the truth?"

In reply, Bartholomew struggled and knelt. Then, with eyes turned heavenward and right arm solemnly raised, he declared in a voice grown suddenly strong: "By the passion of our Saviour, I swear I speak truly!"

"Good!" said the Bishop. "I shall advise the barons immediately!"

The church in those days was not alone the Christian's house of prayer; it was likewise his council chamber, a place of sober deliberation and fateful decision.

When the starving nobles had come together in the Cathedral, the Bishop repeated his conversation with Bartholomew and advised them to hear this man from whose eyes the truth was shining. The princes agreed, if reluctantly, to do so. They could but nod with scepticism. There was no harm in hearing him, although not a man present was prepared to believe his words. Would an Apostle appear to such a simpleton?

"*Spiritus fiat ubi vult!*" the Bishop replied. "Simple he is, but meek of soul."

Bartholomew, his once spritely legs no longer able to support his weakened flesh, was carried in and helped to stand before the altar. Here, for the first time in his life, the penniless seminarian from Marseille faced an assemblage of mighty lords. In the carefree past he had viewed them from a distance; today he was meeting them man to man, and clearly he could read their doubt in their cold, contemptuous eyes. For despite the Bishop's admonition, they were convinced that never would the Divine Spirit deign to choose so disreputable a vessel to receive what it had to impart.

"You say it lies buried here in the Cathedral before the main altar?" Raymond St. Gilles inquired icily. "Precisely in which place?"

"There!" Bartholomew pointed without hesitation to the spot where at that very moment he seemed to see the Apostle Andrew standing. And with that, he began to lose consciousness. Everything of a sudden had grown confused and unclear to his mind. He began to murmur incoherently.

Adhemar poured a few drops of ceremonial wine into the poor fellow's mouth and had him carried back to his quarters. Brother Peter was told to go along and look after him.

After the departure of their witness, the nobles remained seated in solemn council. The youth's words had rung with a sincerity which had moved them to a man. It was not likely the unfortunate fellow would lie deliberately. Moreover, had he not testified under oath? But who was there to say whether or not he had been a victim of hallucination?

"A drowning man will clutch at a straw!" Chaplain Arnuld observed. "Why may not starving men then clutch at a word?"

"I do not understand such allusions," grumbled Godfrey. "Why not accept all this as a matter of simple trust? And as evidence that God desires to save us by a miracle?"

The Chaplain smiled dubiously and shrugged.

"Say as we will," spoke up Boemund, "the least we can do is dig! Small effort will that cost, and then, so having done, we shall know! . . . So long as no one else gets wind of it!" he added thoughtfully.

"Nay, you are mistaken there, My Lord!" the Bishop corrected. "We have no right to do such a thing by stealth. If we are to accept what this boy has told us as the will of Almighty God, then it is our duty to inform the people that a vision has been had, and that we are awaiting the fulfillment of the prophecy. Otherwise, God might punish us for lack of faith!"

"But suppose we announce it and find nothing?"

"We will find that which we seek!" the Bishop shouted. "I am convinced this poor wretch has spoken the truth. For how could he have invented such a lie? And to what purpose?"

"I agree, Your Excellency!" cried Godfrey, his stand being supported at once by Robert of Flanders, Raymond, and Hugh of Vermandois.

"Then call the people together and we shall begin at once. We have no time to lose."

It was unnecessary to summon the people, for a famished throng had been waiting for hours outside the church. The rumor had spread that some manner of miracle had happened and would save them all. What it was no man could say. Perhaps God had miraculously multiplied their loaves, or manna would fall from Heaven, as it had in ancient times. Had not words of that been spoken at Clermont? Or perhaps the Saracen was withdrawing from the city before some miraculous appearance of the Angel Gabriel?

The Bishop Adhemar, weakened from hunger, tottered out onto the balcony above the main entrance of the Cathedral and addressed the people.

"Hear ye, my brothers!" he said. "I bring you good tidings. God has bestowed his mercy upon us and stands ready to save us from our present misery. St. Andrew the Apostle has appeared to one of us to say that within this very church lies buried the Holy Lance with which the Roman centurion, Longinus, pierced the side of Our Lord, Jesus Christ. The Apostle has said that when we shall find this Lance, victory over the Saracen will be ours . . . The strongest among you must come forward to dig; the rest of you must remain in perpetual prayer. The miracle has not yet been fulfilled; it will come to pass only if we draw it fervently into ourselves. God's kingdom has suffered violence. Unclean hands are reaching forth to grasp it. We alone can save it. Our strength lies not alone in our spades, but in our prayers as well. Pray that the Holy Lance may be found, so that we may survive as a people who will see and deliver the Holy Sepulcher!"

Beneath the stone slabs of St. Peter's prison, the earth was pressed as hard as rock, impossible to dislodge with spade or shovel. Picks and battle axes alone served to chop loose a few crumbs of earth at a time to be carried outside in a blanket. Shifts were constantly changing, famished men being unable to deliver more than a few strokes of the pick before dropping with exhaustion. A day and a half of continuous digging and the hole was no more than six ells deep.

The barons, standing in groups or seated on the mound of dug-up earth, watched the diggers at work. Occasionally the ground would yield a metallic sound, whereupon all would leap to their feet thinking that the spear had been found. But their hearts fell each time some foreign object came into view.

The vast interior of the Cathedral was swarming with people, feverishly waiting, swaying in their tracks, bracing themselves one against the other. Other waiting faces peered through doors and windows, bony fingers clutching at the bars.

The pit was slowly deepening. Outside the Cathedral the pile of earth was growing. And as each shift of workers, collapsing with exhaustion, was promptly relieved, faith alone kept hope from wearing thin.

At the edge of the excavation, Peter Bartholomew, weeping with frantic impatience, was struggling with restraining arms in a sudden determination to descend. "Let me go down!" he sobbed. "I have just seen the Apostle again, I tell you! I know I shall find it! Let me go!"

"What will you find?" the diggers protested. "This is no place for a spindle-shanks like you! You couldn't even hold a pick in your hand!

"Nay, let him go down!" others cried appeasingly. "Who knows but he may find it!"

A respectful silence fell when the Duke of Tarentum, attired in a sweeping white cloak, descended into the pit. "Go above and have a rest!" he said quietly, nudging the men who were digging. "Let that blubberer in! Let him search!"

The weary diggers slowly dragged themselves out. This was already the middle of the third day. They had been scratching in the earth for sixty long hours without respite, and the mind of each man was as a taut string which might snap at any moment. These men were nearing the end of their endurance.

Boemund followed after the diggers. Peter Bartholomew was now free to go below and search. Perhaps the Apostle would show him the place.

As Bartholomew was descending the ladder, all eyes burned to assist him. A hundred heads pressed close to peer after him. He was conscious of their breath . . .

"What now? What now?" boomed the crowd. "Has he found it?"

"Bartholomew is praying. He is getting up. His eyes are closed. He is picking at the earth with a spade. Now he has put it aside. He is searching the ground with his hands . . . groping. His head is thrown back, he cannot see. Now he is bending down, and . . ."

The explosive roar from the thousand throats within the Cathedral announced to the masses without, that which already needed no announcement; "The Lance! He has found it! The Miracle! Thank God!"

Bartholomew had found the object of their search. With unseeing eyes, he had found it, there at his very feet just beneath the soil. The diggers had excavated all around it without once coming upon it, so it was clearly the will of God that Bartholomew alone should find it. With lightless eyes and mouth agape in a voiceless shout, Bartholomew stared up from the pit. Then slowly raising his wasted arms, he held aloft— the Holy Lance!

All fell to the ground as though struck down by the sweep of a mighty hand, by a hurricane blast of joyful emotion. Now they were saved! And would conquer the foe! Of that all men were now perfectly sure! They would burst from the gates of the city with this miraculous weapon raised on high, and the very sight of it would smite the infidel with awe!

The enemy, seeing it, would scatter like clouds before the sun. The men of the Cross were saved!

On bended knees and with trembling grasp, the Bishop Adhemar received the holy treasure. Tears of gratitude flowed from his eyes. "Thou hast looked down upon Thy people, Lord, and hast delivered us from our enemies!"

The roaring multitude on the square were milling about like madmen, pushing and trampling each other in a wild endeavor to crowd into the Cathedral. Each man was demanding to see with his own eyes, to touch with his own fingers, to know! It was necessary for the Bishop to appear once again on the balcony, this time to confirm the miracle.

First, respectfully wrapping his hands in golden material, he raised the lance for all to see. Broken it was and eaten by rust, a broad spearhead of ancient design and known to the Romans as *framea*. A man could tell by looking at it that it had lain in the ground for many years. In general appearance and condition it was not unlike the lance which Peter had brought back from the camp of the Saracens.

"Behold the instrument of our salvation!" the Bishop proclaimed. "Lo, the weapon which shall save us! Along this very edge once flowed the Most Precious Blood of Our Lord. Within its sacred metal throbs a power equal to the power of the Holy Grail! That which the bards have celebrated in song for centuries is ours, as a living reality!"

In reply, a mighty shout arose. The square, the nearby streets, the entire city quaked beneath the tumult. Dying men took strength and revived. The Holy Grail—a fountainhead of renewed vigor—had become a reality! High up on his rocky citadel, Yagi-Sian looked out with astonishment. The Franks still lived? Were shouting?

"Move! Move!" the crowd thundered. "Move now against the Saracen!" Disorganized bands were already rushing toward the gates. Let but the Bishop carry the Lance and lead them!

"Stop!" commanded Adhemar. "You cannot go as you are! Eaters of human flesh! Cannibals! First we must pause to cleanse ourselves! I hereby proclaim a two-day fast! This is the eve of the holiest of all Holy Days. The mercy of God has reached us by a miracle! Remain in prayer that ye may be worthy of salvation! Day after tomorrow, on the Day of Sts. Peter and Paul, we shall move!"

"God wills it! God wills it!" roared the blustering, seething throng. A holy fervor, a full consciousness of God's mighty immanence was throbbing in every man's breast. They had been condemned to the most ruthless of fasts for well-nigh a month! Aye, but who would confuse enforced hunger with the voluntary fasting of a vigil? Such was the general spirit that no man would have so much as looked upon a heaping plate had one been set before him. They could wait a day or two longer. They would feast at the rout of the Saracen.

The entire day preceding the attack was devoted to mass confession and receiving of Communion. The Bishop, restored to full vigor since the moment of finding the Lance, went about busily distributing Communion with the aid of a corps of priests, and praying aloud that the Saviour would refresh their souls and bodies with His Most Holy Flesh, thus enabling them to live until the morrow, the day of victory and glory.

While the people were fasting and praying, the leaders were seated in council. They would have to fight on foot for the first time in their lives, a thing no belted knight had ever been called upon to do before. The horses had been slaughtered; no mounts were left. Pray, how did one fight from the ground?

"Rely on me!" urged Boemund. "Grant me full command and your leave to lead the attack. I have been studying a plan all night, and these are the tactics I have developed . . ."

All heads came together in a tight group, as Boemund unfolded his plan.

When an agha-sheik burst into Kerbogha's sleeping quarters and shouted, "Hanum Baraba!" the Emir thought he was dreaming. "In the name of Allah!" he growled, "why do you awaken me with your bleating?"

"Hanum Baraba!" the sheik repeated, prostrating himself. "Your mother! She is here!"

"What is that!" Kerbogha was on his feet.

"She is arriving this very minute in a chair. She is here!"

Still not altogether sure whether he was awake or dreaming, the emir ran from his tent. The inconceivable had happened; his mother absent from Khorassan for the first time in twenty-odd years! and on an incredibly long journey. What possibly could have brought her hence? Could the Calif have become vexed with her because of some untoward prediction?

Before he had time to consider all the numberless possibilities, Baraba and her retinue drew up. Breathless slaves, smeared with sweat and dust, bore her in the light sedan. A score of protectors, mounted and on foot, were surrounding her chair. A train of camels followed. Unable to endure the swaying of camelback, Hanum Baraba had had herself carried the long way hence on the shoulders of a triple shift of slaves.

The moment the chair came to rest on the ground, she alighted, swathed in black veils which fully covered her face, save for a narrow slit through which her black eyes were nervously peering.

"Mother!" the emir cried. "*La illah el Allah, Mohammed rasul Allah!*" In his exclamation there was piety mingled with astonishment.

The woman bowed low, folding her hands on her breast. "My son!" she breathed with equal reverence. Then, following him into a reception room within his pavilion, she sank onto a mound of cushions with an air of great exhaustion.

"Tell me, what brought you hence, Mother?" the emir inquired anxiously. "If you have offered offense to the Father of the Faithful, it would have been wiser had you sought to flee elsewhere! As it is, his disfavor will fall upon me as well!"

The woman waved this suggestion aside. "Have some water fetched me, Son—then you must listen. I have had a vision," she began, after she had drunk, "a vision so imposing and austere that, fearing you would not believe my written word, I have come to speak it to you with my own lips. And this is what I must say: You are to raise the siege forthwith!"

Kerbogha was thunderstruck. "What are you saying, Mother!" he gasped.

"Lift the siege!" she repeated emphatically. "Withdraw your armies to the south this very day!"

"But, by Allah, that is quite impossible! And, pray, why should I withdraw?"

"I know not why! But I see your destruction and the end of all who are with you, if you do not do this! And that is why I have come! Oh, my son—seeing that I, who am so old and ailing, can have made this journey, all the while wondering if I might be fortunate enough to arrive before it should be too late—are you not to be influenced at least by that?"

The emir forced a smile. "By the holy sandals of the Prophet,

Mother!" he exclaimed. "Do you realize the nature of your demand? That I should spare these unclean *Giours*, these Franks, who are already in my clutches! One more week and there will be nothing left of them but corpses. Besides, this is a Holy War—can you not understand? A Holy War! Why, I should be inviting the contempt of the faithful and the ire of the Prophet himself—the Prophet who has said, 'One stand in a Holy War is more agreeable unto mine eyes than a lifetime of prayer in a mosque!'"

"Son of Najaz—although I am but a woman and may not mention the holiest of books by name—I know what is written there, and I know what is meant when it stands written: 'A man shall grasp time when he can, for time forever graspeth after him.' You must grasp this moment before this moment grasps you! That is the warning I have come with. I brought you forth from my womb to be a great strong man, before whom enemies would quake and the faithless would pale. I cannot bear to see you now destroyed. You know me well, my son—do you think I would yield to a whim? I speak solemnly: Lift the siege at once."

Kerbogha, son of Najaz, paced the rug beneath his feet. "But woman," he cried, "what you ask is impossible! At least, pray, tell me the reason! What threatens?"

"I do not know," his mother said simply. "I do not know. I have seen a great cloud of smoke billowing from this city. And the smoke changed into a tree, and the tree grew until it touched the sky, where it burst forth with a hundred branches. And the tree spread forth its branches, and they showered leaves upon you and your men. I saw white turbans whitening the ground beneath, like snow on the mountain top. And I recognized the tree whose leaves were falling to bury the many turbans —it was *Zakkum*, the Tree of Destruction. A great fear came upon me, and I began searching for you, O son of Najaz, O, my son! And I saw you disgraced, and my terror grew—to such an extent that I was determined to fly to you. And I minded not the great distance, nor the haste, nor the difficulties of the journey. And now I am here to warn you! This is the truth I speak."

She fell silent and lowered her head, as though in token that she would speak no further.

Kerbogha looked at his mother with desperation in his gaze. Here was no ordinary woman whose speech was unworthy of heed. She was Hanum Baraba, The Seeress; the Calif himself relied upon her every word. Her prophecies never failed; no one dared ignore her counsel. As he thought over her words, the emir was torn between two considerations; his superstitious dread of the disaster she had foretold and his repudiation, as a sound military man, of any form of irrational, ignominious action. He tried to imagine himself giving orders to his armies to withdraw. The astonishment of the emirs, the jeering smile of Ahmed ibn Meruan, the indignation of Kilij Arslan. How could he explain? What excuse could he give for the command? And the Latins? They would revive, fatten, and grow strong again. Instead of finishing them off while he had them in the hollow of his hand, he was simply to lift the siege? "Ho!" he told himself, as he continued to pace, "if any of my sheiks were to come forth with such a notion, I would have him beheaded on the spot! Besides, what danger can there be? Have we not already had the example of the knight who accepted the true faith for the sake of a mouthful of food? Was he not representative of the condition of the Latins?"

Halting to look his mother in the eyes, he asked shortly: "From whence will this black evil descend?"

"I know not," she repeated in a voice dull with helpless discouragement.

She left that day for Aleppo, well realizing that her mission had failed. Nor did her son attempt to stay her. He bade farewell to her without even inviting her to a repast after her long journey. He wanted to be alone to battle with his thoughts. He was tortured by doubt and suspicion. There was something in all this which his mother had not fully understood. Her warning in itself had been valuable, but in her interpretation of her vision she had gone astray. After all, this was a military situation, and his mother was no soldier.

He considered the problem in terms of his own armies; he sought a solution within his own ranks. Treason! Were some of the lesser emirs plotting against him? In his mind he ran through the list of his subcommanders and stopped at the name of Ahmed ibn Meruan. Could it be he? Everyone knew that this haughty sharif had expected to be appointed commander-in-chief. He had submitted to the will of the Calif, but he was probably harboring anger in his breast. In his attitude toward Kerbogha he had always been arrogant and reserved, if at all times correct. When Antioch should fall, he would enter the city first—no doubt it was his thought to hold it for himself!

Kerbogha was so impressed by this conclusion that, when Yagi-Sian notified him through the underground passage from the citadel that there were extraordinary activity and commotion among the Franks, he paid not the slightest heed. They were about to die and were performing their final rites, he decided. He returned to his contemplation of Ibn Meruan's unquestionable treason. How clear it seemed to him now! Ahmed's army, ten magnificent regiments, stood closest to the walls— just outside the Bridge Gate and the Bridge of the Dog! Ahmed ibn Meruan himself had chosen this position. Obviously, he would be the first to enter the city and would permit no one to follow!

"O my prophetic mother, who foresaw and forewarned me!" Kerbogha triumphed under his breath. " 'Withdraw!' you said. Very well, withdraw it shall be—but not Kerbogha! Ahmed ibn Meruan shall withdraw! He must be given the order at once!"

The assembled emirs listened with no small show of amazement to the order of the commander-in-chief. The Emir of Palestine, flushing with anger, pointed out the harm which could result. To withdraw his forces at the very moment when Yagi-Sian had sent word that the Franks' encampment was seething with activity, like a disturbed ant hill. Why?

The more emphatic Ibn Meruan was in his argument against such a retreat, the more confirmed in his suspicion the Emir of Mosul became. He eyed the angry chieftain with malicious satisfaction. "I have crossed your plans, reptile!" he gloated to himself.

"We have nothing further to discuss," he concluded aloud. "You will simply obey my command. The army of the Emir of Palestine will move to the rear this very day. It will be replaced by—" At this point he hesitated. Upon which of the other emirs could he sufficiently rely? Ibn Meruan might try to gain his ends by bribing another commander into a conspiracy with him, might he not? There were six and twenty commanders. He must weigh his choice carefully. "The division to replace the regiments of the Emir of Palestine will be named tomorrow! I have finished!"

"*Allah akbar!*" the leaders saluted and departed.

Ahmed ibn Meruan was furious. "Now what does he mean by that?" he asked Kilij Arslan.

The former Sultan of Nicaea shrugged.

But Kerbogha, son of Najaz, was satisfied, convinced that his penetrating intellect had stood him in good stead. "Ah, good Mother," he breathed, "without you I might never have seen the truth!"

40.

The Battle of the Lance

THE YEAR BEFORE, UPON LEAVING BYZANTIUM, THE CRUSADERS HAD NUM-
bered three hundred thousand. Today there were fewer than seventy
thousand of them left.

A sizable host, none the less! And all, with a single exception, were
convinced beyond all doubt that before their very eyes a great miracle
had come to pass, a miracle which would deliver them. They were awaiting the morrow with ecstasy. Marching about the city in a vast procession, they were no longer aware of their hunger, indifferent as they were
to everything save the day of their resurrection finally at hand.

Out of this faith, this holy certitude of weakened flesh through which
the spirit poured a spectral light, a surging enthusiasm was born. Above
the heads of the people their corporate will rode like a great storm cloud
wherein thunders and lightnings were brewing. Even the more obtuse
were conscious of the swelling charge; they felt it physically in the crack-
ling and rising of hair, in the flashes of fever which swept through their
limbs to the tips of their fingers and toes. A mighty reservoir of power
was building up above the city, a power almost ready to discharge and
strike. The seed and channel of the brewing storm was the Holy Lance,
exposed upon the altar in a sea of light, the focus of all eyes. And all who
saw it there were fully conscious that the power which would be unleashed on the morrow would be sufficient to cause earthquakes, to divert
rivers from their age-old courses, to level hills and transport mountains,
compared with all of which, the smashing of the Saracen was viewed
as a casual certainty. In holy anticipation, folk moved as in a trance.
With concerted resignation, they obeyed the words of Boemund who
had assumed chief command and who, with tireless activity, was disposing the forces he would use and explaining to each man his duty.

The entire night was given over to the formation of fighting units in the vicinity of the two gates through which they would issue. The enemy had withdrawn from the walls the day before, and the broad plains beyond the river were clear. This unexpected move on the part of the Saracen the crusaders had likewise attributed to the influence of the Holy Lance. Their joy and assurance were therefore even greater than before, as they now awaited the dawn.

Boemund had formed his people into six divisions of two battalions each. On the left was Hugh de Vermandois, together with Robert of Flanders and Swennon the Dane. Behind these was Godfrey of Bouillon and behind Godfrey, Robert of Normandy. On the right, the first division was led by Adhemar in place of Raymond. The Count of St. Gilles with half his people was left in the city; whilst the main army was encountering Kerbogha in the field, he would strike at Yagi-Sian locked up in the citadel. Behind Adhemar came Boemund and behind Boemund, Tancred.

Each division was numerically strong, being able to boast of some ten thousand men, but what an army it was! Armor hung loosely on emaciated bodies as though on so many poles, the loose parts clanking dismally at every step. The knights felt curiously small beneath the arches of the gates which towered above their heads. The heavy armor, never devised for foot soldiers, weighed heavily upon them and impeded their progress.

The sun burst from behind the mountains. Only a moment before, a single wandering cloud had drifted across the sky and dampened the ground with a sudden unexpected shower. Rain in the full of summer, a rarity indeed in this part of the world! As the formations emerged from the gates, everything about them was wet and glistening. Pearls of fallen rain were clinging to the bushes and from the sea far off to the west, a cool breeze was blowing—a wind of freedom and salvation.

Intoning a sacred chant, the divisions in columns of four were leaving the city in exemplary order. Crossing the bridge over the Orontes, they immediately deployed on the open plain beyond. Robert of Flanders to the left, Godfrey to the right, the remainder in the center, save for Tancred who, as rearguard, was to protect the rear from encircling attack. The Bishop, carrying the Holy Lance, otherwise unarmed, was flanked by Peter the Hermit and Peter Bartholomew. Behind the three walked Walter the Penniless, protecting the Bishop with his huge sword.

The Bishop's formation included even women. Many of these had come the day before to clutch at his robes and beg leave to join the battle. They were of no mind to remain idle on such a day, for were they not also crusaders? . . . No longer comely as once they had been before hardship and starvation had taken their toll, they were now but a band of gaunt, grey creatures—widows, mostly, of fallen knights, aging, bereft, uncared for. But devout they had now become and had spent each day from dawn to dark in church. And ever since Bartholomew's contact with the Apostle Andrew, these women had taken to having prophetic visions of their own. One after another, they had come running to the Bishop to report what distinction had been visited upon them from this or that female saint—St. Catherine, St. Agatha, St. Symphronia, St. Pulcheria, St. Margaret, St. Eustachia, and others were appearing almost daily now in a perfect epidemic of revelation, all of which but emphasized the importance of these women of the Cross! The Bishop did not ridicule them, even though the knights turned deaf ears to their entreaties to go forth with them to battle. He found a place for them in the heart of his division, well protected by the mass armor of his men-at-arms. He accepted them, he said, because after all this battle would not be like any other.

Nor was it, as things turned out. The air was curiously tense, like the atmosphere presaging earthquake or solar eclipse. By fits and starts, the wind would lunge and fall away as though intimidated by an unseen hand. The earth trembled beneath the measured tramp of this army of living skeletons. From gardens along the river, a billowing fragrance of jasmine dulled the stench of decomposing corpses within the city walls and assailed the senses with intoxicating sweetness. The air was growing wan before the oncoming heat of the day, and in the swiftly changing light, all things appeared weird and ghostly. And spectral indeed appeared those ranks of infantry forging inflexibly ahead under the spell of a supernatural courage. They had prepared themselves as in a dream and now were going forth to do battle in their continuing trance, with inhuman indifference to death or danger and conscious of but a single necessity—victory!

Kerbogha, already awake, was playing chess with the Atabeg Dokak of Damascus when an agha-sheik rushed in with an astounding report: the Franks had left the city and were already deploying for battle.

"Sound the call to arms!" Kerbogha flung, at the same time raising his hand to detain the Atabeg, when the latter hastily rose. "Nay, first we must finish this game," he said, returning his gaze to the board. "The emirs will require no assistance from us in order to kill off those starvelings! Later on will be soon enough to go forth and view their end!" And in silence, the two men went on moving their handsomely carved chessmen.

The game did not progress well for Kerbogha: in rapid succession, he lost his knight, his rook, and finally his queen. His mind was occupied with the thought that Ahmed was likely to seize this very opportunity for betrayal. Very well, Kerbogha reflected, his reply to that likelihood would be to keep Ahmed out of battle for the time being. And so, as he issued orders for individual commanders between moves, he deliberately ignored the Emir of Palestine. At length, having suffered the inevitable checkmate, he thrust the chessboard roughly aside and angrily arose. "Let us go outside and see how the corpses fight!" he growled.

The emir was astounded by the sight which met his gaze. From the hilltop on which he stopped beneath a triangular *menjuk* and a huge green flag of the Prophet, he had a clear view of the entire field on which the battle was about to engage. The Franks were deployed from the river bank on their left to the hills on their right. From this position his only access to the battlefield was by way of a narrow passage through the hills. Meanwhile, the Franks had fanned out quickly and wisely. In order to encircle them and strike them from the rear, a force would have to swing out around the hills and drive in upon them from the direction of the sea. Kerbogha at once dispatched a courier to Kilij Arslan with orders to execute this maneuver with cavalry. Taken thus from two sides, the ludicrous Frankish turtles would not be able to hold out a single hour.

At the moment, the Franks were moving forward in broad, deep columns, like a densely packed body of ants. For the first time since Roman days, so large a mass of men were going into battle on foot in the manner praised by the Prophet as "the unity of welded lead." This was not the thin, loosely jointed front known as a "fence" to the Latins, who used infantry only for the protection of fortress or encampment. These were solid phalanxes which were forging ahead indifferent to the hail of arrows showered upon them by the attacking Moslems.

Dimming the light of day with their clouds of missiles, Kerbogha's Saracens were already dashing against the enemy with massed cavalry.

The earth was groaning beneath the weight of charging horses. Camels were swaying forward, stretching their necks, spitting yellow saliva. The sun struck sparks from swinging scimitars and blazed down upon the bright silk of multicolored oriental garb. Like a desert hurricane, the cavalry charge descended upon these men plodding so indomitably to meet them—these "turtles," as the emir had so contemptuously dubbed them.

When the first assault failed to break those solid ranks—when the howling, surging tide had been brushed aside as though by an outcropping of rock, the Saracens employed their old tactic of suddenly turning back in the thought of drawing their adversaries along with them into a trap. Indeed, here was an excellent maneuver against enemy horse, but one that was utterly meaningless when employed against men on foot. Limited as to pace and formation, infantry could do no more than plod ahead; thus, instead of breaking ranks and starting off in pursuit, the men of the Cross further compacted their front, in certain instances even by locking arms. They were not to be dispersed by the infidel—nay, by the Holy Wounds of Christ, not ever!

Increasing numbers of riderless horses were now charging about the field; the heap of Moslem dead was mounting. Kerbogha, on his hilltop, angrily stamped his foot.—By the Holy Stone of Kaaba, where was Kilij Arslan! Why was he not attacking from the rear?

Even as he fretted, a mass of flying horsemen appeared in the distance and a thunderous outcry reached the ears of the chief. Out of the west the proud cavalry of Kilij Arslan was racing in to charge the enemy's rear. But the Latins, too, had already spied them, and Tancred was busy disposing his ranks to meet the oncoming assault.

Kerbogha viewed the situation with satisfaction. Already the battle was joined, and the Christians were in a trap! The low, rugged mass of armored foot soldiers had been caught between the two forces and would be crushed like a nut between the jaws of a pincers.

Tancred fought with matchless courage, but such were the odds against him that no man could expect him to hold out for long. But at that moment, Boemund detached three thousand men from the forces of Godfrey, Adhemar, and Robert, and quickly formed an auxiliary division under the command of the brave Renard de Toul to reinforce Tancred's ranks.

But Kilij Arslan was of no mind to surrender his advantage. Seeking to inspire his men by word and gesture, he rode forward to lead the attack in person. With prancing horse and flailing sword, the Moslem bore in with full force.

The knights resisted mightily. And as they struggled, they shouted mutual comfort and encouragement. "Normandy! Lorraine! Toulouse!"

"Toulouse!" Gouffier de la Tour was crying lustily when suddenly, as though in answer to his shout, a penetrating roar reached his ears from a point close by. Then, like a ball of yellow lightning, a tawny beast came bounding at him from a nearby rocky slope to leap on his chest with its forepaws, the while baring its fangs in laughing pleasure and growling at him affectionately.

This unexpected appearance of the lioness created consternation in the ranks of the attacking Saracens. Screaming and pawing, their horses sat back on their haunches. The hands of the men of Islam were trembling as they struggled to hurl their lances.

An untimely cast wounded the lioness. With a roar, this time of rage, she leapt at her assailant. In a flash, she had ripped open the throat of the rearing mount and had broken the back of its rider. Frenzied by the scent of fresh blood, she flung herself at others about her. Left and right, she struck out with a series of fatal blows. The Sultan himself paled with fright, for it seemed that the *Giour* had Satan in his service! At Nicaea, Iblis had transformed himself into a winnowing gale; here today he was appearing as a lion!

Overcome by fear, the horses turned back, despite the efforts of their riders to urge them ahead, with the lioness in roaring pursuit. The Latins struggled to keep up with her, their armor rattling as they hurried forward. More and more knights were pausing to seize riderless mounts, breaking from the ranks to do so. The Latin formation was soon hopelessly scattered, and had the Sultan's men now turned and attacked, they would have easily smashed the Franks. But no power on earth could have controlled their panic-stricken steeds, and even Kilij Arslan himself was in helpless flight. So be it! What man could cope with such sorcery? The tawny form of the lioness was flashing hither and yon, trebling itself as it ran, multiplying itself interminably, until each one of the routed enemy could have sworn that whole regiments of lions were on their heels. The beast's incessant snarling, its thunderous roars were driving both horses and riders to distraction. At length, realizing the necessity of setting up some manner of barrier against the pursuing

Christians, the Sultan ordered the grass set afire. Let flames hold back the unclean!

Soon a low blanket of acrid smoke was spreading over the ground, marked here and there by orange-petaled flames bursting in bloom beneath the whitish pall. Had the Latins been mounted, they might never have cleared this obstacle, since no horse will enter fire. Being afoot, however, and conscious of nothing save the victory foretold by the Holy Lance, the men of the Cross refused to be thus undone. And indeed, the danger was less than it appeared; the grass, being short, scorched only the soles of their feet and only goaded them to greater haste. The loose hay, scattered by the retreating Turks, was damp from the morning rain and yielded more smoke than fire. With reckless abandon, the Franks pressed on; the very rush of their passing served to disperse the smoke; while, seeing them clear the barrier with little or no trouble, Kilij Arslan no longer found any hope of halting them and fled south with the remnants of his army.

Ahmed ibn Meruan, still condemned to idleness, listened angrily to the din of battle. Having received no orders, he was powerless to act. Had the commander not irritated him with his exhibition of curiously personal animosity, Ahmed would possibly have moved on his own authority, acting upon the assumption that the courier had come to grief. There was, however, the possibility that Kerbogha was intentionally withholding him from battle. The haughty emir flushed when he considered this.

The truth was, Kerbogha had dispatched not one but two runners. Perceiving how Kilij Arslan was failing him, he had twice sent orders to Ahmed to swing in from the side and strike at the flank of the faithless. But the Latins this day had been favored at every step by fate. The first courier had been unfortunate enough to run upon the battle and had perished; the second had failed to leap a rocky chasm and had been crushed beneath his horse. Neither had got through to Ibn Meruan.

Livid with rage, Kerbogha had then dispatched a third runner with the message, "In Allah's name, attack!" This courier had succeeded in getting through, but by that time it was too late to deliver an effective blow. Boemund had been given sufficient time to protect his flank by ordering the Flemings to take position in the hills. In the narrow defile, they could hold back even a large force indefinitely.

Dumbfounded, the emir watched what was happening on every hand.

The victory he had long considered inevitable was turning into certain disaster. His best cavalry had been powerless to smash an enemy which was inching ahead on foot like the slow lava from a volcano. Far off in the distance were rising the final wisps of smoke from the dying grass fire which had failed to save Kılıj Arslan from the fury of the Franks, and melting out of sight on the southern horizon were the straggling remnants of the once proud army of the former Sultan of Nicaea. Astride captured steeds, the Latins were racing after them, unmindful of hunger or exhaustion. Indeed, Kerbogha was forced to admit, no ordinary mortals were these who today had engaged him in combat.

Bearing the Lance aloft before his eyes, as though it were a monstrance, Adhemar was striding forward in a daze, overcome by his sense of miraculous accomplishment. On either side trudged Peter and Bartholomew. Behind him stalked the ever watchful Walter. Peter, who had once so feared battle that he had been jeeringly sent to join the women-folk, was on this day no less transported than his fellows, as he walked forward without heeding the arrows whistling overhead.

Seeing that Ahmed ibn Meruan would not soon be able to hew his way through the ranks of the Latins holding the pass, Kerbogha undertook to play his last trump—elephants! Of these he had two. Although both were still young, unschooled, and somewhat shy, the moment was such that Kerbogha could not afford to hesitate.

Atop the lumbering beasts in turret-shaped howdahs, a picked group of archers and spearmen rode, and perched between the ears of each giant a mahout was guiding his charge by means of a slender wand. "Ahuu! Ahuu! Forward!" Like two enormous boulders, these living fortresses began rolling through the ranks, which swiftly parted to make way for them. The large ears rose and fell uneasily; the tiny bloodshot eyes were burning with fierce suspicion. "Ahuu! Ahuu! Forward!"

The sensation created by the appearance of his elephants exceeded Kerbogha's wildest expectation. Not one of the crusaders had ever seen an elephant before, and but few of them had even heard of the existence of such a monster. To them these mighty unknown engines, rolling inexorably forward, appeared horrible beyond belief, and howls of sudden panic arose from the throats of the Latins, who at once began to fall back in a milling, crushing pack. The huge, grey monsters were coming straight toward them at an even stride so ponderous that the very earth trembled and groaned beneath their tread. And as they came, they crushed everything in their path. No man alive would be able to resist such an assault!

Like leaves before a blast, the knights and men at arms were yielding to the advancing elephants. Only the Bishop refused to turn and retreat, and in the end had to be pulled aside to safety. Victory was turning into defeat! A wide path was now open through the ranks; once Islam's cavalry should come charging into that fatal breach, the end of the battle would come quickly.

From the rear, Ostoy was pushing his way through the retreating ranks. With strenuous effort he was able to breast the tide and claw his way forward. "Stop! Stop!" he was shouting. "These are not monsters! They are animals! Elephants! Elephants! We can easily slay them!" —But panic had already seized even the most valiant.

Elephants! Suddenly Imbram Strzygonia, who was following close in the wake of Ostoy, recalled the words of the Abbot Guido. Back home, the old man had told him all about elephants—and here were the very beasts of which he had spoken! Elephants. Monsters of the size of a house. Noses which dangled clear to the ground. Found only in heathen lands. Ho! Ostoy was right! These were not hell's leviathans, they were living beasts!

And so, while the routed Franks were dispersing and crowding to the rear, the two Poles stood firm against the tide. At length they stood face to face with the animals. Ostoy wasted no time, for the first was all but full upon him. One lance in the soft skin behind the front shoulder, another fair in the eye, and behold! another miracle was accomplished! With a roar of pain and fury, the elephant wheeled and began stamping his own people. The mahout was powerless to control it as it bucked and tossed, trampling the Saracens underfoot and hurling the occupants of the howdah on its back to the ground.

"Quick, Imko!" Ostoy cried out in a choking voice. "The other one! A wound in the face! His nose! That will make him turn!"

Imbram was quick to grasp the situation. The second elephant had passed Ostoy and was coming straight for him. The spearmen on its back were already casting lances at him, but without effect at so close a range. . . . Imbram raised his sword and, just as the beast was reaching forth its curling trunk to seize him, swung. With all his might he swung, cutting clean through that curling flesh as easily as though it had been a stalk of hops. The severed end fell like a dead serpent to the ground. Maddened with pain, the now savage beast wheeled and, spouting blood, smashed its way back through the ranks of the Saracens, crowding, trampling, crushing. Both elephants were stampeding now, leaving pandemonium in their wake.

Now encouraged by the seeming ease with which even their supernatural enemies had been put to rout, the Latins quickly reformed their scattered ranks and swept forward in a final attack, invincible against a cowed and beaten enemy. No need for further tactics now; the Saracen, convinced beyond all further doubting that nothing could prevail against black magic, were fleeing on every hand.

Kerbogha's mind was seething with recollections of his mother's prophetic words. O, why had he not heeded the unhappy seeress who had meant him only well. "A great cloud of smoke billowing from this city!" she had seen. "And the smoke changed into a tree—*Zakkum*, the Tree of Destruction!" She had seen the great tree scattering its leaves to bury the snow of his many turbans. She had seen him disgraced. Aye, and forsooth was there a worse disgrace than to flee?

Somewhere south of Antioch, the inglorious paths of Kerbogha and the Sultan Kilij Arslan merged. Together those two once mighty ones put the scene of their disaster behind them.

By sundown the battle was fully ended. Not even one entire day had been required for the exhausted and emaciated soldiers of the Cross to scatter the gallant armies of Kerbogha. The fullness and finality of the victory at Antioch thus led the Latin chroniclers to establish the miracle which had ruled the day—the Miracle of the Holy Lance, the anniversary of which would be solemnly celebrated by the Church throughout the centuries and one which even serious and conscientious Arab historians would likewise be inclined to recognize through their inferences of supernatural powers involved in the battle. "The Franks defeated us," they would one day write, "for the very reason that Satan intervened to assist them by breathing into them his own strength, which no mortal could hope to withstand. Of what avail was even the most gallant bravery, when even wild beasts entered the fray to assist the *Giour?*"

The camp of Kerbogha yielded stores sufficient to maintain the entire Latin army for half a year at least. In addition to food and provender there were treasures surpassing anything the crusaders had encountered except in the vaults of the Basileus. Even when it was divided among them each knight was richer than ever before in his life. There were cartloads of gold and silver service, priceless tapestries and rugs, crystal goblets, amber chalices, and vases of rarest porcelain. Even the most common utensils were works of art—kettles, pitchers, trays, pots, and pans. Of particular interest to the knights were suits of chain mail made of so delicate a mesh that they could be wound around the arm like a strip of silk or drawn lightly through a stirrup.

There was also in the camp an elaborate apothecary well stocked with medicines and herbs and fully equipped with surgical instruments fashioned from gold or finely tempered steel. Finally there was an extensive library, including a rich collection of maps. Carefully the knights gathered all the medicines and books together and burned them. They did not want Adhemar, with his notorious weakness for pagan learning, to come upon them.

The Bishop, however, had other cares than loot. He viewed with growing concern the general mood of the barons, whose thoughts now toyed with worldly wealth and whose hearts were now far from Jerusalem. The East, bursting with riches, was more and more a temptation to them. As the days rolled by in Antioch the leaders of the crusade showed no inclination to gather their men and resume their holy march. They were unmoved even when Ostoy reported that the road to Jerusalem was clear.

"Kerbogha's power has been shattered," he said in council. "Two defeats in quick succession have been more than his forces could survive."

"Two defeats?" said the Bishop.

"First at Edessa, then here at Antioch."

"He fought at Edessa?"

"For a full month he besieged the city, but without success and with heavy losses. Of course, he might have won out in the end had he not abandoned the siege to move to the relief of Antioch."

"Who defended Edessa so brilliantly?" asked Godfrey.

"I was told it was Prince Baldwin, your brother. I thought you knew."

"Baldwin!" Godfrey shouted, leaping to his feet in surprise. "Baldwin at Edessa!"

The barons were speechless with astonishment. The long lost Baldwin, whom they believed to have perished in the desert, was now reigning in Edessa!

"So there is another Latin kingdom in Asia," said Boemund quietly, smiling and rubbing his chin.

"Another?" said Raymond. "Pray, where is the first?"

"Here," said Boemund. "Mine!"

Raymond stood up in anger. "I will not listen to talk of a kingdom!" he said, hitting the table with his fist. "Enough of this nonsense! I will not give up the citadel. I will not yield it until you have renounced your claim to the city. I refuse to countenance perjury. We have sworn that all we take shall go to the Basileus. I will not see our oath broken!"

"It was agreed upon by all that Antioch should be mine," said Boemund. "Had it not been for me Antioch would never have been taken. Kerbogha would have smashed us against its battlements. It cost me dear effort to overpower the garrison. Now, failing your knightly honor, you refuse me what is mine."

"I was not present when the ignoble pact was made," shouted Raymond. "I would not have consented then, and I do not consent now. As for your effort, you bribed one traitor."

"Did any other man make such an effort?" said Boemund. "But that is of no consequence. The agreement was that I would lead you into Antioch and the city would be mine. Well, lead you in I did. Now I want the city."

"You led us into starvation," said Raymond. "Had it not been for the miracle of the Holy Lance you would have died a dog's death with the rest of us. It was the Lance which saved us and the city, and that was all because of my man, a Provençal from Marseilles."

"By the blood of the martyrs!" roared Boemund, "let us for once cease chattering about that miracle! Let the Count St. Gilles inform us what he will have in exchange for the citadel instead of constantly trying to delude himself and us with a fairy tale fit only for children!"

"I wish nothing!" shouted the exasperated Raymond.

"Stay!" the Bishop, stunned, cut in at once. "What call you a fairy tale, sir?"

"That miracle! Sound fodder for the public mind, but—now that we gentlemen are alone—there was no miracle."

"No miracle! We all saw it come to pass!"

"What did you see? Events, not miracles! Peter Bartholomew is only a doltish boy, whose simple mind was not aware of the nature of its own fancies. It's enough to look at the fellow to tell that!"

"But what he said came true—the Lance was there!"

"Indeed it was—placed there for him to find!"

There was dead silence which was suddenly rent by a piercing cry from the choir loft. Peter Bartholomew! It had been his custom to spend a few hours daily in the Cathedral where, high up beneath the vault and unnoticed by any man, he would gaze adoringly at the altar where the Holy Lance was ensconced. Whenever the council met, he would hide behind the balustrade. Today he had involuntarily overheard all that had been said of him and, convulsed with shock and indignation, had hurried down the stairs to confront the wicked gentlemen. What did they mean by saying it wasn't true? Were they out of their minds? Shaking with anger, he quite forgot his usual fear of the nobility—forgot they might suspect him of deliberate eavesdropping and have him flogged or even beheaded.

But, as it was, no man arose to threaten him, for the reason that his sudden appearance had been taken as an act of Providence. "Tell us the truth, Bartholomew—" voices spoke to him—"How came it to pass?"

Boemund shrugged. "What can he possibly tell us!" he suggested. "Obviously he had visions arising out of his hunger—such as might have come to any of us who were starving. The women were always seeing saints. Today, when all bellies are full, there are no revelations. And the Lance, as I have already related, was—hm—arranged."

"That's not true!" Bartholomew shouted, drawing his diminutive figure erect and throwing back his head. So that was it! he thought. It was in their minds to deprive him of the honor—humble peasant that he was—of having been the one whom St. Andrew had chosen to address! But the truth was not to be denied! Never would he permit them to make a fool of him; for had he not seen with his own eyes St. Andrew descend to him from the starry heavens on a beam of light? Not once had that happened—not once, but many times. He had committed no deception, nor had he been deceived. The more he thought about it, the more clearly the whole thing came back to him. It was exactly as though it had happened but a moment ago. He fell to his knees and, beating his breast, shrieked with emotion, "I give you my oath! I do not lie! I saw!"

"And we believe you," said the Bishop with great dignity.

"Well, now," said Boemund in an angry voice, "is not His Excellency speaking too soon? I have been silent long enough—and had not the stubborn attitude of St. Gilles compelled me, I should never have breathed the truth. As it is, being forced, I can only say: it was I myself who put the spear in the way of this boy. And that I swear!"

Adhemar, speechless with horror, looked searchingly at Boemund. Was it possible that he was really telling the truth? Had all that storm of emotion, that holy ecstasy, that certitude of spirit so fully felt by all, been but a rank delusion? When at last he could speak, the Bishop inquired in a quavering voice: "You—did—that—sir?"

"I did," responded Boemund. "I saw them tormenting themselves on the third day without finding anything. Therefore I went down into the pit and placed the lance where Peter Bartholomew could find it. It was the old lance-head the Hermit brought back from Kerbogha."

"To think that nothing is sacred to you!" Raymond St. Gilles flung in Boemund's teeth. He would have said more, had he not been stopped short by the sound of Bartholomew's voice, crying out insanely:

"That is a lie! A wicked lie! It's I who speak the truth! I found the lance right where the Apostle showed me. The Duke had nothing to do with it! I swear I am telling the truth! I will go through fire and water to prove it—I want to be tried by God!"

"I wonder which of us the *prudentissimi seniores et milites* will believe," Boemund remarked coldly, "this dull-witted clerk or me!"

"However that may be, it was the Lance that conquered!"

"Nay, never so much the lance as the happy sequence of events and—may I suggest—the sagacity of the battle plan!"

"Impossible!" the Bishop contradicted hotly. "God's hand was in it! I felt it! The power which led us was beyond our doing."

"I repeat, it was this very hand of mine which fetched the lance and placed it where it was found."

"God shall try me! A trial by God, I beg of you!" sobbed Peter Bartholomew. "Cast me into the water! Or let me walk through fire! Let God prove to you that I am right!"

The Norman chaplain, Arnuld, came to the Bishop in the evening to plead—or rather to advise confidentially—against permitting a trial by God. What possible good could come of it? The Duke of Tarentum was obviously telling the truth. It would be wisest to keep the whole affair secret and run no risk of dispelling the charm of the Holy Lance before the people.

"Do you think I would agree to set forth as a miracle a mere cruel deception? The whole affair is monstrous, monstrous! . . . That would be to provoke God, to take His name in vain, to commit blasphemy!"

"Be that as it may, Your Excellency, the results of the Duke's deceit have proven a blessing! And just suppose he had not done what he did? Have you considered that?"

"Then God would have delivered us in some other way, had it been His will to save us!"

Arnuld's lips curled in a barely perceptible smile. "Very well, Your Excellency," he said quietly. "Let us assume that the All Merciful Creator employed Boemund as an implement of His Divine Will and inspired him with the idea of a harmless artifice. The evil of the matter lies elsewhere, in the fact that this bumpkin overheard a conversation intended not for the rabble but only for the ears of their betters! Undoubtedly, the fellow has peddled the news hither and yon. On my way hence I could not but observe that the entire camp is buzzing with conjecture. We must put an end to that as soon as possible."

"In what way?" the Bishop asked with hostility.

"The Count St. Gilles must yield; then the Duke of Tarentum will recant what he said about the Lance, and everything will be as before."

"The Count St. Gilles would not agree to that; nor should I care to join in any such deception. Besides, we are forgetting about the most important person involved in all this: Peter Bartholomew, who insists upon proving his veracity."

"What will he prove, that giddy nincompoop! He will die a nasty death and will thus further disgrace the Lance. No, Your Excellency, we must send Bartholomew away! We must remove him to a place where his voice will no longer be heard!"

"But he is convinced he is right!" the Bishop protested.

"The flames will devour his conviction along with his hide!"

"Send for Peter Bartholomew!" the Bishop sighed, turning to his page.

"Merciful God, what a horrible situation!" he murmured to himself. "How can it be solved? Our only course is to follow the golden thread of truth wherever it may lead us!"

When Bartholomew appeared, his eyes were red with weeping.

"My child," the Bishop greeted him kindly. "You have demanded a trial by God. You are entitled to this. However, I wonder if you have given the matter full serious consideration? Because once we announce it, you may no longer withdraw, you know. Are you not afraid?"

"Afraid? No, Your Excellency! I cannot fear God or the truth!"

"You are sure?"

"As sure as I am of being a Christian."

"The Duke of Tarentum has declared publicly he fetched the spear."

Bartholomew clenched his fists. Again they were trying to frighten him into retracting! It was they, not he, who feared the trial. And no wonder, for the Duke of Tarentum lied!

"You know not what trial by fire means, fool!" Arnuld hissed through clenched teeth. "When you see the flames, your nerve will fail. You had best withdraw now, while there is yet time!"

"No!"

"Very well, then—let there be a trial! Will Your Excellency permit me to depart? This turn of events would seem to favor the Duke! His claim will be confirmed. I wished to save this zany from himself, but saved he will not be! Well, that is his affair, at least. And to be truthful, I was far less concerned about him than about the populace, in whom the belief in miracles is rather to be cultivated than undermined. I bid Your Excellency goodnight!"

The ordeal was to take place on the plain where the Battle of the Lance had been fought. The ground was spacious enough to accommodate all who wished to witness the unusual event. And indeed, vast throngs poured forth from the city. There was hardly a crusader but who was present. Minds were inflamed, opinions divided. The Provençals, like a solid wall, were there in support of Bartholomew; the Normans and Italians were as solidly opposed.

In the very middle of the plain stood two carefully arranged piles of wood, six ells high, four ells wide, twelve ells in length and precisely one ell apart. Each pile consisted of solidly packed lengths of dry pine oozing with pitch; between these woodpiles a narrow alley ran. . . . The Bishop's face was gray with fatigue. He was striving to remain calm. Before fire was touched to the wood, he ordered both chroniclers to inspect, measure, and verify, so that no one in the future might challenge the exactitude and effectiveness of arrangements. The Canons, Raymond d'Aguilers, representing the Master of Toulouse, and Foucher de Chartres, representing the opposition, inspected, measured, recorded. Their goose quills squeaked as they wrote.

A few paces away, Peter Bartholomew, clad only in a light tunic, stood awaiting the start of the ordeal. The day was blisteringly hot, but the body of the boy showed gooseflesh, so tense was his emotion.

"Is it fear you feel, Bartholomew?" asked Brother Hyacinthus, who was closely attending him.

"I feel no fear," the youth replied. "It's only the delay which concerns me. Pray, let us begin, Your Excellency!" he cried to the Bishop imploringly.

"So be it!" Adhemar replied with great solemnity. "In the name of our God Most High, we perform this test. A man's truth has been called in question! He has sought to be tried by God before the eyes of men. The ordeal will now begin! Touch fire!"

From both sides, squires advanced with brands of flaming pitch and ignited the woodpiles. The Bishop, pale and tense, took from the field altar the Holy Lance. Kissing it reverently, he placed it in Bartholomew's outstretched hands, and covered it with a fine, white, silken cloth.

The wood was soon aflame from top to bottom. In the hot still summer air, the dry wood burned like sheaves of straw. The flames from the two woodpiles united to form a single giant blaze. In awed silence, the crowd pressed forward.

The Bishop, as a final gesture, blessed both Bartholomew and the Lance. Then, turning the boy to face the flames, he pushed him gently forward. "In the name of God, go!" he said.

Walking as though in his sleep, the Lance extended before his staring but unseeing eyes, Peter Bartholomew approached the fire and entered it, as though it was no more than a forest thicket. The flames closed in behind him. He disappeared. The fire roared and showered fresh sparks, as one which had been newly fed. What madness to suppose that a man might enter there and live!

But then, ". . . God!"

The cry which arose from the assembled multitude broke across the plain like a sudden storm. For there beyond the flames walked Bartholomew, swaying on his feet, his eyes still wide and unseeing. Before him, as he walked, the Lance still reposed on his outstretched palms, the silk which covered it unscorched!

Stricken with fear and hardly daring to believe their own eyes, the chief witnesses crowded about Bartholomew—the Bishop, the chroniclers, the lords—Boemund, Arnuld, the foremost knights. They seized him in their arms, to support and caress. Not a man of them was able to utter a word. Against their own faces the heat of the nearby fire was a torture, and yet—the flesh of this youth was unscathed, cool, not even flushed!

The battlefield shook beneath the pandemonium immediately unleashed. Thousands of excited men and women stamped and pushed and shouted. Even those on the outermost fringe of the crowd were fully aware of the miracle. Those too now pushed forward and further compressed the multitude. All eyes were burning to see, all hands were trembling to touch the one whom God had spared and to kiss the Holy Lance which God had so miraculously affirmed.

"I imagine, my Lord," Arnuld whispered to Boemund, "that it would be wise of us to slip from the gaze of the people!"

The exalted tumult increased. One man, stronger than the rest, seized Bartholomew and hoisted him onto his shoulder that the multitude might the better see him. Already other hands were reaching. Each person wanted to touch the boy, to tear a strip from his tunic. They pulled him from each other's arms—tugged and hauled and wrenched. Like a limp sack, he permitted himself to be passed from one embrace to the next, offering neither weight nor protest. Overcome by their adoration of the miracle, the people were beside themselves. And as he was swept away by that seething, maniacal tide, Bartholomew fell to the ground and could not rise, was trampled underfoot.

"Save him!" cried the Bishop. "In God's Name, save him, before they kill him!"

When Gouffier de la Tour, together with several of his knights, rode into the crowd, they found the object of uncontrollable public admiration more dead than alive. Many of his bones were broken, and it was certain he had suffered internal injuries, for blood was welling from his half-open mouth. His tunic had been torn away, and his limp body, stark naked, was bruised from head to foot. But for all that, his eyes were still wide open in the same unseeing, glassy stare.

"Poor devil!" said De La Tour with sincere sympathy as he tenderly raised the inert body. "He has proven to the world the truth of his words, but at what a price to himself!"

Seated in Robert Curthose's tent, Boemund and Arnuld were looking at each other uneasily.

Robert was tittering oafishly. "It would seem the gentlemen came in for a bit of a surprise."

"Had I not beheld it with my own good eyes," Arnuld remarked, "a thousand learned tongues would never have led me to believe it possible!"

"Or me!" Boemund echoed simply. "But see it we did!"

"Before we know it, even you and I will be finding ourselves believing in miracles!"

"I was standing nearby. The heat was frankly unbearable."

"The woodpiles were even sprinkled with resin! I saw to that myself, so that his suffering might be brief."

"What do you think will happen now?"

"Well, to tell the truth, my Lord, it would seem to be but fitting that you yourself should undergo the test! Otherwise, you will be taken for the actual liar!"

"You mean—that *I* should go through fire?" Boemund gasped.

"An engaging thought, at least!" Robert tittered. "My, my! I can just see you in there, beating off the flames with your sword! Only I can hardly help wondering, Boemund, if the Lord will be gracious enough to repeat the miracle in your behalf!"

"I should much prefer to be represented by your pious chaplain!" smiled Boemund, accepting the jest.

"So!" the Chaplain carried on gaily. "The noble Duke would not care to put himself to the test, even when—by another strange form of miracle—for once he spoke the truth?"

"That will do, Chaplain!" Boemund snapped and narrowed his eyes. "I am not Robert, mind! Watch that tongue of yours!"

"A thousand pardons, Your Grace . . ."

Boemund had lost the mood of jest. He was in deadly earnest now. "We have witnessed a singular occurrence, perhaps a miracle! But should ten more like it come to pass, I will not give up Antioch! No, Antioch I will never yield!"

"Of course not," the Chaplain murmured meekly. "For a miracle is but a miracle, a city—hm—still a city!"

In the home of Bishop Adhemar, Peter Bartholomew, the once gay seminarian from Marseilles, lay dying. His life was seeping away, and no hand could stay its departure. As he lay there fully conscious, he gazed about him with quiet amazement. That any man should have been aroused by what had happened! Things could not have turned out otherwise, after God had been called upon to decide the simple truth.

The Bishop, his own tear-stained face quivering with emotion, bent over the dying youth. A great question lay in his heart; for, although he stood in awe before divine mystery, he was at the same time consumed by the curiosity of the scholar. Torn between his conflicting considerations, he looked long and humbly at Bartholomew before at length he asked him shyly: "What felt you in the flames, my child?"

"I do not know, Your Excellency," Bartholomew whispered, mildly perplexed. In truth, he knew—it was the power to describe it that he lacked, and that troubled him. It was so difficult, and he so weak. He recalled how some great, strong breath had accompanied him through the flames, and how it had swept a path for him as he walked. Whether this breath had come from within him or from some mighty outside source, he could not tell. He had *seen* the heat but had not *felt* it. He had seen the flames combed to the sides, stacked like sheaves against both glowing walls.

Yes, and there was one more thing he remembered: how curiously empty he had felt upon emerging, as though there had been nothing left of him, save an empty, hollow shell. And that was why he was dying now. Oh, not because of broken bones and bruises, but because of this terrible void left by his departed spirit! He was dying, but wholly without regrets. Life? He had cared nothing for life since the first moment he had spoken with the Apostle. He was dying willingly, marveling only that God had chosen him, a wretched sinner, for His miracles.

All this Bartholomew was thinking without ever being able to put any of it into words. At the end, with already stiffening lips, he could only whisper:

". . . But they saw I was telling the truth . . ."

The vindication of Peter Bartholomew had no effect on Boemund. He repeated his arguments calmly: he had led the Latins into Antioch; he had planned their battle against Kerbogha, he had planted the lance —miracles notwithstanding—and it was common sense to hold Antioch for the Latin cause rather than turn it over to the inefficient and untrustworthy Greeks. Why go on to Jerusalem and leave behind no bulwark of reinforcement, no haven of retreat? Had not Baldwin saved Edessa, and was he not ruling it well?

Raymond impatiently waved these points aside. Knightly honor forbade them to take Antioch for themselves; it must be given to the Basileus. Most of the knights agreed with him; Tancred even declared against his uncle, something which hurt Boemund deeply. Adhemar pleaded for some kind of a settlement so that the crusade might proceed. Armenian travellers reported that for three months after the defeat of Kerbogha Jerusalem was open for any invader; the garrison had fled in terror. Now large armies from Egypt were moving to defend it.

The Latins stayed in Antioch. Godfrey went off to visit Baldwin in Edessa. The Syrian harlots returned to their knightly lovers. The Christian women ceased to have visions and visitations from the saints; they dreamed instead of lusty men and stayed away from the Bishop.

Adhemar de Monteuil fretted and brooded and at length his health began to fail. "My blood has been poisoned by this fearful procrastination!" he complained to Walter the Penniless. "Each day thus squandered here adds its further drop of poison. I hear a voice from the Holy Sepulcher calling out to me. Day and night I hear the voice. 'Christians! Christians! Where are ye? Why come ye not?' it cries out constantly. And it falls as a sickness upon me, because I cannot answer. Because I cannot render a fair account as to why men, who have taken an oath to journey long distances on a holy mission, should have settled in foul disgrace on the very threshold of its accomplishment without stirring to keep their oath!"

The Bishop had aged fearfully. His features were deeply lined and even Godfrey and D'Haineault appeared young by comparison. For all his famed vitality, his grief too long protracted had at long last laid him low. Bile had entered his blood and his body had given out. Pain, unrelenting pain, tormented him day and night. The thundering steeds of death were rampant in his flesh.

But an even fiercer pain tore at his weary mind. Particularly at night when the light by his sickbed flickered fitfully and sent shadows wavering across the carved beams above his head. His thoughts, as usual, ran riot in the darkness and were magnified by the gloom. The once brave flame of his mind, reduced by sickness to a few dull glimmers of remaining fire, fought feebly against the scarecrow visions which rode shadows in the smoky light of the small alabaster lamp on the wall.

Moses, as he lay dying, had looked forth from his mountain top and seen the promised land. Adhemar in neither fact nor symbol saw the goal of his holy quest. God had dealt more harshly with him than He had with Israel's leader. The miraculous certainty to which the Bishop's mind had once attained in a moment of contemplation on the banks of the Sakkara had withered away and died. In its place had grown up a sense of crushing calamity, born and bred of the unbearable smallness of the human being. The Bishop went through in his weary mind all that God had done to aid the crusade. The miracles, the many other evidences of His special consideration. And how had the people responded? With weakness and strutting vanity! With petulance and saucy indifference! With self-abuse and vicious parade! The Bishop squirmed, and for the first time in his life he found himself hating humanity.

Abominable tribe! Oh, that it might perish from the earth! For it was but a spiritless ooze of slime, an idle dropping of dung! In vain had the great breath of life from beyond descended to animate it! In vain had God nourished it with His great tender hand and motioned it into the light! In vain was a highroad laid forth at its feet! In vain was it given strength! It feels, it hears, it sees—but for all that, the flesh does not lift itself in aspiration. Oh, paltry, crawling, mewling clay which was to have risen and matured and assumed the image of God—out with it!

"Were someone to offer me a pilgrim's shelter deep within the desert, that should I prefer to a kingdom here among people!" the Bishop groaned as he tossed upon his bed. "People! They see the truth before their eyes and strain their tongues with falsehood! They live for nothing but perfidy. Soon enough will the patience of the Lord exhaust itself and His divine vengeance be visited upon mankind. The day of merciless death is drawing nigh, stalking our very homes! The moment is at hand when the Everlasting will say: 'Let them lie like grass in the field, like sheaves behind the reaper that never shall be picked!'

"But pity them not, O my soul! Pity them not! Humanity is degraded and abhorrent. With claws it clings to the muck wherein it crawls and will not be upraised. However sublime may be the helping hand, our race prefers its bed of filth—grovelling, feeding, adultering, and, snoring in uncomely sleep, breeding further sin and wretchedness. Sin is its very nature. Sin is its one expression. And sin is its sole attainment. In vain to speak to it of God. For it craves not the Divine . . . it swears by nothing which transcends the swamplands of its own banality! Even in the presence of a miracle, it is incapable of forgetting its dark, ignoble pursuits, its own small temporal gains. For a brief flash it permits itself to stand erect and sniff the clean air of inspiration, only to collapse again, and the more infamously!

"O, never to see any more people! To know nothing more of their foul affairs, of the misfortunes brought upon themselves by their own surly natures but for which in their eyes God alone is to answer! It would be better that they perished utterly!"

Thus marched the thoughts of Adhemar de Monteuil. His veins flowed bile, his tongue was wet with vinegar and aloes. Cruel, ruthless thoughts he made no effort to dispel.

He would permit no one to visit him. Only Walter the Penniless and Peter had access to his sickroom. No other man might enter. In vain did the barons crowd the corridor outside his door to inquire for his health.

Thoughts noxious and intense persecuted the sick man day and night. He reviewed the events of the world in his mind. He saw that everywhere evil was conquering good, simply because of human failure. No, it was because of human collusion, because of human *will!* The evil lay within. If Satan truly existed, the Bishop decided, his kingdom was not Hell, but the human breast—and the three-fold scepter of his power was indifference, stupidity, arrogance.

"Accursed humanity!"

He glared from his pillow as he spat forth his awesome curse. Had he been holding the stone tablets in his arms he, like Moses, would have smashed them in righteous indignation.

Exhausted by his vehemence, he lay there quietly and traced with his eyes the dark carvings on the vaulted ceiling. To his tired mind they appeared as a jumble of characters and symbols. Then, slowly as he continued to watch, they came together and arranged themselves into a text. What was this? Whose writing was that? Quite suddenly Adhemar knew these were the words of an ancient fable he had once known, but long ago forgotten: the words which the beloved writer, St. Dionysius Areopagita had inscribed for Demophile:

"... *a certain man named Karpencius had but hate for sin and sin-ners. He loved God so dearly that he could but hate all men who sinned against Him. Now it came to pass in that time that two Christians, whom God had blessed in many ways, had come to fear for their goods and so had turned from God before men and gone back to false pagan ways. Karpencius learned of their act and cursed them both for what they had done. He cursed them in the evening when the Angelus was sounding. At midnight, when the hour was dark, he roused to curse them again. And then he fell asleep and had a dream ... He saw an abyss toward which the two sinners were walking. They could see naught before them, for that their eyes were bound ... The pious Karpencius was glad to see that they would walk straight into the abyss where they would surely perish. He waited to see them fall ... Then he saw a stranger walking in haste to halt and save them. At once Karpencius cried out: "Stay! For they are but accursed sinners! The sooner they perish the better!" But the stranger paid no heed. He put forth his arm and warned them. And he had reached them barely in time, for their feet were already on the very edge of the abyss ... Karpencius was angry and raised his arm to strike the stranger. "Begone!" he cried out. "Begone, or I shall smite thee! For those are accursed sinners!" But then the stranger turned his face. And his face was full of light. And Kar-pencius saw that it was our Lord, Jesus Christ. ... When the Saviour spake, he said: "Smite so, Karpencius! For I am ready once more to die that these men may be saved."*

"God have mercy on my soul!" moaned Adhemar aloud. "For I am the truly wretched sinner!" It appeared to him that he himself had been Karpencius so justly rebuked by God. "God have mercy on my soul!" he repeated.

Later, when the Bishop awoke, he saw that it was broad daylight and that someone was standing by his bed. Walter the Penniless had come to report that he had found a physician, a Greek, who would surely cure the Bishop. The man had spent much time practising amongst the infidels but had remained in hiding, after the fall of the city, out of fear for the Latins. Walter had already fetched him. He was waiting just outside the house.

To ease his pain! To ease the mighty suffering which had been tor-

turing him for weeks! To know again sweet slumber, so long, so long un-
tasted! What an enticing promise! . . . But of what use was it to think
about it? To call in a Greek practioner would be to outrage every mind
which considered the use of Eastern drugs a sin.

"Permit me to fetch the man, your Excellency," Walter implored
persistently.

Adhemar closed his eyes the more fully to consider the matter. He
himself was positive no evil lay in the Greek methods of treatment and
that the gaining of medical knowledge through the practice of dissec-
tion was in no way sinful in the eyes of God. But the general belief ran
to the contrary. His people would accuse him of stooping to sin in order
to save his own life. Had he fought this superstition earlier and had
proven its utter baselessness, he might on this day have called in the
Greek physician. But this he had not done and he could not now begin
with himself. Who would believe in his sincerity?

"Send him away, my son!" he said.

"In the name of God, your Excellency! Think only of what will become of us with you no longer here! To remain with us, that is your
highest duty!"

"Nay, I have accomplished little in your midst. Behold the last half-
year! What has my presence meant? If God wills me to remain, He will
spare my life without a physician's hand; if He takes me, it will mean I
was not needed."

"But surely your Excellency does not think it a sin to seek a physician?"

"Surely not, my son! I am convinced no sin would lie in that."

"Then—then, your Excellency—?"

"I have told you! I must not offend against the belief of others."

"But your leaving would be a worse evil!"

"May we really say that? In self-conceit a man may think himself indispensable. Then one day he dies . . . and life flows on the same, neither better nor worse."

"What will become of us?" cried Walter in despair.

The Bishop smiled sadly. "I shall always abide with you in spirit,
Walter," he choked. "You remember my words in the desert? That the
dead may better defend Jerusalem than the living? The time has come
when I must take these words unto myself. Alive, I have been powerless.
In death, I may the more easily attract the aid of merciful God. I shall

not abandon you here. I shall gather together all those who have died on the way and shall lead them. We shall be standing at your side as you enter the walls of the Holy City. You will see me right there at your side. Only, hear me, Son, lose not your spirit! Pray, move! For the love of God, move soon!"

Walter was weeping.

The Bishop put out his hand. "Weep not, my son!" he said gently. "Just go, dismiss the physician." With his eyes, he ushered Walter from the room, recalling how but a few hours before, he had imagined himself hating people! He had cursed them—aye, as had Karpencius, whom Christ himself had rebuked. "Is it possible?" he asked himself, "really to hate people? People like Walter. Or Bartholomew? Bartholomew, who had trusted in the Lord so fully? Or Peter, who had refused to touch a morsel of Kerbogha's food?" A warm, assuaging wave of affection for people swept over him, especially for the meek and lowly, those disinherited of life who are so woefully wronged by the mighty, who live in misery and degradation and amongst whom so often bloom the fairest flowers of humanity! Oh, may God bless them! God, who knew them best and who loved them . . .

A sharp pain assailed him, piercing his flesh with the seven swords of suffering. With difficulty, he gasped for breath. The Greek physician might have deadened that pain. But this was as it should be! All that remained now was to call in the barons for the last time. To utter a deathbed entreaty that they repair their feuds and move on. Afterwards, he would yield his soul to the Lord God with the same trust with which Bartholomew had yielded himself to the flames, fearing nothing, regretting nothing.

. . . *in aeternitate Dei vigere, in veritate Dei lucere, in bonitate Dei gaudere . . .*

Adhemar's passing struck the people and their leaders a heavy blow. His wisdom had been their salvation, his virtue their crutch. He was buried in the cathedral, in the same ground from which Peter Bartholomew had taken the Holy Lance. Peter was buried outside the walls of the church, not far from his Bishop. For a while many people prayed at both graves, but soon there were only a few. Adhemar's death did not break the deadlock between Raymond and Boemund; it deepened it, in fact, for now there was no one to chide their consciences and no one to act as leader. Godfrey returned from Edessa weary and mystified. He had discovered Baldwin in a gay, forgiving mood, ruling like a king and quite willing to shake hands and forgive, since it now was obvious to him that his quarrel with Godfrey had been the means of his good fortune. Leone was dead; she had succumbed in childbirth, along with her son. Baldwin was considering the offer of a Syrian princess, ruler of a neighboring principality.

"She proposed to me!" he said to Godfrey in glee. "Now I shall be ruler of all Mesopotamia."

Godfrey said nothing, but he wondered as he prayed what terrible end would come to the crusade with its rulers succumbing along the road to temptations of power and wealth.

In Antioch, when he returned, the situation seemed permanently insoluble. The barons were indulging their interminable quarrel. To make matters worse, a horrible pestilence had broken out, and the people were dying by the hundred. This cruel foe had thus far spared the Latins; but during the present winter it had invaded their ranks and had reached even the select.

The pestilence did not abate. Zbylut fell a victim to it and lay dying in his tent. Imbram went and sat beside him, brooding about Ofka and his affair with Leah.

Zbylut, rousing from sleep, stared at his brother.

"Water?" said Imbram.

"Not from you," Zbylut answered.

Imbram leaned forward and peered in his brother's face. "Tell me, Zbylut," he asked, "why do you hate me so?"

"You don't know?"—the sick man seemed aghast and opened wide his eyes. Set in so sunken a face, those eyes appeared grotesquely large. "You mean—you don't know?" he repeated.

"Would I ask you if I knew?"

"You know not that I loved—Ofka?"

"Ofka? You loved her? You?"

"And I love her now and always. And she chose you! You whelp! You who betrayed her with a strumpet! You good-for-nothing changeling! Cheat!" He glared with flaming eyes.

Imbram ignored these insults, overwhelmed as he was by this revelation. Not until the very end had his brother given himself away! No one would ever have suspected the truth! How could he have lived so close to this man without ever having known his heart? As he brooded, trifling incidents, words which had hitherto sounded utterly innocent but which now had taken on a deeper significance, kept flashing into his mind as evidence of the sincerity of Zbylut's unexpected confession. Beneath the weight of complex emotion, Imbram bowed his head. Zbylut's words had revived in his mind a clear picture of his beloved—an image which had grown all too tenuous of late. He saw her again as though she were standing before him—her flaxen tresses, her airy nymph-like figure.

"You loved Ofka . . ." he repeated, not knowing what else to say.

The circumstances surrounding the betrayal of his wife—until a moment ago submerged in his memory—now rose to occupy his mind in a light so glaring that he groaned in pain and covered his eyes. Oh, never in this world might Zbylut know how profoundly guilty his brother had really been! Merely to sleep with another woman—almost any man did that, and no husband was likely to attach much weight to such a breach of faith! But what had Imbram done? He had allowed the wench to cast a spell upon his wife, had stood idly by while the weird harlot, Leah, was uttering strange incantations and practising secret rites aimed at harming Ofka, his woman, the mother of his acknowledged son. In permitting that had lain his vilest guilt! Although Zbylut would never know of that, Imbram lowered his eyes. How ever could he have sunk so low?

"I will see her! I will tell her!" The words were rattling in Zbylut's throat.

"You would frighten her thus?" asked Imbram, suddenly alarmed.

"I will rap on the walls. I will whisper in the rafters. The dogs will howl when I come. I will enter her chamber," the half-conscious Zbylut was gurgling.

"Don't you dare!" shouted Imbram in despair.

Zbylut twisted his mouth venomously. "You forbid me?"

"I forbid you!"

"I wonder how!"

"I beg you, entreat you, Brother!" Imbram dropped to his knees and attempted to kiss the hand of the sick man.

"Away with you!" Zbylut croaked. "Get out! Now she is mine . . .

mine!" He was silenced by a fit of hiccoughing. His eyes were staring wildly, but a moment later they rolled back, his mouth fell open and he was silent.

Imbram rose heavily without a word, overwhelmed with a feeling of helplessness and despair. There was no meaning to him in all of Momot's accusing chatter, his fussing and fuming about the details of decent burial. The Zavoras could dress the corpse, could do with it as they liked. The body of Zbylut was offal to be disposed of. What remained was a baleful ghost, a spectre condemned for three days to linger near the rotting flesh. After that, it was free to wander wherever it wished, wherever the dying thought had directed. What could Momot and his less voluble brother, Yashek, know of the dreadful relationship which now existed between that ghost and Imbram, of the pain and anguish, which now were tearing at Imbram's breast? What victory could strangers discern in the glassy stare of the corpse? Enough that Momot and ' his brother might perceive the outward effects of the shock he had suffered and themselves undertake what earthly details now demanded execution.

Not until the heavy iron-bound door of the burial vault had been securely fastened in place and blocked with stones did Imbram experience a sense of relief. His peace of mind was of short duration, however, and before evening came his anguish had returned. For what did a pile of stones mean to a ghost which could penetrate any wall? Nothing could stay a spectre. When, late that night, Imbram was sitting by himself, it seemed to him that his brother was standing there close behind him, laughing sarcastically as he had done while still alive. He attempted to pray. But prayer refused to flow from his lips into his heart.

Suddenly a wave of red hatred—at odds with his gentle nature—swept into his heart and carried him away. His own subconscious sense of guilt appeared to give it force. For had not he, Imbram, permitted a foul spell to be cast upon Ofka, no spectre might now approach her. He himself had permitted a marriage tie, fashioned before Christ's altar, to be severed by a harlot's lewd sorcery. He himself had helped to consign to perdition the flaxen-haired bride who loved him, who had believed in him and who had been loyally awaiting his return! Unable to fall asleep, he continued thus to torture himself, addressing first his brother, then himself. Was there no defense against the dead?

He pondered the problem long and earnestly, and at length the method occurred to him. An ancient method it was, but one said to be infallible. Without hesitation, he rose from his couch and tiptoed out, careful lest he arouse Sobek, asleep in the adjoining room.

Even so, the watchful lad heard his footsteps and raised his sleepy head. "My Lord?"

"Go to sleep!" murmured Imbram. "I have no need for you."

Hearing the lad dive back under the covers, Imbram stepped out into the night and felt his way forward to a clump of trees. There he drew his misericorde and cut away one of the lower branches. From this he fashioned a short, pointed peg, shaped like the tooth of a rake. Concealing the peg in his bosom, he slipped back to the house, and, stealthily as a thief, tiptoed down the stairs to the vault wherein Zbylut's body lay. On one of the stones a small oil lamp, left there by Momot, was burning.

"Since he had to die without light, let this lighten him now!" Momot had said.

Imbram began removing the stones which blocked the entrance to the vault. Utter silence was necessary, lest he awaken those who were sleeping above. It would be a terrible thing were someone suddenly to come upon him here! The stones, taken from a nearby ruin, were smudged with soot and charred wood, and before Imbram was finished with his task, he was as black as the god of thunder.

At length, he had the door free. Taking the lamp in his hand, he eased open the door and entered the vault. He was at once met by Zbylut's pitiless stare, that same mocking leer, from beneath the half-closed lids which poor Momot had unsuccessfully tried to force shut. Imbram recoiled in panic as he saw how turbidly the light from the lamp was reflected from the glazed pupils of the dead man. For a moment, he was beside himself and was on the point of flight. He took himself forcibly in hand, however, and stood firm. The task he had to perform was inescapable, were he to save Ofka. If only because he had failed to restrain Leah, he now must lay a ghost.

He set the lamp on the ground and drew the peg from his tunic. Thrice he crossed himself, each time spitting in four directions: before, behind, to the right, to the left. Then he blessed the peg. Bending over the corpse, he unfastened Zbylut's tunic and laid bare the yellowed chest, already beginning to show signs of decay. He raised his arm to strike. Now. Now!

Was his brother's ghost lurking there within this dead and putrid flesh? Watching every motion through half-closed lids? Ready to seize its slayer in a foul embrace, which would hold him there in the vault forever? Watching? Waiting? Again Imbram felt that he must flee. His teeth were chattering, every hair on his body had stiffened. But run away he would not! Closing his eyes with desperate determination, he raised his hand and struck. The puffy flesh offered no resistance to the smartly driven peg.

Leaving the stake imbedded in the dead heart, Imbram drew back and crossed himself. Sweat was pouring from his face. His knees were bending under him. He was unable to take a step. Not for some time was he able to master himself sufficiently to start for the door. Before leaving the vault, he raised the lamp in his hand and paused to cast a triumphant glance at his brother. "So! Now you will stay here where you belong!" he grated through his teeth.

Slowly and laboriously—for his hands were limp and weak—he replaced the stones in front of the door. At length he managed to finish the task. Leaving the lamp where he had found it, he tiptoed up the stairs.

Daylight was already breaking when he entered his room.

Not all the sick were suffering from the same plague. A new disease had struck, a subtle commentary on the pride of the Latins in their virtue. Some of the men who had lain with pagan women broke out with ugly sores. One of them was Omer de Guillebaut, who had slain his wife. Another was Swennon, the husband of Florine.

"It is a thrust of Lucifer, placed where it will do the most good," said Swennon's confessor. "We have succumbed to the thing we came to conquer. How did you happen to commit this sin?"

"I am held to a foolish vow," said Swennon. "My wife will not take me for husband until we reach Jerusalem. Now we remain in Antioch while the barons argue. Is a man to blame for his nature?"

"What will you say to your wife?" asked the priest.

"I will not tell her," said Swennon. "I will not see her again. I have no more interest in life, no more faith in God. I shall die here, dreaming of Denmark, which I should not have left."

Florine, when she was barred from Swennon's quarters, went weeping to the Lady Elvira.

"He is ill and he will not see me," she cried. "I want to nurse him, to stay with him, but I am not allowed even to speak with him. Why does he behave this way? What has happened? Does he no longer love me?"

Elvira took her in her arms. "There, there, child," she whispered.

Spring came, and the army seemed destined to rest forever in Antioch. Since the Bishop's death, the council of the chiefs had degenerated into a general wrangle of irresponsible minds. Each meeting was now little more than an obscene brawl wherein everyone shouted down everyone else in an atmosphere of rattling words, threats and counter-threats, marching heels, and slamming doors.

Meanwhile, the discontent of the people at large was mounting. Folk wanted to leave the plague-ridden city of Antioch, to move on to Jerusalem, to realize the holy purpose of the crusade. Hugh of Vermandois had left for Rome with a report of the Bishop's passing and an urgent request that His Holiness the Pope appoint a new leader. But Hugh would be gone for months, perhaps a year, and the people were losing all patience.

About their campfires at night, squires and serving folk, fighting men and camp followers were discussing the whole dark problem besetting them. The growl in their voices was unmistakable.

"More than three hundred caught their death in our camp but yesterday!"

"Another two moons in this place and there won't nobody be left alive! It's like I say!"

"We'll all catch our death of the pest, you'll see! And the Princes? What about them? They're fit and will stay fit to the end of our days! Those bastards will set here feuding till we're all gone, now mark me! Poor devils that we are, there's no way out of it! High-born, low-born, it's like I always say!"

"No way out of it? That's where you're wrong! They have their high-born ways, their talk! But as for us, we have ourselves, our weapons. And who is there the more of, the high-born or the low?"

"It's like I always said, there's more of us!"

Such were the words flung out at every campfire. Such were the words picked up by the sharp ears of Walter the Penniless as he strolled about of a night alone. Here spoke the blustering Klimek, there the limping Martin, farther on the cross-eyed Gilbert. And at length, when the general complaint gave voice to a common will, there stood Walter with his towering hulk and the great venom that was in him to lead these people against their masters . . .

That night, while the barons were screaming at each other in council, a din of bells arose outside in the city. Some mighty alarm was sounding. And the cause was not far to behold: blackness no longer stood pressing against the window; a blood-red glow had invaded the night, and the sky was blooming with fire.

"In Christ's name, what is this?" cried Raymond. "Can the enemy have broached our gates? To arms, Toulouse! Provence! To arms!"

"Normandy! To arms! To arms, Tarentum! Amalfi! . . ."

But outside in the Cathedral square, there was no response to the cries of the excited barons. Where were the people—squires, grooms and men at arms? . . . Against bright backgrounds of flame, dark figures were darting hither and yon with torches. Wherever they paused, a fresh fire was born. What was happening? Who were these firebrands?

Obviously the enemy had taken the gates by surprise, had rushed in and slain the guards and servants and were now destroying the city.

"Where are our people? Where are they?" shouted the helpless knights.

The fire roared over the city, shaking its flaming mane. From the thickets of the river marshes, awakened birds were darting aloft with shrill cries and were madly circling the city. The black of the river was mirroring the mounting glow. Terrified horses screamed as houses, surfeited with flame, fell crashing to the ground in a shower of sparks . . .

And then at length it was clear to the barons what was afoot. Dark figures, armed with torches, axes, bars, and other paraphernalia, came darting into the square to form a solid phalanx. And at their head towered the figure of Walter the Penniless.

"You bastard!" shouted Raymond. "You dung-tailed hind! What is the meaning of this! What are you doing here?"

Walter laughed scornfully. "What are we doing here? See for yourselves, good sirs! We are burning the city! We are destroying this bone of contention, this pest hole of yours! The people have acted to end the tragedy of Antioch. The crusade must move on to Jerusalem!"

"On to Jerusalem!" A mighty cry arose from the multitude assembled there in the square, a massed shout which drowned out even the roaring of the flames. "On to Jerusalem! Down with the nobles! On to the Grave of Our Lord!"

For the first time within the memory of any man present, the people had united against their masters. They stood there staring insolently at the barons and watching the flames with calculating eyes. The common man had discovered a powerful weapon within his grasp. He had found also the courage to use it, and the victory gained this night of holocaust was his and his alone . . .

Saving face as best they could, the nobles resolved their personal quarrels and yielded to the will of the people. In the light of the dying fires forgotten oaths were reaffirmed, new pledges taken, tears of humble piety shed. With drawn sword, Raymond St. Gilles recognized a sign from heaven; with drawn sword, he pledged himself to equip the holy expedition with all possible dispatch and to lead it in person south to Jerusalem, where the Holy Sepulcher yearned for liberation.

Amid the ruins of half a city, now left in the sovereign care of Boemund, a bustle of activity supplanted all former indolence. St. Gilles, as determined as he had been in the past to remain as watch dog over the sly actions of the Duke, was now equally determined to move on as quickly as possible. He was in all ways a zealous leader, and the Lady Elvira was proud of him.

And at length the host departed from Antioch and set forth on the road to Jerusalem. Of the original three hundred thousand crusaders, a bare forty thousand now remained to redeem the Holy City. The dust of the road rose over them as they passed through the gates of Antioch and trailed out onto the plain.

Boemund stood watching the departure from a post atop the city wall. His heart was not for this shabby host; reserved it was for the stunning youth who in a moment or two would be passing directly below. Tancred! Bereft of his own retinue and only a common hireling of Godfrey now, he was still no less a nobleman for all that. How gallantly he sat his horse! How proudly he held his youthful head! He had declined the princely offerings of his uncle held out as an inducement for him to remain with him in Antioch. True to the crusade, he had preferred the march to Jerusalem in liege to Bouillon and now was riding forth.

The Duke touched his fingers to his lips and threw a gentle kiss. "Farewell, boy!" he shouted. "Farewell and a safe return!"

Tancred could but turn in his saddle and salute with outstretched arm.

Boemund did not know why his eyes should have so suddenly misted over, but there was something akin to comfort in his heart as he wiped the strange moisture away and descended into the city . . .

Departing from the scene of their misery and dimly recalling past miracles, the crusaders sang a little. But they had almost forgotten the feeling of hope, and prayer sat better on their lips than song.

The year was 1099, and once again it was spring . . .

41.

Jerusalem! Jerusalem!

SOUTH ALONG THE ORONTES, THROUGH TERRITORIES ALREADY SUBDUED, THE advance proceeded without obstacle, save for problems of forage. During the past year, while the main host had stood idle in Antioch, smaller forces led by some of the more enterprising knights had undertaken frequent forays to east and to south and had swept the country clean.

South of Laodicea the situation improved. The route there chosen followed the line of the coast through an earthly paradise of orange and pomegranate groves, of fig and date and olive, of lush grasses and grazing herds, of fresh meat and bulging storehouses.

Ignoring the torrid May sun, the men of the Cross marched on through Tortosa, giving thanks that their chiefs had chosen the coast road, as the shortest route to Jerusalem, in preference to the Sultan's highway through Damascus or the road through the highlands of Lebanon. The Count St. Gilles had been advised by native Christians against taking the shore road, because of the lurking danger at the narrow passes where a small Moslem force would be in a position to deliver a crushing blow from ambush, but he had spurned the advice of his Syrian well-wishers, his sole concern being to reach Jerusalem as soon as possible.

They marched through Tyre and Beirut where an occasional snowy peak pierced the sky. It was in these parts, where off to the left a small enemy force appeared in the distance and vanished without seeking encounter. And it was along this road they learned from wayfarers that the Moslems were massing in Jerusalem.

Passing through Joppa, they turned inland and made for Antipatris. As they drew away from the sea, the pleasant, fertile landscape of the littoral faded into one of gloomy, sullen waste. Ahead loomed the hills of Judah, unblessed by any forest growth or even the slightest sign of bird or animal life. Here and there a sparse grove of small gray olive trees clung frantically to patches of harsh soil. Higher up, the hills were cluttered with rocky debris, with boulders and slabs precariously poised and ready to plunge at a touch. Jutting ledges cast grotesque shadows on the wretched settlements clinging to hillsides below . . . Whoever might have dwelt in these settlements, whether Christian or infidel, had fled at the sight of the advancing host.

On through Lydda they passed, on through the mountains to Ramlah, where they paused to liberate what was said to be the tomb of St. George, the knightly martyr, their patron saint.

Summer was nigh. The sun was beating down unmercifully, parching man and beast, together with the earth on which they trod. Horses dropped with the heat, and many a knight had to struggle to keep from swooning. The riders had covered their heads and shoulders with long strips of white material, looted from Antioch, so that from a distance it was difficult to tell whether they were men of the Cross or Moslems. The rank and file had exchanged their heavier garments for the lightest summer dress and resembled pilgrims, indeed.

The way was exceedingly difficult, leading over mountains, through parched valleys, across dry stream beds whose rocks were whitened and powdered by the heat. In one place it led through a narrow defile, flanked by loose and jutting ledges; the knights looked up at those overhanging slabs which seemed to teeter as they passed and recalled the warnings of the Maronites. Was not this the very spot where an ambush would be most likely to succeed? The chiefs admitted to themselves that had the infidels been lying in wait for them here, this very gorge would have become the grave of the crusade. But they were passing through safely! God was watching over them!

At length they encountered a procession of Syrian Christians who had come forth from Jerusalem to greet their liberators. Persecuted by the Moslems, they had been awaiting the crusaders for two long years. As time passed, they had begun to doubt; of late they had abandoned all hope. But now that the moment of liberation had arrived, they were unable to stem their tears of joy and thanksgiving.

"How far is it to Jerusalem?" the knights inquired feverishly.

"Not more than ten miles . . ."

Ten miles! Not more than ten miles! Their own joy was now well nigh uncontrollable, although tempered with consternation. They could hardly believe that it was possible that they were so near their final goal. How many years had they now been marching toward Jerusalem, with their goal always receding, ayways remote and unattainable! Like death, it had seemed to them somehow unreal,—certain, yet inconceivable. And now it was only ten miles!

"If only the Bishop could be here with us now!" a voice said feelingly.

"The Bishop said that he would stand with us before the walls!" said Peter the Hermit.

Peter had revived during the past year, had regained his health and stood forth a new man. In the course of that unforgettable moment, whilst serving as envoy to Kerbogha, he had recovered his most precious possession, his self-respect, and that had saved him. From an insane half-wit, the laughing stock of all, he had become a man again. Now he had been called to ride with the nobles, for was he not the only one in the entire host who had seen the Holy City? He knew this rocky desert, these forbidding, outflung ledges. With burning eyes he gave directions and mentioned points of interest. He explained to his companions that behind them to the north lay Galilee, that these mountains off to the left were beyond Jordan and that Bethlehem lay in *that* direction. The knights listened greedily and crossed themselves each time he mentioned a particularly holy place.

Thus they marched on, without halting for food or rest the whole day. They watered their horses without dismounting and they themselves thought not of meat or drink, hoping to reach the mountain overlooking the city before nightfall.

Despite their frantic effort, however, dusk overtook them in a valley, not far from what looked like a settlement.

"That is Emmaus!" declared Peter.

Emmaus! At last they had come upon pathways where Christ Himself had walked. These very stones had been sanctified by His holy sandal.

"Let us vow to build a church here!" said Godfrey solemnly. "On the site of our last bivouac!"

The moon was full and the whole valley was washed with silken light when the knights entered their pavilions to seek their last rest before they entered Jerusalem. But no man could sleep! The magic of the moonlight night, the pounding of their hearts on the eve of such a

day, made an impossible fugitive of sleep. They sought each other's
company and talked the night away. They recalled those days four years
ago when they had gathered in Toulouse to discuss the approaching
journey. There had been a night very much like this—a night of moonlight and enchanted dreams—a night of sleepless excitement. They
smiled indulgently as they recalled how they had judged the distance
between Byzantium and Jerusalem as approximating that between
Paris and Metz. Oh, how their conceptions had changed, not only re-
garding distances, but everything. In a hundred years, or even two
hundred years, their forefathers could never have hoped to learn as
much as they had learned in these last four, during which they had
learned how great and wonderful the world truly was. And they also
recalled with the same smile of indulgence how they once had judged
that Jerusalem could resemble no other city in the world, that its walls
would glow like the setting sun and glitter like a diadem in changing
colors, like the rainbow gleam of a peacock's fan, that a wonderful
breath would rush through the air to scatter a refreshing fragrance. But
since then, a sense of reality had crowded out boyish dreams, and they
no longer looked forward to any such miracles. Their enthusiasm had
not suffered for all of that; for, as men who had experienced all, they
realized that the thing they were seeking lay not in color and fragrance.

Now they fell to discussing the details they had learned from fleeing
Christians concerning the Moslem's preparations to defend the Holy
City. Ostoy had reported to them that the garrison at Jerusalem was
commanded by the Emir Iftikar-al-Davla, that he had already collected
more than forty thousand men, that new forces were daily pouring into
the city to join his standard, and that the emir had amassed provisions
and supplies sufficient to resist a siege of a year or more.

"They say he has raised the inner walls ten ells in height," Ostoya
reported.

"Let them raise them to the clouds, and still we shall mount them!"
came the instant reply, to which there was general assent.

The conversation was interrupted by the sound of excited voices outside. Something exceedingly strange and mysterious was happening. The
barons noticed at once that the moonlight, previously so bright, was
now curiously smoky.

"See there! See there! See the moon!" their servants shouted.

Although the heavens were still cloudless, it seemed that some in-

visible curtain was being drawn gradually across the face of the moon.
The entire camp had been aroused and a great buzz of voices rose.
Knights and soldiers threw back their heads to gaze at the sky in alarm,
and all could see that a shadowy disc was crawling slowly across the
moon's bright shield, in the end obscuring it completely. The night
seemed ghostly gray and breathless. It was as though the sky had suddenly died, and the world itself stood afraid. The buzzing of voices
abated and those who had cried aloud before fell silent and were ap-
palled . . . Stillness, utter silence . . . Then the squeal of one panic-
stricken horse.

The silence was then further broken by the voice of Raymond St.
Gilles, their leader, who thundered: "Christians! Fear not! You behold a
divine miracle! You have witnessed the twilight of the pagan moon! It
will melt and disappear forever from this earth. God wills it!"

"God wills it!" A chorus of voices arose. "God wills it!"

Then the obscuring disc moved slowly on, uncovering first one sickle
edge of the moon, then slipping softly away to leave its silvery face
clear, and the night was bright again.

No one now had the patience to wait until morning and, without
waiting for the dawn, the knights quickly mounted and rode off through
the pearly dusk. To the right, they passed the tomb of the Maccabees;
despite the explanations of Peter and the Canon d'Aguilers, they ignored
it completely. Equally unimpressed they were when they passed between
the two mountains whereon the Israelites and Philistines had camped;
nor did they so much as pause when clattering across the stream from
which, as Peter told them, David had picked up five stones with which
he had slain Goliath. Such things mattered nothing to them in the light
of their present devotion, their impatience to deliver their Lord. Swiftly
they charged up the last slope with the dawning day behind them, the
first bright javelins of the sun already launched.

At the summit they halted abruptly and stood there in speechless silence. Dismounting, they could but crowd together and stare. When all
had arrived, they covered the crest of the hill like a thicket of trees.
Then suddenly, as though by silent command, they all knelt and gazed
intently. The valley was lost in violet shadow, but the mountain beyond
was bathed in light, and in the shadow lay the City.

No shimmer of precious stones here met their gaze, no gleam of
marble. A small and shabby town lay before them, a small and wretched

cluster of cupolas and towers and gray stone dwellings which seemed but thrown together, like the piles of rocky debris at the foot of its walls. Compared to the splendors of Byzantium and Nicaea and Antioch, it seemed not to exist at all.

As they knelt and gazed at the Holy City, tears came to their eyes, and men wept without knowing whether it was for joy or for sorrow, or for something which still lay beyond. The knights bowed their heads and kissed the earth with humility and, seeing this, the common folk, perhaps for the first time in their lives, regarded their masters without bitterness or ill-will. An emotion of indescribable joy had enveloped all, an emotion not to be compared to any other they had ever experienced, a divine release, a happiness exceeding all bounds.

The sun was now high and hot. Peter the Hermit, surrounded by an audience, was lecturing to the Canon d'Aguilers, who was jotting down each word that was spoken as fast as he could scribble. "That barren hill off there is Mount Moriah on which stood Solomon's temple, later Herod's. The cupola you see there is part of an infidel mosque. To the right is Mount Zion, and those other small cupolas are the chapels of the Holy Cross and of—the Holy Sepulcher!"

"God have mercy on us!"

With the assurance of an experienced traveler, Peter turned full about and continued his description. That gray rocky slope, darkened by an olive grove, its only spot of green, was the Garden of Gethsemane. On those grey rocks had fallen the bloody sweat of Our Saviour; those same trees had shaded His saintly Head. The narrow valley below, separating the city from the Mount of Olives and cut lengthwise by a dry stream, was the Valley of Jehosephat, the stream bed marking the course of the brook called Cedron.

"The Valley of Jehosephat! Where? Where? Show us!" people cried, marveling how narrow and small it was. How ever would all the people be able to crowd into it on Judgment Day? Where would they all stand?

"God will miraculously widen it," the Canon reassured them, continuing his busy scribbling.

Beyond the city lay the mountainous wilderness where Jesus had conquered temptation, and close by it was the Pool of Siloam. That building off there was the praetorium of Pontius Pilate, where the trial of Jesus had taken place. Between those closely crowded houses, those houses

which resembled but wildly jumbled heaps of stone, wound the Road of
the Cross, from here invisible—the *Via Dolorosa* . . .

Via Dolorosa! How well they knew what that sad way meant; for had
they not already traveled their own Road of the Cross, their own woeful
Calvary, before arriving here at the Feet of God.

Their tears were still flowing on unchecked, their knees were still bent,
when suddenly through the clear morning air came a high-pitched
tuneful song from the city, a chant only too well known to them, the
voice of the muezzin calling all the followers of Mohammed to prayer.
To those kneeling there on the slope, it came as a note of savage discord,
as one which blasphemed against the sacredness of their present mood.

A terrible anger awakened in them, the kind of anger which had
once moved the ancient prophets. It clutched them, tore at them, set
their mighty breasts aflame. Without pausing, just as they stood, forgetful of yesterday's all-day march without halt and the sleepless night
which followed, they hurled themselves together and descended the
slope in a rushing wave which would beat upon the city. The force of
their impetuous assault would shatter every obstacle which might rise
to stand in their way.

"My brothers!" shouted Raymond St. Gilles. "Tonight in the city the
Angelus will be heard—not the prayers of infidel dogs!"

An answering roar greeted his words: "God wills it! God sees us!
God watches! Forward! God wills it! Now!"

Transported by emotion, overcome by a holy madness, strengthened
by an unshakable certitude, they raced down the hill at breakneck speed,
brandishing their swords as they ran. They swooped down into the
valley like vultures, stumbling over the rocks, surging across the dry
bed of the Cedron with the fury of a hurricane, with the heedlessness of
an ocean wave, scrambling up the opposite slope, on toward the walls,
toward the gates. They would break down those gates with their bodies,
chop them to slivers with their swords. It seemed that in their madness
they would bite down the walls with their teeth. They stood upon each
other's shoulders. Whole ranks bent forward that others might climb
upon their backs. Others scrambled upon these, until they were piled
three, even four high. Some men were hurling ropes, while still others
attacked the gates.

The defenders, however, were not idle, and soon a mounting bank of corpses served as a first step aloft for the attackers; for the sudden assault found the Moslems well prepared for defense. They loosed on the frantic crusaders a steady hail of missiles—rocks, javelins, arrows, boiling water, hot tar, and Greek Fire.

But nothing could stay the fury of the men below. Their courage was of a sort never known to any of them before. The newly found strength of each man was incalculable; it was as though he had multiplied himself by ten, or a dozen, or more. Despite the frenzied opposition of the enemy, four knights were actually successful in scaling those terrific walls. They fell immediately, cut to pieces, but at least they had the satisfaction of saying with their dying breaths that they had been the first to enter Jerusalem.

For three, four and at length, five hours, the crusaders continued their assault. But in the end they were forced to withdraw. So many of them had fallen that their dead would have completely filled the Valley of Jehosephat. The survivors, at the end of their resistance to thirst and hunger and fatigue, retired from the wall in a daze.

When men recovered themselves sufficiently to think, they became desperately conscious of their bitter disappointment. The Angelus would not sound in the city that night; already a muezzin was hastening to call his faithful to prayer.

Why had God permitted this? they asked themselves. Why had He forsaken the crusaders?

Aloft on the very hilltops where they had experienced their unforgettable exaltation of the early morning hour, night descended upon them, a night of inconceivable woe, the worst these men had ever spent. Into their burnt-out hearts, seeped the bitter realization that they had made the long journey hence but to meet defeat, unexpected, incredible defeat. There in the Garden of Gethsemane their hearts had been mortally wounded and were slowly bleeding to death.

Only man is capable of such extremes of feeling within so comparatively short a time: from the heights of faith and hope to the depths of blasphemy and despair from dawn to dusk. Indeed, some of those who had fought had become so dismayed that had anyone but flung out the slogan: "Save yourselves who can! To Joppa! To the ships of the Genoese!" they would have taken to their heels. God had misled and forsaken them, they mumbled; He had failed to respond to their glorious enthusiasm. They had kissed the earth with pious joy, had scrambled on the walls unmindful of death; they had lost more than five thousand of their comrades, and yet had been repulsed.

The knights, lying on the ground wherever they had dropped with fatigue, were suffering the torments of the damned. Had the Moslems but emerged from the city and taken the Latins by surprise, not a hand would have been raised to oppose them. The unconquerable Franks would have fled like sheep. Indeed, it was fortunate that the Moslems did not suspect the depths of despair to which these men of the cross had sunk. The reckless courage they had displayed, their attack repulsed with such difficulty, had inspired the Moslems with a healthy respect for their enemy. He spake the truth who said that the Franks had Satan at their service.

Daylight restored a certain measure of confidence to the Christian host. They began to view what had happened with greater calm and realism. "We struck like children," declared Robert of Flanders when the council met, "and like children were we chased away. It's not God's fault, but our own."

Slowly their minds became calmer. To be sure, they still mourned the fallen, still raged against the infidel, but no longer were they so ready to blaspheme. Now they realized that, before all else, they would have to set up a proper encampment, secure it against assault, and undertake an effective siege.

This siege would be more difficult to carry out than earlier ones, owing to the city's peculiar situation. Jerusalem was built upon three hilltops which sloped sharply into the valley. Because of this, the walls seemed even higher than they were, and the approach to them was rugged. Only on the east flank of the city was there a field broad enough for the deployment of a sizable force and the rolling up of siege towers, but even there the deep moat would first have to be filled in.

The walls of the city were amazingly high and thick. Only now, as the knights studied them calmly, could they fully appreciate the madness of their premature attempt to surmount them without ladders and towers. These walls had grown by stages during succeeding epochs, from the time of David or Solomon, or perhaps even earlier; they had been repaired and heightened by the Romans, and finally, foreseeing the assault of the Franks, the Arabs had raised the walls by another ten ells at least. Gazing at those sheer faces, the crusaders recalled that twice already had they constructed siege towers, both times unnecessarily and at great cost of time and effort. Those built at Nicaea they had had to leave to the Greeks, whereas at Antioch they had had to burn their towers at the approach of Kerbogha. Fortunately, the work would go quickly this time, the carpenters being considerably more experienced. But, indeed, what good did their experience do them, when there was no wood? In that gloomy, inhospitable land of Judea, trees simply did not grow. Here and there were sycamores and olives—as in the Garden of Gethsemane—but these were gnarled and stunted and good for nothing. The natives had learned long ago to manage without wood; their homes were all of stone; dry manure served as fuel. For yokes and furniture and other necessities, they had to go as far away as Galilee where wood was abundant and where the settlements, especially Nazareth, were famed for their skilled carpenters and joiners. No wood, no water, no forage, soon the crusaders would be short of even daily bread. In truth, never had a siege been undertaken under such inauspicious conditions.

Almost at once the Moslems succeeded in poisoning all but one of the wells that surrounded the city, and hundreds died in agony, among them Momot Zavora. With this savage affliction upon them, few men retained their courage. Only Raymond St. Gilles preserved a stout heart, and it was at his command that a party under Godfrey succeeded in making its way to Jordan and returning with water for the suffering host.

42.

The Pirate's Gift

THE COUNCIL HAD DECIDED TO SEND MOST OF THE HORSES TO JERICHO
There the animals would have sufficient water and pasture. At the camp were left only the camels, which in long trains were continually shuffling the long way over the mountains to Jericho to fetch food and water in leather bags. The water thus delivered could only prove insufficient, and the general suffering from the heat was intensified by thirst.

As June neared its end, the heat increased. Never before had the crusaders experienced a sun so inexorable, so ominous as it burned mercilessly down upon them. It would bound from the mountains at dawn and resume, without a moment's delay, its murderous attack of the day before. And there was nowhere that a man might hide from it.

Swarms of flies, impossible to chase away, fed upon them; filth, which they had no means of cleansing, had accumulated upon their bodies. The siege was utterly static. They were no nearer the moment of assault than they had been weeks before. There was no wood for the siege towers and the other necessary engines of war. They prayed for wood as they were praying for rain or for a new spring to burst from the earth. But there was no forest, and it was necessary to send all the way to Galilee for building material.

A fair-sized expedition commanded by Tancred and Robert Curthose was dispatched with a number of horses and wagon frames for that purpose. The men afoot muttered unhappily as they trudged off and cried, "To the dogs with such work!" They complained that their number was all too few; there would not be enough of them to cut all the needed wood at one time, and several trips forth and back would be necessary. Was it sensible to lose all that time?

The Count St. Gilles stoutly maintained, however, that no larger group could be spared, and the Chaplain Arnuld convinced Robert of the wisdom of such a decision. Raymond was right, he insisted, for any serious depletion of the siege forces would invite a crushing Moslem attack. The enemy, perceiving the dire straits of the crusaders, were already becoming bold. They would stand in groups on the walls and call out in Arabic, Syriac, and even Greek, all manner of words highly uncomplimentary to the Latins. They would scoff and jeer and would make a great show of spraying each other with water, as though to prove that they themselves had more of the precious element than they needed.

The Latins, perishing of thirst, would grit their teeth at the sight. Their own helplessness was devouring them. After their first bitter experience, they made no further attempt to take the walls with their bare hands. Their rancor grew as they patiently waited for wood. It was bitter to recall that, after the defeat of Kerbogha, Jerusalem had for months remained entirely without garrison, and that, had the crusade moved south immediately, the city might have been taken without a struggle. They preferred not to think of that lost opportunity; instead, they devoted themselves to coddling their hatred of the Moslems. The very sight of them, chattering like magpies atop the walls, uttering their foul mockeries and sneering at the plight of the crusaders, was driving the knights to distraction. Here was no armed opponent, possessed of admirable bravery and fighting ability, but a nagging personification of Satan himself. And the hatred in the Latins' hearts swelled until it passed all human bounds; it became a mad obsession, a mania, a morbid disease of the mind. The seeds of this hatred had been sown at Nicaea, and by now it had become a full harvest of emotion. Even the more pious souls were today thinking less of the Holy Sepulcher than they were of at last getting the infidels into their clutches in order that they might stamp on their throats and crush out their breath! And it was of the foulest of revenge that these men of the Cross dreamed night and day.

"What a country!" complained Robert Curthose, riding along beside Tancred at the head of their crew. "Not a soul anywhere about! What happened, did the pagans kill off all the people, or are they all hiding somewhere off in the mountains? There are houses enough but not one of them seems to be occupied!"

"A man cannot say to look at them, whether these dwellings were abandoned yesterday or a century ago," sighed Tancred. "It would not be pleasant to dwell in such a desert!"

"It would be perfectly hellish! Could not our Lord have chosen a better place to live in, since He had the whole world before him?"

"It is not our right to judge!" said Tancred.

"Hush," said Robert, reining in his horse. "I think I hear someone coming our way!"

"More than one—I hear them."

"Thank God there is still something left to remind a man what his sword is for!"

"Armed horsemen are ahead, riding in our direction!" shouted Sebastian de Monte Scabioso, galloping up to Tancred.

"We have heard them, too . . . Here, you!" he called to his squire. "Pass me my shield! The moment they appear we shall attack!"

The knights stood there in silence, their reins held taut in their hands, their lances at the ready.

The strangers were drawing near but were still obscured from view by a curve in the gorge, through which the road passed. At length, they emerged from behind the jutting wall . . .

"Normandy! Amalfi! Forward! God wills it!" the waiting knights shouted, as they began charging forward at full gallop.

"God wills it!" came an answering shout from the strangers.

Before the two groups met, all horses were brought to a rearing halt, but not until the last moment did any of the knights raise his lance.

"Ours!" cried Robert. "Ours! Welcome! From whence has God sent you?"

The newcomers, however—although they too had reined up—did not return the greeting. Still distrustful, they continued to point their lances defensively.

"Look you, it's Stephen!" Robert cried incredulously. "Stephen! Don't you recognize me?"

The Count de Blois who, together with a youthful knight resembling Paul Engelram, was heading a cavalcade, shook his head uncertainly. "In the name of God, who are you?" he asked.

The Duke of Normandy shook in his saddle with laughter. "Stop pretending!" he chuckled. "Don't you know Tancred? Don't you know me?"

"Is that you, Robert?" asked Stephen suspiciously, but edging closer.

"Who else could it be? We are live Christians, not spectres!"

"Forgive me!" the Count de Blois apologized. "But it's hard to tell—"

Although he did not finish, Tancred and Robert nodded their heads understandingly, for they had suddenly realized that to Stephen and his fresh and neatly groomed company their own appearance must have appeared outlandish indeed. From beneath their helmets, which everyone wore for protection from the sun, flowed a width of material on the order of an Arabian *kouffie*. Their beards, unshaven for many months, had grown halfway to their chests. Their eyes were as red as a rabbit's, their cheeks black and emaciated, their garments faded and worn, and, from a distance, it was not easy to tell whether they were knights or pagan bandits.

"We are on our way to Galilee from Jerusalem in order to fell timber for siege towers," Tancred said. "I say, Count," he added haughtily, "not one of us ever expected to see you again!"

"I know," said Stephen quietly. He had gained weight since their days together in Antioch, and had aged greatly. "But even so, I have returned and have brought several good knights with me. This is Eustache of Lorraine, the brother of Godfrey and Baldwin."

The youthful knight bowed respectfully.

"Is my brother Godfrey in good health?" he asked shyly.

"He is alive," Tancred responded grimly. "We have no other standard of health. I believe he knows nothing of your coming?"

Eustache blushed. "No, he left me in the care of my uncle. But I ran away to join you."

Tancred smiled cordially. He had taken a liking to this boy. He made a point of ignoring Stephen. That Stephen had returned was well, but, after all, he had once deserted them, and no man could forgive him that!

"Did you come with the Genoese?" he inquired of Eustache.

"Only as far as Alexandria. From there we were brought by a pirate of Boulogne who says that he, too, is a crusader—a knight."

"Guynemere?" cried Tancred.

"That's the man. He brought us to Joppa. A few Genoese galleys were there in the port, but they fled at our approach."

"Ho, now that Guynemere has arrived, there's a chance that he will give us people with axes," suggested Robert.

"Yes, Guynemere could give us people—experienced carpenters and such," said Tancred. "Before we go any farther, I must see him!" And with no more delay, he called his squire and departed.

As the dust settled behind the departing riders, Robert and Stephen sat down together.

"You are the last man in the world any of us would be expecting to see again," said Curthose. "I could hardly believe it when I saw who you were. But—they won't be receiving you kindly in the camp! You know that?"

"I had suspected as much."

"As it is, I am happy that our meeting took place out here away from the city . . . And that I am not going your way! Otherwise, I should find myself in no end of trouble because of you. I am sure you can understand that you are—hm—hardly a man to consort with!"

"Never fear, I have not the slightest hope that you will—hm—consort with me!" said Stephen stiffly.

"Now, now—as to that! I speak with you quite as of old!" Robert hastened to add. "Because, you understand, I have a soft heart and I—hm—I must bear in mind that you are my brother-in-law, and all that, but—ah—there are others, you understand . . ."

Stephen uttered a dry, unpleasant laugh. "I understand perfectly well why you are speaking with me! It's not because of a kind heart or because of our relationship at all, but because you are simply burning with curiosity. As for the others, I know precisely how they will greet me! I know what you crusaders are like . . ."

"Now, now. But tell me, Stephen, why did you really come back?"

"I had to return," Stephen answered briefly. "I had to." He wrinkled his brow angrily, painfully. Suddenly he could no longer contain himself and burst out, "I had to, I tell you. You could never imagine how I was received at home. 'Coward! Coward! Chicken heart!' I was called. I had abandoned the Holy Expedition! No one cared to talk with me . . . In all Europe they think only of you; they worship you as saints and heroes. When I tried to tell them the truth, they would come at me with their swords. Right to my face they told me I lied, I who had come from you direct, who had been in the East and had seen! They did not believe me! They knew better! I was given no chance to utter a word. Even were a man to swear on the salvation of his soul, they would simply decline to believe. Adele refused utterly so much as to welcome me home! Great were the riches I had brought with me—riches given me by the Basileus as compensation for all I had lost—she would not even look at them—or me! She would lie in bed beside me all night long and weep until I could only groan with anger and pity. 'Why do you weep?' I asked her. 'Because I have returned?' 'Because you are a coward!' she told me. 'Once all envied me my crusader husband and now—' My son, Egmont, had no word to say to me, but I knew that his thoughts were the same. It was enough to drive a man mad! I assured them that I alone had been saved, that all the rest of you had foolishly perished—when, all of a sudden, as though in mockery, the Genoese brought home the news of your great victory. They told of signs and miracles; after that, there was no chance at all for me. And so I left to rejoin you! I shall never return home."

"And what about Hugh?" asked Robert.

"I've heard he is still in Byzantium. He has not even been to Rome! He was afraid they would receive him as they did me, and he has no appetite for further fighting. But on the other hand, new knights in strength are coming forth to join you! They are gathering in bands to come by sea to the Holy Land. In a few months a good number will be at your side."

"God grant they come soon! I doubt that, all told, our forces stand at a man over five-and-twenty thousand."

"Great God, man! What are you saying!"

"Five-and-twenty thousand. If those you are promising us do not make haste, it's doubtful they will find anyone but Moslems here . . . Well, well—so that was how they received you! And here there was many a man that envied you!"

Guynemere, self-styled knight of the sea, was genuinely pleased to see Tancred boarding his vessel. "A marvel how often we meet!" the old pirate observed in greeting. "Only this time I have no ladies by me! How now—will the Duke forgive me?"

"Believe me, Sir Guynemere," said Tancred with great dignity, "not a man of us is thinking of women today!"

"Yo-ho! Our knights are praiseworthy! But for all of that, I still say that what a man always needs is meat, drink, sleep—and a woman! So be he's not too old to drag his legs . . . And how is the Countess d'Haineault?"

Tancred, no less himself than usual, blushed as though he were a culprit. In a few words, he related the sad fate of Ida.

The old bandit opened wide his bird-like eyes. "Never in this world! Why, really, this tears my heart! Just to think—that dear, sweet lady! And I who guarded her as a holy sacrament! How ever could you yield to such a pass, Duke?"

"She was not with me at the time!" retorted Tancred haughtily. "I had sent her back to her husband. The small company escorting her were captured by Saracens."

"You sent her back? Ho-ho, Duke! You do have your own way of handling women, don't you? A way completely your own! I recall—"

"Enough of that!" hissed Tancred, already furious. "I abhor your jibes! Were you but a true knight, I would meet you at once. Even so, you may find yourself in trouble!"

Guynemere narrowed his eyes in a sneer. It gave him real pleasure to plague this young hotspur. "You say, Sir, that I am not a true knight?" he wailed mournfully. "I thought I told you at Nicaea that I was. And I remember that you spoke with me as with an equal there and that you did not then abhor my assistance."

"It's one thing to speak and quite another to duel. And a man may quite honorably accept help from one and all when our holy aspiration is at stake."

"A hearty world, forsooth, is this you've laid out for yourselves, my good and noble Sirs! So be it, friends—since considering is the thing, mark you, I consider myself no less a true and noble knight, even though I do not ride a horse, but sail! I wear a belt!"

"A belt will not veil a pirate's trade!"

Guynemere darkened with anger but controlled himself and burst forth with a hearty laugh. "Ho-ho! My trade was dropped in my lap by destiny. An old witch once told my mother that her son would set all the seas a-boil with his pranks. This she foretold three years before my mother met the warrior rightly or wrongly considered by her to be my father. And today I'm known from Danzig to Alexandria! With the girdled elite I have never jousted, chiefly because one so rarely encounters a gentleman at sea."

"Let us stop this nonsense, my dear Guynemere! No one expects that you shall be a true knight, any more than it's demanded of a wolf to become a lion. You are not even in a position to judge what true knight-hood is. But no matter! We have a favor to ask of you. Tell me truly: are you a Christian and a crusader, or not?"

"I am a crusader," answered the king of the pirates morosely.

"Then the moment has arrived when you can be of great service to the crusade. We cannot take Jerusalem without siege towers, and—to build them we have no wood. In the whole of Judea there exists not one stick of wood! What an accursed country! Wandering about the sea, you cannot imagine what it is like there. Naught but rocks—barren, blistering rocks! It's a rocky hell! Water—not a drop, since the pagans have poisoned all the wells! What water we have has to be hauled in bags over ten leagues of mountain desert. And that in scorching heat! If the siege is to last two months longer, not one of us will be left alive, and we shall not succeed in freeing the Holy Sepulcher. The Duke of Normandy and I have been dispatched to Galilee to fell timber for building materials. But we find we have too few people, and too few saws and axes. We shall have to make two, perchance even three trips there and back. Pray, help us with men and tools!"

"They are yours!" Guynemere was quick to respond. "I am a crusader as I say, so all that is understood! I shall keep but a small watch aboard; the rest of my crews go with you. So it is that bad before Jerusalem, is it? I can see it just to look at you, Duke. Now, take no offense, but you are a sorry sight!"

"I! I appear none too badly, for I am young and strong—but if you could only see the others!"

"I will call my people together and order them to prepare," said Guy-nemere shortly and disappeared below.

But when he reappeared with a brass whistle in his teeth, Tancred, in a sudden impulse, clutched his arm. "Stay a moment, Sir Guynemere! I have something more to say!"

"My ears are open!" the old pirate growled, taking the whistle from his lips.

Tancred feverishly ransacked his mind for the appropriate words, for he realized the enormity of the request he was about to make. The galley was to these pirates their native home, a part of their fatherland, their only estate, their only means of livelihood, and at the same time a thing precious above all else in the world. Tancred had once spent a few days aboard one of these pirate galleys and, during the siege of Nicaea, had

had an opportunity to observe with his own eyes that these people, seemingly devoid of all human feeling, nevertheless loved their vessels with a devotion at once fierce and tender. How then could he ask them to give up their ships? By what eloquence could he draw Guynemere into his plan? For, as Tancred realized, anything like compulsion was utterly unthinkable. Who could be bold enough to think of forcing free sailors to part with their vessels? He and his lone squire were aboard merely as guests. The good will of the old pirate alone could decide the fate of the host before Jerusalem.

"My ears are open!" Guynemere repeated, peering from under his brows.

Tancred swallowed with some effort. "You are a Christian and a crusader, my dear Guynemere?" he began.

"Ho, that again! I told you once before that I am! What is plaguing you?"

"Just a moment—hear me out, I pray you. Listen carefully. Our people at Jerusalem are wasting away. The pagans on the walls are reviling our God, are mocking the Cross and its defenders. True, you are giving us people, and God will repay you for that, but before we can go with them to Galilee and return to Jerusalem with the timber, at least four weeks will have passed, four long weeks! And meanwhile, we are losing men every day. But—your galleys, Guynemere—*they* are—of wood! Wait, friend—hear me further! If you would be willing to give up—not all, but only a few of them—you have ten—we could start building at once. We will offer you all in our power, whatever price you ask. And thus you would save us all. The Holy Sepulcher, thanks to you, would be liberated. As for me, I possess nothing in the world. I myself had to take service after all I owned went up in flames at Antioch. Oh, but others still have much to their name and they will give you all they have. I speak for them, knowing them as well as I do; be it Godfrey, the Count St. Gilles or the Fleming, not a man will hesitate. I know what a sacrifice it would be. I understand. Like asking a knight to part with his sword. But, by the wounds of Christ! the fate of the entire crusade lies in your hands!"

"Enough!" Guynemere cut in harshly. Without another word, he strode across the deck to the opposite rail, where he halted with his back to Tancred. There he stood while angry thoughts swarmed in his brain. So! he thought, that was what they wanted! Those mighty nobles! Aye, today they were dancing about in a lather, but what about a year ago? No haste then! Only now they have the gall to say, "Be good enough to haste our cause by giving us your galleys. We'll accept you as a knight then. We will even 'meet' you if that's any satisfaction!" Guynemere snarled, "Ho-ho-ho! there's a handsome reward, my hearties! Ho, by my arse, it is. Let the devil reward them. I need none of your gold. Give up my galleys! Ho-ho! By all means!"

He let out his breath and wheeled about in order to say that if this silly knight still wanted his people, let him take them—and that if not, he could get ashore. But before he opened his mouth, he paused, for it would be a fine thing to take Jerusalem, after all, he thought. Didn't that young jackanapes say that you are a Christian and a crusader? he said to himself. Why, of course; Guynemere is, by God, a Christian! It hardly warms his heart to hear that the pagans are defiling the holy places. And Guynemere can rescue them? Yes, sir, he said to himself with a secret smile. There is something better than a bandit's glory! And even all glory aside, he could also win favor with the Lord. The old pirate, Guynemere, could have his name written down in Heaven!

So be it! He would deliver the Holy Sepulcher! Aboard these galleys nothing had yet happened to give the angels cause for rejoicing. Well, then—let it happen now! Let these vessels of his be broken up for timbers! Let them be turned into siege engines. Guynemere himself would buckle on his sword and help storm the city! Ho-ho-ho! There would be a fine jest—to storm the walls of Jerusalem with his own vessels!

Resolutely he straightened his back, threw back his head. "Ahoy, there, Duke! Come here!" he barked imperiously.

Tancred reddened and bit his lips. He endured this insult only because of the wood he needed. Struggling with himself to assume an air of outward calm, he approached the pirate.

"My galleys are yours!" Guynemere blurted hoarsely. "Take all of them, if necessary! Only don't talk to me of payment! Because if you do —by the net of St. Peter—duke though you are, I'll be delivering you such a kick in the arse that you'll go flying right off this deck here! Understood? What I do, I do out of Christian zeal and I don't need any payment from you—any more than I need 'to meet' you, as you say! I am a pirate—not highly born—and I should not care to soil your sacred honor! Now then—you have no need to go to Galilee at all. My vessels are sound; they're strong; they'll do. They'll set you up six towers to the last tie and stay!"

Tancred paled and flushed by turns, alternately enraged by this fellow's insolence and sentimentally affected by the brotherly alliance offered. "We will not meet, if you do not wish it," he was finally able to say—"but nevertheless, I hold you, Sir, for a true, good knight and shall strike down with my lance the man who would dare dispute it in my presence!"

"Bravo! Bravo!" Guynemere mumbled indifferently. "Now ride forth and fetch your people! We have no time to waste!"

43.

It Came to Pass

THE TIME HAD PASSED WHEN ONLY CARPENTERS AND COMMONERS HEWED, while knights and squires looked on. Today all hands were busy, and although there were far fewer than before to do the work, two days now equalled a fortnight.

At Nicaea, Pantopulos had purposely delayed construction. Again at Antioch, the carpenters had not known how to organize their tasks and had lost much time to no avail. But here at Jerusalem, all things ran smoothly.

The oaken beams from the demolished galleys were of sound timber and two huge towers were taking shape on the plain—two grim, four-storey, mobile fortresses. In addition to these, there were to be three smaller auxiliary towers.

Imbram was handiest to hew and trim, and all eyes were on him with envy. In other hands, accustomed only to sword or lance, the axe would slip out of grasp or would gouge too deeply. Imbram, as he stood there delivering his steady, measured strokes, was wondering if God might be observing his work and whether, as a reward, He would restrain the vengeful soul of his evil brother. At another time, deep grief for his lost comrades would overcome him. Those comrades of his who, being forest people, had been skilled in carpentry—as able with the axe as with the sword. Today, of all those who had started out from Silesia, only he and Yashek Zavora remained!

While some worked, others would mount guard, in order to prevent the infidels from making a sudden destructive sally. The attempt had already been made on several occasions, but each one had been success-fully repulsed. The sun was as hot and blinding as ever, but the people appeared to have become accustomed to its tortures. All had lost them-selves in frenzied activity and were indifferent to heat and thirst.

Women, with the Lady Elvira at their head, passed among the workers with water, warm, repulsive and stinking of leather, yet welcome.

The morrow would be the seventh of July, exactly a month since the crusaders had first taken their stand before the Holy City. In another week they would launch their assault, according to their present resolve. But one more week of painful toil and then—either they would have perished or they would have entered a free Jerusalem!

To the quarters of the Danish prince had come, for the first time in nearly a year, the wife he had spurned—Florine. Inwardly, as well as outwardly, it was clear how much she had changed. Her pride had vanished, leaving only the torturing loneliness which had driven her here, poor, bedraggled, and humiliated. She wanted nothing in the world but to see Swennon. She knew he still lived. In fact, it was said that he was even to join the assault.

In a tremulous voice, Florine implored Olaf, standing guard not far from the tent, to go within and tell the Prince that she, his wife, was there, begging him to take pity on her and permit her to see him.

The huge, blonde Dane turned his sunburned face and gazed down at her from beneath his helmet crowned with urus horns. There was restrained sympathy in his stare, but nothing more. Olaf and his fellow-Vikings, simple, honest men that they were, had long since stopped trying to understand the riddle of their Prince's marriage. All that had happened since his wedding day—including even his illness—they had been content to attribute to witchcraft. But which had been the evil magician and which the sorry victim, they neither knew nor would think.

"I will tell him," Olaf said deliberately, then turned and tramped ponderously off toward the tent, unaware that Florine was stealthily following in his tracks. Close behind him, she entered the tent and crossed the main enclosure to a farther wall where a curtain hung before Swennon's private quarters.

It was dark beyond the curtain, although not so dark but that the figure rising from the couch could be seen by those who entered. Florine had not the presence of mind to suppress her scream.

The Prince buried his face in his arms and turned toward the wall. "Go! Go!" he shrieked. "Go! Who gave you leave to enter?"

"I asked no leave. I came . . . I shall not look, Swennon! I have already bound my eyes with my kerchief! I cannot see you, Swennon! I cannot see!"

"Go at once, do you hear!"

"O, I will not go! O, my beloved—it's I, your wife! Pray let me stay, only for a moment! I cannot live thus any longer!"

"Go, go! I am not here!" wailed Swennon. "I have died! I no longer exist! Add not to my hopeless misery. Go!"

"Swennon. I am to blame for all that has happened. I will go, but first you must hear me! Pray, let me speak! All that has happened is my fault, my sin! Forgive me, if you can. I am not as I was. See! You are putting me from you—and yet here I stand ready to fall at your feet. O, Swennon."

"Go! Go!" the Prince continued to repeat, pressing his face into the canvas of the tent. "Go! You know nothing! My sickness comes from— because I . . . I"

"I know everything. Do not speak!"

"You know and even so—you came?"

Both were weeping now. But each was finding comfort in the other's tears. Swennon had long since renounced all earthly life, but Florine had not yet surrendered. She was already catching at a spark of hope, was groping for her beloved in the darkness before her eyes.

"I will never leave your side!" she cried fiercely. "You may never drive me from you, my dear one! We shall storm the city together. You will lower your visor. No one will see you. I shall be at your side . . . If we are spared, we will kneel together before the Holy Sepulcher and pray that you may be healed. I know that God would never refuse us; our Lord healed lepers—would He not therefore heal you, too? We shall yet be happy. Only let me stay now, Swennon!"

"You must leave me, my love, my sweet! You must go. And God bless each moment of your life!"

"No, I will not go! I will not go!"

"You must! I am not yet wholly debased, Florine! If you love me, you will go!"

"Promise me then that we may join the attack side by side!"

"Oh, Florine—well do I know what you are! You will do battle far better than I—I who can no longer so much as raise a sword and can wish for one thing only: to perish there on the tower, so that my men

can carry the news home to Denmark that I fell in battle, as fully became a knight. So that my mother's grief may be lessened! That is all
I wish—death and nothing more."

"You cannot refuse me! You owe it to me—for the whole past terrible
year! We shall stand side by side and let God do with us as He wills."

"As God wills," Swennon whispered, but he did not move a step
nearer to her.

No man closed an eye that night. In the morning they would begin
the assault and they were only waiting for daybreak. Quietly they had
rolled the mighty siege towers forward across the filled-in-moat, where
now, like great black spectres, they stood just beyond reach of the foe.
At dawn they would be moved close against the walls. The stone-
casters were in position; all weapons and ammunition were assembled
and stood in readiness.

The defenders had been equally busy. On top of the walls rose special
barricades of sand bags and sacks of wool to protect the walls from
catapulted rocks. Suspended horizontally on heavy chains, great wooden
fenders dangled along the walls to fend off the blows of the battering
rams or soften their terrific impact. Behind the barricades vast stores of
rocks and tar and incendiary weapons had been prepared and, together
with massed spears and arrows, were waiting to defend the city.

But the crusaders had fasted and partaken of the Eucharist and, when
morning came, they went forth refreshed and confident as they had
been upon emerging from Antioch to smash Kerbogha. They had placed
themselves wholly in the care of the Lord and were ready to accept His
will.

Before moving to the attack, the entire host joined in a solemn procession and slowly circled the walls. All personal quarrels and grudges had
been spoken and mutually forgiven and a spirit of perfect brotherhood
now cemented the ranks.

Raymond St. Gilles and Tancred, formerly so savagely at odds, shook
hands and embraced each other before the multitude and now were
leading the procession. Peter the Hermit was bearing the Cross, followed
by the Chaplain, Arnuld de Rohes, carrying the holy relics of the French
patrons. In close procession behind Arnuld walked all the nobles and
their women. Swennon in armor, his visor lowered to cover his face.
Florine, in squire's garb, was close by his side, just as she had promised

—so close, in fact, that each one was conscious of the other's heartbeat. Florine was holding her husband by the arm, not alone from tenderness, but also from fear that he would fall. For Swennon, in truth, was very weak. Both were singing with the others:

Awake, awake; shake thyself from the dust, O Jerusalem!
Loose thyself from the bands of thy neck, O captive daughter of Zion!

All knights and squires had joined the holy march: De La Tour, with his faithful lioness close beside him; Ostoy, Imbram, Yashek Zavora—those three the only ones left from the Polish retinue; Andrew and Bela de Kolosvar, the last of the Hungarians; the brothers Salviac de Viel; Raymond de Chartres, Gaston de Beziers, and Eberard du Puiset; the inconsolable D'Haineault; and the brave Konon de Montaigue. Yes, and Walter the Penniless. Their voices rose thunderously as they sang:

Awake, awake; put on thy strength, O Zion;
Put on thy beautiful garments, O Jerusalem, the holy city!

Pirates, men at arms, shield-bearers, lancers, bowmen, servitors, villeins, even the meanest rabble—all today were marching and singing together as equals. From their throats the voice of the Prophet Isaiah broke upon the rocks:

Break forth into joy, sing together, ye waste places of Jerusalem;
For the Lord hath comforted His people, He hath redeemed Jerusalem.
The Lord hath made bare His holy arm in the eyes of all the nations;
And all the ends of the earth shall see the salvation of our God.

The Moslems gathered in multitudes upon the walls to mimic the procession. The infidel throngs kept pace with the marchers below, in their own hands carrying a cross which had been robbed from one of the churches and bearing aloft a picture of the Blessed Virgin. Blasphemously the cross was carried head down, while people rushed up to revile it and smite it with rods.

The crusaders looked up and saw, and a great wrath swept over them. They saw, and their hearts were bursting with hatred. A storm of vengeful emotion swept through the ranks and set them to surging and heaving.

But with effort they managed to restrain themselves. They must finish the procession first, must completely surround the walls, as Joshua once surrounded Jericho, must seal them tight within a magic circle of united passion and prayer. Only then might they attack . . .

Atop the mighty four-storeyed tower shone a golden cross, and beside it Godfrey stood, together with his brother Eustace, De Montaigue, the old pirate Guynemere, Raynald de Chartres, and Robert of Flanders. On the stage below were Swennon and Florine, Robert of Normandy, Stephen de Blois, and the fighting men of Denmark and Lorraine. With a creaking and groaning of timbers, the enormous structure was jolting forward, creeping toward the wall. Great catapults mounted on the upper stages were casting heavy boulders at the rampart. Iron-shod rams were battering at the lower courses with the impact of rolling thunder which shook the earth. Upon the advice of Guynemere, heavy beams swung by warriors in crews were sweeping along the top of the wall and knocking the defenders from their feet.

As the battle increased in violence, a flood of flaming pitch and Greek fire was directed from the embrasures upon the tower. The air was filled with flying missiles—arrows, lances, jagged rocks. Howling like demons, the men of Islam pushed and shoved at the tower with beams and iron pikes, preventing it from moving closer and meanwhile assaulting it with every available weapon. In spite of its sheath of hides, the tower began to burn from two sides. Not having water to spare, the knights and their soldiers beat out the fire with their cloaks, some even with their hands. They grasped the pikes of the Saracens and tugged with all their might; they would move the tower forward by this means or pull the defenders from the walls. The complex sounds of battle combined to split the air in a hellish din.

"Heave-ho, down there! Lay to it!" Guynemere bawled down to the crews on the ground who, by means of lever and windlass, were straining to keep the tower's great wheels moving. "Heave! On we go! Again! What in Satan's name? Another fire?"

The tar-soaked timbers taken from the galleys were highly inflammable. The pagans shrieked with joy each time a new fire broke out. The scant supply of water fetched from Jordan the day before and reserved for the tower fighters to drink, now had to be used for quenching the flames.

Along the walls away from the tower, fierce duels were raging between defending Moslems and the masses of crusaders attacking them

from the ground. Behind massed shields the assailants crouched, while
their bowmen exchanged volleys with the crack archers of the enemy,
who were fighting off the efforts of the crusaders to mount the walls by
means of ropes and scaling ladders. The stone-casters on both sides were
busy and the numbers of the dead and dying were mounting steadily.

The second siege tower, commanded by Raymond St. Gilles, was
furiously attacking the wall on the opposite side of the city. Accom-
panying Raymond were De La Tour, the brothers Salviac de Viel,
Ostoy, Imbram, the Hungarians, De Foix and Walter the Penniless.
De La Tour's lioness was roaring amid the clatter of raining stones.
Otherwise, the battle was but a counterpart of Godfrey's assault. Flames,
blood splattering on wall and tower . . . The swishing and booming
of heavy beams . . . The ropes of the catapults groaning and hissing
. . . The squealing of windlasses as the wheels ground slowly forward
. . . Prayers and curses mingling in the smoky, dust-laden air . . . Air
made doubly choking by the heavy scent of steaming sweat and blood.

The Moslems were feverishly heightening the ramparts by means of
beams and bags and loose rocks, determined to get above the tower
with their weapons and to make it more difficult for the drawbridge
to find a level seat on the wall.

The swaying tower had edged forward several paces. That, too, was
already being heightened. Without hesitation, Raymond had ordered
the smaller auxiliary tower dismantled. "Hand up those timbers there!
Quickly! By the body of St. George, more haste! Faster! Now then—
we'll add another stage!"

It did not matter that the tower was already swaying and complaining
in every joint and that it was ready to collapse at any moment. The only
thing that mattered was added height. They must keep pace with the
growing wall—a race with death.

The carpenters and artisans worked like many times their number.
Up went beam and joist, stud and stay and rafter. Now sound planks
for the floor. The new stage was complete. The catapults ceased firing
while strong hands lifted them to their new level.

The Count St. Gilles was one of the first to leap recklessly to the
added stage. With satisfaction, he looked down on the walls. The race
had been won!

Barely able to keep his balance on the teetering, lightly joined timbers
of the new stage, the Count directed the aim of the stone-casters at

points on the wall where the defenders were thickly massed. At one time, in his excitement, he even seized an archer's bow and himself drove arrows into the ranks of the enemy.

Below, the infidels were attempting to set fire to the tower by sending over thick logs flaming with pitch and Greek Fire. But the ever vigilant knights would catch these on their pikes and, with the strength of combined effort, would cast them back on the walls where they would ignite the inflammable scaffolding and the piled sacks of wool.

Noon had already passed and evening was drawing near, but the battle raged on unabated. The walls of the city were encased in a deafening roar, a hellish tumult, as though the Day of Final Judgment were at hand. The ground beneath the ramparts was piled high with the dead; the fields and rocks beyond were littered with the wounded and the dying.

Night fell and the city still stood. The savage attack, the heavy losses, all seemed to have been in vain. In vain had men sacrificed themselves beneath the blazing sun, in vain had they burst their hearts with superhuman effort. The dead looked up with sightless eyes, and before the living, the walls of Jerusalem still loomed tall and dark and impregnable.

But no man thought of sleep or rest. Unaware of their dreadful fatigue, they stood like watchful cranes aloft on the towers. The city's defenders, too, remained wide awake. All night long they strove to repair breaches in the wall and to raise their level wherever possible. About the ramparts Arab hags went about performing their sorceries, muttering their secret curses, designed to sap the strength of the foe, and weaving them into the air with torches of galipot. The night was moonless but fevered with stars; all nature lay awake, vigilantly waiting. A curious night, more weird than even that night in Emmaus, when an unknown darkness had swallowed the moon, and the knights hastened to murmur their matins to protect themselves from evil spirits.

As the night wore on, the tension imperceptibly eased and a great calm sense of fellowship crept over them. The darkness was flowing with an unseen force and was washing into them, as they watched, a strange new sense of encouragement. It seemed as though vast trains of reinforcements were mounting the towers and crowding every stage, and as the moments passed, this perception became less and less a vague impression and more and more a reality. Dark figures they were indeed; arm against arm they took position there with the watchers.

Raymond St. Gilles, fearing for the safety of the tower, viewed with sudden apprehension those who were pressing about him. "Don't push!" he whispered. "The tower can barely stand as it is!"

"We won't be adding much weight!" the man nearest him said with a chuckle.

Raymond could not say who had spoken. The voice might have been that of Adhemar de Monteuil, save that the Bishop was long dead. Then again he imagined he heard the voice of the knight, D'Armillac. Pray, how could that be? Raymond vaguely wondered.

But Raymond was not alone with such strange impressions. Pressed against the knight, De La Tour, it seemed that Saint-Pierre de Luz was standing; and Imbram could have taken his oath that he had just seen the serious face of Glovach and that great stubborn head of his; and to the brothers Salviac de Viel, it seemed that Raoul de Beaugency was standing close at hand.

Old comrades were crowding in from every side. Wherever one looked, their pressing ranks could be seen, and the air grew warm and heavy from the influx of those spirit legions. But even more curious than their coming was the fact that the presence of men long dead frightened no one—it all seemed so natural, so inevitable.

Hardly had a new day dawned when the battle began afresh. Back and forth between the opposing forces swirled a continuous tempest of flying stones and lances, groaning beams and whistling arrows, boiling water and flaming pitch, fiery rags and torches. The situation of the besieged had not changed since the day before, but the situation of the attackers had grown considerably worse—since fewer and fewer were left to carry on the fight. The phantom host had vanished with the light, and the towers looked strangely deserted now, so many of those who had manned them yesterday lay below in the heaps of the dead.

It was becoming increasingly difficult to protect the towers from fire. The dried wood ignited as though it were straw. In spite of every effort of the attackers, fresh flames were forever breaking out and the lower stages were continuously smouldering. The women and servants were doing their utmost to keep these fires under control, but they were finding it a hopeless task, and the knights aloft on the topmost platform were well aware that their remaining moments were numbered. Unless they were successful in laying a bridge now, the fire which would shortly come bursting up through the tower would consume them along with everything else.

Paul Salviac de Viel, struck in the temple, fell. His twin gazed down at the prostrate form and it was as though he himself had taken the blow.

Weak from exhaustion, Stephen de Blois battled persistently but without conviction. He saw in their frantic efforts but a spirit which was pathetic and a little ludicrous. The beam which felled him left him with just enough breath to call up to Robert: "Remember what you promised me! Tell Egmont that I fell like a . . ."

The rock which killed the old pirate, Guynemere, glanced and struck Swennon on the stage below. He fell without a word. The arms of Florine were helpless to stay him. Forward he fell to the ground where flames were eating away the base of the tower. His body, like those of his Viking forefathers, had found its last resting place on a funeral pyre, and Florine looked down with tearless eyes.

On the upper stage, Godfrey, assisted by his brother, Eustace, and Robert of Flanders, was vainly trying to drop the bridge onto the wall where a forest of Moslem pikes pushed it away again and again. A mere handful of knights remained to do battle from the platform. The choking, smoke-laden air was like fire itself: from above burned the sun, from below the mounting flames. And yet they struggled on.

Up through the curling smoke a slight figure nimbly climbed. It was Florine. Her helmet, too large for her head, was sent spinning through the air by some glancing missile. "Burgundy!" she cried in a voice which was fresh and young. "Burgundy!" And at that moment she fell. Her body went hurtling below to join the body of Swennon on his couch of flame.

Still they battled on. Even though all odds were now pitted against them, they stubbornly continued to assail the infidels with whatever came to hand. No reinforcements could reach them now, for the flames were out of control. Despite the concerted efforts of hosts of fire-fighters, passing forward water from the poisoned wells, it was clear that the tower was doomed. At any moment now it would collapse with a crash and an eruption of fiery sparks.

The moment had arrived when the men on the platform could remain on the tower no longer. They could but choose their manner of dying: whether by fire or on the spears of the infidels. As a man, they chose the great wild leap; they would set foot on the walls of Jerusalem and there perish.

"God wills it!" With this outcry, Godfrey and his comrades acknowledged their imminent death. God willed that they should perish here and now.

"God wills it . . ."

"God wills it!" a long-drawn echo answered from the hills, an echo so vast and tumultuous that no echo quite like it had ever been heard in the world before. "God wills it!" Like the voice of a thousand mighty seas, it rose from beyond the furthest hill and came beating down on the rocks which lay about Jerusalem.

Godfrey paused before he leaped. With incredulous eyes he turned and looked, and this is what he saw:

From the crest of the Mount of Olives to the Valley of Jehosophat a thundering host of wildly riding horsemen were flying down the slope. Rank on rank in endless waves, and more were appearing all the while. Who could they be? No, who could doubt they were Latins! The sun struck golden fire from the crosses they bore and glinted in flashes of silver lightning from their swords. Their own! Their own! These riders were their own! Above those flying ranks of glittering armor the gonfalons whipped proudly. Normandy! Lorraine! Flanders! Toulouse! At the head of the charging cavalcade there rode a man on a great gray horse, a man who looked strangely familiar. A towering man he was as he rode, with a cross in one hand and a sword in the other. But what manner of man was he that he rode with no reins in his hand? And what manner of steed did he ride which stumbled not nor fell?

Nearer and nearer they came in a surging, plunging, headlong tide. Into the Valley of Jehosophat, on across the Cedron. And the speed of their coming raised a great wind. A great rushing breath which suddenly tautened each lifeless banner and carried all smoke and flame to the walls. A quick bursting gale which fanned not the flames in the tower but tore them away and laid them upon the pagans.

The bags of wool on the walls began to burn. The pitch prepared for the crusaders caught fire. The barricade began to smoke. The Moslems

Not pausing to wonder whence or how had come these unexpected reinforcements, Godfrey took instant advantage of the enemy's sudden screamed and fell back before the menace.

panic. Down went the bridge at last and he leaped across onto the wall, into the midst of the milling enemy. With flailing sword, he carved out a space where he could stand. He carved out room for Eustace, for Robert, De Montaigue, Letold, Engelbert. Together they cleared the way for others who, now that the fires were out, were piling up through the charred and smoking towers.

The Moslems, demoralized by this sudden turn of events, were unable to make a stand before the flashing swords of the crusaders who were now pouring out upon the wall, across the bridge from the tower, in endless chains from the scaling ladders, made fast by the earliest arrivals. Before they quite knew what had happened, Godfrey and his men had cut their way through to the Gate of St. Stephen, where Tancred's forces were clamoring. As the gate swung open, a thousand hands wrenched them from their hinges and threw them lightly away. Into the city Tancred and Robert of Normandy led the invading host.

The crusaders had entered Jerusalem.

It was the third hour of the afternoon, the hour at which the Lord Jesus Christ had been nailed to the Cross. It was the fifteenth day of July in the year 1099.

The city was soon teeming with Latins. The battle was passionate, insane, merciless. The men of Islam defended themselves like wounded lions, with a dark, wild, scornful bravery. They could afford to be scornful, for on this day, without fail, they would join the Prophet in Paradise.

But the Moslem warriors were not the sole occupants of the city. There were also masses of frightened women with infants in their arms. There were the peace-loving citizens, the dark-eyed youths, and maidens. There were the aged, the children. Back through the narrow streets they crowded in panic-stricken flight before the flashing swords of the advancing invaders. In vain they screamed and begged for mercy. In vain they fell to the ground and clung to the knees of their slayers, for the Latin sword spared no one. Nor age nor sex nor frailty existed for these rampaging men of the cross. They saw before them but infidel flesh. Each shrieking victim was to them the contemptible pagan that had defiled the Cross and befouled the face of the Blessed Virgin.

In every narrow street flowed blood. It gurgled, rose, spilled forth in red streams, formed itself into steaming pools where the streams converged in the squares; there were lakes of blood through which horses waded to their fetlocks. In the deadly rush of mass murder many a pilgrim perished at the hands of the knights, and of those who lived in the city, Christians and Moslems were treated alike. The aged Armenian patriarch, Varam, was within a sword's length of being butchered like a pig. The Arab chroniclers, in discussing this day, later reckoned their own dead at more than seventy thousand.

In the holy mosque of El Sakra, on the heights of Mount Moriah, a throng, consisting mostly of women and children, had gathered. Some had huddled together on the octagonal roof; others were clinging to a bare, gray rock, which rose in the middle of the colorful, fairy-like interior. This rock had once served as a sacrificial altar in Solomon's temple, and at its base was a trough-like drain which had once carried the blood of the victims away to the brook called Cedron; it was believed that on this very rock Abraham had intended to sacrifice Isaac, and that from here Elijah had ascended to heaven in a whirlwind. And now at this rock, the pagan women, mad with fear, were seeking refuge.

But the men of the cross swung their bloody swords, and down that ancient drain, blood flowed again in a swift stream.

While the hecatomb was at its height, Tancred burst into the mosque. With the rays of the sun behind him, he was like an archangel of wrath. His nostrils were quivering at the scent of blood and he stared about him wildly and greedily, only to be met by the shrill moans and the desperate clamor of women and children! He looked at the victims, and the eyes which gazed back at him were round and frightened and tearful.

"Stay you!" roared Tancred in a voice of indignation. "You shall not slay women and children! These have not fought against us! These have not desecrated the Cross! Stay!" He pressed forward to the rock, then turned and faced his people. "Plant my standard before this mosque!" he commanded. "Now it is mine with all that is in it! No man may molest anything here—neither things nor people!"

Leaving Sebastian de Monte Scabioso and a company of knights to guard the mosque, Tancred left and ran on further. The Moslems had ceased to defend themselves and sat about on the ground with their cloaks thrown over their heads. They sat there waiting indifferently for the sword of the enemy.

The sun had already set and the sudden dusk of the East was descending. In the darkness agonized groans and the rattles of death mingled with the panting breath of the killers.

Now in the distance the twinkle of torchlights: a small procession of dancing lights, here and there reflected in the blood pools, winking and beckoning where their images were cast from the more swiftly running streams. That was Godfrey, barefoot, bare-headed, swordless, who, like a penitent, was leading a little company of knights and squires forward to the Sepulcher. They were murmuring a low chant as they marched.

Raymond, Tancred, the two Roberts, threw down their swords and helmets and fell in behind the procession. Blood splashed underfoot—warm and slippery. And they had difficulty keeping their footing on the wet stone.

Now silence lay over the city.

To come to the Holy Sepulcher the bare-footed penitents had to climb over many a ghastly heap. This they did coldly, unfeelingly, even a little impatiently. The events of the day had settled into the depths of forgetfulness like useless dregs precipitated from their consciousness by the dream they were about to realize. As they brushed against walls, splashed with blood to the height of a man, they wept tears, not of repentance, but of holy joy.

They carried in their breasts nothing but the feeling that in a few moments they would be seeing That toward which they had been struggling since the beginning of time. The years of their wandering had swelled and become eternity, and nothing lived in their past save their pilgrimage. All that had actually happened before the start lurked obscurely in their minds, as though on some distant, foreign shore separated from their conscious life by a gulf of forgetfulness so wide that each man would have been ready to swear that his life on earth had begun on that fateful day at Clermont—that within this span of years lay all he ever knew of life: his infancy, his youth, his maturity.

Advancing on their knees, crawling over mounds of cold and lifeless flesh and as indifferent to them as to the cobbles of the street, they had no notion of how their goal would actually appear, for they had yielded to no fancies. They were fully prepared to accept whatever they saw. They possessed no knowledge of the history of the Holy places—and, if they knew nothing, they cared less. They continued on their way over fallen columns and broken tiles—shattered by the tides of history—and did not even notice them.

With tightening hearts they crowded into the Church of the Resurrection and knelt beneath its defaced and shabby cupola. Before them stood a formless face of rock, in which a spacious opening yawned. This was the entrance to the Sepulcher, the outer chamber wherein the family and mourners had gathered for the burial. In the farther wall of this grotto-like antechamber was a low opening which led to a further recess. Beside it rested a large round stone which had once blocked the entrance to the Sepulcher itself. On this stone had sat the angel of the Lord to tell the mourning women that the One they were seeking had risen. The stone was now rolled aside and the passageway was free.

With a mysterious sense of having grown far beyond themselves, they crept on their knees through the narrow opening and on into the tight grotto beyond. There in the dark their groping hands came reverently upon a bench carved from the rock to their right. It was on this bench that the Holy Body of the Saviour of Man had rested from Friday evening until Sunday morning. To the pilgrims, weeping with exaltation, it seemed that they could see It shining there in the dark—an indescribable presence which blessed the purple shadow with a great pure holiness of light. With loving tenderness they covered the rough stone with kisses and moistened it with the steady flowing of their tears.

Outside, in the antechamber, within the church and in every nearby street and square, the knights knelt, motionlessly awaiting their turn to enter the Sepulcher. Creeping, crawling, they covered the earth with a gently undulating expression of their own combined nostalgia, like a flock of exhausted swallows. The torches had long since died and the night was approaching its end. But who of these could say whether it was night or dawn or day?

44.

The Return to the Past

"NOW WE MAY RETURN HOME," OSTOY WAS SAYING TO IMBRAM. "WE must find out when the Genoese will sail . . ."

"Return?" Imbram repeated absently.

"Aye, and why not? Why should we stay here any longer? We have fulfilled our pledge. Our mission stands accomplished. The Grave of the Lord is free."

Imbram looked at his comrade with sudden alarm. Return? That he and Ostoy—the last of the Polish knights—were actually free to return in the flesh, and not as ghosts, like all the rest, he could not force himself to comprehend.

"Enough of the others are remaining to defend the Sepulcher," Ostoy went on. "And the time for that will be coming along soon enough! For they say that a great new force of Saracens is gathering to march against us in strength. Stubborn bastards! The Caliph himself has called his chiefs together, and it may even be that he will lead his forces in person. St. Gilles is getting ready for them . . ."

But Imbram was not following his words. For a long time now he had ceased entirely to consider the possibility of ever returning home, as flesh and blood, at least. If ever he was to see the forests of Silesia again, it would be as a ghost, he had convinced himself. He would join the train of phantoms and haunt the halls of his ancestors as a draught of cold air through the crannies, as a creaking step within the timbers, as a great lonely sigh in the rafters. How was he alone, out of that once proud retinue, to survive this accursed expedition? All had been doomed from the start, of that he had long been sure; and that, very likely, was as it should be. For the sake of those at home, they had all gone forth to die, and one by one, they had perished. None had been destined to return, and, knowing this, they had broken all ties connecting them with their

451

old life. Those who lived had become changed; they had become creatures of a strange new existence, an existence that knew no past. And
now . . . to return? That he and Ostoy had been singled out to return
to a life which no longer existed?—He shook his head over its impossibility.

"Farewell! Godspeed!" Ostoy cried, as he turned off to the left with
his people.

Imbram Strzygonia, followed by a few servants driving the baggage
train, waved goodbye and went on. Now he made no effort to unsnarl
his feelings as, hour by hour, he neared his home; with neither joy nor
impatience in his heart, he felt but a kind of boundless wonder to discover that nothing here had changed but himself. While riding with
Ostoy, he had not fully yielded to this sense of surprise, because of the
knight's ceaseless chatter.

"What will you be doing with yourself after you have been home?"
he had inquired several times.

Imbram had looked at him indecisively, and was silent. Then, "Go
on living," he said slowly.

"Ho, not for me—it's not for that I roved the world!" the other had
cried with a flourish. "Should I squat in a backwoods tower and gape
at passing bears? Not I, my friend. I'll take myself to some princely
court . . . perhaps to lead an embassy! I'll take it upon myself to stir
up our fine lords a bit and make them stick their noses for once outside
their forests. But first of all, I'll settle with that treacherous rascal,
Shechec! I'll get even with him, I can promise you! He'll be wishing he
had never been born—that dust-eating snake! He will see! But I'll not
show my hand at once—not until I have had an opportunity to look
about the country and study the lay of the land. I must know whom
it will pay to join up with! Then you will be hearing from me . . . The
first thing, of course, is to rid ourselves of Shechec. After that, I'll draw
the lords together and put them to work. We might restore the kingdom,
for example! It's about time we were heading the nations again, instead
of limping along at the tail!'"

"Restore the kingdom? Oh, heavens!" Imbram had sighed. He recalled the many, many times during their wanderings when they had
mourned the lone position of their mere handful of knights, their lack
of a king of their own or any powerful lord to lead them.

"Wait and see!" Ostoy had shouted. "They will all follow us, never fear! There is no one in our country, let me remind you, who knows as much or who has seen as much as we."

"As for me, I know nothing any more!" Imbram had replied.

"Nonsense! You are a capital knight! Didn't I see myself how you felled that elephant of Kerbogha's? There was a thing which no one but we ourselves—you and I—would have dared to attempt! Mark you, together we shall accomplish great things!"

Imbram had listened, but there was so little promise in the way he was wagging his head, that Ostoy had at length lost patience.

"If only your brother were alive, I'd not have to repeat that twice! There was a red-blooded knight!"

Brother? Imbram had winced. That venomous foe! What about him? Had he returned home as a ghost, as he had threatened, or had that peg in his breast broken his evil will and left his spirit captive in Asia?

Ostoy's shout of farewell had roused him from his gloomy reverie. "Fare thee well!" he had responded lifelessly. "Godspeed!"

The hills of Cracow lay behind and about him now was the wilderness of Silesia—his native forest. It was early March and the trees were bare. Here and there a patch of dirty, lumpy snow remained, but the lapwings were already beginning to clamor.

The patches of packed snow were honeycombed and water gushed beneath the hoofs of the horses. From the open world beyond, a strong spring wind was blowing; it whistled and roared above the forest roof, sometimes swooping down among the trees to sing along the ground. The poignant scents of early spring were in the air which, still cold enough to excite the blood in one's veins, was nevertheless warm enough to provoke the sap in the trees. The scudding clouds swam low above the forest and left here and there a wisp of mist clinging to the taller treetops. Occasionally through a rift in the clouds the glowing sun would peer—a sun quite different from the sun of Asia—a precious, life-giving radiance awaited by all nature.

The farther Imbram rode beneath the arching vault of the forest, with every inch of the trail becoming more and more familiar, the more stubbornly grew within him the sense that he was gradually bogging down in the primitive soil of his fathers, that like a tree he was striking root and developing a tough bark and that the creeping vines of his own past were weaving themselves into his life to imprison forever his spirit. All the things that he had lived through and experienced were falling away from him like so many dry pods and, strangely enough, he now felt closer to the moment when together with his brothers he had ridden through this selfsame wilderness from Krushvitsa than to the events of the past few months.

Day after day, hour after hour, he was drawing nearer and nearer the home he had left five years before. By now he knew every turning in the trail, every pool, every rock and clearing. But these he greeted with a curious absence of feeling, always being under the impression that his return was a violation of some supernatural law. Zbylut had wanted to return even after death, but it was he, Imbram, not dead but alive, who was returning in his stead.

With envy, he thought of Ostoy who was returning with such haste and excitement, who was bursting with plans for the future and boiling with a desire for action. But although he envied him, Imbram did not feel it within his power to emulate his comrade. In nature they were so different. Ostoy was arrogant, impetuous, passionate, bold. Life and its pitfalls were a challenge to his will; he was ready at the drop of a gauntlet to wrestle with circumstance as with a bear in the forest. On the other hand, Imbram—soft, emotional, sensitive, Slavic —participated in events only to the extent that he was dragged into them against his will. Even his homecoming was to him but another event to be approached listlessly and without spirit, simply as something which had been somehow prescribed. He looked about him half-consciously at trees as familiar to him as his knightly gear, at the tracts which Glovach, before their departure, had ordered cleared—at the manor's outlying fields, now carpeted with the blue-green feathers of winter wheat.

Another turning, and there stood the manor—the row of horse-skulls glistening white atop the stockade—the chapel and the house itself, the two joined together by a covered wooden passageway. Everything seemed curiously shrunken and small—far different from the magnificence Imbram recalled! He stared, unable to comprehend what change could possibly have taken place here.

The entrance gate was closed, as it should be. The gate from which he had once turned back to call out that they would soon return! His squire ran forward to open it with hands trembling with emotion and it creaked as of old. And now an uproar of barking dogs—the same dogs he had left—greeted him at the house.

Imbram dismounted and opened the door; the main hall, running the full width of the house, was filled as usual with smoke, swirling in a great blue cloud among the rafters of the ceiling.

Before crossing the threshold, Imbram remembered to draw from his bosom the tiny bag of soil taken from beneath this very doorsill five years before and which had lain against his heart throughout his wanderings. With great care he restored the pinch of earth to the very spot from which he had taken it. Then, patting the threshold three times in greeting, he at last stepped into the house.

More than ever, he seemed to be lost in a dream. As in a dream, he heard footsteps and the sound of voices in the adjoining rooms. A door opened cautiously; a number of girlish faces peeped out, then quickly withdrew in alarm. Glovach's daughters, no doubt, how they had grown! Behind the door a remembered swish of skirts, and there, boldly entering the room, was Bogucha. His sister-in-law had not changed in face or figure; in manner, she was as vigilant and protective as always. Her face was aggressively expectant now, but at the sight of the newcomer still standing motionless in the doorway, she stopped short and half raised her hand. Bogucha may not have changed, but it was only now that Imbram realized how greatly he himself must have changed with the years, for his sister-in-law did not recognize him.

"Imko, is that you?" she at last asked uncertainly.

"Yes, that's who it is."

"And my man?"

"Dead these three years."

"*Oi lelum, lelum!* A widow I am, then! . . . And Zbylut?"

"Dead, too."

"And the rest? Nagodzits? Osventa? The Zavoras?"

"All dead. Only I came back."

Silence . . .

The old man stirred in his corner. Something fluttered behind Bogucha's skirt. Only then did Imbram notice that a child, a little boy of some five years, stood peering curiously out from behind his sister-in-law.

"We thought you'd never be back," said Bogucha slowly. "We thought as how you were lost. Where have you been?"

"Out in the world."

Again silence. . .

Bogucha looked at him distrustfully. Was this her brother-in-law or not? God help her, was not this a changeling who stood before her? He did not praise God, spoke no greeting and had not a word to say for himself! He simply stood there stiffly. . . . "See—this is your boy!" she cried out suddenly and drew the lad from behind her skirt.

The little one, by no means timid, stared up at the strange knight before him—not into his face, but at his sword, his coat of mail, his girdle. The child had flaxen hair which fell to his shoulders; his eyes, as blue as cornflowers, were set in a frame of healthy tan.

"Mine," Imbram whispered and felt that he could bear it no longer. He had to blurt out the question which was choking him. "Where . . ." he asked, "is Ofka . . . ?"

Bogucha brushed the air with an indifferent arm. "Dead, too, this long time. It will soon be two years she is dead."

"Dead—?" Imbram murmured weakly. "You tell me . . . Ofka is dead?"

"That's what I said. But it was not from any sickness she died, but only because she pined to death. She had no hand for work—you know that—so she just let herself eat out her heart. Such a one!" Bogucha could afford to speak boldly, for she could see that Imbram was no longer listening.

So she was gone! It could not have been otherwise! He had somehow felt it all along! And now he knew . . . How ever could he have expected to find her? She had died because he had allowed a spell to be cast upon her. Or it might be that the ghost had drawn her blood.

"But why don't you look at this young one?" Bogucha asked offendedly and pushed the child toward his father.

With strange shyness, Imbram tried to take him by the hand, but the boy was not even looking at him. His attention was fixed on the people and horses and carts that he could see through the open door. His bright eyes were burning with curiosity. Then, no longer able to contain himself a moment longer, he was suddenly off with a bound, and how like Ofka's were his airy movements as he leapt across the threshold and began dancing about the yard! "Aunt! aunt!" he cried. "Just come here and see! Oh, my!"

Neighbors and kinsfolk who, in spite of the spring thaws, had come to the Strzygonia manor to see and hear the crusader, had gone away disappointed, for Imbram had had little or nothing to relate. When questioned, he had replied, but his words had been few and reluctant.

The reason for Imbram's reluctance was not only his abiding sense of personal guilt, in his utter brokenness of spirit, but also because of the difficulty he found in expressing himself. During recent years he had been accustomed to speaking and thinking exclusively in Latin, a tongue so rich and flexible that it had a name for every thing and every condition of soul. Returning now to the native Polish language, hard, poor in word and idea, he was at a loss to express in it anything of his wealth of experience. Never, as things stood, would he be able to share his experiences with a living soul here at home. The Abbot Guido alone would have understood his Latin and would have listened to him with rapt delight, but it was in the presence of the Abbot of all persons that Imbram was most careful to conceal his excellent knowledge of the western tongue, for he feared the penetrating gaze of the Abbot and the man's shrewd omniscience. He feared that, in the course of his accounts, he might inadvertently mention Leah or Zbylut's death!

And so, instead of telling anyone about himself, he would listen with painfully greedy attention to everything that was told him about life at home during his absence. Evenings, he would lie stretched out on the bench and would gaze at the shooting sparks of the hearth fire. In the wall crickets were chirping. Now and again there would be strange knocks and rustlings, like footsteps—ghosts were circling the manor. In the next room it seemed as though someone were weeping—or laughing.

Bogucha, wrapped to the eyes in homespun kerchiefs, as became a widow, sat spinning with her daughters, meanwhile recounting convincingly and precisely the household chronicle. Her voice rang with self-conscious superiority, at the moment considerably inflated by the discovery that the great foreign world, stretching itself afar—a world she had never seen—was neither more interesting nor wiser than the wilderness here at home, for had not Imko been far abroad in that world for several years and come home with nothing to tell, while she herself would require many an evening to sit and relate all the things she knew? How many, many important things had transpired here, immensely interesting details, closely connected with the life of the home, the livestock, the land and the staff. There was above all, for example, the armed attack by Shechec's men who had come seeking the absent knights shortly after their departure; the manor had been plundered, horses taken away, all the provisions in the storehouses devoured. Only the courage of Bogucha, stubbornly defending her husband's estate, had prevented the greedy monsters from destroying or pillaging everything. More than this, she could tell about the sickness of the little one who had had such a hard time cutting his teeth; and about the mare who had broken her leg on the icy ground; about the toll taken by wolves in the sheepfold, about the luckless calving of cows, and about the escape of two serfs—accursed runaways! It was only about Ofka she never spoke, nor did Imbram question her further on that subject. It was as though they had bound themselves by some secret compact to keep silent.

Occasionally Bogucha would pause, weary with talking. "And now you say something, why don't you?" she would challenge him, lowering her spindle. Glovach's daughters would stop their wheels and stare expectantly into the face of their uncle.

"What shall I talk about?" Imbram would ask with a wan smile.

And, indeed, of what was he to tell them? And how? To women whose feet knew only clay floors, how was he to explain that he had walked upon mosaics designed to resemble a pool of water rippled by a breeze into tiny wavelets beneath whose vibrant transparency shone golden fish at play? How was he to tell such inhabitants of a damp and shady wilderness about sun-burnt waterless deserts? He would have to start at the beginning and recount his experiences day by day, step by step—and for that he possessed neither the strength nor the courage, and so he hid himself behind a barrier of silence and was satisfied to note that gradually they were ceasing to harass him with questions. It mattered to him not in the least that they had concluded that he must have seen nothing in his wanderings, since he never had anything to say . . .

Bogucha was managing everything. On the first day, she had stepped aside, having impressed upon her brother-in-law that he was now the master here and that all should report to him for orders. Seeing, however, that Imbram was continuing to walk about as though in a daze, starting everything wrong, allowing his people to do as they wished, and caring little for household economy, she had again taken up the reins of management and was now ruling again with her highly capable hand. To her quiet surprise, Imbram had not become angry, nor had he in any way objected to the change.

Spinning her wheel one evening, she considered bitterly that the two sensible men of the house had perished and that only this changeling remained. She cast a sidelong glance at him. Hm, he was indeed a sluggard, but he was none the less tall and handsome! More than that, she had to admit, he had brought home from his journeyings a gentility hitherto unknown to her. He moved and spoke differently from all the others. What was there about him, she wondered.

Her spindle kept falling to the floor, her thread was constantly breaking. Bogucha tightened her lips.

And as time went on, she became increasingly restless and irritable. She would scold her daughters frequently and would take savagely after the serving folk. She was forgetful in her tasks and, in the presence of Imbram, would grow nervous and expectant, stopping in the middle of remarks. Uncommon symptoms these were in one as wise and well-balanced as Bogucha.

The days were growing longer; the spring plowing was under way. The steward's son was turning the soil in the south field when Imbram came along the road and stopped to watch him. Again the feeling he had had while on his way home through the forest came over him—the feeling of being a tree which had struck root and which was developing a tough bark, a curious sensation, hard to say whether it was pleasant or otherwise.

Suddenly yielding to impulse, he pulled off his boots and walked barefoot over the soil, feeling with pleasure the sun-warmed earth between his toes. He thrust the boy aside and seized the handles of the plow. His sense of relief was so sudden and so clear that it struck him that the secret of spiritual calm lay here in just such homely tasks as this. The plowboy strode behind him, watching suspiciously to see whether the master had forgotten how to plow, and Imbram, feeling that boring gaze upon him, fixed his entire attention upon the proper laying of the furrows. In this way, he covered the entire field from end to end, once, twice, a third time. His spirits rose, and with a smile he tried to recall the last time he had guided a plow. No doubt at home before his departure! But no—it was at Antioch! At Antioch!

The memory of that moment and its terrible consequences struck

him so suddenly that he dropped the plow and walked away. Let
Pobieda finish!

Imbram turned toward home, staggering as though ill. The sky-blue
kirtle at the edge of the woods. That blue kirtle, never again to appear,
never again.

No miracle might ever conjure her forth. No prayers could raise her
from the dead!

His grief for the loss of his beloved wife whom he had betrayed—
grief so long suppressed—now burst forth with full violence and tore
his breast with hopeless anguish. Incapable of mastering his despair, he
struggled forward like one condemned. Every few steps he would halt
to lean his head against a tree and to sob with tearless woe. Why had he
returned? Oh, why? He might better have perished of thirst in the
desert, or starved to death in Antioch! Better to have burned in the tower
before Jerusalem, to have fallen there in battle, than to remain alive here
at home—without her, and with only the consciousness that he had
caused her death.

The spinning wheels whirred harmoniously this day, as always. The
crickets sang on the hearth. The little one had already gone to sleep in
Bogucha's big bed in her chamber. As usual, Imbram was relieved by the
absence of his son. He loved his little boy, but the mere sight of him
always cut him with memory: every gesture, the sound of his voice, were
but reminders of Ofka; the airy step, the endearing childish charm, those
blue eyes—all were hers, only hers!

Unable to utter a word, he took a seat far from the fire. He was afraid
that Bogucha would begin again to scold. But tonight she was silent.
Her broad, square face, on which the firelight played, was expressive of
only a steadfast determination to execute something which had been
long considered. Her lips were clamped tight shut, quite as though she
were prepared to beat down the opposition she expected to encounter.
Her wheel whirred faster, more briskly than usual.

Soon the servants retired, and a little later, the girls. Imbram did not
stir from his corner and Bogucha kept on spinning.

Suddenly Imbram spoke. "Talk to me—how was it when Ofka died?"
he asked in a hoarse voice, unlike his own.

Bogucha lowered her spindle and pushed aside the distaff, as though
she were preparing for a long conversation. "But I've already told you!"

she retorted with some impatience. "She wasn't sick—only her thoughts bothered her. She took no interest in anything. I was the one that brought up your young one. Remember that, Imko, it's the truth! Without me, she'd have spoiled him, as sure as you're alive—that crazy girl, always laughing and crying! And he's well brought up, too, you can see —strong and healthy and never afraid of a thing. You can box his ears all you like, he'll never whimper. He'll be a fine knight. Have you watched him shoot an arrow or sit a horse?—And all because of me!"

"I know . . . But tell me more about her."

"I've told you and told you and there's nothing more to tell. After you went away, she cried and cried. She wandered about like one without a head. Sometimes there was work here enough for five, washing and baking and all that, and there she'd be, looking up and down the road, just as though we had nothing to do!"

"She was waiting."

"Waiting! She was always afraid you would forsake her for another woman. That's all there was to that! I scolded her and told her she was wronging you, a good true knight, by thinking the way she did—but she kept right on till it killed her. Bah! She had no sense!"

"Stop speaking of her like that!" Imbram implored in a whisper.

"I'll say no more, if you don't like it. But certainly you must see that she never did anything for you! What can you expect from a cry-baby? But I . . . It was I who hid your colt when Shechec's ruffians came. They took all the horses—but not that one! Such a horse! I hid him in the pitch-house. Oh, yes, and I saw to all the stock, so that not much of anything was lost!"

"Well done, Bogucha! Not many men would have managed as well as you. But tell me more about her!"

"Some other time. It won't run away! But now . . ." She swallowed, folded her hands in her lap. In spite of her pretended poise, she was embarrassed, even alarmed. She looked at him entreatingly; never before had he seen her thus. "Only now," she said hoarsely, "I'd like to know what's to be done."

He looked at her without understanding.

"You will be getting married, no doubt—then—what about me? My man left me unprovided for. I can only become a housekeeper for someone. Where will I go?"

"I'll not be getting married," he assured her.

"Then how can we live under one roof? Are you wanting to give me and my daughters a bad name?"

"It's hard to please you," he smiled.

She lowered her eyes and smoothed her shawl with her hands. "Doesn't it seem only fitting and proper, Imko," she whispered, "that you should marry me, taking it to mind that if it hadn't been for me, you'd never have found your son or your cattle here at home and would have to live like a beggar?"

Imbram sat up, opened his mouth and stared at her, dumbfounded.

"I'm still sprightly enough to give pleasure," she quickly added. "Still young enough to have children . . ."

A dark curtain descended before Imbram's eyes. In blackness he wrestled with his sudden thoughts. Ofka had sensed his betrayal and had died. And he was now to take Bogucha to wife? It seemed to him that once again he was sitting at a wake, as that night at Doryleum, but this time the corpse was he—Imko; not Glovach, not Zbylut, but Imbram Strzygonia had died.

"I will marry you, Bogucha," he said aloud. "We can announce our betrothal even tomorrow."

Glossary of Characters

A

Adele, wife of Stephen de Blois
Adhemar de Monteuil, Bishop of Puy, leader of the Holy Expedition
Alberon, a worldly archdeacon
Alberta, wife of a Norman noble, friend of Willibald
Albert, Bishop of Nimes
Alexius, Basileus of Byzantium
Anisa, wife of Firus, the Greek renegade
Anna Porphyrogenita, royal Princess of Byzantium
Anselm de Ribeaumont, an elderly Norman knight
Gaston d'Armillac, a Provencal knight of the court of Raymond St. Gilles
Arnuld de Rohes, chaplain of Robert of Normandy
Strategos Argyros, a Greek envoy to the West

B

Baldwin du Bourg, a follower of Godfrey of Bouillon
Baldwin of Lorraine, brother of Godfrey of Bouillon
Bartholomew of Marseilles, a seminarian
Blaise, a servant of the Count de Blois
Blanche de Montbeliard, daughter of Lady Salviac de Viel Castel
Boleslas, King of Poland
Boemund, Duke of Tarentum
Bogucha, Glovach's wife
Bonina, servant of Florine
Butumitos, Captain of Alexius' Eastern Armies

C

Luigi Chiaco, Genoese merchant

D

Djurisha, wife of Kilij Arslan
Dudon de Contz, a follower of Godfrey of Bouillon

E

Elvira, wife of Raymond St. Gilles, daughter of the King of Castille
Von Emich, a German knight associated with Gottschalk
Paul Engelram, ward of Anselm de Ribeaumont
Wilfried d'Esch, a follower of Godfrey of Bouillon
Eustace of Lorraine, brother of Baldwin

F

Firus, a Greek renegade in the employment of Yagi-Sian
Florine, daughter of the Duke of Burgundy, wife of Swennon, Prince
    of Denmark
Foucher de Chartres, chronicler with Robert of Normandy
Fulgence de Guines, wife of the Sire de Guines

G

Godfrey, Duke of Bouillon, Lord of Metz, Toul, and Verdun
Gontrane, wife of Baldwin of Lorraine
Gouffier de la Tour, a Provençal knight
Gottschalk, a German knight, leader of the pogroms
Count du Grai, a Norman knight
Abbot Guido, a Silesian priest
Robert Guiscard, father of Boemund
Guynemere de Boulogne, "King of the Pirates"
Guenon, wife of a Norman noble, friend of Willibald
Giselle, daughter of Raymond St. Gilles
Guy, half-brother of Boemund

H

Hanum Baraba, mother of Kerbogha
Henry, Duke of Normandy, son of William the Conqueror

Helgund, servant of Gontrane
Brother Hyacinthus, a copyist
Hugh de Vermandois, brother of the King of Paris
Gaston d'Haineault, a follower of Godfrey de Bouillon
Ida d'Haineault (Ida de Montferrand) wife of Gaston d'Haineault

I

Ibrahim, son of Mudjahid, a Saracen warrior
Emir Iftikar-al-Davla, commander at Jerusalem
Imbram Strzygonia, a Silesian knight, brother of Glovach and Zyblut
Irene Dukas, wife of Alexius
Isaac, son of Firus

J

Jacob the Pimplefaced, a farmer

K

Euforbenos Kalatos, captain of Alexius' southern armed forces
Sultan Kilij Arslan
Kuropastos, a Greek
Emir Kerbogha of Mosul
Klimek, a Polish servant
Count Konon de Montaigue, a follower of Godfrey de Bouillon

L

Lawrence, squire of Gaston d'Armillac
Leah, Imbram's paramour
Leone, Baldwin's mistress and second wife
Bishop Lambert of Arras
Ladislas, Prince of Poland
Ladislaus, King of Hungary

M

Paladin Magnus
Sir William de Melun, follower of Hugh de Vermandois
Macar, a farmer
Marco de Santa Leone, follower of Tancred

Emir Mudjahid, commander of Nicaea
Emir Ahmed ibn Meruan, lord of Palestine

N

Novina the Babbler, a Silesian knight
Novina the Oak, his brother

O

Omer de Guillebaut, a Norman knight
Oleg, a Russian knight
Ostoy, Polish knight who escapes from slavery and joins the Crusade
Ofka, Imbram's wife

P

Philip, Duke of Burgundy
Philip, King of Paris
Saint-Pierre de Luz, squire of Roger de Foix
Father Placid, Florine's Confessor
Peter the Hermit
Pobieda, the steward of the Stryzgonia family
Pantopulos, Greek military construction expert

R

Raoul de Beaugency, a follower of Godfrey
Raymond St. Gilles, Count of Toulouse
Robert, Duke of Normandy (Robert Curthose)
Robert, Duke of Flanders
Roger de Berneville, follower of Hugh de Vermandois
Roger de Foix, follower of Raymond St. Gilles
Canon Raymond d'Aguilers, chronicler of the Crusade
Emir Rodoan of Aleppo

S

Paul and Stephen Salviac de Viel Castel, followers of Raymond St. Gilles
Lady Salviac de Viel Castel, mother of Blanche de Montbeliard
Simon Dukas, a Greek nobleman

Stephen de Blois, a follower of Hugh de Vermandois
Sykelgaita, mother of Guy, stepmother of Boemund
Schechek, a Polish prince
Simeon, the Greek patriarch of Byzantium
Sobek, servant of Imbram
Emir Sokman ibn Ortok, a Saracen warrior
Swennon, Prince of Denmark
Sukki de Squka, the Zupan Geza, leader of the Hungarian knights
Moymir Stiborovits, a Polish knight

T

Tatikios, Captain of the Basileus' Western Armies
Tancred, nephew of Boemund
Abba Thoros, Christian ruler of Edessa

U

Pope Urban II

V

Vitoslav Strzygonia (Glovach), brothers of Imbram and Zbylut

W

Walter the Penniless, leader of the peasants
Willibald de Guillebaut, wife of Omer
William the Red, brother of Robert of Normandy

Y

Yagi-Sian, commander of the Saracen forces at Antioch

Z

Momot Zavora, a Silesian knight
Yashek Zavora, his brother
Zbignev, bastard son of Prince Ladislas, pretender to the Polish throne
Zbylut Strzygonia, brother of Glovach and Imbram

.

CPSIA information can be obtained
at www.ICGtesting.com
Printed in the USA
BVHW062120030522
636072BV00009B/203

9 781379 241881